An African Exploration of the East Asian Education Experience

An African Exploration of the East Asian Education Experience

**Edited by Birger FREDRIKSEN
and TAN Jee Peng**

THE WORLD BANK
Washington, D.C.

© 2008 The International Bank for Reconstruction and Development / The World Bank
1818 H Street NW
Washington DC 20433
Telephone: 202-473-1000
Internet: www.worldbank.org
E-mail: feedback@worldbank.org

This volume is a product of the staff of the International Bank for Reconstruction and Development / The World Bank. The findings, interpretations, and conclusions expressed in this volume do not necessarily reflect the views of the Executive Directors of The World Bank or the governments they represent.

The World Bank does not guarantee the accuracy of the data included in this work. The boundaries, colors, denominations, and other information shown on any map in this work do not imply any judgement on the part of The World Bank concerning the legal status of any territory or the endorsement or acceptance of such boundaries.

Rights and Permissions

ISBN: 978-0-8213-7371-2
eISBN: 978-0-8213-7372-9
DOI: 10.1596/978-0-8213-7371-2

Library of Congress Cataloging-in-Publication Data has been requested.

Cover design: Critical Stages.

Contents

BOXES

FIGURES

TABLES

Foreword

Nelson Mandela, one of Africa's foremost elder statesmen, once remarked that education is the most powerful weapon you can use to change the world. This belief in the power of education is widely shared by ordinary African parents who, like parents everywhere, make extraordinary sacrifices to secure an education for their children in the hope of equipping them for a successful future. The sentiment was resonated in the 2006 decision by the Heads of State and Government of the African Union to launch the Second Decade of Education for Africa and to motivate many African governments to invest substantial shares of their national resources in education.

The concerted effort of Africans and their governments and development partners has produced good progress in recent years, particularly in ensuring that all African children are given the chance to complete a full cycle of primary schooling. But Africa is impatient for faster and broader progress—not just in primary education but across the whole education sector, including higher level technical and vocational education and training. Underlying this impatience is the widespread recognition that a good and strong education system has the potential to foster social cohesiveness as well as deliver the skills required by individuals and nations to succeed in today's global economy.

In their quest for educational development, African leaders are keen to examine the experience of other countries for possible adaptation to their own contexts. The story of East Asian countries holds special appeal in this regard. Four or five decades ago many of these countries started from conditions quite similar to those of African countries, and since have managed to turn their colonial-era systems into highly effective instruments for national development. They have grappled with and overcome many of the difficulties faced by most African countries today: seemingly impossible trade-offs in the allocation of scarce public budgets; severe shortages of teachers and large shares of underqualified staff; overcrowded and inadequate school facilities; overburdened and irrelevant curricula; scarcity of good learning materials; misalignment between the education and training system and the job market; poor articulation between different parts of the system; and huge losses from wasteful patterns of student repetition, dropout, and poor learning outcomes. For Africa's policy practitioners, there is therefore a special interest in the approach adopted by their East Asian counterparts to address these problems.

Responding to this interest, the World Bank sponsored an education study tour to Singapore and Vietnam in June 2006. Among the participants were senior education policy makers from six African countries—Cameroon, Ethiopia, Ghana, Lesotho, Madagascar, and Mozambique—accompanied by World Bank staff working on these countries along with staff from partner organizations. The program included site visits and presentations on Singapore and Vietnam as well as presentations on Korea, China, Hong Kong (China), and Thailand. Importantly, it also created throughout the two-week period of the study tour ample opportunities for formal and informal exchanges, both between the study tour participants and their Asian counterparts and among the African policy makers themselves.

Out of this rich dialogue and joint-learning process emerged several important lessons about East Asia's development practice in education. Perhaps the most striking is the indispensable role assigned to the education and training system as a driver of sustained economic growth and social development. Investing to prepare the next generation for good jobs in tomorrow's economy should be treated as a long-term national priority. So clear is this vision that it motivates active and sustained leadership at all levels of government and encourages close coordination of effort in policy and program implementation across sectors and ministries. The focus is two-fold: ensuring a well-functioning system of schools and institutions that delivers student learning and skills development; and fostering appropriate mechanisms to link what is taught in institutions to what employers seek and value in their workers.

These insights from the study tour and their operational implications are elaborated in this book and in the companion volume copublished by the Singapore National Institute of Education and the World Bank and which focuses on the development of education in Singapore. Taken together, the two books capture information that should interest a wide range of readers regarding East Asian countries' experience in developing and positioning the education and training system as a source of economic strength and social progress. The hope is that lessons from this part of the world over the past four or five decades will both inspire and inform African countries' efforts to shape their own path for educational development in the coming years.

Yaw Ansu
Director, Human Development Department
Africa Region
The World Bank

Acknowledgments

This book was made possible by contributions from a large number of individuals and institutions associated with the June 2006 education study tour to Singapore and Vietnam. The tour was jointly organized by the Government of Singapore and the Human Development Department of the World Bank's Africa Region, in cooperation with the Government of Vietnam and the Human Development Department of the World Bank's East Asia and Pacific Region. The coeditors of this volume—a byproduct of the study tour—wish to acknowledge with thanks the special role of several groups of people.

First, the chapter authors, whose work has helped to consolidate the knowledge gained from the study tour for wider dissemination: Chong Jae Lee for the chapter on Korea, Goh Chor Boon and S. Gopinathan on Singapore, Luis Benveniste on Thailand, Nguyen Quang Kinh and Nguyen Quoc Chi on Vietnam, Daniel O'Hare on Ireland (a case study added for reasons explained in chapter 1), and Mamadou Ndoye on education in Sub-Saharan Africa.

Second, the study tour organizers: on the Singapore side, special thanks are owed to a number of institutions and persons who worked tirelessly to make the tour a success. They include Anna Ng, Alan Ng, Wai Yin Ho, and G. Jayakrishnan of International Enterprise Singapore (IESingapore); Professors Sing Kong Lee and Leo Tan and their colleagues at the National Institute of Education; Dr. Song Seng Law and his colleagues at the Institute of Technical Education; Mr. Cheng Ton Lin and his colleagues at the Nanyang Polytechic; and Professor Tommy Koh, Tin Fook Koh, Teng Hoe Chua, and Emilyn Poh at the Ministry of Foreign Affairs. In Vietnam, the design of the tour benefited from guidance from Christopher Thomas, Christopher Shaw, Jeffrey Waite, and Binh Thanh Vu, whose deep knowledge and contacts greatly facilitated the consultations with counterpart officials in the Vietnamese Ministry of Education where special thanks are owed to Hung Ngoc Nguyen of the International Cooperation Department. The generous hosting of the tour by the Ministry and by the staff of the institutions visited in Hanoi and Ho Chi Minh City added to its success. Help with event management came from Julieta Watlington, Mavis Ku, Linh Van Nguyen, and Nguyet Minh Nguyen, whose collective efforts made the whole program of the study tour run like clockwork.

Third, the tour participants from the six African countries—Cameroon, Ethiopia, Ghana, Lesotho, Madagascar, and Mozambique—as well as the World Bank staff and those of other partner agencies working on these countries: their active engagement prior to the tour and in the formal and informal discussions during the tour have enriched the study tour program. Their valuable contributions, particularly in the summary session in which each country delegation presented their insights from the tour, have benefited the preparation of the overview chapter of this volume. While these participants are too many to name individually here, they are listed in annex 2 at the end of chapter 1.

Fourth, our friends who helped improve the book and facilitated its publication: sincere thanks are owed to Christopher Shaw, for his collaboration with the two authors on the chapter on Vietnam to finalize the English version after translation from the original in Vietnamese; to William Saint, who reviewed in detail the whole manuscript and made many incisive suggestions for improvement; and to Richard Crabbe, Valentina Kalk, Abdia Mohamed, and Dana Vorisek for guiding us through the publications process.

Finally, the coeditors wish to acknowledge with gratitude the management support of Yaw Ansu for the study tour, as well as the financial support received from the Government of Singapore through the Ministry of Foreign Affairs, the Government of Norway through the Norwegian Education Trust Fund, and the donor partners of the Education for All Fast Track Initiative through the Education Program Development Fund.

About the Authors

Luis BENVENISTE is country sector coordinator in the East Asia and Pacific Region's Human Development Department of the World Bank.

Birger FREDRIKSEN is an international consultant on the development of education policies and programs in developing countries, following 20 years of experience at the World Bank.

GOH Chor Boon is an associate professor and associate dean of the External Programs Office at the National Institute of Education, Nanyang Technological University, in Singapore.

S. GOPINATHAN is a professor at the National Institute of Education (NIE), Nanyang Technological University, in Singapore, and vice dean (policy) at the Centre for Research in Pedagogy and Practice at the NIE.

Chong Jae LEE is professor of educational policy and administration in the Department of Education, Seoul National University.

Mamadou NDOYE is executive secretary of the Association for the Development of Education in Africa.

NGUYEN Quang Kinh has served in several capacities in Vietnam's Ministry of Education and Training, most recently as General Director of the Ministerial Bureau.

NGUYEN Quoc Chi is a member of Vietnam's Ministry of Education and Training Mid-Decade Assessment Unit on Education for All.

Daniel O'HARE is a nonexecutive director of Calor Teoranta and Framework Solutions and a member of the board of Ireland's Commission on Electronic Voting.

TAN Jee Peng is regional education advisor in the Africa Region of the World Bank.

Abbreviations

ADB	Asian Development Bank
A-NET	Advanced National Educational Test
BK 21	Brain Korea 21
BMR	Bangkok Metropolitan Region
CDIS	Curriculum Development Institute of Singapore
CHIU	Conference of Heads of Irish Universities
CYS	Children and Youth Survey
DGE	Department of General Education
DTI	Dublin Institute of Technology
EBS	Educational Broadcasting Station
ECCE	Early Childhood Care and Education
ECGD	Export Credits Guarantee Department
EEC	European Economic Community
EFA	Education for All
EGFSN	Expert Group on Future Skills Needs
ESA	Education Service Areas
EU	European Union
EXIM	Export Import Bank of the United States
FDI	foreign direct investment
FETAC	Further Education Training and Awards Council
GAR	gross admission rate
GCE	General Certificate in Education
GDP	gross domestic product
GER	gross enrollment ratio
GNI	gross national income
GNP	gross national product

GPP	gross provincial product
HEA	Higher Education Authority
HEP	High School Equalization Policy
HRD	human resource development
IBEC	Irish Business and Employers Confederation
IBRD	International Bank for Reconstruction and Development
ICL	Income Contingent Loan
ICT	information and communication technology
IDA	International Development Association (chapter 5)
IDA	Industrial Development Authority (chapter 7)
IEA	International Association for the Evaluation of Educational Achievement
IES	International Enterprise Singapore
IFSC	International Financial Services Centre
ITE	Institute of Technical Education
IUA	Irish Universities Association
KBE	knowledge-based economy
KDI	Korean Development Institute
KEDI	Korean Educational Development Institute
KERIS	Korean Educational Research Information Service
KFTA	Korea Federation of Teachers Associations
KICE	Korean Institute for Curriculum and Evaluation
KIST	Korean Institute of Science and Technology
KOTMC	Korean Occupational Training Management Corporation
KRIVET	Korean Research Institute for Vocational Education and Training
LCAP	Leaving Certificate Applied Programme
LCVP	Leaving Certificate Vocational Programme
LGO	local government organization
LLECE	Latin American Laboratory for the Assessment of Quality in Education
MNC	multinational corporation
MOE	Ministry of Education
MOET	Ministry of Education and Training
MOI	Ministry of Interior
MOLISA	Ministry of Labor, War Invalids and Social Affairs
MUA	Ministry of University Affairs

NCCA	National Council for Curriculum and Assessment
NCEA	National Council for Educational Awards
NEA	National Education Act
NEC	National Education Convention
NEDS	National Education Development Scheme
NEIS	National Educational Information System
NER	net enrollment rate
NES	New Education System
NFE	Non-Formal Education
NFQ	National Framework of Qualifications
NGO	nongovernmental organization
NIE	National Institute of Education
NIETS	National Institute of Education Testing Services
NIHE	National Institutes for Higher Education
NSO	National Statistics Office
NURI	New University for Regional Innovation
OBEC	Office of Basic Education Commission
OEC	Office of Education Council
OECD	Organisation for Economic Co-operation and Development
OECF	Overseas Economic Cooperation Fund
ONEC	Office of National Education Commission
ONESQA	Office for National Education Standards and Quality Assessment
O-NET	Ordinary National Educational Test
ONPEC	Office of National Primary Education Commission
PASEC	*Programme d'analyse des systemes educatifs de la CONFEMEN*
PCER	Presidential Committee for Educational Reform
PIRLS	Progress in International Reading Literacy Study
PISA	Programme for International Student Achievement
PLC	Post-Leaving Certificate
PROGRESA	*Programa Nacional De Educación, Saludy Alimentación*
PRTLI	Programme for Research in Third-Level Institutions
PSLE	Primary School Leaving Examination
R&D	research and development
RSEs	research scientists and engineers
RTC	regional technical college
RTG	Royal Thai Government

S$	Singapore dollar
SACMEQ	Southern and Eastern African Consortium for Monitoring Educational Quality
SAT	Scholastic Achievement Test
SCL	Skill Certification Law
SDF	Skills Development Fund
SES	[Household] Socio-Economic Survey
SFADCo	Shannon Free Airport Development Company
SFI	Science Foundation Ireland
SIF	Strategic Innovation Fund
SMI	Strategic Management Initiative
SPR	school participation rates
SSA	Sub-Saharan Africa
TIMSS	Trends in International Mathematics and Science Study
TSLN	Thinking Schools, Learning Nation
TVET	technical and vocational education and training
TVETPL	Technical and Vocational Education and Training Promotion Law
TVHS	Technical-Vocational High Schools
UNDP	United Nations Development Programme
UNICEF	United Nations Children's Fund
UNKRA	United Nations Korea Reconstruction Agency
VITB	Vocational and Industrial Training Board
VSIP	Vietnam-Singapore Industrial Park

CHAPTER 1

East Asia Education Study Tour: An Overview of Key Insights

Birger FREDRIKSEN and TAN Jee Peng

INTRODUCTION

The study tour to Singapore and Vietnam began as an idea at a workshop on textbooks organized by the World Bank in May 2005. The workshop was designed for African countries to discuss the problem of textbook scarcity and options for overcoming it. At that workshop, a delegation from Singapore presented their country's 40-year experience with textbook provision, an experience that encompassed the transformation of a modest Ministry of Education unit struggling with its mandate to prepare and distribute high-quality textbooks with relevant content, into what is today an internationally competitive private sector publisher of multimedia learning materials. Several participants requested that a study tour to Singapore be organized to enable participates to examine the experience.[1] It soon became clear, however, that a study visit focusing on textbooks alone would be too narrow in scope. Instead, given the key role of education behind what economists have termed the East Asia miracle, it seemed more appropriate to seize the opportunity to learn not only about Singapore's approach to education sector development at the strategic and operational levels, but also about the experience of other East Asian countries that have made similarly impressive strides in education and economic development over the past few decades.

Accordingly, in June 2006, delegations of African educators from six countries (Cameroon, Ethiopia, Ghana, Lesotho, Madagascar, and Mozambique[2])—each typically led by the minister of education or other senior policy makers and accompanied by World Bank staff and managers along with representatives of other development partners[3]—traveled to Singapore and Vietnam. These educators participated in a program that included site visits to education institutions in the host countries, attendance at presentations on selected aspects of education sector policies in these countries by local experts and policy makers, and participations in discussions with invited experts from China (the mainland), Hong Kong (China), the Republic of Korea, and Thailand.[4] As part of their pretour preparations, each country delegation drafted a short note summarizing the key education challenges in their country and their learning expectations for the visit. At the end of the tour, each delegation delivered presentations to the other participants that captured their impressions and lessons learned.

OBJECTIVE AND DESIGN OF THE STUDY TOUR

The study tour program did not showcase the high standards attained by East Asian countries.[5] Instead, it focused on the choices and implementation strategies that have allowed these countries to propel their education and economic systems, over a period of 30 to 40 years, from a situation similar to that in many Sub-Saharan African countries, to their present standing among the more industrial countries of the world.[6] To make the best use of the limited time available during the tour, the agenda addressed four broad themes associated with noteworthy features of the East Asian experience over the past few decades:

- The education sector's central role in nation building and national development.
- Rapid scale up of basic education of good quality for all.
- Management of the pressures on postprimary education as progress toward universalizing primary education was made.
- Alignment between education and the economy, particularly at the postbasic education levels and in technical and vocational fields where responsiveness to labor market needs are especially important to support economic growth.

The last of the themes listed above attracted the most interest, given the success of East Asian countries in fostering dynamic, responsive, and productive links between the education system and the economy. For the past 5 to 10 years, many African countries have achieved sustained economic growth averaging about 5 percent a year, a clear break from the nearly two decades of economic decline and stagnation that occurred from the mid-1970s to mid-1990s. Yet this growth remains fragile and probably too slow to reduce poverty on a large scale. An emerging consensus is that getting onto a path of faster and more sustained growth will require a more strategic, proactive, and systemic approach to skills development in Africa than has been adopted to date. In this regard, East Asia's decades-long experience offers an interesting laboratory of successful experimentation with policy design and implementation. The study tour program thus created opportunities for participants to interact with practitioners of technical and vocational training institutions during site visits to training facilities in Singapore and Vietnam and through discussions with the experts who made formal presentations.

OVERVIEW OF THIS BOOK

Because the lessons distilled by the study tour participants are interesting to other African countries, this book collects a set of papers associated with this study tour. This introductory chapter summarizes the insights from the visit and relates them to the education challenges faced by countries in Sub-Saharan Africa today.[7] Chapter 2 contains a detailed discussion of these challenges, including an analysis developed from a presentation offered during the study tour. The three chapters that follow—on Singapore, Vietnam, and the Republic of Korea—were commissioned as background papers for the study tour. Chapter 6 on Thailand is based in part on the presentation made during the tour and on information from ongoing analytical work by World Bank colleagues. Although the inclusion of Ireland in a volume on Asia may be surprising, it was motivated by the resemblance of the country's spectacular economic development over the past few decades to the experience of its high-performing counterparts in East Asia (which also explains why it has been nicknamed the "Celtic Tiger"). Many of the problems Ireland has confronted parallel those experienced in Africa, and its skill development strategy shares additional similarities with Asia. Fortunately, a paper on the Irish experience had been commissioned for other World Bank work and was readily available for adaptation to suit the purpose of this book.

ORGANIZATION OF THIS CHAPTER

This chapter draws on other chapters in this book and adds insights from the rich discussions held during the study tour—among the participants themselves, as well as between them and their East Asian counterparts. The formal and informal exchanges and question-and-answer sessions during the tour exemplify the value of a well-planned program to provide a framework for structured conversations. Many of the approaches summarized below arose out of these conversations. These interventions may not be directly applicable to the specific education challenges of African countries, but they do represent a source of practical know-how about education strategy and reform, and thus inspire successful leadership and management of the sector's transformation. The experience of East Asian countries over the past few decades contains useful lessons that are worth exploring as African policy makers seek to reform and improve their education systems.

Although East Asian countries fit no single model of success, the policies and strategies they followed in the education sector share a few critical features. *Adaptability* is one such feature. These countries invariably customized the reform effort to their initial national conditions and continue to adapt it as conditions inevitably evolve. *Pragmatism* is another important commonality. A pragmatic approach puts flexibility in pursuit of an agreed development objective above national pride or ideological dogmatism. This approach embodies a willingness to learn by doing and to improve implementation by closing the feedback loop to capture lessons learned. Attention to building national *institutional capacity* is a third common factor. The leaders of East Asian countries understood the value of technical expertise as well as the importance of building a *national consensus* around the policies adopted. These countries have systematically built their own national capacity in these dimensions to better develop and implement sound policies and strategies. They also used *foreign assistance* strategically in the education sector to support their national policies. Within the education and training system, the high priority given in the early years to *adult literacy and universal primary education* is particularly noteworthy. Additionally, the constant attention paid over the last decades to developing a *technical and vocational education and training* (TVET) system has enabled these countries to consistently upgrade this system to respond to rapid changes in the skills demanded by the economy. Finally, education success in East Asian countries hardly would have been possible without the support of more general factors such as *sound macroeconomic policies* and *strong, committed political leadership.*

These common features are an admittedly stylistic and simplified description of the diversity of experiences in the region. Yet they capture well some of the key factors behind these East Asian countries' success in achieving *consistently high rates of long-term economic growth* and in *rapidly raising the quality of their human resources.* The interaction between economic and human resources development and the mutually reinforcing nature of their relationship are among the most admirable features of the East Asian story.

This complex narrative unfolds as follows. The next section elaborates on the enabling conditions that contextualized education development in East Asia. This discussion is followed by education sector priorities, policies, and strategic choices in East Asian countries, and highlights of key features in their approaches to policy implementation. In each of these areas, the region's developmental experience yields interesting insights into the sources of the region's extraordinary progress in education. The last section provides a summary of participants' impressions of the study tour as reflected in their final presentations and includes a tentative agenda for follow-up.

ENABLING CONDITIONS FOR EDUCATION DEVELOPMENT IN EAST ASIA

Foremost among the enabling conditions for education development are the following: (a) high rates of economic growth; (b) the emphasis on "shared growth" in the countries' overall development policy; (c) rapid demographic transition; and (d) strong public institutions. Success in establishing these (and other) enabling conditions provided the bedrock for successful education policies, which in turn nurtured these conditions, thereby creating a virtuous cycle of mutually reinforcing interactions. To be specific, rapid economic growth generated the domestic resources necessary to finance a scaling up of education development, which in turn boosted economic growth by providing the skilled labor required to raise productivity. These enabling conditions did not materialize by chance. Creating and sustaining these conditions was the result of deliberate and persistent effort guided by visionary and determined political leadership, an effort that was arguably even more strenuous than that required for success in the education sector.

RAPID ECONOMIC GROWTH

A full explanation of the extraordinary economic success of East Asian countries is not included in this chapter.[8] But clearly, this success facilitated the development of education in a way that is generally absent from the experience of most African countries during the last quarter of the twentieth century. Between 1970 and 1997, per capita gross domestic product (GDP) in East Asia rose by 355 percent (from US$157 to US$715 in constant 1987 U.S. dollars), or at a rate of 5.8 percent a year. By contrast, it *declined* over the same period by 36 percent in Sub-Saharan Africa (from US$525 to US$336 in constant 1987 U.S. dollars) (World Bank 2000a, 8).[9] This decline was uneven, however. Per capita GDP had actually been expanding up until the first "oil-shock" in 1973. It then stagnated between 1973 and the second oil-shock in 1980, which was followed by a long decline that lasted until the mid-1990s. Thereafter, and especially since around 2000, growth has picked up in a significant number of African countries.

Looking at individual countries, per capita GDP was US$104 in Korea in 1962, US$430 in Singapore (which is a small urban nation state), and US$117 in Thailand, compared with Sub-Saharan Africa's average of US$142 (World Bank 2006c). During the 34-year period between 1965 and 1999, the per capita GDP grew at an average rate of 6.6 percent a year in Korea, 6.3 percent in Singapore, and 5.1 percent in Thailand. Thus, measured in constant prices, at the end of this period, the per capita GDP had multiplied by a factor of 7.8 in Korea, 7.0 in Singapore, and 4.4 in Thailand (World Bank 2001a, 25–26). Of the 35 Sub-Saharan African countries for which data are available for the same period, 19 experienced a decline in their per capita GDP between 1965 and 1999, including three of the six countries that participated in the study tour, namely, Ethiopia (declining at −0.3 percent a year), Ghana (at −0.7 percent a year), and Madagascar (at −1.7 percent a year). The other three countries underwent modest increases: Cameroon (at +1.1 percent increase a year), Mozambique (at +1.3 percent a year), and Lesotho (at +2.8 percent a year) (World Bank 2006).[10]

These dramatic differences in economic performance between countries in East Asia and in Sub-Saharan Africa affected the education sector in a number of ways.

Below we highlight how they affected the countries' ability to (a) finance education development; (b) implement politically difficult education reforms; and (c) generate employment for school leavers and graduates.

Impact on Education Financing. Early on, East Asian policy makers demonstrated their strong commitment to education by allocating increasing shares of the GDP for investments in education. African policy makers made a similar choice and, on average, the share of the GDP devoted to education in Sub-Saharan African countries has exceeded that in East Asian countries.[11] However, these comparable levels of financial commitment to education translated into different trajectories in terms of the governments' actual ability to pay for education. East Asia's steady increase over time in education's share of GDP, combined with strong economic growth, produced a sustained increase in the absolute size of the education budget. By contrast, in Sub-Saharan Africa, the steady increase in the share of GDP devoted to education was undercut by economic stagnation or decline, which implied slow-growing or even shrinking education budgets in real terms. As will become clear, the differences in economic growth have had a profound impact on the countries' ability to manage classroom conditions (for example, by avoiding excessively high pupil-to-teacher ratios) and, perhaps most important, to finance the wage bill for teachers.

In the context of Sub-Saharan Africa's current efforts to reach Education for All (EFA) targets, the impact of economic stagnation on the countries' ability to finance universal primary education is particularly illuminating. Between 1960 and 1980, Sub-Saharan Africa's gross enrollment ratio (GER) grew from 45 percent to 80 percent, and enrollment rose by 260 percent, a rate of expansion hardly experienced over a 20-year period in any other region at any time. Unfortunately, the next two decades of economic stagnation and decline severely constrained public budgets,[12] which stifled the education supply. This stagnation forced governments to resort to the use of fees to mobilize resources for education, which increased private costs and reduced education demand. The GER declined from 80 percent in 1980 to 72 percent in 1992, and only slowly regained its 1980 level by 2000. The 70 percent expansion in enrollment during the period from 1980 to 2000 was barely sufficient to absorb the increase in the primary-school-age population that occurred during this 20-year period, thus leaving the GER unchanged.

The adverse impact of economic stagnation, when combined with rapid growth in the population of school-age children, is reflected in the pattern of primary education development in individual countries. In addition to the countries with a sustained GER above 100 percent,[13] at least nine other countries reached a GER exceeding 100 percent sometime during the period 1965–1985. In these nine countries, however, the GER dropped well below 100 percent by the mid-1990s, including three of the countries that participated in the study tour.[14] The resumption of economic growth in the late 1990s has facilitated a strong rebound in primary enrollment growth in most Sub-Saharan African countries.

Impact on the Political Economy. East Asian countries have been able to establish and implement clear national education priorities, even when this has required difficult tradeoffs unfavorable to better-off groups (for example, giving strong budgetary priority to primary rather than higher education). Sub-Saharan African countries generally have been less successful in this regard. Although they have made many attempts, these initiatives have remained largely rhetorical.

Various factors explain why some countries are more successful than others in moving from political rhetoric to actual policy implementation. One factor that may not be sufficiently recognized in explaining Sub-Saharan Africa's often weak performance in this area is the impact of economic stagnation on these countries' political ability to successfully implement reforms. Most Sub-Saharan African countries are challenged by high unmet social demand for education, fueled by young and fast-growing populations, and slow-growing, largely rural-based economies. These economies do not generate the tax revenues necessary to achieve universal primary education and also provide publicly financed secondary and higher education in response to social demand. Nor do they generate the modern sector jobs that graduates seek. In fact, many countries are trapped in a vicious circle in which a low skill base constrains economic growth and, in turn, low growth severely limits their fiscal potential to improve skill levels and create the political space necessary to introduce difficult education reforms. East Asian countries managed early on to avoid this vicious circle by setting clear priorities for their public education spending and managing their cost structures (for example, teacher salaries, class size, and use of double-shift teaching) to ensure the early universalization of primary education.

Three examples will illustrate the difficult political economy of education reforms in slow-growing, low-income Sub-Saharan African countries. First, in the absence of growth, increased public expenditures to reach EFA often require redistribution of the benefits generated by the present use of public budgets, away from postprimary education—which favors the better-off population groups—and in favor of those who are not entering primary schools, that is, largely the rural poor who have a weak political voice. Such redistribution of a shrinking pie is difficult politically, especially when the children of those in charge of implementing the change would be the principal losers. Second, contrary to many Asian countries in the early stage of their development, Sub-Saharan African teachers generally have strong unions, and the success of education reforms depends on their support. This is difficult to obtain when teacher salaries are falling, as will be discussed. Third, to successfully participate in the knowledge-based global economy, Sub-Saharan African countries must revitalize their higher education subsector. For most countries, this means limiting access to the many traditional academic programs that respond poorly to current job opportunities and prioritizing quality improvement and the labor market relevance of all programs. Again, to develop and implement such reforms requires strong political commitment and an ability to provide alternatives to deal with student opposition.

In short, many of the nonimplemented education reforms long advocated by African politicians become controversial and politically risky in the absence of economic growth. Not to pursue reforms, however, also has a serious cost. This cost takes the form of slower economic growth, low job generation for a rapidly growing population of youth, a high degree of inequity in access to education, and a risk to social stability. The East Asian countries have demonstrated ways to overcome such obstacles to reforms, generally through a combination of factors such as good technical preparation, development of political commitment, strong advocacy in relation to the public, and consensus building with key stakeholders. Thus, the resumption of economic growth in Sub-Saharan African countries may remove one of the major obstacles to success in education reforms.

Impact on Job Creation for Graduates. Complaints about the weak capacity of the education system to produce graduates who are "employable" is a common topic of education policy discussions throughout the world and, especially, in Africa. As will be discussed, East Asian countries have a particularly good track record in adapting their education programs to their rapidly changing labor market demands. But this effort would have had little impact on employment if they had not also generated high economic growth and created the flexible labor markets needed to translate this growth into effective demand for skilled labor.

Korea's development illustrates well the workings of this virtuous circle originating from strong economic growth, well-functioning labor markets, and an education system responsive to labor market demands. In the early 1960s, Korea was saddled with an excess supply of low productivity, low skilled labor. By 1967, a shortage of skilled labor had begun to be felt as a result of accelerating growth, and by the late 1970s, the labor market was tight for most categories of workers. As these pressures increased, they created incentives to improve the quality of both labor and employment. Consequently, an increasing number of Koreans found work in professional, technical, and clerical jobs, and fewer found work in manual jobs. This led real wages to grow by 6.7 percent a year on average between 1960 and 1985, which means that real wages over a 25-year period were multiplied by a factor of four. During the 1980s, the differences in earnings between lower- and higher-paid workers narrowed, caused partly by the rapid increase in the supply of skilled workers (World Bank 1987). In short, as summarized in chapter 5, "Korean education owes much of its rapid expansion to economic growth, which provided the financial resources and job opportunities for recent university graduates."

EMPHASIS ON SHARED GROWTH

Shared growth is an important principle of the strategies followed by East Asian countries to reach national consensus on the policies required to achieve high economic growth. "To establish their legitimacy and win the support of the society at large, East Asian leaders introduced the principle of shared growth early on . . ." (World Bank 1993, 13).

Explicit policies and mechanisms were established to implement this principle. Some of these policies will be highlighted in the discussion of institutional factors. Although these policies varied by country, and extended well beyond the education sector,[15] rapid development of education was a common—and arguably the most important—instrument to achieve the objective of shared growth. Thus, in addition to investing in education to develop the human capital required to sustain the economy, the configuration of these investments also reflected a desire to ensure that the benefits from growth were shared among all population groups (see chapters 3–7 for examples of such policies). Rapid attainment of universal adult literacy and primary education was particularly important in this regard. Early universalization of primary education ensured that the gender gap in education was closed more rapidly in East Asia than in other developing countries. In turn, this enhanced the "equalizing effect" of growth by improving women's access to gainful employment. It also allowed women, families, and society to take advantage of the universally accepted benefits associated with the education of girls and women.

As a region, Sub-Saharan Africa has perhaps the world's highest income inequality.[16] In addition, the region's stagnant economies have not provided much growth to share. Furthermore, Sub-Saharan African countries have not been as propoor as East Asian countries in the pattern of their public expenditures on education. Sub-Saharan African countries put less emphasis on universalizing adult literacy and primary education, and they do not rely as heavily as East Asian countries on private financing for tertiary education. For example, in 1965, primary education received 58 percent of the education budget in Singapore, 66 percent in Thailand, and 66 percent in Korea. The corresponding share for Sub-Saharan African countries averaged 49 percent in 1970, and it fell to 44 percent in 1975 and 1980 (World Bank 1988).[17]

This difference in policy emphasis has major implications for the distribution of public education expenditures across population groups. For example, late-1990's data for eight Sub-Saharan African countries show that the 20 percent of the population with the highest income received 34 percent of public education expenditures, whereas the poorest 20 percent received only 12 percent. For countries such as Malaysia, the distribution is the reverse: about 28 percent is allocated for the poorest 20 quintile of the population, and 11 percent for the richest.

As the demographic transition in East Asia got under way, the primary-school-age population fell while that of older cohorts of youth rose, and the relative distribution of education budgets shifted as well. As a result, by 1995, the share of the education budget devoted to primary education had decreased to 26 percent in Singapore, 45 percent in Korea, and 50 percent in Thailand.

RAPID DEMOGRAPHIC TRANSITION

East Asian countries' rapid transition from high to low fertility rates helped to accelerate both education and economic development in these countries. In turn, rapid development of the education system and the economy are major factors in determining the onset and speed of fertility decline. The resulting decreases in family size and in the overall magnitude of the primary-school-age population made it possible for families and governments to spend more per primary school student and gradually shift their resources to postprimary education.

The impact of the demographic transition on the size of the primary-school-age population began to be felt at different points in the four East Asian countries covered in chapters 3–6. In Singapore, this population expanded at 0.4 percent a year between 1965 and 1970, and then decreased by 1.8 percent a year during 1970–85.[18] In Korea, it also increased between 1965 and 1970—in this case, by 2.5 percent a year—and then declined during 1970s and into 1985, at a rate of 0.6 percent a year. Thailand's school-age population increased sharply between 1965 and 1975, at an average of rate of 2.9 percent a year, and continued to grow between 1975 and 1980. But the rate of increase was already tapering off at 0.8 percent a year. In the early to mid-1980s, the growth rate was negative (Lockheed and Verspoor 1990, 166–67). In Vietnam, the decline in the primary-school-age population started in the 1990s and is projected to fall by 20 percent between 2000 and 2012. Clearly, this decline facilitates Vietnam's ongoing efforts to reduce class size and increase spending per student in primary education, as well as to attain its goal of universal lower-secondary education by 2010.

Several attempts have been made to estimate the benefits that East Asian countries accrue as a result of their rapid demographic transition. One such estimate compares the share of GDP actually allocated to primary education in Korea, Singapore, and Thailand with what would have been required if the school-age populations in these countries grew as rapidly as those in Kenya (at that time, probably the fastest-growing population in Sub-Saharan Africa) (World Bank 1993, 195).[19] The estimates suggest that Korea would have had to allocate 5.6 percent of its GNP to primary education rather than the 2.8 percent it actually allocated, that is, twice as much. The corresponding estimate is 4.2 percent for Singapore compared with the actual allocation of 2 percent, and 3.9 percent for Thailand, compared with the actual allocation of 2.6 percent.

Because of several factors, including the scarcity of quality family planning services and low contraceptive prevalence levels, the benefits of an early and rapid demographic transition have not been available to Sub-Saharan African education systems. Thus, in most countries, this transition is only in its early stages. On average, the region's primary-school-age populations expanded by about 95 percent between 1960 and 1980 (an average rate of 3.4 percent a year) and by about 70 percent between 1980 and 2000 (an average rate of 2.7 percent a year). Even though the school-age population is now growing less rapidly in this region than before, the demographic momentum of past high fertility and the slow transition to lower fertility imply that Africa's primary-school-age population will continue to grow for some time to come. Sub-Saharan Africa's school-age population is thus projected to grow by 24 percent between 2000 and 2015 (that is, at an average rate of 1.4 percent a year), compared with a *decrease* of 13 percent in East Asia over the same period.

STRONG PUBLIC INSTITUTIONS

Institutional strength is the last enabling factor that we identify as a key factor behind East Asia's success in education. Building effective public institutions is a complex task and the insights from this study offer only a glimpse into how different institutions were created, how they evolved, and what role they played in facilitating education development in each setting. Furthermore, this glimpse is limited by the fact that it comes mostly from the visit to Singapore, and development experience clearly shows that, in this area as in others, one size does not fit all.

Notwithstanding the above reservations, the study tour generated some useful perspectives that may be of particular interest to African countries, particularly given their ongoing struggle to build and retain institutional capacity, including in the education sector. These insights are presented below under three related rubrics: (a) political will and visionary leadership; (b) quality of the civil service; and (c) consultative and consensus-building mechanisms.

Political Will and Visionary Leadership. The crucial importance to education development of strong political will at the highest political level is underlined in all the presentations as well as in the overview papers, including the one for Ireland. For example, Ng states that "[t]he economic and education success of Singapore did not happen by accident. Strategic planning, a strong political will, and stable government are key factors in charting the success of Singapore" (2008, 39). As underlined elsewhere in this chapter, strong political will manifests itself in many ways: (a) in the governments' overall policies, including the volume of resources devoted to the education sector; (b) willingness to implement politically sensitive education reforms; (c) concerted and sustained effort to build consensus and support for these reforms beyond the education sector; and (d) attention to ensuring that the education system responds explicitly and demonstrably to the country's national development agenda. Furthermore, as discussed below, East Asian countries were effective in ensuring that national policy decisions were given the follow-up attention needed for implementation at the sector level.

Reputable and Reliable Civil Service. To achieve and sustain growth—be it in the economy or in the education sector—a country needs solid institutional capacity to formulate effective policies and implement them. In analyzing the good performance of East Asian countries in this area, the importance of cultural factors such as Confucianism (which places a high value on education) has often been invoked. But even if cultural factors have played a role, it is important to note that East Asian countries have labored tenaciously to develop a technically competent civil service as well as an overall institutional environment in which professionalism, performance, and integrity are required and rewarded. Specific measures to implement such policies included merit-based and highly competitive recruitment and promotion, and a level of total compensation, including pay, perks, and status, which are generally competitive with the private sector (for further discussion, see World Bank 1993, 174–75). Finally, a job in the civil service is associated with prestige, and civil servants generally enjoy considerable insulation from undue outside interference.[20] Aspects related specifically to developing the institutional capacity of the education sector will be discussed below.

Consultative and Consensus-Building Mechanisms. East Asian countries emphasized the principle of "shared growth" and chose among their policy options accordingly. This approach—

> raised complex coordination problems. First, leaders had to convince economic elites to support pro-growth policies. Then they had to persuade the elites to share the benefits of growth with the middle class and the poor. Finally, to win the cooperation of the middle class and the poor, the leaders had to show them that they would indeed benefit from growth (World Bank 1993, 13).

To create and maintain a viable social compact, countries developed institutions and mechanisms dedicated to promoting overall economic development (such as the Economic Development Board in Singapore, and the Korea Development Institute in Korea); attracting private investments; and very important, minimizing debilitating conflicts in the labor market.[21] Korea and Singapore established formal deliberative councils that included such members as government officials, journalists, labor representatives, and academics. This type of arrangement facilitated coordination between government agencies and firms, and generally improved the flow of information. These councils may have strengthened the commitment to shared growth among the general public and contributed to a reduction in rent-seeking behaviors (World Bank 1993, 352–53).

EDUCATION PRIORITIES, POLICIES, AND STRATEGIES

The policy decisions taken outside the education sector by East Asian governments were essential, but not sufficient, to sustain success in education. Equally critical were the forward-looking policies and strategies within the education sector itself and the strong follow-through in policy implementation. Accordingly, the study tour program focused on the evolution of the education priorities chosen, the policy tradeoffs made, and the strategies adopted. This section summarizes insights with regard to the (a) exercise of visionary leadership in the education sector; (b) adoption of an "integrated" approach to policy development; (c) validation of the importance of TVET; (d) mobilization of resources for education; and (e) use of external resources catalytically to advance national goals in education.

EXERCISING VISIONARY LEADERSHIP

East Asian leaders at the highest levels of political office have been strong and effective advocates of education as a foundational asset for and driver of their development agendas. Typically, the Ministry of Education itself is led by one of the stronger ministers in the cabinet. This visionary political leadership has been a key ingredient in ensuring that the country's education system has (a) shaped future citizens by teaching moral values, (b) fostered national cohesion among groups with diverse backgrounds, (c) helped build a national identity, and (d) equipped students with the skills required for individual as well as national progress.

Understanding how to align the education sector with the national development agenda has been a central topic of debate in most developing countries over the past half century. To this end, weighty statements have been adopted at both national and international conferences about ways to achieve this alignment. However, political leaders in East Asian countries have often done better than their counterparts in most other countries at translating this rhetoric into explicit policies and substantive implementation. This leadership is exemplified by actions such as follows:

- *The sustained priority given early on to enrolling all children in primary school* and, as progress toward this challenge was made, to universalize 8 to 10 years of basic education. In Korea, this meant concentrating education subsidies in rural areas and tolerating, for a time, huge class sizes (in some cases, more than 90 pupils per class). In Vietnam, it meant bringing all schools up to a minimum standard of quality for inputs (under the so-called Fundamental School Quality Level program). In Singapore, it meant spreading resources evenly across schools and operating all schools on double shifts for most of the 40 years after independence. The priority of universalizing primary education so clearly stated by African leaders just after independence could not be maintained when the economic stagnation started in the early 1980s.[22]

- *The priority given soon after independence from colonial rule to revamping the school curriculum* and gearing it to serve the country's own goals for nation building and economic development.[23] This orientation, which is shared by Korea, Singapore, and Vietnam, stands in sharp contrast to the situation in many African countries, where today, some 40 to 50 years after independence, many political leaders still complain that their education system is burdened by a colonial heritage that responds poorly to their national conditions (this aspect is discussed further in chapter 2).

- *The priority given to ensuring that education programs respond to labor market needs* is strongly underlined in the chapters on Korea, Singapore, and Vietnam. As discussed further below, this priority manifested itself particularly in the attention paid to ensuring consistency between education policies and wider national development goals, and in the priority accorded to TVET.

ADOPTING AN INTEGRATED APPROACH

East Asian countries deal with education in an integrated manner, thus avoiding the error of treating subsectors as separate, special-interest silos with tangential links to the rest of society. It is tempting to leave educators alone to their task of teaching and learning, but East Asian policy makers have side-stepped this pitfall by explicitly recognizing the mutually dependent and reinforcing interaction between education (at all levels), economic performance, and national development.

To achieve the desired result in practice, policy makers use institutional arrangements to reduce potential inconsistencies in the relationship between national and sector goals. In Singapore, the minister of education at the time of the study tour held a concurrent position as the second minister of finance. His job is thus not only to make claims on the state budget, but also to keep these claims in balance with other national priorities in light of the contribution of education to national development. Moreover, all large expenditures in education (as in other sectors) must be approved by a three-party committee made up of a representative each from the Ministry of Education (as the sponsoring ministry), the Ministry of Finance, and a third ministry with no direct stake in the matter—an arrangement made to ensure that sectoral interests are evaluated within a broader context. Recently, the Singapore government has even broached the idea of cluster ministries, which would further emphasize the cross-cutting nature of policy choices.

In Vietnam, the top leadership is likewise fully engaged in guiding the development of education in an integrated manner. The minister of education at the time of the study tour was also the deputy prime minister and was thus very well-versed on the country's education strategy and maintained continuous discussion at the highest level of government by chairing monthly meetings to discuss education and training issues. Such practices not only put education at the center of the development agenda, but also ensure that it stays on track in implementation. At the institutional level, particularly in Singapore's vocational and technical training institutions, this integrated approach is evident in the composition of their governing boards. Typically, these boards include a large number of industry leaders who give direction to the design of course curricula to maintain a tight link to the professional world.

Interestingly, the chapters on Korea, Thailand, and Ireland all show that similar concerns arose in these countries regarding the need to ensure close links between education and economic development. And they have responded with approaches that resemble those used in Singapore and Vietnam.

VALIDATING THE IMPORTANCE OF TVET

For most participants, the discussions on TVET and the visits to TVET institutions in Singapore and Vietnam were perhaps the single-most interesting aspect of the study tour. There are many reasons for this, including the following: (a) the key role TVET has played in the rapid industrialization and economic growth of Korea and Singapore, and now also Vietnam; (b) the urgency of revitalizing TVET institutions in Sub-Saharan African countries—outdated and dilapidated after decades of economic stagnation; (c) the growing problem of creating employment for Africa's rapidly growing youth population;[24] and (d) the urgency of adapting to the competitive realities of globalization.

Successful cultivation of TVET capacities is perhaps the most complex of all the education and training challenges facing industrial and developing countries alike. Over the past few decades, countries have struggled with such issues as the role of vocational subjects in general secondary education, the level in secondary education at which to introduce vocational and technical specializations, the balance between general and specialized TVET streams, and the role of industry and the public sector in providing vocational training. In addition, as the experience of East Asian countries demonstrates so well, in high growth economies, the TVET system needs to be dynamic so that it can adapt and evolve constantly to rapid changes in the labor market and in the demand for skilled workers.

The study tour offered good opportunities to explore these and other questions. East Asian countries consider skilled and technically competent workers indispensable ingredients to transform their economies from being driven by factor endowments, to being driven by knowledge and innovation. Therefore, these countries have developed training systems to support this change process. In Singapore, study tour participants learned about the remarkable changes to most aspects of TVET programs and the delivery mechanisms that have restructured the traditional vocational workshops and training centers created in the early years. These original programs have been integrated into today's full-fledged system with multiple ladders and built-in opportunities for students to move from TVET streams to the polytechnics and universities.[25] In Vietnam, participants saw a system that appeared to be headed in the same direction.

The openness of Singapore's current system fosters connectedness across courses in terms of curricular content and objectives. The current system offers options to young people who shift interests and develop capabilities at different stages of their lives. The site visits revealed other attractive aspects of the Singapore system. For example, the teaching equipment at all the TVET institutions typically was current by industry standards; students routinely worked on projects commissioned by private industry as part of their final-year studies; and graduates enjoyed high rates of employment. By creating a strong demand from employers, the "poor image" problem traditionally associated with TVET institutions has been kept at bay.

In Vietnam, the emphasis on TVET was equally palpable. Study tour participants were especially struck by how strongly the Vietnamese felt that they needed highly skilled technical workers to compete successfully with their neighbors. They are working hard to attract foreign direct investments (FDIs), and provisions for skilled worker training are a vital part of the packages they negotiate. One such example is the Vietnam-Singapore Training Center in Ho Chi Minh City (HCMC), which the tour participants visited. The center trains workers for firms in the Vietnam-Singapore Industrial Park (VSIP), as well as those in the vicinity, and it is funded by the two governments and VSIP. The skilled workers trained at this center are viewed as assets that the government can use to attract additional FDI.

Study tour participants also visited HCMC Industrial University where the same emphasis was placed on skilled workers. The hosts for the visit explained that foreign companies may take perhaps 10 years to scale up their operations, using a phased approach that buys them time to assess whether Vietnam can indeed supply the skills required. More generally, this approach enables foreign companies to determine whether cultural and other business climate factors are sufficiently favorable to justify a major scaling up of investment. The hosts underlined the need for Vietnam to compete with other East Asian countries to attract FDI and the associated high-end jobs. To attract cutting-edge firms was considered crucial to realize Vietnam's goal of becoming an industrialized country by 2020.

In Korea, the importance of TVET has been stressed since the creation of the Republic in 1948 (see chapter 5 for a summary and the data). But in the early days,

TVET graduates found it hard to obtain good jobs, which naturally dampened demand for this course of study. In the early 1960s, the government reformed the TVET system to sharpen its capacity to train the type of skilled workers required by the country's labor-intensive light manufacturing industries. As a result, by 1970, TVET accounted for 47 percent of all high school students. During the 1970s, the focus of the training shifted to align with the goal of developing the country's heavy-chemical industries. TVET's share of high school enrollment stayed above 40 percent through most of the 1970s and 1980s, and made a marked contribution to Korea's rapid economic growth during this period.[26]

In the 1980s, when Korea's economy was making the transition toward technology-intensive industries, the demand for technically trained workers shifted from the secondary to the tertiary level. Despite the government's efforts during the 1990s to maintain a high share of high school enrollment in TVET— and indeed even to increase it to 50 percent—the share actually dropped steadily, from 42 percent in 1995 to 36 percent in 2000 to 29 percent in 2005. The trend reflects the increasing demand for workers with technical training at the tertiary rather than secondary level (see chapter 5 for details on the ongoing debate in Korea regarding the future role of the TVET high schools).

In Thailand, policy makers were concerned about the balance between the academic and vocational tracks of secondary education, as chapter 6 indicates. A recent external evaluation suggests that low-quality equipment and a shortage of qualified teachers are compromising the quality of instruction. Thus, Thailand appears to be facing similar issues as those faced by Korea and Singapore at an earlier stage of their development. In 2004, 12 percent of Thailand's secondary students were enrolled in TVET programs, but the share was higher at 29 percent in upper-secondary education. Chapter 7 on Ireland tells a similar story to that of Korea and Singapore regarding the second-class label attached to TVET institutions in the early years, and discusses how these institutions were upgraded to become indispensable sources of the technical skills required to support the Irish "economic miracle."

The study tour offered multiple opportunities to explore how successful economies have addressed some of the most vexing issues of TVET development. Given the complexity of these issues, Africa's urgent needs in this area, and the wealth of experience in East Asia, this is one of the most promising areas for follow-up cooperation between East Asian and African countries.

MOBILIZING PUBLIC AND PRIVATE RESOURCES

East Asian governments have acted on their belief that skills, beginning with literacy and numeracy, are fundamental drivers of growth. This belief has sustained for decades a policy of allocating a significant share of the public budget to education.

Sub-Saharan African countries have allocated comparable shares of their GDP to education. But while East Asia's faster economic growth and effective population management have enabled this policy to generate rapidly growing education budgets, the combination of economic stagnation and continued rapid population growth has produced severe budget constraints in Sub-Saharan Africa.

Public education spending in East Asian countries is supplemented by significant financial contributions from families. One calculation for Korea puts family inputs at 50 percent of the national total, and the estimate for Vietnam appears to be of a similar order of magnitude. African families also contribute in a major way to education financing—at a level that has increased during the economic crisis of the 1980s and 1990s—through payment of fees at public schools and financing of teacher salaries at community schools (established largely in rural areas with no public school). In contrast to the Sub-Saharan African approach, however, public financing in East Asia has favored basic education and relied more heavily on private financing for higher education. For example, in 1989, Korean households paid only 2 percent of total expenditures for primary education, but paid 42 percent for junior secondary education, 73 percent for senior secondary education, and 72 percent for colleges and universities (Yoon 2001, 18). Most Sub-Saharan African countries, especially francophone countries, traditionally have spent a high share of public education budgets on providing tuition-free higher education with generous scholarships,[27] while parents contributed to the financing of primary education. For example, a study of 12 francophone countries in 2002 found that on average almost one-third of all primary school teachers were paid by parents rather than by the government (Mingat 2004).[28] A similar survey for Cameroon in 2001 concluded that parents' education expenses corresponded to 44 percent of total expenditures in primary education (World Bank and Pôle de Dakar 2003).[29]

USING EXTERNAL RESOURCES CATALYTICALLY

Foreign aid played a positive role in the development of education during its early stages in Korea and Singapore. When expressed in terms of its share of the education budget, however, that share was lower than currently prevails in Africa, and because it focused on strengthening technical and vocational skills and science research capacity, the aid was different in nature. Early on, aid made an important financial contribution to education reconstruction in Korea, first through the United Nations Korea Reconstruction Agency (UNKRA) and U.S. donations, and later through loans from different development banks, the two largest of which were the World Bank (59 percent of all loans) and the Japanese Overseas Economic Cooperation Fund (24 percent). Over the period 1969–99, the World Bank financed 11 projects in Korea focusing on upper-secondary vocational schools and junior technical colleges. About 80 percent of these loans were used to equip labs and training facilities.

In addition to external financial support and technical advice, East Asian countries have used a number of mechanisms to actively strengthen their technical and scientific skill base and to acquire foreign technology and experience, for example, through licenses, capital good imports, foreign training, use of foreign technical expertise, FDI, and country visits to acquire knowledge.[30] The region's approach has been—and continues to be—characterized by pragmatism and a willingness to test new ideas, adopt what has been found to work, and drop or change what does not work.

Singapore is an excellent example of this approach. Since gaining self-governance in 1959, the government has consistently sought cooperation with industrialized countries and foreign firms to upgrade the technical skills of its labor force. It started by the government requesting the United Nations Development Programme (UNDP) to send a team of experts "from small, developed countries so that Singapore could learn the lessons of development from their experience" (Chan 2002, 5). The resulting report convinced the political leaders that continued dependence on entrepôt industries would not ensure economic survival and that Singapore urgently needed to train the technicians and engineers needed for industrial takeoff. [31]

This training started a process that continually upgraded the country's capacity to develop the various skills required to support its evolving technologically based economy. Although the instruments used have changed over time, the process continues. It includes the creation of specialized training centers with aid from UNDP (by 1968, six centers had been created) and three apprenticeship training centers in cooperation with leading external firms (Tata in 1972, Rollei in 1973, and Philips in 1975). These and other facilities later merged into the Institute of Technical Education, created in 1992, which since has evolved into a world-class postsecondary institution focused on developing vocational and technical skills.[32] Similarly, three institutes were established to provide high-level technology training in cooperation with, respectively, Japan (1979), Germany (1982), and France (1983).[33] In 1993, these three institutes became core elements of the Nanyang Polytechnic. Today, world-class foreign institutions such as the Wharton School of Business are establishing campuses in Singapore, thus providing the country with new opportunities to acquire the necessary skills to undergird an increasingly global and skills-based economy.

The presentations and site visits in Vietnam demonstrated that a similar deliberate and pragmatic process is under way there to develop a TVET system that responds to rapidly evolving labor market demands. In HCMC, study tour participants visited the Royal Melbourne Institute of Technology-Vietnam, a 100 percent foreign-owned private tertiary-level institution (tuition fees are US$6,000 a year), which started with 2,700 students in 1998 and is projected to enroll 10,000 students within the next five years.[34] Rather than see this private enterprise as a threat to the country's socialist ideology, our hosts noted that it adds value by accomplishing what the government cannot do on its own—that is, provide a performance benchmark for the rest of the system, thereby stimulating competition and creating market pressures for improvement, particularly in terms of the alignment of course offerings with labor market conditions and student expectations for the quality of services.

Also noteworthy is Vietnam's view on external aid, which now finances almost 10 percent of the country's investment in education. The Vietnamese government has made it clear that it expects all external aid to fund what the country has determined are its own national priorities. In other words, if an external donor were to come with tied resources that fail this test, the government was quite prepared to forgo the money rather than be side-tracked from its plans. This does not mean that external partnerships are merely tolerated. On the contrary, the deputy prime minister stressed during his meeting with the heads of the study tour delegations that these relationships were indeed highly valued as channels of expert technical assistance, sources of knowledge, and benchmarks for external validation of Vietnam's education performance.

IMPLEMENTATION OF EDUCATION POLICIES

Good policies and strategies will not produce results without determined implementation and follow-up. What seems to characterize implementation in both Singapore and Vietnam is a consistent ability to choose pragmatism over ideology through a deliberate and pragmatic process of testing new ideas, adopting what has been found to work, and dropping or changing what does not work. One member of a country delegation commented that he now saw what Deng Xiaoping meant when he said, "it doesn't matter whether the cat is black or white, as long as it catches mice."

The discussion below highlights a few areas for which deliberate actions have been particularly important in explaining the progress achieved: (a) sequencing of reforms; (b) benchmarking for excellence; (c) retaining high-quality staff; (d) ensuring availability of high-quality yet low-cost training materials for all students; and (e) pricing policies in education.

SEQUENCING REFORMS

Over the past 40 years, many Asian countries have built education systems characterized by a strong foundation of quality universal basic education, diversified options for postbasic education, and multiple (but not haphazard) routes to acquire skills before entry to the labor market, as well as an emphasis on science and mathematics. In Singapore, a skills development fund, financed by employer contributions, has been established to upgrade skills or retrain those already in the labor market, creating a system that practices the concept of lifelong learning. Similarly, in Korea, a number of initiatives have been taken—by the government and the private sector—to promote lifelong competency building. Vietnam has also developed proactive policies designed to reach this goal. Asian countries are beginning to reap significant benefits from their sustained investment in science and technology capabilities, as seen by a pattern of economic development that increasingly draws its strength from skills, technology, knowledge, and innovation. Against this backdrop, tour participants were keen to understand how Asian countries have sequenced their reforms to achieve the remarkable transformation of their education systems.

At risk of oversimplification and without implying a strict sequencing of interventions, the pattern, particularly in basic education, has generally been as follows:

- First, expand quantity to ensure access while tolerating "low quality" in terms of inputs such as less qualified teachers, large class size, and multiple shifts (the "low-cost approach" described in chapter 5)
- Next, upgrade the worst-off schools to meet minimum standards of inputs
- Finally, upgrade the quality of inputs and tighten management of the inputs, especially teachers, to meet standards for performance as measured by learning outcomes

These steps make up a continuous series of overlapping interventions intended to move the system forward and position it to perform even better in the next phase. This attitude of seeking progressive and continuous improvement is applied to the whole system, not just basic education. In other words, while emphasizing basic education as a first priority, Asian countries simultaneously grow and reform the rest of the system and expect these other parts to perform to ever higher standards as well. For the latter, indicators of results include the employment status of graduates, employer satisfaction with their job performance, and the graduates' aggregate contribution to moving the economy up the technological and economic value chain.

In Singapore, the approach to sequencing was accomplished in three phases: a survival-driven phase (1965–78), an efficiency-driven phase (1978–97), and a knowledge- and ability-driven phase (1997–present) (the content of each phase is described in chapter 3). The focus in the early years had been to put together the building blocks to align the education system with the national development agenda, an effort that involved (a) rationalizing the curriculum and addressing language-of-instruction issues to create a unitary system; (b) developing textbooks to go with the curriculum; (c) reforming the examination system and certification framework; (d) standardizing procedures and processes in schools to lay the groundwork for school-based management; and (e) investing in staff development programs for school heads and teachers to professionalize and strengthen the teaching service and its managers. As the institutional structure took shape, the shift toward the efficiency- and knowledge-driven phases meant intervening to make the system more efficient and ever more responsive to the economic agenda. In vocational and technical education, the system is now sufficiently mature that institutions routinely use tracer surveys of graduates to evaluate the effectiveness and relevance of course offerings.

Korea also placed clear priority on universalization of primary education. To achieve this goal at a time when the infrastructure was largely destroyed because of the Korean War, during which time the primary-school-age population was still growing and the education budget was severely constrained, the government gave clear priority to quantitative expansion through the "low-cost approach" described above. This policy choice was a temporary measure, followed by measures to address quality issues when the quantitative objective of universal primary education had been reached in the late 1950s. It is interesting to note that a similar "low-cost approach" was followed to universalize lower-secondary education during the 1970s and 1980s and to achieve the rapid expansion of higher education during the 1980s. For example, average class size in lower-secondary education stayed above 60 during the period 1955–85 and reached a peak of 65.7 in 1979. Average class size was brought down through a combination of fewer students and more teachers, reaching 35 in 2005. Similarly, in upper-secondary education, average class size remained around 60 until about 1985, and then started to decline, reaching 34 in 2005. Once enrollment targets were attained, efforts were redirected toward education quality enhancement.

In Vietnam, a similar sequencing of interventions is under way. The country has completed the early stages of reform and is now implementing quality standards and outcome-based management of the education system. It is entering the equivalent of the efficiency phase experienced in Singapore, but the country is simultaneously attempting to leapfrog toward the knowledge-driven phase (and perhaps also the ability-driven phase). The desire to strengthen and expand TVET is strong, and some of the arrangements that worked in Singapore (for example, governance structures that engaged industry leaders in determining the course curricula) are being scaled up in Vietnam.

Thailand likewise gave strong priority to achieving universal primary education, reaching a GER of about 83 percent in 1970 and 96 percent in 1980. The strong priority on universalizing primary education—targeting the enrollment of children from poor families—was maintained until the early 1990s when

Thailand started a drive to rapidly develop secondary education[35] as well (the GER at that level increased from 31 percent in 1990 to 82 percent in 2000).

Ireland, like all western European countries, gave high priority to achieving universal primary education, using "low-cost" approaches to provide education in rural areas close to the families. Even in year 2000, more than a quarter of all classrooms were multigrade, combining two grades (or age-groups), and 16 percent had more than two grades. But in the twenty-first century, the emphasis has shifted to tertiary education, where one-third of the workforce now holds a university degree.

BENCHMARKING FOR EDUCATION EXCELLENCE

The drive for excellence was particularly evident in Singapore, but it was interesting to note how strongly the Vietnamese also embraced it. In fact, the value placed on education achievement goes back a long, long way as we learned in Hanoi. There study tour participants visited the Temple of Literature, the 1,000-year-old site of Vietnam's first university, where the most successful candidates sitting for imperial examinations were honored by having their names carved permanently onto large stone tablets.

East Asian countries have an ancient tradition of merit-based professional mobility based on exams. Korea provides an excellent example of this system, which created a "virtuous circle" of quality. Formal academic credentials—the principle criterion for merit—were achieved through highly competitive exams, the results of which formed the basis for selection into jobs in both the private and public sectors. Rules of examinations were the same for everybody, and the content was confined to what was covered in textbooks. Absence of corruption in the examination and selection process encouraged students and parents to do their best and to accept the outcomes.[36]

As described in chapter 5, however, competitive examinations also presented disadvantages, including an emphasis on memorization, high examination pressure on students, and extensive reliance on private tutoring, which poor families could ill afford. Therefore, in 1968, the government abolished entrance exams in lower-secondary education and introduced a lottery system for student placement in high schools, designed to provide equal opportunity of access to the most prestigious schools. In 1974, the government also adopted the High School Equalization Policy, intended to equalize such school inputs as operating expenditures, class size, and education facilities. As a result, no discernable quality difference can be found across public schools or between public and private institutions. In short, the examination system has accompanied education progress, as Korea universalized first lower, then higher, secondary education, and expanded tertiary education to almost two-thirds of the relevant age-group.

The tradition in East Asian countries to measure their learning against high standards continues today with an interesting twist—by measuring themselves against world standards and taking deliberate action to reach those standards. For school education, the benchmarks include the international assessments of student learning, such as the Trends in International Mathematics and Science Study (TIMSS), in which several Asian countries have participated for many years now. In the 2003 survey, the top five countries for eighth-grade performance in mathematics were all from East Asia, with Singapore on the top,[37] followed by the Republic of Korea, Hong Kong (China), Chinese Taipei, and Japan. Singapore was on top of the 2003 survey for eighth-grade science, with Chinese Taipei second, the Republic of Korea third, Hong Kong (China) fourth, and Japan fifth.[38] In Africa, only three countries—Botswana, Ghana, and South Africa—participated in TIMSS 2003, although many of these countries do take part in regional assessments (for example, Francophone countries in PASEC [Programme d'analyse des systèmes éducatifs de la CONFEMEN, or Conférence des ministres de l'éducation des pays ayant le français en partage] and Anglophone countries in SACMEQ [Southern Africa Consortium for Monitoring Educational Quality]).

Singapore continues to rely on the British system of "O-" and "A-level" examinations, for the simple reason that these examinations offer an external validation of the quality of instruction and open doors for students to pursue studies overseas. Both Singapore and Vietnam send their best and brightest students to compete in international academic Olympiads (mathematics and the sciences) in which the young competitors test their mettle against other bright students, and get a chance to mingle with and be inspired by the Nobel Laureates who frequently attend these events (eight of them will participate in this year's Physics Olympiad in Singapore). Winning is clearly only part of the story: The goal is to provide role models for the country's budding talent and through them to inspire the rest of their cohort.

Finally, the trend toward establishment of branches of renowned foreign universities in East Asian countries (such as Singapore and Vietnam) is another important way for these countries to benchmark the standards in their higher education institutions against the best in the world.

ATTRACTING AND RETAINING HIGH-QUALITY STAFF

Attracting and retaining high-quality staff is relevant at the systemic level, at which the concern is about the connection between education and goals of nation building and social and economic development, and the individual school and institutional level, at which the concern is about schooling outcomes. In each case, effective management is vital for efficient resource use as well as for the choice and implementation of cost-effective learning strategies. Effective management depends not only on the skills of school managers and administrators but also on the management capacity of teachers who, in addition to their main pedagogical duties, are given important management functions with respect to how they manage classroom instruction and how they use school resources.

With respect to teachers, East Asian countries recognized that devoted and quality teachers at all levels of education are fundamental to achieving quality education. These countries have used a combination of financial and nonfinancial incentives to achieve this quality. Salary level is not the only factor affecting the attractiveness of the teaching profession, but it is an important factor. In the initial stages of their economic takeoff, East Asian countries did not pay their teachers high salaries. Even in the 1990s, data for a sample of countries indicate that the average pay was about 2.5 times the per capita GDP. Similar to other salaried workers, however, teachers benefited from the rapid increase in average national income.

This pay increase is quite different from the situation in most Sub-Saharan African countries. These countries suffered sharp declines both in GDP per capita (by 36 percent on average between 1970 and 1997) and in primary school teacher salaries expressed in per capita terms (from 8.6 times GDP per capita in 1975 to 6 times GDP in 1992 to 4.4 times GDP in 2000) (Mingat 2004).[39] The combination of these two factors eroded the salaries of Sub-Saharan African teachers (like those of most other civil servants) during the last two decades of the twentieth century, especially in Francophone countries. The loss of income, and the absence of explicit validation of their role in society, further undercut the professional morale of educators. Apart from affecting salary levels, the decline severely constrained the overall education budget, thus limiting teacher recruitment, increasing class size, and causing extreme shortages of other pedagogical inputs.[40] Following the recent resumption of growth, many countries are trying to address this problem. The tradeoffs in the use of these increased public budgets among competing needs—such as higher salaries, better trained teachers, smaller classes, more training materials, or abolition of school fees—are extremely difficult in a situation of continued high population growth and strong demand pressure on postprimary education.

This contrasts with the situation in East Asia, where economic growth has made it possible to raise the pay of teachers over time. In Singapore, teacher pay is now highly competitive. It is comparable to that of recent law school graduates, for example, which explains the surplus of candidates over available openings in teacher-training programs. In Korea, the entry level salary in 1995 for a primary school teacher was already slightly above the average in member countries of the Organisation for Economic Co-operation and Development (see chapter 5). In Vietnam between 1999 and 2001, the pay of teachers rose at all levels of education, but especially in primary education where a fourfold increase occurred (albeit from a very low base, see chapter 4). Incentives are in place to attract teachers to less popular rural postings. Notably, the study tour presentations for Vietnam and Thailand underlined the strong financial incentives reserved for teachers who accept and remain in rural posts.

Apart from these financial incentives, Asian countries are also using nonfinancial rewards to attract and retain good teachers. In Singapore, for example, better rewards and recognition combined with comprehensive in-service professional development has improved the image of the profession and attracted higher-quality teaching talent. Singapore motivates teachers by recognizing that teachers mold the nation's future; they offer teachers meaningful career tracks leading to positions as master teachers, school principals, and senior administrators or specialists. This policy is backed up by a pay structure that keeps the incentives for the various tracks in balance. At the same time, they encourage continuous professional upgrading by allowing teachers to earn credits from in-service training that accumulate toward formal certification (for example, master's and doctoral degrees).

Vietnam has likewise launched efforts to raise the status of the teaching profession, beginning with the pay increase mentioned above, as well as through a stock-taking exercise to establish a baseline of teacher qualifications (or "profiles") to inform the design of a strategy to strengthen pre-service and in-service training. Parallel efforts are under way to improve the effectiveness of teacher deployment, organization, and utilization, as well as to address the skill development needs of teachers and managers in areas such as computer competence and mastery of foreign languages (primarily English). More generally, while the high social status of teachers is well-established and requires little development in the Confucian-influenced societies of East Asia, the political leadership nonetheless relies on social marketing as well as pecuniary and nonpecuniary rewards to reinforce and affirm their status, including regular opportunities for staff development.

Over the last three decades or so, East Asian countries—similar to the experience of most European countries in the 1950s and 1960s—have been upgrading the training of their primary school teachers from secondary-level programs to postsecondary degree programs. In Korea until the 1960s, primary school teachers were trained at secondary-level teacher-training colleges. In 1962, these colleges were upgraded into junior teacher-training colleges at the postsecondary level and again in 1982 to colleges offering four years of postsecondary training leading to a degree. The four-year programs were introduced after enrollment levels had peaked as a result of the decline in fertility rates. This gradual upgrading increased the attraction of the teaching profession and positioned the education sector to compete successfully for qualified staff during a period of rapid economic growth.

In Vietnam, the upgrading of teacher-training programs—from lower-secondary education plus three years of teacher training to programs of upper-secondary

education plus one year of teacher training—is ongoing. To be considered "qualified," primary school teachers must hold an upper-secondary pedagogical
diploma. In school year 2004–05, 82 percent of teachers met this requirement,
while 10 percent held college or university degrees.

Many African countries are seeking to provide primary school teachers with
opportunities to pursue postsecondary degree programs. But because of continued
rapid growth in the primary-school-age population, countries find it difficult to
cope financially with the impact this has on the teacher salary budget. Before
recruitment of teachers holding postsecondary degrees becomes affordable, many
Sub-Saharan African countries are implementing intermediate measures (similar
to those adapted earlier in Singapore and Korea, and now in Vietnam) to improve teacher qualifications by increasing the entry requirements to primary school
teacher-training programs from completion of lower-secondary education to completion of upper-secondary education, followed by one or two years of pedagogical
training. African countries can also learn from the approach of East Asian countries,
which extends systematic in-service training and other support to existing teachers.

Regarding education mangers, Singapore has done a lot to validate the role of
managers at all levels and to empower them to lead. The debate about what kind
of manager should be put in charge of education institutions—professional business managers or educators—appears to have been resolved by combining both
qualifications. To this end, educators who seek to become school heads are
selected carefully and given specific training as managers, ensuring that they not
only can handle their institution's day-to-day operations but also can make strategic choices informed by their personal knowledge of the teaching and learning
process. Vietnam is also upgrading the management expertise, computer skills,
and professionalism of its education managers.

Seniority plays almost no role in a competency-based system. Rigorous screen-
ing and recruitment of potential principals and leaders in education is as important as the training provided to this small pool of candidates. Within the technical
institutions, managers are often either technical specialists with managerial training or former industry leaders who naturally would be keenly aware of the skills
required to run a competitive business. For all managers, the performance expectations are clear—that is, achieve global standards for learning outcomes and
economic impact.

PROVIDING HIGH-QUALITY LOW-COST TRAINING MATERIALS FOR ALL

In addition to qualified and committed teachers, no other education input is
likely to be more important to the quality of the learning process than the availability to all students of high-quality written learning materials. This is especially true in countries where many teachers have little training, classes are large,

duration of the effective school year is comparatively short, and homes are lacking in alternative reading materials. The two countries visited, as well as Korea, did exceptionally well in ensuring early on that their drive to universalize primary education included universal access to quality textbooks. Again, this experience is relevant to Sub-Saharan African countries where schools generally suffer from a severe shortage of textbooks and where book prices often are much higher than in East Asian countries.

After attaining self-governance in 1959, the government of Singapore chose as an urgent national priority to inculcate students with shared civic values and responsibilities to achieve social and racial harmony.[41] The textbooks available at that time were produced by private publishers only in English with content largely not relevant to the issues faced by the new state. The Ministry of Education set up a Civic Training Subject Committee (1966–73) to develop a syllabus and produce civics textbooks, which first were developed in Chinese. More textbooks were developed by seconded textbook writers working under a University of Singapore editorial board. To ensure low cost, the Ministry established the Education Publishing Bureau (EPB) in 1967, tasked with producing affordable textbooks that promoted national objectives such as social cohesion and nation building. As a government agency, EPB was able to make textbooks available in the three main languages by cross-subsidizing development of textbooks for the two smaller groups (Malay and Tamil) with income from the sales of textbooks for the largest group (in Mandarin for the Chinese). A textbook-to-student ratio of 1:1 in key subjects was reached at an early stage.

Over time, the Singapore government implemented various mechanisms to ensure that syllabuses and textbook materials evolved in a way that reflected successive changes in education policies made to respond to changing national economic and social priorities. For example, after the introduction in 1979 of a major education reform (the New Education System, NES) to support the restructuring of its economic strategy, the government set up the Curriculum Institute of Singapore (CDIS). The CDIS changed the syllabuses and textbooks so that they were consistent with NES objectives. Following successful implementation of the NES, the CDIS was closed down in 1996 and its staff transferred to the Ministry of Education to serve other functions. At that time, the responsibility for textbook publishing returned to the private sector, based on syllabuses and specifications defined by the Ministry. In the process, the EPB was privatized. Schools now choose among various Ministry-approved textbooks.

In short, over a 30-year period, Singapore went full circle in textbook publishing. It began with commercially produced textbooks mostly unsuitable for Singapore schools; transitioned to textbooks developed by education ministry agencies to be consistent with education reforms and complement the shortage of well-trained teachers, but printed by private printers; and then shifted back to commercially produced textbooks reflecting syllabuses approved by the Ministry.

This evolution reflects the maturation of the Singapore education system and economy. The quality of Singaporean textbooks is now recognized internationally, and Singaporean publishers export textbooks and other training materials and help developing countries establish national publishing capacities.

Vietnam has also had a positive experience with respect to textbooks, and learning about this experience was an important part of the study tour program. In particular, the role played by the Education Publishing House in managing the different stages of the "textbook chain" is interesting and highly relevant to African countries—for example, the way textbook manuscripts are developed and tested; the printing and distribution of the books (based on outsourcing through competitive bidding); and the way foreign technical assistance (for example, from Singapore) has supported this process. The way textbooks are financed is also noteworthy (about 80 percent of children have to pay for their textbooks, while 20 percent of children living in poor areas get them free).

The financial contribution by parents is facilitated by the fact that Vietnam has managed to develop excellent-quality textbooks at a price (covering all costs) that ranges from the equivalent of one-third to about two-thirds of a U.S. dollar. This compares favorably with the US$2 to US$4 textbook price in most Sub-Saharan African countries. The way textbooks are distributed to areas that are difficult to access and how teachers are trained in their use are other valuable techniques. The importance given to textbooks in Vietnam's education policy is well illustrated by the following statement in chapter 4 of this book: "The replacement of textbooks at all schools—the most important task in the third education reform and completed in 1996—brought consistency to general education across the nation."

Wide access to textbooks also formed a key component of Korea's education development strategy. During the reconstruction period after the Korean War, UNKRA helped Korea publish textbooks for primary education. Later on, Korea developed a system that relied both on textbooks developed by the Ministry of Education and on textbooks developed by individual authors. Each type of textbook reflected the curriculum developed by the Ministry, and each needed Ministry approval before schools could use them. Up to 1980, textbooks developed by the Ministry accounted for the largest share of the textbooks used. Since then, this share has declined, and the role of the Ministry is increasingly limited to review and approval of manuscripts. Commercial publishers also produce a variety of reference materials and workbooks.

PRICING POLICIES IN EDUCATION

Some of the tour participants were surprised to discover that charging fees for public education is standard practice in East Asia. To protect disadvantaged groups, the fee policy is invariably coupled with provisions to identify and exempt children from these groups rather than to provide blanket subsidies to all. This seems to be a common attitude among Asian policy makers. Such realism is reflected again in chapter 4 of this book: "the people, however, thought that their children's education, even vocational or higher education, should have been subsidized. . . . The people's expectations of state subsidies were inappropriate in a poor and developing country like Vietnam, especially in the context of a postwar period and economic crisis. . . ."

In East Asia the cost to parents rises with level of education (primary education is now tuition free in most cases). Families are typically expected to pay for textbooks, even at the primary level, on the argument that when families pay for them, children take better care of the books. Compared with the situation in Africa, it is important to note that this policy of charging for textbooks at the primary level is made more affordable to parents by the following factors: (a) the comparatively low costs of textbooks (see above reference to Singapore and Vietnam); (b) the low number of children per family; (c) well-developed systems for targeting subsidies to poor families; and (d) rapid economic growth that has produced much lower poverty levels, including in Vietnam.

In Korea, although primary education was compulsory, parents initially had to buy textbooks and pay supplementary fees to operate the schools. Later, a special scheme was set up to eliminate fees and provide free textbooks to poor families. The abolition of fees for primary education started in rural areas before the benefit was spread to urban schools. The 1968 decision to abolish entrance examinations to lower-secondary schools set the stage for extending the duration of compulsory education to include lower-secondary education as well. As part of this policy, the government again implemented a financial support policy that included the abolition of tuition fees and payment for textbooks for lower-secondary education, starting with remote rural and fishing communities and for low-income families. China has reportedly sent officials to Korea to study this approach and is learning from the experience to inform its own efforts to promote economic development and reduce poverty in rural areas. The Thai and Vietnamese governments have adopted similar approaches to promote schooling in rural areas (for example, free tuition and textbooks, scholarships, secondary boarding schools for ethnic minorities, and so on).

PARTICIPANT IMPRESSIONS AND FOLLOW-UP PLANS

This final section summarizes the impressions formed and reinforced during the study tour among the participants, and considers a tentative agenda for follow-up.

PARTICIPANT IMPRESSIONS

On the last day of the study tour, a structured discussion was organized to allow participants to share the key lessons they drew from the event, particularly regarding teachers, textbooks, school facilities, education finance, management of the education system, development of postprimary education, and leadership in education. Each national team made a formal presentation based on their team discussion and outlined a plan for post-tour action. Each team's action plan was unique, but a careful review suggests two themes are common in the plans of all six countries:

- Strengthening the link between education and the economy through a variety of mechanisms, among them the diversification of options beyond primary education, focusing on skill development and lifelong learning, and the institutionalization of engagement with key stakeholders from industry, particularly employers, in this effort.
- Promoting excellence in schools by paying close attention to teacher training and school management issues, developing curriculum and textbooks, and benchmarking through the use of continuous student assessments.

On the link between education and the economy, all of the six African countries face serious concerns about the development trajectories of both general secondary education and TVET. The demand for secondary education is growing as these countries advance toward the EFA goal, and these countries are grappling with issues[42] that most Asian countries have successfully addressed—that is, universalizing lower-secondary education in a fiscally viable manner; managing the inevitable need for selective admission to publicly funded upper-secondary and tertiary education; striking a balance in the curriculum between vocational and general subjects; and so on. With regard to TVET, the depth of concern is evident from the interventions of the country delegations during the tour. Developing appropriate national policies for TVET is perhaps the *single-most difficult education and training challenge facing African countries today.* This is due to the following reasons:

- The economic stagnation in Africa during the 1980s and 1990s has stifled the development of TVET. The systems that exist today in most countries are generally obsolete in terms of equipment and management, and they are poorly positioned to assist with a resumption and acceleration of economic growth.
- There is no obvious correct model, the way forward is filled with blind alleys, and the scope for costly mistakes is large.
- African countries have limited access to high-quality international expertise in this area to help them evaluate options in TVET and make good policy choices.
- The modern sector is nascent in most African countries, making it difficult to match investments in TVET with current and projected labor market demand.
- Policy makers sometimes hold a misguided perception that secondary and tertiary graduates cannot find jobs *because they lack the "right" technical skills.* This line of reasoning suggests that the employment problem can be "solved"

simply by investing in TVET in an attempt to supply the missing skills. Yet focusing on the supply side alone is unlikely to work. To succeed, supply-side action must match the skill requirements implied by the country's development strategy, as well as by the specific worker characteristics desired by prospective employers. East Asian countries, particularly Singapore, have applied the supply-chain logic to plan their investments in TVET, taking their cue from industry and employers to work out the skills and training implications; and they have been particularly adept at finding effective institutional arrangements to connect the supply and demand sides of the education equation.

On promoting excellence in schools, it is striking that the main ingredients for excellence are standard features in practically all World Bank–financed education operations in the Africa Region, including teachers, curriculum, textbooks, management, and student assessments. In budget support operations, these ingredients may remain in the background, but they play an important part in the story, in the sense that such operations transfer resources that eventually fund operating expenditures in education through the sector's claim on the government budget.

The Asia study tour highlighted just how important good management is as a quality-enhancing complement to the more traditional inputs of teachers, books, and classrooms. The plentiful supply of books at affordable cost in Asia was a distressing discovery for tour participants, because the reality in Africa after decades of donor support for textbooks is that school books are limited in choice, expensive, and often unavailable for countless African children. The need for good textbooks and other written pedagogical materials, along with the in-service teacher training to go with them, is clear. But many African countries will need to make a decision on what is perhaps a more fundamental issue—that of language of instruction. As long as this issue remains unsettled, it would seem difficult to make significant headway with curriculum reform and textbook development (for further discussion see chapter 2).

The challenges in the above two priority areas identified by the participants are huge. Tackling them will require much stronger national leadership than typically has been observed in Africa in the past. But it will also need catalytic support from Africa's development partners. To offer such support, it is important in each setting to reflect on such fundamental questions as the following: Do we have sufficient knowledge to articulate a time-bound roadmap for tying the education and training system more tightly to the economy and for fostering excellence in education? Are the basic building blocks for reform in place? Is the implementation plan realistic and well-sequenced? Do we have a good sense of where countries are currently located in the reform agenda? Are we helping countries develop systems with interconnecting parts, or are we reinforcing silo mentalities? Have we paid sufficient attention to promoting national leadership throughout the system (for example, fostering a culture of learning by doing and being responsive to feedback)? Are we finding ways to help mobilize sustained support for education from the country's top leadership? Are we helping counterparts in the education sector establish an appropriate communications strategy to reach key audiences with information that will engage them and garner their support for education? These are just some of the issues to keep in mind as development partners consider ways of providing more effective assistance.

AN AGENDA FOR FOLLOW-UP

In the best of circumstances, study tours may generate some impact on the development of education in the participating countries, thanks to follow-up actions taken by committed individuals among the tour participants. More often, however, study tours tend to end up as isolated events with questionable impact in the absence of structured and systematic post-tour action. To avoid this outcome and to take advantage of the ideas stimulated by the tour, various follow-up options were discussed. Interest centered on the following possibilities:

- Support to the participating countries to implement their action plans as developed and presented during the study tour. This includes facilitating direct interaction between the six African countries and countries in East Asia.
- A conference to report on progress made in carrying out the national-level action plans and to share related experiences.
- Broader dissemination of insights from the study tour.

As of this writing, some progress has been made on each of these ideas, as outlined briefly below.

On the post-tour support to the participating countries, the World Bank education task team leader for each country will manage this work as part of their normal responsibilities, drawing on support where needed and feasible from the broader development community. Several countries on the tour have expressed a desire to develop institutional ties with Asian countries, particularly Singapore, to facilitate continued knowledge exchange and to benefit from support for implementation of their action plans. Accordingly, the Africa Region of the World Bank signed a Memorandum of Understanding (MoU) in December 2006 with the government of Singapore as a framework for continued collaboration following the study tour. Under the terms of the MoU, the Singapore government will host a second workshop in January 2008, this time targeting a larger number of participants from a smaller number of countries, to form a critical mass of policy makers with a shared exposure to Asia's story in the education sector. The specific purpose of the workshop is to achieve the following:

- Better understand the *nature and scope of the visionary and strategic leadership* required to align the education and training sector to the economy.
- Acquire practical ideas to facilitate reforms in the TVET sector now being prepared or implemented in the participating countries that will result in the development of a *high-performance skills development system.*
- Gain practical know-how to foster *leadership for excellence in schools.*

To translate ideas into action and tangible results, the workshop will enable the participants to achieve the following:

- Prepare an *action plan* that crystallizes specific ideas from the workshop for implementation as part of the ongoing education sector programs in their own countries.
- Establish *contacts with specific institutions* in Singapore for potential postworkshop collaboration.

On the follow-up conference to report on progress with the national action plans, an idea was mentioned in the closing remarks of the study tour. The purpose of such a conference would be to create a forum for the national teams to share their experiences with implementation of their action plans and to learn from each other, thereby keeping up the momentum for progress. Given its purpose, the event should be timed to occur after a suitable time lag, to allow a sufficient interval for plans to mature and to be implemented. As a first step toward such a conference, a session on the study tour and the follow-up workshop will be included in the program of the Biennale of the Association for the Development of Education in Africa (ADEA), currently scheduled to take place in Mozambique in May 2008.

On the broader dissemination of insights from the study tour, the outcomes of the study tour were presented to World Bank staff and others at the Bank's Human Development Forum (October 30 to November 1, 2006), with the participation of resource persons, particularly those from Singapore. More important, in addition to this publication, another publication is in the pipeline and a video of the visits to Singapore and Vietnam (with an abbreviated and a full-length version) has been completed. The video was shown at the World Bank conference on Secondary Education in Africa (April 1–4, 2007), which was attended by 28 ministers of education and some 300 participants from 36 African countries. As part of the continuing dissemination effort, the video will also be made available to participants at the 2008 ADEA Biennale.

Further learning from Asia's experience in education is both attractive and feasible. The attraction lies in the fact that many East Asian countries started off in circumstances that were quite similar to those of African countries and yet they have managed to shed the limitations of their colonial heritage and carve a path toward national development and economic prosperity. The feasibility flows from the opening created by the study tour to Singapore and Vietnam, and by the promise of follow-up exchanges and dissemination through print and video. The Asia–Africa comparison does not mean that lessons from Asia can be adopted wholesale for application in Africa, because each African country faces unique challenges that call for custom approaches adapted to local conditions.

An examination of the Asian experience reveals common elements across countries that provide opportunities for reflection. Not surprisingly, a consistent element is visionary leadership at the highest level of government—leadership that prioritizes investments in education as an integral part of the strategy for national development, which in turn creates mechanisms to foster productive dialogue and consensus building among the relevant stakeholders, and matches political rhetoric with attention to follow-through in policy implementation. Within the education sector, other commonalities across Asian countries include the use of an integrated approach to policy development across all levels of education and training; the emphasis on TVET; and the mobilization of private resources to supplement public spending on education. Last but not least, East Asian countries have demonstrated the importance of using external resources catalytically to advance their own national goals in education. Hopefully, these lessons from Asia's experience will prove useful in helping African governments revitalize the education and training systems in their countries.

NOTES

1. Past study tours organized by the World Bank's Africa Region Human Development Department include a visit in 2000 to Guatemala and El Salvador for delegations from Benin, Guinea, Madagascar, Mali, and Niger; followed by a second tour in 2001 to India and Bangladesh for delegations from Cameroon, Nigeria, Rwanda, Sierra Leone, and Tanzania. In 2004, the Department sponsored a tour organized by UNESCO's International Institute for Capacity Building in Africa to Thailand and Malaysia for delegations from The Gambia, Lesotho, Nigeria, Kenya, and Zambia.

2. These countries were chosen for this visit largely because they were all implementing major education sector development programs with external support and faced issues on which East Asia's experience offered potentially useful lessons.

3. These included a representative from a bilateral donor (United Kingdom's Department for International Development) and the executive secretary of the Association for the Development of Education in Africa. One other bilateral donor and UNESCO were invited to send a representative each, but the invitees were eventually unable to participate because of scheduling conflicts.

4. The program was designed through an iterative process of internal consultations with World Bank education sector staff and through them, with the African country delegations; and through consultations with officials from Singapore and Vietnam. The Singapore

government agreed not only to host the visit, but also to co-sponsor it and finance all the local costs in Singapore, including lodging for the African participants. International Enterprise Singapore bore responsibility for the logistics of the program in Singapore, while its content was developed in cooperation with the Ministry of Foreign Affairs and the National Institute of Education. In Vietnam, the staff of the World Bank's team working on education provided the essential link to government counterparts and facilitated collaboration with the relevant government counterparts on the substantive and logistical design of the visit in Vietnam. The quality of the cooperation and the resulting program was truly outstanding in terms of both substance and organization.

5. Throughout this chapter, the term "East Asian countries" refers generally to the countries covered in the presentations made during the study tour. The coverage coincides broadly with what the literature commonly refers to as the "Four East Asian Tigers"—that is, Hong Kong (China), the Republic of Korea, Singapore, and Taiwan (China)—but also includes other newly industrial East Asian countries such as Malaysia and Thailand.

6. See Annex 1 for the study tour program.

7. Many African countries share experiences and challenges in the education sector common to those faced by Asian countries in the early years of their development experience, but African countries also grapple with issues that are unique to their circumstances. The discussion in this chapter is thus offered in the spirit of illustrative information, based on an admittedly limited though rich exchange. It does not replace, but complements, the more in-depth comparative analyses that would be required to paint a more complete picture of the similarities and differences between Asian and African countries in the education sector.

8. A World Bank study of economic growth in East Asia during the three decades ending in the early 1990s concluded that "[t]heir rapid growth had two complementary elements. First, getting the fundamentals right was essential. Without high levels of domestic savings, broadly based human capital, good macro-economic management, and limited price distortions, there would have been no basis for growth and no means by which the gains of rapid productivity change could be realized. . . . Second, very rapid growth . . . has at times benefited from careful policy interventions" (World Bank 1993, 23–24).

9. The figure for Sub-Saharan Africa excludes South Africa.

10. In the 1990s, four of the six countries experienced annual per capita GDP growth: Ethiopia (1 percent), Ghana (1.7 percent), and Lesotho and Mozambique (3 percent), whereas Cameroon and Madagascar saw an average annual *decline* of 1.2 percent and 1.3 percent, respectively. During the period 2000–04, all countries except Madagascar saw growth, ranging from 0.8 percent in Ethiopia to 6.7 percent in Mozambique. The decline in Madagascar continued during this period at an annual rate of −1.8 percent.

11. The following figures on public expenditure on education as percentage of GDP illustrate this point:

Country	1960	1989	2004
Korea, Rep. of	2.0	3.6	4.6
Singapore	2.8	3.4	3.1 (2005)
Thailand	2.3	3.2	4.3
Vietnam	—	3.5 (1994)	4.6
Sub-Saharan Africa	2.4	4.1	4.6

In Africa, the level of spending varies more widely across countries, ranging from less than 2 percent of GDP to about 9 percent (for example, Lesotho in 2004). Apart from Lesotho, the other five countries participating in the study tour devoted between 3.3 and 4.6 percent of their GDP to education around 2002–04. See World Bank (1993, 198) for 1960 and 1989 data, and UNESCO (2006) for 2004 data. Data for Vietnam are from chapter 4. Data for 2005 for Singapore was taken from Ng (2008) for government expenditures on education and from World Bank (2006c) for GDP.

12. As will be discussed, in addition to the budgetary constraint resulting from poor economic growth, Sub-Saharan African countries also gave much lower priority to primary education in their education budgets than did East Asia.

13. These mainly included the richer countries: Botswana, Cape Verde, Mauritius, Namibia, the Seychelles, South Africa, and Swaziland. A GER of 100 percent does not indicate universal primary school completion, which is the EFA target.

14. Cameroon, Ghana, Kenya, Madagascar, Nigeria, Republic of Congo, Tanzania, Zambia, and Zimbabwe. Of these countries, all but Congo and Ghana had in 2004 regained a primary GER of 99 percent or above, see UNESCO (2006, Annex Table 5).

15. Examples include land reforms in Korea and massive public housing programs in Singapore and Hong Kong (China).

16. In the mid-1990s, Sub-Saharan Africa's Gini coefficient was estimated at 51.0, as compared to 38.1 for East Asia. The richest 20 percent had 51 percent of national income as compared to 44 percent in East Asia. The poorest 20 percent had 5 percent in Sub-Saharan African countries as compared to 7 percent in East Asia (World Bank 2000a, 92–93).

17. These figures refer to the median for Sub-Saharan African countries.

18. Singapore has had particularly rapid changes in its population since its founding in 1819. In the early periods, the growth was rapid (admittedly starting from a low base). For example, the total population increased tenfold between 1891 and 1964, and doubled between 1947 and 1965. When fertility levels started to decline in the mid- to late-1950s, however, the speed of the decline was spectacularly fast (resembling that of postwar Japan). For example, the crude birth rate was almost halved in a little more than a decade, declining from 42.7 in 1957 to 22.1 in 1969 (see Jones 1975, 169).

19. The estimates refer to 1988–89 for Korea and Thailand and 1980–81 for Singapore.

20. This factor has been noted as important for the "takeoff" on sustained economic growth in the Nordic countries. For example, among the favorable "preconditions" for the start of long-term growth around 1830 in Norway was ". . . a rather well-developed bureaucracy staffed with fairly competent and incorruptible officials" (see Fredriksen 1985, 73).

21. The paper on Ireland also stresses the importance of government policy dialogue with labor organizations in helping solve the economic crisis that country faced in the mid-1980s. Such dialogue has become a cornerstone of development in the Nordic countries.

22. At their first regional education conference after gaining independence, organized by UNESCO in Addis Ababa in 1961, Sub-Saharan African countries agreed to reach universal primary education by 1980. At a similar regional conference held in Karachi in 1960, Asian countries agreed on the same target year for this goal. The progress actually achieved by 1980 in reaching this target is reviewed in Fredriksen (1981).

23. As described in the paper on Ireland, curriculum reform was also the first major education reform introduced in Ireland after independence in 1922.

24. The key role of skill development in the transition from school to work is reviewed in Adams (2007).

25. Korea and Singapore's proactive use of foreign aid to strengthen their TVET capacity is further discussed below.

26. In 2004, the enrollment in technical and vocational programs in Sub-Saharan Africa included on average only 6 percent of total secondary school enrollment (3 percent in lower secondary and 11 percent in upper secondary). Only 7 of the 29 countries for which data were available had more than 10 percent of their secondary enrollment in such programs (see UNESCO/Institute for Statistics 2006, 102–104).

27. The situation in Senegal illustrates this point. In 1990, 78 percent of higher education students had scholarships, and public expenditures on scholarships, student food, lodging, and so on, represented 52 percent of the higher education budget, which, in turn, accounted for 25 percent of the education budget. Put a different way, public support for higher education students for scholarships and student support services (that is, excluding all pedagogical costs) amounted to more than three times the per capita GDP and was 16 times the per student public financing in primary education (see World Bank 1992).

28. Moreover, teachers paid by parents received only about one-fourth of the salary of government teachers. This means that these children on average have less qualified teachers than their counterparts in urban areas.

29. Despite the official elimination of school fees in Cameroon in year 2000, low public funding meant that, in 2002, parents still paid for one out of four teachers in public primary schools (mainly in rural areas). Added to this fact, 23 percent of all primary teachers are employed in private schools (only slightly subsidized). This means that not far from half of the total number of primary school teachers are paid by parents.

30. Also Japan—for the first 15 years or so of its modernization process during the Meiji era (starting in 1868)—also followed an approach in which it devoted considerable resources to systematically acquiring foreign technical knowledge, mainly through use of foreign experts and through training abroad (see Emi 1968).

31. The "Winsemius Report," published in 1961, was named after its author, a Dutch economist and industrialist who was closely involved in developing the postwar industrialization program in the Netherlands.

32. "Postsecondary education" in Singapore means education continued after completion of six grades of primary and four grades of secondary education.

33. Lin (2002) describes the deliberate strategy and process followed in setting up these various training facilities to respond to the evolving needs of the economy.

34. Financed by a loan from the World Bank's International Finance Corporation and contributions from a U.S. philanthropist.

35. An early analysis of reasons why Thailand needed to expand its secondary education is given in Tan (1991).

36. The way this system functioned and evolved is described in Yoon (2001, 29–31).

37. The TIMMS survey is conducted every four years, and Singapore has ranked first in science and mathematics since 1995.

38. Based on Japan's experience in six African countries, Nagao (2007) assesses the extent to which Japan's approach for reaching excellent results in math and science teaching is "transferable" to the conditions in African countries.

39. The drop was largely due to a sharp decline for Francophone countries, from 11.5 times per capita GDP in 1975 to 4.8 in 2000. By contrast, the ratio for Anglophone countries declined from 4.4 times GDP in 1975 to 3.6 in 1992 and then increased to 4.2 in 2000.

40. The situation in Cameroon illustrates this point well. It also shows that while the 1973 and 1980 "oil-shocks" were a key trigger of Sub-Saharan Africa's economic stagnation during the 1980s and early 1990s, the decline also affected education in oil-exporting countries. Cameroon's strong growth during the 1960s and 1970s was followed in the mid-1980s by a severe economic crisis that lasted nearly 10 years, reaching a social climax in 1994 when salaries of civil servants (including teachers) were cut by half. The education system suffered greatly from this economic crisis. Public education spending per child ages 6–15 years old was more than halved between 1990 and 1995, and the 1990 level of spending per child has not yet been regained. The share of the government's budget allocated to education declined from 23.3 percent in 1990 to 12.9 percent in 1995, and was still only 15.2 percent in 2005. The share of the education budget allocated to primary education was just 36 percent in 2003–04.

41. The summary in this and the next paragraph draws on Ang (2006).

42. Verspoor and others. (2008) provide a comprehensive review of issues and policy choices in secondary education in Sub-Saharan Africa. The review summarizes the outcomes of a multiyear cooperative study program carried out by the "Secondary Education in Africa" (SEIA) team led by Jacob Bregman of the Human Development Department of the Africa Region of the World Bank.

ANNEX 1: ASIA EDUCATION STUDY VISIT FOR AFRICAN POLICY MAKERS, SINGAPORE AND VIETNAM, JUNE 18–30, 2006

Sunday, June 18, 2006

Start	End	Duration	Program	Presenters / Panelists	Session Moderator/Chair
Day	Day	—	Arrival of World Bank and African Delegates in Singapore	NA	NA
17:30	18:00	0:30	Registration and Informal Cocktail	Study tour organizers	
18:00	19:00	1:00	Study Visit Briefing	Jee-Peng Tan, Birger Fredriksen, and Anna Ng	
	Evening		Free Evening; Own Arrangements for Dinner		

Monday, June 19, 2006

Theme: Education for Growth—Singapore's Experience Over 40 Years

Start	End	Duration	Program	Presenters/Panelists	Session Moderator/Chair
9:00	9:10	0:10	Introductory Remarks	Ms. Tan Jee Peng, World Bank	Mr. Dzingai Mutumbuka, World Bank
9:10	9:20	0:10	Opening Remarks by World Bank	Mr. Yaw Ansu, World Bank	
9:20	9:30	0:10	Address by Guest of Honor	Mr. Lee Yi Shyan, Minister of State for Trade & Industry	
9:30	9:45	0:15	Group Photo		
9:45	10:05	0:20	Coffee Break		
10:05	11:05	1:00	Education Challenges in Africa: Overview and Country Perspectives	Six African education ministers & Mr. Mamadou Ndoye, Exec. Sec., ADEA	Mr. Dzingai Mutumbuka, World Bank
11:05	11:50	0:45	Development of Education in Singapore since Independence	Prof. Lee Sing Kong and Prof. S. Gopinathan, NIE	
11:50	12:35	0:45	Discussion		
12:35	14:05	1:30	**Welcome Lunch Hosted by Mr. Lee Chiong Giam, Deputy Secretary, Ministry of Foreign Affairs**		
14:05	14:50	0:45	Strategic Management of Education Development in Singapore	Dr. David Ng, NIE	Prof. Lee Sing Kong, NIE
14:50	15:35	0:45	Discussion		
15:35	15:55	0:20	Coffee Break		
15:55	16:55	1:00	Panel Discussion: Singapore's Experience in Education over 40 years	Drs. P.Y. Huang, Wee Heng Tin, Mr. Gerald Pillay	Prof. Lee Sing Kong, NIE
16:55	17:55	1:00	Discussion		
	19:00		**Welcome Dinner Hosted by Mr. Alphonsus Chia, Deputy Chief Executive Officer, International Enterprise Singapore**		

Tuesday, June 20, 2006

Theme: Successful Teaching and Learning

Start	End	Duration	Program	Presenters/Panelists	Session Moderator/Chair
7:45	8:45	1:00	Meet in Lobby for Departure to NIE		
8:45	9:30	0:45	Singapore Teachers' Pre-Service Training and Professional Development	Prof. Lee Sing Kong, NIE	Mourad Ezzine, World Bank
9:30	10:15	0:45	Discussion		
10:15	10:35	0:20	Coffee Break		
10:35	11:20	0:45	Curriculum Development & Textbooks in Singapore	Dr. Ang Wai Hoong, former MOE Head of Curriculum Dev. Dept.	Don Taylor, DFID Education Advisor, Ghana
11:20	12:00	0:40	Discussion		
12:00	13:30	1:30	Lunch Hosted by National Institute of Education (NIE)		
13:30	14:15	0:45	ICT Masterplanning for Education: Singapore's Experience	Dr. Koh Thiam Seng, Director, Ed. Technology Division, MOE	Dzingai Mutumbuka, World Bank
14:15	15:15	1:00	Discussion		
15:15	15:35	0:20	Coffee Break		
15:35	16:20	0:45	ICT Serving Educational Needs in Rural Areas: China's Experience	Prof. Kang Feiyu, Tsinghua University	Gary Theisen, World Bank
16:20	17:05	0:45	Discussion		
			Free Evening; Own Arrangements for Dinner		

Wednesday, June 21, 2006

Theme: Skills for Development

Start	End	Duration	Program	Presenters/Panelists	Session Moderator/Chair
8:15	8:45	0:30	Meet in Lobby for Departure to Suntec		
8:45	9:00	0:15	Study Tour Participants' Arrival at the World Education Forum		
9:00	9:10	0:10	Welcome Address by International Enterprise Singapore	Ms. Euleen Goh, Chairman IE Singapore	WEF organizers
9:10	9:20	0:10	Welcome Address by World Bank	Yaw Ansu, World Bank	
9:20	9:45	0:25	Opening Address by Guest of Honor	Mr. Gan Kim Yong, Min. of State for Education and Manpower	
9:45	10:15	0:30	Welcome Reception		
10:15	11:00	0:45	Education for Growth: Korea's Experience over 40 years	Prof. Chong Jae Lee, Seoul Nat. Univ.	Yaw Ansu, World Bank
11:00	12:00	1:00	Discussion		
12:00	13:30	1:30	World Education Forum Networking Lunch		
13:30	16:00	2:30	Site Visit to ITE Balestier Campus	ITE Staff	
16:00	16:45	0:45	Thailand's Experience in Addressing the Challenges of Secondary Education Development	Dr. Khunying Kasama Varavarn, Permanent Secretary, Ministry of Education, Thailand	Jacob Bregman, World Bank
16:45	17:30	0:45	Discussion		
18:00			Visit to the Asian Civilizations Museum		

44

Thursday, June 22, 2006

Theme: Skills for Development (*Continued*)

Start	End	Duration	Program	Presenters/Panelists	Session Moderator/Chair
8:00	9:00	1:00	Meet in Lobby for Departure to ITE Simei Campus		
9:00	9:45	0:45	Tertiary and University Education in Singapore: A 40-Year Perspective	Prof. Leo Tan, NIE	
9:45	10:30	0:45	Discussion		
10:30	10:50	0:20	Coffee Break		Prof. Lee Sing Kong, NIE
10:50	11:35	0:45	Technical and Vocational Training in Singapore	Institute of Technical Education (ITE)	
11:35	12:05	0:30	Discussion		
12:05	12:50	0:45	Tour of ITE Simei Campus	ITE staff	
12:50	14:00	1:10	Lunch Hosted by Institute of Education (ITE)		
14:00	14:45	0:45	Lessons from Singapore's 40-year Experience with Textbooks	Mr. Sim Wee Chee, Director, Educational Publishing, Panpac	Prof. Lee Sing Kong, NIE
14:45	15:30	0:45	Discussion		
15:30	15:50	0:20	Coffee Break		
15:50	16:35	0:45	Post-Primary Education: Implications of the Global Economy	Prof. Cheng Kai Ming, Univ. of Hong Kong	Yaw Ansu, World Bank
16:35	17:20	0:45	Discussion		
Evening			Free Evening; Own Arrangements for Dinner		

Friday, June 23, 2006

Theme: Skills for Development (*Continued*)

Start	End	Duration	Program	Presenters/Panelists	Session Moderator/Chair
8:00	9:00	1:00	Meet in Lobby for Departure to Nanyang Polytechnic (NYP)		
9:00	9:45	0:45	Polytechnic Education: Singapore's Experience	Mr. Lin Cheng Ton, Principal and CEO, Nanyang Polytechnic Nanyang Polytechnic	Prof. Lee Sing Kong, NIE
9:45	10:30	0:45	Discussion		
10:30	10:50	0:20	Coffee Break		
10:50	12:50	2:00	Site Tour of Nanyang Polytechnic & Departure for IES	NYP staff	
12:50	14:20	1:30	**Buffet Lunch at International Enterprise Singapore**		
14:20	16:20	2:00	Group Work by African Delegations to Consolidate Lessons and Prepare Country Reports	N/A	N/A
16:20	16:40	0:20	Depart for Suntec		
16:40	18:10	1:30	Singapore Heritage Tour		
Evening			**Free Evening: Own Arrangements for Dinner**		

Saturday, June 24, 2006

Rest Day

Start	End	Duration	Program	Presenters/Panelists	Session Moderator/Chair
AM	PM		Free/Own Arrangements		
Evening			Check Out of Hotel and Settle All Personal Bills		

Sunday, June 25, 2006

Transit to Vietnam and Cultural Activities

Start	End	Duration	Program	Presenters/Panelists	Session Moderator/Chair
6:45	10:00	3:15	Check Out of Hotel and Leave for Airport		
10:00	12:30	2:30	Flight to Hanoi		
12:30	13:30	1:00	Arrival in Hanoi and Transfer to Hotel		
13:30	15:00	1:30	Luncheon (Own Arrangement)		
15:00	18:00	3:00	City Tour Followed by Theater		
Evening			Free Evening; Own Arrangements for Dinner		

Monday, June 26, 2006

Theme: Vietnam—Overview of Education

Start	End	Duration	Program	Presenters/Panelists	Session Moderator/Chair
8:15	9:00	0:45	Audience with Vietnamese Deputy Prime Minister, He Pham Gia Khiem	African Heads of Delegation; Yaw Ansu, Dzingai Mutumbuka, Jee-Peng Tan; Jeffrey Waite	Mr. Nguyen Ngoc Hung, Deputy Director of International Relations Dept.
8:15	9:00	0:45	Registration		
9:00	9:30	0:30	Welcome by Vietnamese Hosts	Deputy PM & outgoing Minister of Education and Training (He Nguyen Minh Hien)	Mr. Nguyen Ngoc Hung, Deputy Director of International Relations Dept.
9:30	9:45	0:15	Welcome by World Bank	Mr. Yaw Ansu, World Bank	
9:45	10:15	0:30	Challenges of Educational Development in Africa	Mr. Mamadou Ndoye, Exec. Sec. ADEA	
10:15	10:35	0:20	Coffee Break		
10:35	11:20	0:45	Overview of Education in Vietnam	Dr. Nguyen Quang Kinh	Hon. Mohlabi Kenneth Tsekoa, Lesotho
11:20	12:05	0:45	Discussion		
12:05	13:35	1:30	Welcome Lunch Hosted by the World Bank		
13:35	14:35	1:00	Vietnam's EFA Strategy: Successes and Challenges (FSQL, Disadvataged Groups, Targeting Support)	Dr. Nguyen Quoc Chi, Mr. Dang Tu An, Mr. Truong Thanh Hai, and Mr. Bui Hong Quang	Ms. Josiane Rabetokotany, Madagascar
14:35	15:20	0:45	Discussion		
15:20	15:35	0:15	Coffee Break		
15:35	17:05	1:30	Panel Discussion: Vietnam's Experience and Its Relevance to Africa	African Ministers, Mamadou Ndoye and Bridget Crompton, DFID	Mr. Yaw Ansu, World Bank
Evening			Official Reception Hosted by Vietnamese Ministry of Education and Training		

Tuesday, June 27, 2006

Theme: Vietnam—School Education

Start	End	Duration	Program	Presenters/Panelists	Session Moderator/Chair
9:00	9:30	0:30	Teacher Development—Professional Competencies	Dr. Nguyen Tri	Hon. Mme. Ana Paulo Samo Gudo Chichava, Mozambique
9:30	10:00	0:30	Panel Discussion by Vietnamese Teachers	Alumni teachers of the assessment program	
10:00	10:30	0:30	Discussion		
10:30	10:45	0:15	Coffee Break		
10:45	11:15	0:30	Student Assessments (Asian and Other International Experience)	Luis Benveniste, World Bank	Hon. Mme. Hamana Adama, Cameroon
11:15	11:45	0:30	Student Assessments (Vietnam's Experience)	Dr. Nguyen Quoc Chi	
11:45	12:15	0:30	Discussion		
12:15	13:30	1:15	Lunch Offered by the World Bank		
13:30	14:30	1:00	Press Conference		
13:30	14:30	1:00	World Bank Staff Meeting		
14:30	15:15	0:45	Vietnam's Textbook Program (Publication, Distribution, Financing, etc.)	Mr. Nguyen Dang Quang, EPH	Hon. Mme. Baiden Amissah, Ghana
15:15	16:00	0:45	Discussion		
16:00	18:00	2:00	Visits to Textbook Publication Facilities	2 parallel groups	
Evening			Free Evening; Own Arrangements for Dinner; Ghana-Brazil Soccer on Large Screen in Hotel (10:00 PM)		
Evening			Settle Hotel Bills & Early Check-Out		

Wednesday, June 28, 2006

Theme: Secondary Education & System Financing

Start	End	Duration	Program	Presenters/Panelists	Session Moderator/Chair
8:00			Luggage Ready for Pick-Up by Hotel Bell Boys		
8:30	9:00	0:30	Development of Lower and Upper Secondary Education	Mr. Le Quan Tan	Hon. Mr. Fuad Ibrahim Oumar, Ethiopia
9:00	9:30	0:30	Discussion		
9:30	9:45	0:15	Coffee Break		
9:45	10:45	1:00	Panel Discussion: Education System Financing in Vietnam	Overview: Mr. Nguyen Van Ngu, MoET; External Financing: Mrs. Nguyen Hong Yen, MoF; Sector budget implementation: Mr. Truong Thanh Hai, MoET	Ms. Binh Thanh Vu, World Bank
10:45	11:45	1:00	Discussion		
11:45	12:15	0:30	Preparation for Departure		
12:15	13:15	1:00	Bus Departs for Airport—Box Lunch Provided on Bus		
13:15	15:15	2:00	Airport Check-In		
15:15	17:15	2:00	Flight to HCMC		
17:15			Hotel Check-In		
Evening			Free Evening; Own Arrangements for Dinner		

Thursday, June 29, 2006

Theme: Visits in HCMC—Technical and Vocational Skill Development

Start	End	Duration	Program	Presenters/Panelists	Session Moderator/Chair
7:30	11:45	4:15	Parallel Visits to TVET Institutions: (a) Singapore-Vietnam Technical Training Centre		MOET officials
9:00	11:45	2:45	Parallel Visits to TVET Institutions: (b) HCMC Industrial Univ.; (c) HCMC Nat. Univ. (IT Campus); or (d) RMIT-Vietnam		MOET officials
11:45	13:15	1:30	**Lunch Hosted by Each Institution**		
2:30	3:30	1:00	Debriefing of Site Visits to the TVET Institutions	Rapporteurs for each group	Mr. Dzingai Mutumbuka, World Bank
3:30	3:45	0:15	Coffee Break		
3:45	5:45	2:00	Country Delegations Prepare Their Reports for the Friday Presentations		
Evening			**Free Evening; Own Arrangements for Dinner**		

52

Friday, June 30, 2006

Reflections on Asia's Experience and Its Relevance to African Countries

Start	End	Duration	Program	Presenters/Panelists	Session Moderator/Chair
8:00	8:10	0:10	Introduction	Jee-Peng Tan, World Bank	Yaw Ansu, World Bank
8:10	8:15	0:05	Key Ideas from the Study Tour: Session A		
8:15	9:15	1:00	Discussion	Country delegates and other study tour participants	
9:15	9:30	0:15	Coffee Break		
9:30	9:35	0:05	Key Ideas from the Study Tour: Session B		Yaw Ansu, World Bank
9:35	10:35	1:00	Discussion	Country delegates and other study tour participants	
10:35	11:35	1:00	Country Presentations (10 Minutes for each Country)	Representative from each country delegation	Birger Fredriksen, World Bank
11:35	12:35	1:00	Discussion & Comment on Country Presentations	Study tour participants	
12:35	12:45	0:10	Wrap Up & Evaluation	Jee-Peng Tan, World Bank	
12:45	12:55	0:10	Closing Remarks by Sponsors	One representative each from Singapore and Vietnam	
12:55	13:10	0:15	Closing Remarks by World Bank	Yaw Ansu, World Bank	
13:10	14:10	1:00	Lunch		
14:10			Free Time		
18:30			Departure for Dinner		
19:00			End-of-Tour Dinner Hosted by Mayor of HCMC		

Saturday, July 1, 2006

Start	End		Program	Presenters/Panelists	Session Moderator/Chair
	Day		Departure of Study Tour Participants	NA	NA

ANNEX 2: LIST OF PARTICIPANTS IN ASIA EDUCATION STUDY VISIT FOR AFRICAN POLICY MAKERS, SINGAPORE AND VIETNAM, JUNE 18–30, 2006

Name	Title
CAMEROON	
HE Halimatou Kangue Mahonde HAMAN ADAMA	Minister of Basic Education
Mrs. Koung BESSIKE Jacqueline	Secretary Gen., Ministry of Employment and Vocational Training
Mr. Apollinaire TCHAMENI	Coordinator for Education Sector Strategy Basic Education
Mr. KOMO Walter Paul	Inspector of Pedagogy for Science
Mr. Pierre TITTI	General Manager Department of State Budget Ministry of Economy and Finance
ETHIOPIA	
H.E. Dr Sentayehu WOLDEMICHAEL	Minister of Education
H.E. Mr. Fuad IBRAHIM OMER	State Minister of Education in Charge of General Education
Mr. Dereje Asfaw JETLL Kiros	Head, Oromia Regional State Education
Mr. Abrha Kiros KEFEY	Head, Tigray Regional State Education
Mr. Tilaye Gete AMBAYE	Head, Amhara Region Education Bureau
GHANA	
HE Angelina BAIDEN-AMISSAH	Deputy Minister
Prof. Daniel Afedzi AKYEAMPONG	Co-Vice-Chairman, National Education Implementaion Review Committee
Mr. Victor Kofi MANTE	Deputy Director, Teacher Education Division
Mr. Asamoah DUODU	Director, Technical/Voc. Education Division
Ms. Benedicta Naana BINEY	Director of Education, Basic and Second Cycle

ASIA EDUCATION STUDY VISIT FOR AFRICAN POLICY MAKERS (*Continued*)

Name	Title
LESOTHO	
HE Mohlabi Kenneth TSEKOA	Minister
HE Ntsebe Idlett KOKOME	Principal Secretary Ministry of Education and Training
Dr. Mapere Benedict KHOBOLI	Chief Inspector, Secondary Inspectorate
Ms. Mapaseka KOLOTSANE	Inspector, Tertiary Education
Mr. Nkopane Paul RAMAPHIRI	Director, Technical and Vocational Training
Mrs. Mamongoli TSEKOA	Secretary-General National Commission for UNESCO
MADAGASCAR	
HE Haja Nirina RAZAFINJATOVO	Minister
Mr. Fils LAHATRA-RAZAFINDRAMISA	Director of Higher Education
Mr. Ernest TSIKEL IANKINA	Director of Tech. & Vocational Education and Training
Mr. Romain Kleber NDRIANJAFY	Director, National Institute of Pedagogy
Mrs. Josiane RABETOKOTANY	Coordinator of the Technical Support Unit
MOZAMBIQUE	
HE Ana Paulo Samo Gudo CHICHAVA	Permanent Secretary
Mr. Adalberto ALBERTO	National Director of Higher Education
Mr. Abel ASSIS	Director National Institute for Education Development
Cristina TOMO	National Director of General Education
Zeferino MARTINS	Executive Secretary, Commission for Reform of TVET

Name	Title
WORLD BANK STAFF, SPEAKERS, CONSULTANTS, PARTNER AGENCIES	
Yaw ANSU	Director, Human Development Dept.
Jee-Peng TAN	Education Advisor/TTL for Study Tour
Dzingai MUTUMBUKA	Sector Manager, AFTHD
Mourad EZZINE	Lead Education Specialist
Gary THEISEN	Sr. Education Specialist
Peter DARVAS	Sr. Education Economist
Eunice Yaa DAPAAH	Education Specialist
Patrick Philippe RAMANANTOANINA	Sr. Education Economist
Xiaoyan LIANG	Sr. Education Specialist
Aidan MULKEEN	Sr. Education Specialist
Jacob BREGMAN	Lead Education Specialist (SEIA)
Birger FREDRIKSEN	Tour Director (consultant)
Fook Yen CHONG	Education Specialist
Susiana ISKANDAR	Sr. Education Specialist
Lynette PEREZ	Human Development Specialist
Sophie NADEAU	Operations Officer/Education Specialist
Florence M. CHARLIER	Country Economist—Cameroon
Julieta WATLINGTON	Logistics/Administrative (consultant)

ASIA EDUCATION STUDY VISIT FOR AFRICAN POLICY MAKERS (*Continued*)

Name	Title
MULTILATERAL PARTNER AGENCIES	
Mamadou NDOYE	Executive Secretary
Donald TAYLOR	Education Advisor
SPEAKERS AND PRESENTERS (SINGAPORE)	
Dr. Khunying Kasama VARAVARN	Permanent Secretary, MOE, Thailand
Prof. Feiyu KANG	Professor, Vice Provost The Teaching Evaluation Office Tsinghua University, Beijing, China
Prof. CHONG Jae Lee	Professor, Seoul National University
Kai-ming CHENG	Chair Professor, Faculty of Education University of Hong Kong
MINISTRY OF FOREIGN AFFAIRS, SINGAPORE	
Emilyn POH	Assistant Director, Technical Cooperation Directorate
Adrian QUEK	Technical Cooperation Officer Technical Cooperation Directorate
IE SINGAPORE	
Ho Wai Yin	Director, Planning and International Organizations
Anna NG	Project Manager, International Organizations Division
Joe D'CUNHA	Project Manager, Events Management Division
SHOW LOGISTICS SINGAPORE	
Mavis KU	Project Manager
NIE INVITED PRESENTERS/ PANELISTS/GUESTS	
Professor Leo TAN	Director, National Institute of Education
Professor LEE Sing Kong	Dean, Graduate Programmes and Research

Name	Title
NIE INVITED PRESENTERS/ PANELISTS/GUESTS (*Continued*)	
Associate Professor GOH Chor Boon	Associate Dean, External Programmes
Professor Saravanan GOPINATHAN	Vice Dean, Centre for Research and Pedagogy Centre for Research in Policy & Practice
Associate Professor David NG	Associate Dean, Graduate Programmes and Research
Associate Professor Quek Jin JONG	Dean, Academic
Mr. Sim Cheng TEE	Divisional Director, Corporate Planning and Development
Assoc. Professor Cheah Horn MUN	Dean, Foundation Programme
Dr. Ang Wai HOONG	
Mr. WEE Heng Tin	Advisor to Ministry of Education
Mr. HWANG Peng Yuan	(Past Chairman, Economic Dev. Board)
Mr. Gerald Francis PILLAY	Consultant
Dr. Koh Thiam SENG	Director, Educational Technology Division
LIAISON OFFICERS (L.Os)	
Victor DUMONT	LO for Mozambique
Mohamed Faizal Bin Osman	LO for Lesotho
Leo Ann Lock	LO for Cameroon
Hee Peng Liang	LO for Ghana
Chew Foong Ming	LO for Madagascar
Pearl Cheng	LO for Ethiopia

ASIA EDUCATION STUDY VISIT FOR AFRICAN POLICY MAKERS (*Continued*)

Name	Title
SPEAKERS AND PRESENTERS (VIETNAM)	
Mr. Nguyen Quang KINH	Consultant
Mr. Nguyen Quoc CHI	Consultant
Mr. Nguyen TRI	Project Director
Mr. Nguyen Dang QUANG	Vice General Director
Mr. Le Quan TAN	Director of Secondary Education, MoET
Mr. Nguyen Van NGU	Director General of Planning & Finance, MoET
Mr. TRUONG Thanh Hai	Planning and Finance Department, MoET
Mr. DANG Tu An	Project Director
Ms. NGUYEN Thi Hong Yen	External Finance Department
MINISTRY OF EDUCATION AND TRAINING, VIETNAM	
Mr. NGUYEN Ngoc Hung	Deputy Director General of International Cooperation, MoET
Mr. LUU Anh Tuan	Expert
Mr. NGUYEN Hoai Nam	Expert
Mr. Jeffrey Waite	Senior Education Specialist
Ms. Binh Tanh Vu	Senior Education Specialist
Ms. Linh Van Nguyen	Program Assistant
Ms. Nguyet Minh Nguyen	Team Assistant

CHAPTER 2

Education in Africa: Knowledge Makes the Difference

Mamadou NDOYE

INTRODUCTION

Educate or perish.
—Ki-Zerbo 1990

The alternatives Professor Ki-Zerbo posed for Sub-Saharan Africa on the eve of the Jomtien Conference in 1990 in reality were not a choice. Education is a categorical imperative for the continent because Africa cannot be an exception in this area relative to the rest of the world. There are two reasons for this assertion. If education is a fundamental human right—and it surely is—this right can be achieved only when it becomes effective, and therefore cannot be limited to an abstract formality. Education must be universal, that is, acquired by all people without exception, and inseparable from the recognition of human dignity. On this basis, no economic, social, or other argument is justified if it deprives a human being of this fundamental right on grounds of gender, social origin, place of residence, cultural affiliation, or special needs. It is this ethical obligation of "having a duty and being able to fulfill it" that Africa cannot escape. Moreover, this fundamental right proclaimed by the Universal Declaration of Human Rights and solemnly confirmed through the commitments made by the governments of all countries and the international community at the Jomtien Conference in 1990, was reaffirmed in 2000 at the International Forum of Dakar on Education for All (EFA). In this context, the concept of education emerged as a worldwide public good.

A second concept can be added to this moral and even legal principle, and this stems from the relationship between education and development. The relationship remains complex from the standpoint of scientific analysis. Beyond the unresolved question of causality, however, historical observation permits us to recognize a strong correlation between education and development. No country in the world has entered a sustainable cycle of economic growth without first having eliminated illiteracy or, in other words, without having given its people a minimum of what can be called basic education. Once the process has begun, the successive stages of development require continually raising the population's general education level. Today, postindustrial competitiveness plays out at the levels of higher education and research. This does not mean that education alone is a sufficient condition. But it does mean that it is necessary for such progress. In this sense, the transitions under way in Asia and North Africa clearly fit in with the transformation processes that took place in Europe and America. This impels Africa to recognize the urgency of the challenge that Ki-Zerbo posed.

Beyond the two major arguments put forward above, Africa's development is now placed in a twenty-first-century context in which the accelerating progress in education has become an even more vital necessity. Internationalization is a reality, achieved through the globalization that reduces distances, tightens the links of interdependence around the world, and shrinks the earth to a global village in which Africa does not constitute an island. Africa's development is therefore integrated—whether it likes it or not—into a universal economic competitive arena in which the criteria for success are called effectiveness, profitability, and innovation. In these processes, knowledge has become the principal factor for production and exchange because of the changes propelled by the revolution in scientific and technical progress, to which must be added the communications explosion. In a world governed to such a great extent by knowledge and by the production and dissemination capacities of this knowledge developed through education and training, the following questions should be asked: What is the situation in Africa today? What are the challenges the development of education and training face? What types of reform are needed to meet these challenges? And what are the chances for success?

PROGRESS AND SUCCESS

The answer most often given to this question is limited to stressing the various ways in which Africa lags behind the rest of the world. This narrow comparative view is based on statistical averages that mask the diversity of African situations. This feeds Afro-pessimism, which—by presenting a generally dark picture—conceals the progress and success that actually exist. By starting with the advances made, progress can be objectively measured and the challenges that remain can be assessed to evaluate future prospects.

A HISTORY OF SUCCESS

For almost all the African countries south of the Sahara, the school—as it is presented today—is not an internal product of the development of indigenous societies. The school in its original form was imposed from the outside by colonization. The function of the school was to follow, support, and anchor a conquest imposed by arms. Resistance to colonization consequently extended to resistance to the school. Furthermore, colonial education policies, whether they were assimilative or not, had limited ambitions in terms of access, equity, and relevance. The basic goal was to recruit, select, and train an allied local elite. This history explains the major handicaps that constrained education in Africa from the beginning and throughout the colonial period.

Despite—but also because of—these constraints, from the 1960s to the mid-1970s, the newly independent countries had to devote extraordinary efforts to accelerate the development of education. It was particularly necessary to deal with the pressing needs of training middle and upper-level managers who had to ensure the immediate takeover of the colonial administration and also eliminate the ideological stereotypes that were harmful to the African persona. In this period, the rhythm of growth in school enrollments averaged about a 5 percent increase annually. In several respects, this was exceptionally high and had practically no equivalent anywhere else in the world.

What then followed was a period of relative stagnation mainly in the 1980s. This was linked to the combined effect of the economic crisis that followed the oil crisis in the mid-1970s and the strong demographic growth of the school-age population. Gross domestic product (GDP) per capita in Sub-Saharan Africa decreased annually by 1.1 percent during this period. Between 1980 and 1990,[1] the annual increase (2.5 percent) in primary education enrollment was less than the overall increase (3.1 percent) in the number of primary-school-age children. This resulted in a decrease in the primary education gross enrollment ratio (GER) in Africa, from 79.5 percent in 1980 to 74.8 percent in 1990 (UNESCO 1999). A detailed analysis of this average trend shows that at a time when 17 countries experienced a decrease, 20 others recorded an increase in their enrollment ratio in primary education. In secondary education, GERs increased between 1980 (17 percent) and 1990 (22 percent), and notably more for females (+7 = 12 percent to 19 percent) than for males (+3 = 22 percent to 25 percent). Remarkable performances of about a 60 percent increase in enrollments were recorded in Mauritius, Namibia, and South Africa, whereas there was less than a 10 percent increase in eight other countries. Out of 14 countries for which data are available, 11 increased their transition rate from primary to secondary school. There was a remarkable rise for Botswana, while Sudan and the Republic of Congo each recorded a considerable drop.

During the same period, the enrollment rate in higher education virtually doubled, generally increasing from 1.6 to 3 percent. This increase was even stronger for females (for which the rate more than doubled, from 0.7 to 1.9 percent) than for males (from 2.5 to 4.1 percent). Except in three countries, strong increases in the number of students in higher education per 100,000 inhabitants were recorded everywhere in Africa, particularly in Botswana (from 119 to 299),

Table 2.1 Development of Pupil-Teacher Ratios, 1980–90

Year	Preschool	Primary school	Secondary school
1980	41	39	27
1990	32	37	22

Source: UNESCO 2002a.

Cameroon (from 135 to 288), Mauritius (from 197 to 330), and Zimbabwe (from 127 to 588). Thanks to expanded intake capacity of local institutions, nearly the entire continent registered a considerable decrease in the ratio of higher education students who studied abroad, compared with those who studied in their own country (about 20 percent in 1980). Mauritius illustrates this decrease in a spectacular drop from 320.8 percent in 1985 to 29.4 percent in 1995.

At all levels of the education system, considerable efforts were made to increase the number of teachers. Between 1980 and 1990, the number increased from 38,000 to 101,000 for preschool, from 1,307,000 to 1,720,000 for primary school, from 338,000 to 676,000 for secondary school, and from 43,000 to 78,000 for higher education. Contrary to the impressions conveyed, the student-teacher ratio generally improved during this period (see table 2.1).

The situation was different for each country for which statistics were available. In primary education, in 1990, 18 countries had a ratio below 40, whereas for another 18 countries the ratio was above 40. In Burundi, for example, the ratio went from 37 to 67 in primary school, whereas in Ethiopia, the same ratio decreased from 64 to 36. For secondary education, the pupil-to-teacher ratio decreased from 45 to 29 in Benin, while in Mali, it rose from 28 to 45.

Globally, this progress can be explained by the efforts to increase education expenditures as a percentage of the gross national product (GNP) (from 5.1 to 5.3 percent between 1980 and 1990) and by decreasing unit costs notably following a decrease in teacher salaries expressed in GDP terms, especially in Francophone countries (Mingat 2004). In real terms, a substantial increase in GNP allocated to education was observed in the Gambia, Kenya, Lesotho, Malawi, Mauritius, Senegal, South Africa, Swaziland, Tanzania, and Zimbabwe. As for the breakdown of expenditures by education level in 1990, seven countries allocated more than 50 percent of these expenditures to preschool and primary education. By category, these expenditures were absorbed by the salaries of teachers (40 to 90 percent) and didactic material (less than 10 percent). The unit costs, which ranged between 0.1 in the Comoros and 0.37 in Ethiopia in terms of GDP per capita, generally declined with a few exceptions in the case of higher education in Ethiopia, Guinea, Malawi, Burundi, Swaziland, and Zimbabwe.

The trends in the data illustrate the unequally divided efforts in the development of education among the countries of Sub-Saharan Africa between 1980 and 1990.

On the eve of the Jomtien Conference in 1990, one African child out of four did not have access to primary education, and one African adult out of two (48.7 percent) did not know how to read or write. The relative internal inefficiency of the system was marked by high repetition and dropout rates, with the result that one pupil out of two never attained the minimum level of acquisition of primary school learning. Here, too, certain countries did better than others. In 15 countries, the repetition rate was greater than 20 percent, and in nine others the rate was more than 30 percent. Francophone and Lusophone countries generally had much higher repetition rates than the Anglophone countries. Some countries—including the Seychelles, Sudan, and Zimbabwe—instituted an automatic promotion system from one class to another.

A PERIOD OF ACCELERATION

The Jomtien Conference on EFA was considered an important occasion for advocacy and for mobilizing a process to accelerate an increase in access to schooling. The 2000 Dakar International Forum on EFA, the Monterrey Conference, and the general assembly of the United Nations on the Millennium Development Goals (MDGs) and children's rights (2000) confirmed and accentuated the international commitment to education as a fundamental human right, and as a factor in the fight against poverty and for the pursuit of economic and social development.

Regarding results in Africa, it is striking to contrast the period 1990–99 with 1999–2004. The average annual rate of increase in primary school enrollments in Sub-Saharan Africa was 3.2 percent between 1990 and 1999, compared with an average annual rate of increase of 4.9 percent between 1999 and 2004 (UNESCO 2003b, 2004, 2007). Moreover, Africa saw an increase in enrollments at all levels of education between 1990–91 and 2002–03.[2] Progress began slowly at the start of the 1990s, then accelerated as new supporting policies were enacted: EFA plans, building institutional and technical capacities, reforms in the recruitment and initial training of teachers, strategies to include girls and generally to promote equity of access, abolition of school fees, decentralization of management, participatory governance, and most important, an increase in education financing resulting partly from resumption of economic growth, and partly from an increased budgetary priority for education as reflected in an increase in the share of GDP allocated to the education sector.

Whereas nearly a fourth of all African children did not have access to the first year of primary school in 1990–91, the statistics for 2002–03 show that the number of children without access in that period was less that 10 percent of the school-age population. With a gross intake ratio (GIR) of 95.8 percent in 2002–03 (see table 2.2), school admission capacity in Sub-Saharan Africa had considerably improved. Among the African countries for which data are available, 23 had the

Table 2.2   Gross Intake Rate in Primary School
(percent)

	1998–99				2002–03			
	Total	M	F	GPI (F/M)	Total	M	F	GPI (F/M)
South and West Asia	105.1	111.2	98.5	0.89	105.6	108.1	105.6	0.98
East Asia and Pacific	108.4	112.5	104.2	0.93	110.8	115.0	108.0	0.94
Sub-Saharan Africa	88.7	91.3	86.1	0.94	95.8	98.4	94.9	0.96
Industrial countries	100.3	101.1	99.6	0.99	99.4	100.5	98.3	0.98
Developing countries	104.2	104.0	104.7	1.01	104.3	106.0	102.1	0.96
Countries in transition	93.7	92.7	94.8	1.02	102.6	102.7	102.5	1.00
World	101.1	102.0	100.2	0.98	101.1	100.2	102.1	1.02

Source: UNESCO 2005, 310.
Note: GPI = Gender parity index.

capacity in 2002–03 to admit all school-age children, and only two (Niger and Djibouti) had a GER lower than 50 percent. As for primary school completion rates, the positive change in this same period was remarkable for most countries. The exceptions were Burundi, the Democratic Republic of Congo, Kenya, Zambia, and Zimbabwe. At the other end of the scale, countries like Mauritius and the Seychelles had practically attained universal primary school attendance. This compares with an average 56.5 percent for Central Africa and 52.2 percent for West Africa, the subregions that lagged behind. Parity between females and males also evolved positively, considering the GER in 2002–03 (females: 95 percent, males: 98.4 percent) compared with 1990–91 (females: 68.3 percent, males: 86.7 percent). The gender parity index for completion rate was 0.87 in 2002–03, and this rate rises to 0.96 if we consider the gross intake rate (see table 2.2). Here, too, as for the first rate, at least two-thirds of the African countries recorded an index higher than 0.80. The second rate reveals promising prospects for parity between boys and girls at the primary level.

As for progress in literacy, African performance has been among the strongest in the world. Nearly two-thirds (60 percent) of African adults could read and write in 2000–04 compared with 50 percent in 1990 (see table 2.3). The majority of African countries display dynamic progress. Disparities exist between males and females, as well as marked progress toward parity. This is notable in Lesotho— where the population of literate women is higher than that of men—and in the Seychelles, Zimbabwe, Namibia, and Botswana. At the top of African performers in terms of literacy rates in the adult population, Central Africa (73.7 percent) is followed by East Africa and countries in the Indian Ocean (62.4 percent).

In general secondary education (lower and upper), African countries recorded notable progress between 1990–91 and 2002–03. The average GER rose 7 points, from 28.3 to 35.4 percent. Transition rates improved considerably. Whereas

he Developing World

	90	2000–04
		59.6
		60.9
		89.3
		91.3
		58.5
		89.2
		76.4
		71.6

...rolled in the first year of
lo   ...u to 46 percent in 2002–03, a rise
of   ...as rapid for access to the first year of upper
seco   ...ess significant as it rose from 18 to 22 percent.

C   ...pular conception, it is in higher education that Africa recorded
the str ...gest relative growth in enrollments between 1990–91 and 2002–03. During this period, the number of students per 100,000 inhabitants went from 232 to 449, an increase of 94 percent. All the African countries except three showed a dramatic increase. Growth was particularly high in East Africa and the Indian Ocean (180 percent) and in West Africa (100 percent). Mauritius, Mali, the Comoros, and Djibouti recorded growth rates above 300 percent.

Several positive trends emerge from this analysis. The progress Africa achieved includes the following:

- Considerably broadened admission capacities at all levels of education. This is encouraging with respect to the prospects for increasing access to education and increasing the number of graduates in the future.
- Improved transition rates that strengthen retention; this trend should facilitate managing student flows particularly to extend the length of time children are enrolled in school (primary plus lower secondary) and to rationalize admission to higher education, starting with access from upper secondary.
- Positive evolution in terms of equity between females and males that should accelerate, in interaction with the broadening of admission capacities and the improvement in transition rates, to be even more favorable to the enrollment of females (see table 2.4).
- Increased investment in education from national budget allocations and an increase in external aid.
- Substantially increased literacy rates.

Table 2.4   Evolution in Access to Education in Sub-Saharan Africa, 1990–91 to 2004

	Primary education gross enrollment rate						Secondary education gross enrollment rate						Higher education gross enrollment rate					
	1990–91			2004			1990–91			2004			1990			2004		
	M	F	Total	M	F	Total	M	F	Total	M	F	Total	M	F	Total	M	F	Total
Sub-Saharan Africa	86.7	68.3	77.5	96	85	91	22.6	17.8	20.1	34	26	30	2.4	0.9	1.6	6	4	5
World	105.7	93.1	99.5	109	103	106	55.4	46.1	50.7	67	63	65	10.0	18.8	14.3	23	24	24

Sources: For the 1990–91 figures, UNESCO (2002b), table 6, p. 254, for primary education, and table 7, p. 252, for secondary education. For the 1990 figures for higher education, UNESCO (2003b), table 8, p. 358. For the 2004 figures, UNESCO (2006), table 5, p. 269, for primary education, table 8, p. 293, for secondary education; and table 9, p. 300, for higher education.
Note: M = male; F = female.

PERSISTENT AND NEW CHALLENGES

Despite and sometimes because of the progress underlined above, long-term challenges persist and new ones appear. Globally, it may be said that despite the meritorious path most African countries have followed, quite a distance still must be traveled to raise levels of knowledge and skills in the populations at large, and to bring about greater openness to technological change and behaviors required for these countries to enter the virtuous circle of education-development-education. Moreover, new challenges are rapidly becoming more pressing, notably that of bringing the "last quarter" of school-age children into school to achieve universal primary attendance, and responding to the pressing demand to raise the right to education beyond primary school. The requirements linked to upgrading and deploying production methods to support different stages of development are increasingly intertwined with the dynamic of globalization. The most blatant illustration of this connectedness is the planetary expansion of the revolution in information and communication technology (ICT).

AN INSUFFICIENT STOCK OF EDUCATED CITIZENS

Despite its recent achievements, the stock of educated African citizens remains insufficient to launch a cycle of sustainable economic growth. The continent remains the most affected by illiteracy, with a rate of 40 percent compared with the considerably lower world average of 18 percent. Moreover, the figures show that Africa remains not only well below the world average but also behind practically all the world's regions, including regions composed of many developing countries.

The average duration of school attendance on the continent was estimated at 6.8 years in 2001 compared with an average 12.8 for all developed countries. The

Table 2.5   EFA Development Index, 2004

EDI	Number of countries in Sub-Saharan Africa	Countries in Sub-Saharan Africa
High EDI	1 country out of 47	Seychelles
Medium EDI	8 countries out of 49	Botswana, Cape Verde, Mauritius, Namibia, South Africa, Swaziland, Zambia, Zimbabwe
Low EDI	21 countries out of 29	Benin, Burkina Faso, Burundi, Chad, Djibouti, Equatorial Guinea, Eritrea, Ethiopia, Ghana, Guinea, Kenya, Lesotho, Malawi, Mali, Mauritania, Mozambique, Niger, Nigeria, Rwanda, Senegal, Togo

Source: UNESCO 2007, Table 1, 200–01.
Note: EDI = EFA Development Index; EFA = Education for All.

overall education development index remains low (see table 2.5). Even if the initial handicaps and the current obstacles in the African environment (AIDS pandemic, wars and civil conflict, the digital and scientific divide, and so on) remain difficult to overcome, it is imperative that African countries meet the challenge of accelerating education and training to make up for their historical lag. The effort will mean differing priorities and differing types and levels of investment depending on the specific national situation. Although a holistic approach to the development of education systems is required, at the very heart of this approach, it is essential that less advanced countries give basic education priority. And, in fact, most of these countries are in Africa.

UNEQUALLY DISTRIBUTED EDUCATION LEVELS

In Africa, the insufficiencies in education levels of the population are not equally distributed, which handicaps the base for development. This not only presents a challenge of equity, but also a challenge of development from the perspective of the impact of education on professional skills, openness to technological change, work productivity, expansion of social capital, and economic growth. Because labor is massively invested in the so-called informal sector of the economy (urban and rural), this sector suffers the most from the shortages in education and training. In fact, the greatest social disparities are evident in the rural areas in which the majority (71 percent) of the African population lives and where the GER and the primary completion rates were 70.9 percent and 28 percent, respectively, in 2000, compared with 103.5 percent and 61 percent, respectively, in the urban milieu. For the poorest 20 percent who are generally found in the rural and periurban areas, the rates were 63.1 percent and 23.4 percent, respectively, whereas they were 106.7 percent and 68.6 percent, respectively, for the richest 20 percent in 2000. The broadest social base of the economy of African countries is thus atrophied in its level of education and skills. Persistent inequalities between the genders are joined to these disparities, worsening them with disastrous social consequences for health, nutrition, and demographic regulation at the family level—particularly considering the eminent role that women play in these areas. The stakes here are enormous because they affect factors of economic growth and social and human development on a macro level. Additionally, they have an impact on social cohesion and prospects for training a democratic citizenry, the lack of which is an underlying cause of frequent wars and civil conflict.

LOW-EFFICIENCY EDUCATION SYSTEMS

In Africa, low efficiency produces an enormous waste in the use of education resources. The repetition and dropout rates are particularly high, notably in primary education. As a result, for 2002–03, on average, 40 percent of all children who entered school did not finish their primary education. This figure was 49 percent in 1990–91. Repetition and dropout correspondingly weaken retention and completion rates; it has been observed that repetition causes dropping out. Early dropout from primary education puts most of the victims on a return path toward illiteracy. In other words, at the time when the challenge is to reach higher enrollment levels with fewer resources—considering the scarcity of the latter and the immensity of the needs to be met—the opposite is what is occurring. Enormous resources have been invested in the effort to enroll cohorts of African pupils, yet, as noted above, nearly 40 percent drop out prior to completing the primary cycle. Apart from the waste in terms of investment, this constitutes a major obstacle to universal school attendance in Africa. Thus, the challenge of acceleration must be combined with the challenge of achieving greater efficiency of education systems through strategies that drastically reduce repetition and dropout.

MEDIOCRE QUALITY

Mediocre quality has a negative impact on internal and external efficiency of education systems. What would the fate of an industry be if 50 percent of its products did not meet market demand? African schools cannot be closed in the same manner in which an unprofitable business would be closed, but it is not acceptable that half of the pupils in Africa who complete primary school have not mastered fundamental learning. It is therefore urgent and indispensable to make the necessary changes to considerably improve learning outcomes. Research and reflection point out that among the obstacles to be removed are the following: weaknesses in the qualification of teachers and their supervisors, the lack of didactic materials, insufficient teaching-learning time, and inappropriate management of schools. It is not enough for schools to be ready to admit children; children must also be ready to learn. From this viewpoint, the early child development programs—which are the poor relation in African education systems—constitute a major challenge for ensuring preparation in respect to health, nutrition, and awakening of the intellectual, affective, and physical potential of future pupils.

LACK OF UTILITY OF SCHOOL LEARNING

The utility of school learning is not always demonstrated in the African environments. The necessity to adapt education to the realities and needs of African societies was identified from the beginning as the decisive element in decolonizing Africa (the 1961 Addis Ababa Conference on Education). However, most of the African countries reduced this to a simple trimming and pruning away of the most shocking elements of colonial ideology for the African persona, notably in history and literature. A few rare countries exhibited the meritorious political determination to design and implement in-depth reforms based on new economic and social needs, but this was not supported with the expertise required to explore unknown territory. Founded on a basis that was mostly intuitive, these experiments did not turn up successful results, and were challenged and halted for the most part. The encyclopedism and formalism of the traditional programs in primary, secondary, and university education—which at the time were no longer even being used by the former colonizing countries—continued to prevail in most African countries. In terms of the aspirations and expectations of communities and individuals, and needs of the popular economy and national development, what was taught in school and training programs was generally perceived to be out of step and not useful for solving problems in everyday life, work, and social practice.

At every level of the education system, the links between education and the surrounding economic, cultural, and social milieu were weak. These connections largely were not seen as the basis of learning and training, action and reflection, construction, and transformation. It is otherwise in this very interactive confrontation that education can be put to the service of development. The insular nature of education systems relative to African societies persists, as is demonstrated by the exclusion of African languages and local knowledge from most official curricula.

From the macroeconomic point of view, education planning is rarely integrated into national development planning and rarely fosters approaches apt to develop endogenous potential. In this respect, higher education and research are rarely equal to their mission of producing and disseminating relevant information and competencies in the African contexts. Faced with globalization, higher education and research in Africa—just like the continent's entire education system—suffers from the atrophy of its scientific and technological programs. The symptoms of atrophy are especially obvious in the areas of technical education and professional training, in which the trend has worsened in recent years, drastically reducing the shares of these programs in secondary education. Furthermore, studies in these areas are often disconnected from the realities and needs of economic development and working life in the different countries.

These issues constitute major challenges to orienting, structuring, and planning education and training systems in Africa so that the objectives, content, and processes of learning provide the outputs to correspond with expectations in terms of their economic, social, political, and cultural utility. Once again, the nature and scope of the challenges differ from one African situation to another. Certain countries have been involved for many years in major reforms to adapt their education systems to the realities and needs of their contexts. These reforms only need finishing touches. Other countries are behind in their efforts to undertake reforms and must continue to pursue them. Finally, some countries are not yet engaged in meaningful reform for various reasons.

The analysis of challenges is not yet exhaustive. Also, the challenges affect each education system differently, and this is instrumental in determining the specific priorities among changes to be made. The most promising policies are those that match response strategies to specific challenges. Access and equity without quality lead to wasted effort and resources if the question of why education is necessary—namely, to obtain learning outputs—is not clarified. Quality without access and equity results in education systems that reproduce and reinforce the existing social inequalities. The search for relevance without quality is most often corrupted into mundane cognitive empiricism. Quality without relevance results in the acquisition of formal knowledge whose sense and usefulness are not obvious. Efficiency without quality is an illusion of performance that disappears when learning output is evaluated, and so on. A combination of these strategies therefore is extremely desirable to create springboard effects through catalytic interactions that will propel the dynamic of the whole. This perspective brings out other challenges, not the least of which are the challenges of mobilizing the resources necessary to tackle all needs, planning the evolution of education systems, and efficiently allocating financing among the different priorities. Additional challenges include establishing governance mechanisms for education systems and schools with a view toward involving all the actors and partners needed to participate in the conception and implementation of this transformation, and holding them accountable.

REFORMS TO TRANSFORM THE EDUCATION SYSTEM

The challenges raised a call for changes both inside and outside the education systems. The next sections will define the strategic framework and philosophy that orient reforms to address the challenges. This discussion is followed by a review of the most pertinent reforms in the current African situation.

GENERAL REFORM ORIENTATION

The general orientation of the education reforms in Africa must be founded on a long-term view that gives coherence and continuity to the concrete changes to be undertaken. For a successful integration into the world economy, Africa is forced to draw up and gradually implement development strategies focused on knowledge and innovation. This focus is necessary to meet the requirements of a competitive global system of production and exchange that is structured around knowledge. Education must be placed at the heart of such development strategies in terms of priority, planning, and financing. The structural evolution of education systems must be oriented toward increasing the broad dissemination of scientific and technological culture with the following strategic objectives:

- Forming a critical mass of scientific human capital possessing knowledge, technologies, and management skills.
- Developing and mobilizing all the delivery modes possible for education (formal, nonformal, informal, face-to-face, remote, and free learning) by taking advantage of the tremendous ICT opportunities to promote learning throughout life, build knowledge societies, and promote open and dynamic cultures.
- Developing scientific and technological training, research, and innovation that favor the creation of endogenous development potential and yields the components capable of fomenting growth and increasing the value of exchange with other parts of the world.

To engage in these long-term undertakings, Africa must create new partnerships to mobilize increased investments for the appropriation and development of science and technology. This assumes, at a local level, that the capacity exists to be open and to adapt. A precondition for training these endogenous capacities is the transformation of the current systems toward an acknowledgement and consideration of local realities and needs, which should be the point of departure for building openness and capabilities to adapt.

In this dialectical perspective, rooting and at the same time opening up the African education systems are not mutually exclusive. They are, in fact, intimately linked. Rooting (and centering) is not a synonym for withdrawal into oneself, but rather implies the mastery of one's status and role, one's values and social practices of reference, one's strong points and limitations, and one's resources and needs. Rooting is essential to be able to have a meaningful exchange with others. In the case of education systems, the issue is one of a total revamping, considering the congenital relationship of rupture between the school and African societies. The introduction of African languages as the first languages of instruction in the framework of bilingual education, consideration of local knowledge in the curricula, and the interaction between the processes of the surrounding milieu and learning represent, among other changes to be made, the facilitating factors for education acquisition. These processes provide the intuitive basis required for the conceptual understanding and opening of the fields of observation and experimentation that are embodied in a transformation. Through these processes a literate environment in the native languages is built from broad dissemination of scientific knowledge and the technological opening of society. The birth of such sources of knowledge and information certainly will favor dynamic exchanges between African cultures and other cultures in the world to overcome the paralyzing myth of a static African identity.

Once these strategic reform options have been set out, the choice and rhythm of the changes will depend on the state of progress, and on the particularities, realities, and needs specific to each country. In view of the challenges identified above, the range of possibilities is broad. Considering the experiences analyzed in Africa and elsewhere, the following trends have proved to be the most promising for the different levels of the education system.

ACHIEVING UNIVERSAL PRIMARY EDUCATION

Policies must be resolutely oriented toward equitable access for all and accelerated progress toward universal primary education on the condition that they are understood and implemented with the goal of quality education for all. Such policies imply strategies targeted to excluded populations (girls, rural children, the poor, nomads, orphans, and the disabled), including the following: (a) improved school mapping and reorganization where needed into multigrade classes to bring schools closer to households, (b) consideration of the specific needs of the local context in the curriculum and the school schedule, and (c) integration of local languages and cultures. Positive discrimination policies efficiently complement these strategies, including such incentives as free schooling policies, scholarships, meal programs, and funding that gives more to those who need it most. Moreover, it is advisable to combine these strategies and measures to strengthen the internal efficiency of the systems and to improve learning outputs. Success for all must replace the spirit of selection and training for an elite population that often guides teacher evaluations and decisions on promoting students to the next grade. This change must be supported with strengthened provision of the basics for quality learning, namely, the essential inputs of trained and motivated teachers, an adequate number of books and didactic materials, and children who are ready to learn. The rest falls under the dynamic of each school that itself depends on the quality of the management and accountability of the grassroots actors according to the skills and resources allotted. This demonstrates the importance of school leadership training, institutionalization of a culture of quality within the school, and decentralization that strengthens schools' autonomy and accountability to and ownership by the stakeholders and direct beneficiaries.

EFFICIENTLY RESPONDING TO THE INCREASED DEMAND FOR EDUCATION

The progress achieved in primary education has increased the demand to educate families, communities, and countries. It is estimated that the number of students completing primary school will triple by 2015. To finance this expansion, the extension of the length of obligatory schooling that stems from this demand has already started in a number of countries that have designed a basic program of 8, 9, or 10 years in which lower-secondary education has begun to be expanded. The observed trends of broadening access to lower-secondary education in the statistics of several African countries are also part of this movement.

The movement from an elitist model to a mass model, however, raises many problems and requires changes that must be developed, steered, and successfully implemented. The need for a greatly increased number of teachers, classrooms, equipment, and didactic materials necessitates that models be adapted to local resources. Broadened and more cost-effective use of these strategies is needed so that the financing of this development is affordable for countries whose resources remain limited. The decentralization of school construction and management favors the participation of communities and increases the efficiency of expenditures following the example of the community lower-secondary schools in Burundi or the lower-secondary schools of proximity in Senegal.

Curricula must be revised to match the developing skills that young people require to deal efficiently with the current and future challenges they meet, particularly when faced with the requirements of an evolving society and economy. In this respect, the AIDS pandemic, the fight against drugs, the media explosion, the ICT revolution, and scientific and technological progress must, among other factors, require great attention.

Will it be necessary to have a common-core syllabus or diversify the programs at this stage? Is it advisable to professionalize or preprofessionalize? The answers to these questions will depend on national policy choices that consider the requirements of strengthening the scientific and technological dimensions of education and understand the fact that this education will be the end of schooling for most pupils and thus must prepare youth for active life and the job market. From this latter point of view, the diversification of programs and modes of delivery appears to be a realistic option to regulate student flows through processes of orientation and selection rather than selection to eliminate. In this respect, it is in Africa's interest to learn from the failures and the successes of other regions of the world.

As for upper-secondary education, its access, content, and objectives should be determined by the goal of selecting and preparing pupils for higher education, either general or professional. The regulation of flows in higher education could operate in the same way as the restructuring of training streams on the condition that upper-secondary education incorporates technical education and professional training. This would open other possibilities for orienting and continuing training for larger numbers of learners.

BROADENING TECHNICAL EDUCATION AND PROFESSIONAL TRAINING

Almost everywhere in Africa, the traditional views of technical education and professional training have wound up in dead ends. A broadened view of professional skills development is needed. The considerable investments made in these training streams, for which job possibilities are quickly saturated, raise recurring problems of financing and the search for a training-job fit that remains elusive. In the meantime, the vast majority of labor that is found in the informal sector of the economy is ignored by the training system. Despite attempts made sporadically, appropriate solutions remain difficult to find, notably because of the state of the economies. To mobilize the potential of the formal education and training systems as well as the nonformal systems, three major reform tracks should be explored. The first strengthens the preprofessional contents and objectives of general education at all levels, including basic technical training in agriculture and industry, familiarization with production processes and trades, professional orientation, and so on. The question will be one of increasing the capacity of general education to contribute to skills development. The second reform is oriented toward the separation between technical secondary education as a transitional program and professional training considered as a final program. This reform will make it possible to strengthen the scientific dimensions of technical education to prepare future engineers and mid- and upper-level technical managers for the economy. In the third reform, professional training at the secondary level would be linked to the vast system of traditional nonformal learning to restructure, modernize, and massively gear up to meet the enormous needs and structural changes in the informal economy. Evening courses for apprentices, work-study programs that alternate learning between professional training centers and sites for traditional learning, common systems of qualification or recognition of performances, and other collaborations could be instituted in the framework of contract programs.

Success will depend on the flexibility of training mechanisms for constant adaptation to the evolution of the work place and on the quality of the public-private sector partnerships that will require a more open and participatory management structure.

RELEGITIMIZING THE HIGHER EDUCATION PARADIGM

The higher unit costs per student in higher education require not only the regulation of access but also an improvement in internal efficiency. The management of student flows should be based on planning geared to the country's estimated needs for high-level skills, particularly in the more dynamic sectors of the economy. The objectives of higher education and research must be tightly linked to economic growth, the achievement of the MDGs, and the creation of endogenous development potential. This assumes relegitimizing the public service mission of higher education and research that serves communities and requires a change in paradigm to redirect the teaching, training, and research toward an applied emphasis on the identification, evaluation, and development of the potential and strengths of national development. From this perspective, the trends toward diversification, specialization, and professionalization will be asserted according to community and corporate demand. Higher education and research will then be oriented toward the creation of a critical base of knowledge and expertise to strengthen the internalization and production of science and technology tailored to needs in the context of Africa's development. In this way, higher education and research could contribute to openness to change and adaptation necessary to position African countries favorably in the overall environment of global change and competition. To evolve in this direction, it is necessary to reform management and financing to strength the autonomy, competitiveness, and accountability of the higher education and research institutions, engage in more planning, and refine accreditation and quality assurance mechanisms. These changes should be based on the creation of public-private partnerships involving the state, the private sector, and civil society, and should encourage the pooling of regional resources through networks and communities of practice and expertise, centers of excellence, and exchanges of teachers and students as well as through south-south and south-north partnerships.

CONCLUSION

Africa is steadily progressing toward expanding its access capacity to educate and train all its children and youth and to gradually eliminate adult illiteracy. High demographic growth and the constraints of limited economic resources are certainly slowing this momentum on a continent already heavily handicapped by the colonial legacy.

To confront the challenges currently involved in developing education in Africa, it is important, first, to accelerate the momentum to make up for the historical lag. It is necessary to give prominence to the requirements of building a knowledge base for scientific and technological advancement in the African economies while fully ensuring that this knowledge base is rooted in the foundation of sustainable indigenous development. To engage resolutely along this path, three major orientations should guide action: (a) holistic vision, (b) education for all, and (c) collaboration.

Holistic Vision. Africa must break with the incomplete and fragmented vision of education development and adopt a holistic vision. This requires taking account of the vertical dimension of different levels of the systems, the horizontal dimension of different streams of training, and the diversity in delivery modes—notably, the new opportunities offered by the ICT revolution.

Education for All. At the center of this holistic vision is the priority of education for all pursued through policies resolutely oriented toward equity. This is an ethical priority that stems from the recognition of human dignity. It is also a developmental priority. No managing elite can successfully meet the challenges of triggering sustainable development (agrarian revolution or industrial revolution) without a critical mass of the population (farmers, fishermen, artisans, and other skilled workers) capable of assimilating the processes and tools to improve work productivity, management, openness to technology, hygiene, health, and so on. Obviously, the question as to whether education for all should include 6, 7, 8, 9, or 10 years depends on the level of development, policy choices, and resources of each country. In any case, the priority accorded to education for all can only be realized coherently and efficiently if it is centered in a holistic vision that allows for regulating the sum of the parts in line with this priority. This diversified and integrated approach to education for all benefits from the mobilization of increased resources—including diverse modes of service delivery in formal education, nonformal and informal education, face-to-face and distance education, open and mutual learning, and so on—to respond to the diverse needs inherent in educating an entire population. Also following such a holistic vision, secondary and higher education, including technical education and vocational training, can be reformed congruently to contribute to the sectoral priority (education for all) as well as to external priorities (economic, social, cultural, and political aims of development). These reforms require combined responses to different and even contradictory issues that must all be reconciled for success. These issues include (a) massively increasing supply while at the same time raising the level and quality of education and training; (b) raising the level of training to meet international standards while concomitantly promoting the values of indigenous development; (c) regulating the flow of students even while expanding opportunities for lifelong learning; (d) mobilizing private financing, including household spending on education, without endangering equal opportunity for all; and (e) ensuring an adequate fit between training and the needs of the economy while also promoting the other cultural, social, political, and individual dimensions of education.

Collaboration. These reforms require abandoning the traditional isolation of sectors and adopting intersectoral approaches and collaboration in the conception and execution of education policies. In this connection, it is necessary to situate education for all at the heart of initiatives, strategies, and programs of development, including accelerated economic growth, fight against poverty, construction of democratic institutions, realization of the MDGs, and so on. Oriented this way, the education sector will be positioned for interaction and alliance with the economic, health, environmental, community development, and other sectors. Through this articulation with the key issues of development, education will be enriched by the contribution of other sectors in terms of content, objectives, approaches, and resources as well as by their demands for relevance and effectiveness. These new relationships for education should provoke a paradigm shift that implies the pluridisciplinary elaboration of strategies to orient education and a partnership for implementation and management of education.

The challenges are numerous and complex. The associated tensions will not be easy to manage. To create the conditions for success, it is advisable to pursue the following:

- Mobilize the political will at the highest level to seize the opportunities of the Second Decade of Education in Africa[3] to undertake advocacy and include major education reforms in the agenda of the heads of state summit.
- Promote policy dialogue and stakeholder participation to establish consensus and partnerships as widely as possible on the goals and strategies of reforms as well as to mobilize resources and enhance implementation.
- Encourage the exchange of experience, mutual learning, and strategic partnerships to build countries' capacities in meeting similar challenges.
- Reduce environmental obstacles, including the AIDS pandemic and other endemic illnesses, wars and civil conflict, poverty, and discrimination on the basis of gender and other factors.

In all these areas, it is possible and useful to continue to learn from the successful, promising, and innovative experiences that exist on the African continent and elsewhere, not to necessarily reproduce them but to recreate in one's own context the conditions and factors for success. The process of transformation to knowledge societies is also a learning process and is achieved through the creation of learning institutions and societies.

NOTES

1. All the numerical data for the period 1980 to 1990 are taken from UNESCO (2002a).

2. The figures for the periods 1990–91 to 2002–03 are from the document UNESCO-Breda (2005).

3. After evaluating the first decade of education in Africa (1997–2006), the Conference of African Ministers of Education, meeting in Maputo, Mozambique, in September 2006, after a declaration at the Heads of State Summit in Khartoum, launched a second decade (2006–15) of education reform. The action plan for this second decade set out seven priority areas.

3

Education in Singapore: Developments Since 1965

GOH Chor Boon and S. GOPINATHAN

INTRODUCTION

The aftermath of World War II in the Pacific region created severe social and economic dislocations for the people of Singapore. Although the British rulers reclaimed control of the trading port, the halo of British invincibility was totally shattered. The people now clamored for political freedom and economic opportunities. Frequent industrial strikes and unrest forced the closure of many British firms and, subsequently, spurred an exodus of British capital out of Singapore. The population grew from about 960,000 in 1948 to about 1.6 million in 1954, but the colonial administration was slow in reviving the economy and in providing enough jobs. There was high unemployment and an acute shortage of public housing. Many squatter colonies sprouted up throughout the suburban and rural areas. In the 1950s, racial integration did not exist and within the plural society the main ethnic groups considered themselves to be Chinese, Malays, or Indians, rather than Singaporeans. Religious differences, if exploited, could lead to communal trouble, and this became a reality in the infamous Maria Hertogh riots.

Besides the economic and social woes, British colonial policies relating to education, language, and citizenship were responsible for stifling the growth of racial integration and the establishment of a common destiny and identity shared by the people of Singapore. In education, for example, the government did not attempt to regulate and support the number of Chinese schools but, at the same time, encouraged the growth of English-stream schools. The Chinese-educated became an underprivileged group; they had no opportunities for tertiary education nor could they hope to be employed in the civil service. In short, the government failed to recognize the more dynamic and vocal Chinese-educated group. These "gaps" were quickly exploited by the Malayan Communist Party in Singapore and contributed to a decade of political turbulence in the 1950s.[1] Singapore thus had, at this time, many of the features of a "failed state."

The years 1959 to 1968 represent some of the epochal years in Singapore's modern history. In 1959, the British colony became completely self-governing and in August 1965 Singapore became a sovereign state after separating from Malaysia. Singapore's political leaders were faced with the unenviable task of ensuring the political and economic survival of the small city-state. Colonialism had produced a lopsided economy strongly dependent on entrepôt trade. Increasingly, science and technology became the vital ingredients that dictated a country's level of competitiveness. The overriding priority of the Singapore government in 1965 was to find the quickest and most effective way to develop an industrial economy and to develop its own military capability. To compete as a viable economic entity, the immediate task was to break away from the long dependency on entrepôt trade and embark on an export-oriented industrialization strategy. To do so, the government developed a "developmental state" strategy.

The developmental state ideology propagated the inseparability of economic and political survival. The successful fusion of economic and political survival required the internalization of an entirely new set of social attitudes and beliefs by the people of Singapore. The call was made for the sacrifice of self-interest for the "national interest." In the process of catching up, important policies, especially those in the field of education and manpower development, were speedily implemented. In the late 1960s and 1970s, the state was successful in ensuring that individual survival matched well with the state's ideology of survival.

This chapter highlights key features of the development of education in Singapore over the last 40 years, focusing on how Singapore has been able over this period to develop its education system from a level in the early 1960s quite similar to that of many developing countries, to reach a level comparable to and in some aspects surpass the best member countries of the Organisation for Economic Co-operation and Development (OECD). This analysis is done in the context of the economic and social transformation of Singapore since 1965.

SURVIVAL ECONOMICS, SURVIVAL-DRIVEN EDUCATION, 1965–78

Since the 1950s, industrialization has been widely acknowledged by the procapitalist, independent states of Southeast Asia as the key to survival and economic growth. But the task was not easy as long periods of colonialism had produced unbalanced economic structures that confined the rising indigenous capitalist class to comprador trading activities and limited small-scale manufacturing and processing. The initial response was the adoption of the development strategy strongly recommended by the Argentine economist Raul Prebisch, that is, Import

Substitution Industrialization (ISI), which was aimed at the reduction of dependence on imported goods (Dixon 1991, 152). Essentially, it involves the small-scale production of nondurable consumer goods whose production requirements are compatible with such conditions as abundant unskilled labor and unsophisticated technology that exists in countries without previous industrial experience. High growth rates were indeed experienced by the countries in Southeast Asia, but by the mid-1960s, the limitations and inherent contradictions of the ISI strategy began to be felt. In the case of Singapore, apart from assembling consumer goods, there were few signs of a transition to capital goods production. Manufactured imports were merely replaced by raw materials, capital goods, and components. Pressure for accelerated growth through the development of export markets was emerging from local manufacturing capitalists. The situation was compounded by Singapore's expulsion from Malaysia in 1965. It seriously undermined the ISI strategy by dramatically reducing the size of the domestic market. When the country was part of Malaysia during the years 1963 to 1965, it was able to take advantage of the wide hinterland market to its north. The development strategy adopted by the Singapore leaders gradually shifted toward Export Oriented Industrialization (EOI), which, by the early 1970s, became the "new orthodoxy" strongly advocated by Bela Balassa of the World Bank for economic growth in developing countries.

In the case of Singapore, by the late 1950s, it remained primarily an entrepôt, with 70 percent of its gross domestic product (GDP) derived from these entrepôt activities (Dixon 1991, 158). The country had a small and limited industrial base. The predominant industry was the shipbuilding and repairing industry that was largely in the hands of governmental and public bodies, such as the Singapore Harbour Board and the British Naval Base. The small manufacturing sector consisted mainly of light engineering, assembly of vehicles, marine engineering, printing, and processing (Colony of Singapore 1955). Though employment in the manufacturing sector grew from 22,692 in 1955 to 44,295 in 1961, manufacturing development was slow and stagnated at about 12 percent of GDP in 1960. In the meantime, the postwar baby boom in the early 1950s and the free immigration policy had resulted in an average annual population growth rate of 4.4 percent between 1947 and 1957, and the unemployment rate stood at 5 percent, rising to a high of 9.2 percent in 1966. It was clear to the government that solving the rising unemployment problem was a matter of high priority.

The government became more focused on the need to expand the industrial base, although it still advocated that Singapore must continue to "jealously guard its position as an entrepôt" (*The Malaya Tribune* March 13, 1953). But the task of expanding manufacturing activities for a trading port was not expected to be smooth because of the "dearth of skilled labor in Singapore" (Colony of Singapore

1954).[2] The year 1968 was a watershed in terms of a shift in industrial strategy to more export-oriented manufacturing activities. To support the EOI strategy, and given the lack of natural resources, the development of the country's human resources was of paramount importance for the government. To achieve this end, a task was started to build an education system that would support the development of a literate and technically trained workforce.

While under British colonial rule, education was used as a tool to meet British political interests and to pacify ethnic groups that were political aspirations. In 1965 and after, an intimate link between education and economic development of the small city-state was strongly emphasized. The government took the conventional path in developing new skills and work attitudes to accommodate new economic strategies. While the economics of education was in focus, the role of education in the socialization and nation-building process, especially in terms of developing a Singapore identity, was not forgotten. National integration through a national education system was seen as the key condition for economic survival. To attain these national objectives, the government rightly recognized the necessity to provide every child with at least six years of education from the age of six—without discrimination of race, language, sex, wealth, or status.

Given the multilingual nature of the population, bilingualism inevitably became a key component in Singapore's education system. In 1960, learning a second language was made compulsory in all primary schools, and in 1966, the policy was extended to all secondary schools. The decision on bilingualism was not just for the achievement of social cohesion in a largely plural society (at least, during the early 1960s). The English language was seen as a primary utilitarian tool in Singapore's effort to make the world its marketplace. It was a politically difficult decision, because English, the language of the colonial powers, was met with much hostility. With the increasing demand for English, however, the danger that the young could become deculturized and forget their mother tongues increased. The bilingual policy assured parents that their children would not grow up culturally ignorant. Today, Singapore's bilingual policy is perhaps the most unique of its kind in the world. It is an Eastern-Western Hemisphere model that allows Singaporeans to attain competency in the use of the English language, the language of the so-called West, as well as in the use of the Chinese language (or other indigenous languages, such as Tamil and Malay), the languages of the so-called East. This approach is particularly useful for Singapore's business internalization strategy. The Western concept of bilingualism in schools is based more on a Latin model in which pupils will usually learn, say, German and English or Italian and English.

The years 1959 to 1965 were significant, even epochal, in the history of Singapore's education transformation. In May 1959, Singapore was given self-government status, and a Five-Year Plan (1961–65) to boost the education standards of the people was implemented. The priority was to provide universal free primary education. The plan consisted of three main features:

- Equal treatment for the four streams of education—Malay, Chinese, Tamil, and English
- The establishment of Malay as the national language of the new state
- Emphasis on the study of mathematics, science, and technical subjects

The philosophy behind these aims "[c]onserved equal opportunity for all citizens, established the means of maintaining unity in diversity and instituted a program for training a new generation for the needs of a forward-looking, modern, industrial and technological society" (Ministry of Education 1966).[3] Today, this philosophy, broadly speaking, stays intact. Although the government continued to provide for vernacular education, a major consequence of the transformation of the Singaporean economy from 1959 onward was the consistently strong tendency for parents to enroll their children in the English language schools. In 1959, only 47 percent of children entering primary grade one were in the English stream, and 46 percent were in Chinese schools. Twenty years later (in 1979), the English stream enrolled 91 percent of all children in primary grade one with only 9 percent in the Chinese stream and a negligible number in the Tamil and Malay language streams. This dramatic shift was brought about by the free choice of pragmatic parents in response to the nation's drive toward high value-added industrialization and to an economy where the language of business is English.

Primary education was freely made available to all. In 1962, out of a population of 1.7 million, the student population stood at nearly 400,000. This led to a period of rapid construction of schools. Under British rule, government English schools and missionary English schools had good buildings. In mainly the rural areas, however, vernacular schools, built and supported by private organizations or individuals, were made of wood. Beginning in 1959, the responsibility of building all new functional schools was passed on to the Ministry of Education.

Primary and secondary education enrollment rose from 320,977 in 1959 to a peak of 530,079 in 1968. Table 3.1 shows enrollment since 1959. The early 1970s saw a decline in primary enrollment because of successful family planning strategies implemented by the government. By 1965, a total of 83 new school buildings were completed—at about the rate of one school a month for seven years. The accelerated building program matched the demand of the primary-school population by 1964. Even with this program, however, it became necessary for school buildings to be used by two sets of children, that is, double sessions were held, to accommodate the rapid increase in enrollment. In the words of Ong Pang Boon, the then minister for education, "The people of Singapore are becoming so education conscious that we have achieved universal primary education without making it compulsory . . . and once admitted, they [the children] are assured of a

Table 3.1   Pupil Enrollment in Primary and Secondary Schools

Year	Primary	Secondary
1959	272,254	48,723
1960	290,576	59,314
1961	307,981	67,857
1962	324,697	72,308
1963	341,620	84,425
1964	353,622	99,592
1965	362,672	114,736
1966	370,899	132,088
1967	373,437	144,448
1968	379,828	150,251
1972	354,936	161,371

Source: Department of Statistics (Singapore), various years.

10-year primary and secondary education finishing at the minimum age of 16″ (*Straits Times* September 26, 1965; November 25, 1965). Because of the rapid construction of schools, universal lower-secondary education was achieved as early as 1970. The overall growth in secondary education, from 48,723 in 1959, to 114,736 in 1965, and to 161,371 in 1972 is impressive evidence of the importance attached to education (beyond primary education) that is perceived by parents. From a societal point of view, secondary education was the most profitable investment (Pang Eng Fong 1982, 94–95). The rate of return to society is 18.2 percent for a completed secondary education for males and 17 percent for females. In terms of types of education, an English-stream education had greater monetary payoffs to society than vernacular-stream education.

Although statistics indicated successful outcomes, it was increasingly difficult for the Ministry of Education to meet the intense desire of the people to educate their children. Some obstacles were logistic in nature. The population in most urban areas and in certain rural areas was unevenly distributed. Suitable school sites in the densely populated areas were unavailable. This problem was compounded by the parents' selection and preference for certain schools, such as those with personal affiliation and language stream. Nevertheless, with careful planning, budgeting, and ensuring that there were sufficient teachers, universal primary education was attained by the mid-1960s.

In 1965, the government allocated 28.8 percent of its total budget to education; of this, 59 percent went to primary education, 27 percent went to secondary education, and 14 percent went to higher education (as compared with 65 percent, 20 percent, and 15 percent, respectively, in Japan) (*Straits Times* November 25, 1965). Table 3.2 shows the annual expenditure on education during the years from 1959 to 1967.

Table 3.2 Annual Expenditure on Education, 1959–67

Year	Expenditure on education (S$ millions)	Percent of national expenditure
1959	60.00	23.6
1960	57.10	23.5
1961	65.84	17.1
1962	82.31	23.4
1963	94.64	15.8
1964	103.36	31.7
1965	112.81	28.8
1966	124.08	23.4
1967	135.05	22.8

Source: Department of Statistics (Singapore), various years.

Education in Singapore was financed almost entirely from state revenue. The Ministry of Education made its own estimates of expenditure annually, which were presented to the Ministry of Finance for submission to Parliament for approval. Hence, except for a handful of private schools run by private organizations such as clan associations, schools in Singapore were (and are) public or state-supported schools. In addition to the generous funding from the government, two other strategies were adopted to cater to the rapid expansion of the schooling population: teacher recruitment and the availability of textbooks.[4]

Corresponding to the increase in pupil enrollment, the number of teachers in the teaching service increased rapidly, from 10,590 teachers in 1959, to 16,986 in 1965, and to 19,216 in 1968. These teachers were trained or qualified, and the strategy used to achieve these numbers resorted to large-scale recruitment of teachers-in-training at the then Teachers' Training College. During this period, a part-time teaching program was introduced—training in the morning and teaching in the afternoon and vice versa (depending on the type of program). This was a realistic approach during the years of rapid expansion.

In tune with the government policy of equal treatment for the four language streams of education, the Government Scheme for Loan of Free Textbooks offered assistance to all pupils studying in these four language streams. This was done in accordance with the Textbook for All policy, which stated that no needy children from lower-income families should be denied an education merely because of an inability to purchase textbooks. The free textbooks scheme was administered by the schools, and the books were obtained directly from the Education Publications Bureau (EPB), which was set up by the government in 1967 to produce common and affordable textbooks for all. The rising cost to the government of this form of aid to needy children can be seen from the annual expenditure on free textbooks—rising from S$79,606 in 1959 to S$259,200 in 1965. The textbook ownership-to-student ratio was close to 1:1 thanks to the low cost of production achieved through a competitive tender system administered by the EPB with private printers. The cost recovery associated with textbook development was not a primary concern, because "Singapore has so far been able to finance its own educational expansion program largely because of the resourcefulness of its people" (*Straits Times* November 25, 1965).

The period of survival-driven education also saw the review and upgrading of technical and vocational education. As early as 1964, the government established secondary vocational schools for the first time, with an enrollment of 4,910 pupils. These pupils did not pass the primary leaving examinations to enter academic secondary schools. The curriculum, aimed to equip pupils for employment in establishments where basic vocational skills are required, consisted largely of vocational subjects, such as woodwork, domestic science, art and crafts, and technical drawing. By 1968, it was becoming increasingly apparent in the Ministry of Finance that the prospective output of technically trained workers produced by the school system would be insufficient to meet the requirements of new industries. It did not require any elaborate process of manpower planning to reach this conclusion. In 1968, out of the 144,000 students in secondary schools, only some 18,000 were enrolled in technical and vocational streams. Accordingly, the government accelerated the plans for the expansion of technical education. A Technical Education Department was set up in the Ministry of Education in June 1968, and from 1969, all male lower-secondary pupils were required to have two years of exposure to technical subjects. Girls were given a choice between technical subjects and home economics.

The Technical Education Department used all available training facilities (located in four newly built vocational institutes) to train skilled workers, such as welders and machinists, to service the shipbuilding, oil refinery, electro-chemical, electro-mechanical, precision engineering, metalworking, and woodworking industries (Clark 1971). From 1970 to 1973, for example, 1,789 trainee welders received formal technical training. Although Singapore succeeded in attracting a wide range of foreign-owned new industries, the industrialization effort benefited immensely from the technical and financial assistance provided by a number of foreign governments and from the United Nations Development Programme aimed at producing industrial skills. Foreign governments who donated machinery and expertise included Japan, Britain, and France. Several vocational training centers were set up as a result of this external support.

To keep pace with the rapid developments in technical and vocational education, extensive teacher training and retraining programs were developed, and the Finance Ministry made funds freely available for such purposes. The number of technical teachers increased from 425 in 1968 to 1,950 in 1972. This was by no means an achievement, because the labor market was getting increasingly tight. In addition to teachers who were specifically trained in technical subjects, academic subject teachers were also encouraged to be retrained as technical subject teachers. In 1968, some 4,000 teachers received training in metalwork, including fitting and sheet metal, woodwork, printing, motor mechanics, radio and television servicing, and electrical fitting and installation. The flexibility inherent in teacher retraining proved to be highly cost-effective in meeting the demand for these technical teachers.

The survival-driven system of education continued into the 1970s with the continual propagation of an industrial-oriented education to produce the manpower needed for industrial development. The Vocational and Industrial Training Board (VITB, the predecessor of the current Institute of Technical Education) was created in 1979 to take in secondary school leavers who were less academically inclined. Vocational training institutes under the VITB offered a wide range of courses, the most popular of which were electrical, electronics, maintenance and repair of motor vehicles, refrigeration, air conditioning, carpentry, masonry, and plumbing.[5] Enrollment at the secondary level continued to grow, rising from about 148,000 in 1969 to 176,000 in 1979. Enrollment in VITB institutes also rose from 2,800 to 14,000 during the same period. By 1976, only a decade after independence, close to 20 percent of the secondary school population was receiving technical education. At the tertiary level, the total intake at Singapore's two main polytechnics at this time—Singapore Polytechnic and Ngee Ann Polytechnic—rose from about 3,500 in 1966 to about 11,000 in 1980. Thus, the decision to promote technical education proved successful, even though it was not initially popular with parents.

Britain's laissez faire policy did not produce systemic changes to the education landscape in colonial Singapore, but the Singapore leaders introduced a flurry of "haphazard changes" (*Straits Times* March 24, 1976). Singapore's planners in education failed to see early enough that the bilingual requirements of the system were not differentiated in terms of pupil ability. Those who failed to make the grade at the Primary School Leaving Examination (PSLE), which was a selection to secondary school, left the system and only some went on to vocational institutions. As a result, the growth in secondary education was slow, with an average of about 70 percent of the leaving primary cohort entering secondary schools. As many as seven different ministers were at the helm of these education changes and, at one stage, Singapore had three education ministers within a span of less than 15 months. No attempt was made to listen to the views of teachers or parents before new policies were implemented. As pointed out by one member of Parliament, "The point is we were so concerned with objects and objectives that we lost sight of the fact that we were dealing with children and people" (*Straits Times* March 24, 1976). A serious communication gap was recognized between the Education Ministry and the schools. This lack of dialogue led to all kinds of interpretation of policy decisions that, at one point, totaled 78 notifications issued to schools within just nine months. The necessity of establishing channels of regular communication between the Ministry and the schools was an important lesson learned from this experience.

The low status and morale of teachers was also high on the list of complaints. As voiced by the Singapore Teachers' Union, resignation of teachers and principals was consistently high in the early 1970s. In 1973, 379 teachers resigned, or 2.1 percent of the teaching force; in 1974, 350 teachers resigned, or 1.9 percent; and in 1975, the figures were 306 resignations, or 1.7 percent.[6]

The year 1978 was a watershed in Singapore's education development. To support its broad "catching-up" economic strategy, and working on the premise that senior servants and talented bureaucrats should assume major roles in decision making, spearheading changes and managing large government enterprises, the government introduced a technocratic ethos in its education framework. A high-level review committee, led by Dr. Goh Keng Swee (the then deputy prime minister) and his team of systems engineers, reviewed the education system and totally overhauled it. Its report (popularly known as the "Goh Report") brought to light the education doldrums embedded in the system, as reflected in two sets of statistics, those relating to education wastage and to the literacy level of the students. Education wastage, in the form of failure to achieve the expected standards and premature school leaving, for the years 1971 to 1974 was high. Out of 1,000 pupils entering primary grade one, on average, 206 dropped out of school nine years later, without acquiring any useful qualification or skill. It was recommended that those pupils who did not have the ability to proceed satisfactorily in the academic stream would be screened and prepared for vocational careers. In this way, reduced student wastage rates contributed to increases in education access.

The low education standard in the 1970s was reflected in the poor literacy level, which was measured in terms of proficiency in the English language (an average 40 percent pass rate in the Ordinary Level Cambridge Schools Examinations in the 1970s), of those pupils who passed their PSLE and young national servicemen with education levels ranging from no formal education to secondary grade three. This low literacy was despite the fact that the nation's literacy rate increased from 72.7 percent in 1970 to 77.6 percent in 1978 (*Straits Times* August 11, 1978). The low English proficiency resulted in the overall low education standard.[7] Out of 1,000 pupils entering primary grade one, only 440 reached secondary grade four after 10 years and, of this number, only 106 obtained 3 or more "Ordinary" level passes at the Cambridge Schools Examinations.

By the mid-1970s, the adoption of the EOI strategy had enabled the country to enjoy full employment. But it was apparent to the political leaders that to sustain robust growth rates, the people must develop additional competencies in science and technology. British colonialism did not leave behind a well-planned education system that emphasized the development of technical and vocational skills. The earlier-than-expected British military withdrawal from 1971 also created the pressing need for the supply of skilled labor resources to fill the positions formerly occupied by skilled British workers. The long time lag had made it difficult for the government to introduce measures to quickly close the technological gap. The problem was compounded by the severe shortage of local expertise in the field of science and technology. Such expertise could have contributed to the development of appropriate science and technical education in schools. A study report in 1970 by Dutch economist Albert Winsemius highlighted the deficiency in terms of the shortage of skilled workers, such as engineers, management personnel, and technicians.[8] Whatever limited pool of engineers the country had was largely taken up by the multinational corporations (MNCs) that dominated the fast-expanding manufacturing sector (Goh 1972, 275). The Singapore government had adopted an aggressive open-door policy to attract MNCs and foreign expertise to the small city-state to provide the impetus for an industrial takeoff and to close the technological gap. As explained by Goh Keng Swee, then deputy minister, in his 1970 budget speech, "When foreign corporations bring their expertise, what we experience as a developing nation is a brain-drain in reverse . . . in the long term the scientific know-how and technological processes which we now borrow from abroad must in course of time develop on an indigenous base at our institutions of higher learning" (Parliamentary Debates Singapore March 9, 1970).[9]

Although new government institutions were set up to deal with science and technology policy problems, quite often the measures recommended did not endure for long. Instead, there was a bewildering succession of ad hoc committees, councils, and agencies, each of which sent out different signals and directions. The confusing situation was further reinforced by the existence of a rather-inept Ministry of Science and Technology (set up in 1968), suffering from a shortage of high-level administrators and overseeing a wide range of activities, ranging from coordination of technical education to the promotion of research work.[10] Young Singaporeans had indifferent attitudes toward "blue-collar" jobs. The magnitude of the problem was seen in some shocking 1976 statistics—of the 150,000 clerical and related workers, only 2 percent were work permit holders; but of the 1,600 metal process workers, 46 percent were work permit holders, reaching 56 percent of the 4,700 woodworkers and a staggering 60 percent of the 55,000 building construction workers (*Straits Times* August 9, 1976).[11] Recognizing the backwardness in the development of science and technology in the country, the Singapore government, in the 1980s, adopted development strategies designed to push the economy and society higher up the technological ladder. With this vision, more education changes were introduced to prepare the people for the country's "Second Industrial Revolution" in the 1980s.

SUSTAINABLE DEVELOPMENT THROUGH EFFICIENCY-DRIVEN EDUCATION, 1978–97

Quite remarkably, by the end of the 1970s, social and economic indicators pointed to a rich and progressive environment in Singapore, which, in the midst of developing countries in the region and elsewhere, was still battling with the problem of poverty. In 1980, after two decades of intensive expansion of the manufacturing sector largely through the aegis of foreign MNCs, the manufacturing sector contribution had risen to 28 percent of GDP, compared with 12 percent in 1960. As countries in Southeast Asia began to compete effectively for foreign investments in low-skilled, labor-intensive industries, Singapore's previous comparative advantage in labor-intensive manufactured products was gradually being eroded.

The response was a shift to a strategy that could accelerate Singapore's transition from a third-tier labor-intensive industrializing country to a second-tier capital-intensive economy. Thus, the Second Industrial Revolution was launched in 1981, accelerating Singapore's transition to a more sophisticated technological base, and thereby taking it out of competition with the lower-wage countries and lessening its reliance on labor expansion for economic growth. The two main strategies of the restructuring program were as follows: (a) a continuation of the policy of attracting MNCs to invest in high-technology operations, and (b) the promotion of science and technology, such as activities in research and development (R&D).[12] To provide a labor force for this stage of industrialization, the government revisited the education system, not only using it as a major vehicle in nation building, but with the state acting as a strategic player through manpower planning, also applying it to the wider process of economic development. The ability of the state to successfully manage education and skill demand, as well as supply, was and continues to be a major source of Singapore's competitive advantage.

After two decades of rapid expansion of education opportunities for all young Singaporeans, during which universal primary and lower-secondary education was achieved, the government now shifted its focus to quality rather than the fulfillment of mere quantitative demands. The emphasis was on upgrading and providing quality education. It was recognized that survival-driven education was structured on the premise that children of different levels of intelligence and learning ability were expected to progress at the same rate. With the pace of teaching geared to the average pupil, the more intelligent students found school to be boring, and those with learning difficulties found it difficult to keep pace.

To support the drive toward sustainable development and reflecting the economic restructuring strategies, education was revamped with an emphasis on efficiency. Aimed at reducing education wastage, a New Education System (NES)

Figure 3.1   The New Education System, 1979

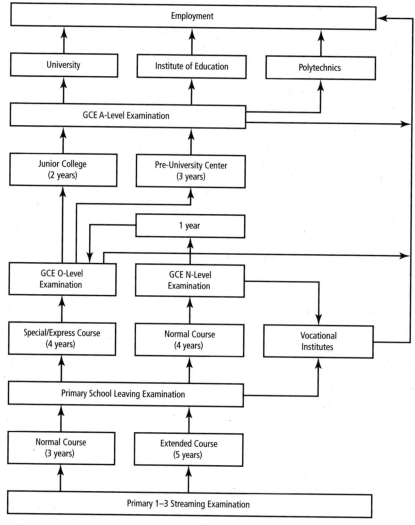

Source: Adapted from Low et al. 1991, figure 4.1.
Note: GCE = General Certificate in Education.

was introduced in January 1979 (see figure 3.1). The NES provided for three streams in both primary and secondary school, to allow pupils to progress at a pace more suited to their abilities. Slower primary pupils were allowed up to eight years to complete primary education, whereas secondary pupils could take up to five years to acquire the General Certificate in Education (GCE) "Ordinary" Level and a further three years for the "Advanced" Level. A new lower-secondary school certificate, the GCE "Normal" was introduced. In manpower terms, the intention was to reduce attrition and enable each pupil to go as far as possible in school, and thereby achieve the best possible education takeoff for further training and employment.

By the early 1980s the key features of the efficiency-driven education system were in place—a national curriculum with a stress on bilingualism, moral education, and civics; an emphasis on science, mathematics, and technical education; regular student assessment regulated by the Ministry of Education's Research and Testing Division; differentiated curriculum materials tailored to the needs of different streams produced by the Curriculum Development Institute of Singapore; and clear lines of progression to the university, polytechnics, and vocational institutes. By 1984, the education system featured a systematic and year-long professional training program for principals and heads of departments. Primary streaming (at primary grade three) and secondary streaming (at secondary grade two) began in 1979 and 1980, respectively. Taken together, these changes motivated student enrollment and performance by eliminating education dead-ends and enabling each student to advance as far as their interest and ability might take them.

On the whole, the NES saw improvements in terms of academic results. Before implementation of the new system, more than 60 percent of pupils who sat for the PSLE and the O-level examination failed in one or both languages. By 1984, the overall percentage passes of the PSLE in English and a second language were 85.5 and 98.7 percent, respectively. For the O-level English exam, the passing percentage jumped to more than 90 percent. At the same time, high attrition rates at the primary and secondary stages of education declined sharply, as noted in the Goh Report (1978). In 1986, for example, only 3,772 pupils (or less than 1 percent of the total school population below 16 years of age) left school without having at least 10 years of education. The country's success in reducing education wastage provided the city-state with an educated workforce able to cope with the demands of a rapidly expanding economy. As in the previous decades, education in Singapore in the 1980s and beyond, being both a public and merit good, was (and is) heavily subsidized by the government. In 1989, private expenditure on education was only 0.55 percent of GDP (compared with 0.86 percent in 1960) (Low, Toh, and Soon 1991, 135–38).[13]

Within the education system, however, there were still teething problems. The strictly top-down approach in planning, disseminating, and enforcing education changes was a clear reflection of the Singapore government's paternalistic style of rule. In the process, it produced three unhealthy trends.

First, it generated the "yes-man" syndrome and the acceptance of instructions without question. Second, it inculcated an over-reliance on the top leaders for direction. Third, it nurtured a spoon-feeding culture. The end result was an education service that lacked autonomy, initiative, and a general sense of detachment from the policy makers. Within schools, teachers and children alike were mechanically fed by a bureaucratically designated and rigid curriculum. The double-session system imposed constraints on schools by restricting the availability of its physical facilities and imposing severe inconveniences on teachers. Not surprisingly, even by the mid-1980s, principals and teachers suffered from low morale and lacked the deep commitment to implement effectively the changes demanded by leaders. Teachers had to endure poor social status, ineffective supervision and guidance, and bleak promotion prospects especially for the non-graduate-level teachers.[14]

With the appointment of Dr. Tony Tan Keng Yam as minister of education in 1985, the pressing problems in the education system were tackled with great vigour. The guiding philosophy for Singapore's education system in the 1980s was explicitly expressed by the former banker who answered the call of duty to serve in the Cabinet:

> I would say that our education system in the 1980s should be guided by three considerations: Firstly, preparing the child for work in a Singapore which is rapidly becoming a modern centre for brain services and technological industries. This means that he will need to have a sound knowledge of English. Secondly, equipping him with a sufficient knowledge of his mother tongue so that he will retain a link with his cultural origins. This is the rationale for our policy on bilingualism. Thirdly, inculcating in the child an awareness of the necessity of moral and traditional values so that he will grow up to be a responsible adult, conscious of his obligations to himself, his family, his neighbours and his nation (*Business Times* July 8, 1980).

From 1985 to 1991 a series of well-planned education changes were introduced that reduced wastage, increased flexibility within the school system, gave greater autonomy to schools, and provided greater access to higher education. All pupils leaving the primary school system were placed in the appropriate secondary school courses that matched their learning pace, ability, and inclinations. An education program for gifted students was started in 1985, English was made the main medium of instruction in all schools, and a scheme to have all secondary schools move to only a single session was initiated in 1989. Changes were also made to tackle the teacher shortage. In the words of Dr. Tony Tan, "The basic solution to the problem of attracting high-quality people to join the teaching profession is to pay them sufficiently" (*Straits Times* July 8, 1980). In response to these needs, training programs at the then Institute of Education were revamped and full-time training for nongraduate and graduate teacher trainees started in July 1980.

A critical issue that continued to fester was the failure of the education system to inculcate positive values and attitudes toward technical training and blue-collar jobs. Though much had been done to equip the school leavers with technical and vocational skills and to change attitudes, vocational training was (and is) specifi-cally aimed at providing a form of continual education for the less academically inclined pupils. Before 1992, those who failed their PSLE and the examination at the end of secondary grade two were channelled into vocational institutes. Unlike in the Republic of Korea, where vocational and technical training is held in high esteem, Singapore's system had failed to project the same image. Vocational insti-tutes continued to be perceived as "dumping grounds" or "catch-nets" for those who failed to master the academic rigor curriculum.

As a result, Singapore continued to be severely hampered by shortages of labor at three critical levels—skilled labor, qualified technical and engineering person-nel, and management trained in modern techniques. Clearly, it is not an easy task to reconstruct a trading culture into a manufacturing culture, especially one that has strong underpinnings in science and technology. In the first place, education in Singapore has long been historically characterized by a white-collar mentality. In part this characterization is due to its colonial origins and to the high standing the civil service has in Singapore because of its contribution to Singapore and its contribution to Singapore's socioeconomic transformation. The majority of school leavers wished to go to university and obtain academic and professional qualifications. They gravitated toward clerical and administrative posts in the ter-tiary sector, mainly in insurance, banking, trading, and government service. A use-ful sociocultural explanation for the continuation of this white-collar mentality is the perception held by many Chinese families that administrative posts were seen as compatible to the scholar class under the Confucian social hierarchy. They com-mand high prestige, prospects, and job security (*Straits Times* April 10, 1968). The white-collar mentality at this time was undesirable and inconsistent with the gov-ernment's policy to shift toward a science- and technology-competent blue-collar workforce. Unfortunately, some vestiges of this historical legacy remain.

The negative perception of vocational and technical training was tackled seri-ously by the Singapore government in the late 1980s. As the young continued to show an aversion toward blue-collar jobs, the danger of the country not possess-ing a sufficient pool of technically skilled local workers became obvious. This sce-nario prompted a serious warning by Lee Yock Suan, then minister of education, in June 1994: "Singapore will be poorer if everyone aspires to and gets only academic qualifications but nobody knows how to fix a TV set, a machine tool or a process plant. We need a world-class workforce with a wide variety of knowledge of skills to achieve a world-class standard of living" (*Straits Times* June 14, 1994).

Several institutional changes were introduced in the 1990s to enhance the image of technical and vocational education in Singapore. In 1992 the VITB was totally revamped and renamed the Institute of Technical Education (ITE). ITE campuses, with excellent education and sports infrastructure and cutting-edge technological support, were built in several locations throughout the island. Beginning in 1992, pupils who did not fare well at the end of their primary education were channelled to a new Normal Technical secondary stream before gaining admission to the new postsecondary ITE. The secondary curriculum was restructured to allow the necessary time to master basic skills, especially proficiency in the English language. Scholarships were available for top ITE graduates to pursue diploma courses in the polytechnics (*Straits Times* December 30, 1993).[15] Beginning in August 1994, ITE launched its attachment programs for Secondary Two Normal (Technical) Technical stream students. The objective was to familiarize these students with the state-of-the-art campuses and, more important, to "remove any fears of machinery and tools or hang-ups about blue-collar jobs" (Chiang 1998, 64). Market demand for the well-trained ITE graduate, especially by some 650 participating companies under ITE's apprenticeship scheme, led to a rise of their starting salary, from an average of about S$700 per month in 1994 to about S$1,200 per month in 2005. Many success stories were highlighted in the newspapers that showcased ITE students making it to the polytechnics and eventually acquiring university degrees. In short, although enrollment in these training schools is limited to those who find it difficult to go the academic route, the image of vocational training has greatly improved.

At the tertiary level, in line with the government's effort to enlarge the pool of scientific and technical manpower and its overall economic vision to transform Singapore into a developed nation, total enrollment in local degree and diploma courses increased by more than 200 percent (20,305 students in 1980 to 62,683 students in 1992) (Ministry of Education, various years).[16] Increasing university enrollment, however, does not hide the fact that Singapore was critically short of university graduates to run the economy. In the early 1980s, only 9 percent of annual cohorts of students entered universities or polytechnics (compared with 20 percent in Taiwan (China), and 40 percent in Japan). Rigidities in the education system and, more specifically, in the admission process to the two local universities also prevented the rapid expansion of the graduate population. Admission was (and is) based on the student achieving acceptable A-level results. Further restrictions included enrollment quotas for the various faculties (for example, law and medicine) and the second language requirement.

Although the increasing number of polytechnic and university graduates helped change the profile of the workforce, the government recognized that, to become a technologically advanced city-state, the country needed a sustainable supply of indigenous scientists and engineers. For Singapore to develop its own indigenous technological capabilities, the lion's share of the supply of scientists and engineers had to come from native-born students educated and trained in local universities and polytechnics.[17] In 1990, out of every 10,000 Singapore

Table 3.3   Output of Degrees, 1980–89

Courses	1980–85	1986–89
Arts	3,792	4,542
Science	3,180	4,105
Engineering	2,467	5,005

Source: Calculated from Department of Statistics 1989, tables 15.12 and 15.13.

workers, 114 were engineers by qualification, but only 29 were research scientists and engineers (RSEs).

Concerted efforts, including better employment prospects and higher baseline salaries, were made in the public-private sector to entice young Singaporeans to take up science and engineering disciplines in the universities. These efforts resulted in an increase in the output of science and engineering graduates during the 1980s, as seen in table 3.3.

This increase in the number of graduates in science and engineering was sustained throughout the 1980s. Most significant, the number of engineering graduates doubled between the periods 1980–85 and 1986–89. This was an indication of the success of the government manpower planning "in meeting the needs of the economy for trained personnel at all levels" (Lee 1988, Vol. 50, Col. 1503). The government confirmed that

> [T]he major constraint on the expansion of technical education has been the number of qualified trainees, not the demand for graduates or the availability of places . . . the Engineering faculty at the University, which expanded rapidly, had difficulty in filling its places, and admitted some marginal students, and then suffered high failure rates in its five year examinations . . . (Lee 1988, Vol. 50, Col. 1504).

The shortage of able students studying engineering was compounded by the fact that "[t]he biggest misallocation in our tertiary education is the very low proportion of girls doing engineering" (Lee 1988, Col. 1505). Girls, some of whom outperformed the boys at A-level examinations, were more interested in courses like accountancy and business administration because "they think [that in engineering] they may get their hands dirty" (Lee 1988, Col. 1505).

In terms of the needed research and development manpower, the increase in the number of science and engineering graduates contributed to a steady rise in the pool of RSEs. Results are shown in table 3.4.

It was also in the mid-1980s that Singapore launched its National Information Technology (IT) Plan, which marked its development as a "wired" nation.[18] Although measures were introduced in schools to promote computer literacy, the

Table 3.4 Research Scientists and Engineers (RSEs)

Year	RSEs	Labor force (thousands)	RSEs per 10,000 labor force
1978	818	975	08.4
1981/82	1,193	1,128	10.6
1984/85	2,401	1,188	20.2
1987/88	3,361	1,252	26.8
1990	4,329	1,516	28.6
1991	5,218	1,554	33.6
1992	6,454	1,620	39.8

Source: National Science and Technology Board (Singapore) 1992.

buy-in was slow and it was not until the 1997 IT Master Plan was implemented that concerted efforts were made to pursue this agenda.

TOWARD A KNOWLEDGE-BASED ECONOMY THROUGH ABILITY-DRIVEN EDUCATION, 1997–PRESENT

By 1995, the efficiency-driven education model was producing positive outcomes. Singapore's youth performed exceptionally well in international mathematics and science tests (TIMSS 1995, 1999). The 1995 research study involved schools in 41 countries. It compared scores of 13 year olds in mathematics and science tests. The international average score was 500. Singapore was first with 643, followed by Korea, Japan, and Hong Kong (China). This feat was again achieved in 2003. Although some have credited Asian values as the success factors for this achievement, the policy of streaming students according to academic abilities in Singapore at both primary and secondary levels helped teachers to better respond to the learning requirements of their students. The pupils benefited from major changes to the mathematics syllabus in 1990 and to the teaching of science since 1985 (when a greater emphasis was placed on thinking skills and understanding concepts, rather than rote mastery of content). The attrition rate for secondary schools decreased significantly from 19 percent in 1980 to 3.5 percent in 1999.

Globalization, powered in part by rapid technological advances, has redefined the competitive framework of nations. In the new economy, national wealth is increasingly determined by discovery and application of new and marketable ideas. The transition to a knowledge-based economy (KBE) shifts the emphasis of value away from traditional factors of production and industrial production toward the use of knowledge in innovation and creativity. For Singapore and Singaporeans, the faster the country's economy changes, the harder it is for the citizens to be confident of their skills and employability. In short, the new economy carries a steep price—more frenzied lives, less security, more economic and social stratification, and the loss of time and energy for family, friendships, community, and self. These trends required Singapore's education system and structure to be redefined and realigned to meet the challenges of the new century. Stakeholders, especially the parents and the community at large, were now actively engaged. Singapore and its education system now entered into an ability-driven phase to meet the demands of the KBE.

The major education milestone of the 1990s was a shift in the country's strategic paradigm—from that of an efficiency-driven education to an ability-driven one. Initiated in June 1997, the new paradigm encapsulated the "Thinking Schools, Learning Nation" (TSLN) vision.[19] The vision of TSLN hinges on the premise that, devoid of natural resources, the future sustainability and wealth of Singapore depends on the capacity of its people to learn—and to learn continuously throughout their lives. The decision to make a radical shift toward ability-driven education in the late 1990s was timely and imperative. Undoubtedly, for nations to survive and prosper in the twenty-first century, the quality of education would be a critical success factor and would differentiate the wealth of nations. Singapore's leaders learned much from the examples of the United States, Britain, and Japan. Although the Americans were (and are) unsurpassed in producing highly creative and entrepreneurial individuals, serious concerns remain about the low average levels of literacy (including technological literacy) and numeracy among young Americans. Similar trends were also evident in the United Kingdom. The Japanese acknowledged the limitations of their mass-oriented school system, with its government-controlled curriculum. They, too, had begun to refine their education system, from primary to postgraduate education, to sustain the country's standing as one of the most innovative and competitive nations in the world. Like Japan, Singapore seeks to keep the best of the old in the education system while forcing needed changes.

Ability-driven education was designed to give all youth a well-rounded 10 years of general education, including six years of compulsory education at the primary level, during which time they could participate in a variety of programs according to their differences in ability (see figure 3.2). The school system continues to feature a national curriculum, with major national examinations administered at the end of the primary, secondary, and junior college years. The ability-driven education model provides greater flexibility and choice. Upon leaving primary school, the young Singaporean now has a range of education tracks that cater to different strengths and interests. For example, brighter students can apply to join the Integrated Programme—a new component in the education system. It spans secondary and junior education without the intermediate O-level examination at the end of secondary school. For students with different abilities the Academic and Technical tracks provide a mixture of academic and technology-based subjects. The streams are no longer rigid barriers, and opportunities exist for lateral

Figure 3.2 Ability-Driven Education System, 2007

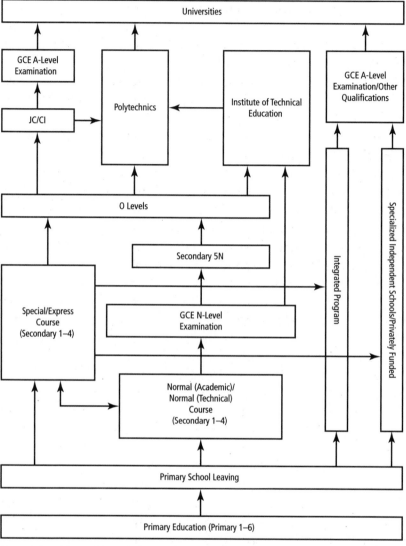

Source: Adapted from Ministry of Education (Singapore) 2006.
Note: GCE = General Certificate in Education; JC/CI = Junior colleges/centralized institute.

transfer. Schools have the flexibility to offer options that match student interests and closer teaching-learning opportunities with links to polytechnics and the ITE. Schools have been encouraged to build on niche strengths in nonacademic areas, for example, sports and performing arts.

A flexible and responsive education structure that better caters to diverse abilities is now in place. The overall objective is to motivate Singaporeans to continually acquire new knowledge, learn new skills, gain higher levels of technological literacy, and develop a spirit of innovation, enterprise, and risk-taking, without losing their moral bearings or their commitment to the community and nation (Gopinathan 1999).[20] To achieve a "quantum improvement" in Singapore's whole process of education, several major initiatives were launched, including revamping career paths for teachers, teaching creative thinking, introducing collaborative learning strategies, stressing national (or citizenship) education, making better use of new technologies in teaching and learning, and giving schools more resources and greater autonomy.

Schools are strongly encouraged to take ownership of the curriculum and cocurricular activities to better respond to student talents and abilities and to develop custom programs that meet student aptitudes and skills. These specialized programs now include music and art elective programs and specially designed physical education and Chinese language classes. As discussed, vocational training under the ITE was given a strong boost. Government recurrent expenditure on technical and vocational education per student increased from S$4,883 in 1991 to S$8,018 in 2004. Infrastructure, facilities, and technical equipment are consistently upgraded to ensure that they match industrial needs.[21]

These structural changes and education initiatives were matched with changes in education funding. During the last two decades or so, several new moves related to the financing of education were created by the Ministry of Education. The first was the government committing itself to increasing spending on education from 4 to 5 percent of the GDP, if the need arose. In 1991, an innovative program, known as the *Edusave Scheme*, was announced that enabled grants to be given to each child between 6 and 16 years old to meet specified education expenses, such as expenses for education visits to other countries, enrichment programs outside the formal school curriculum, and so on. The *Edusave* financial provision thus incorporates an element of choice in the use of funds, serving to customize the use of education facilities according to needs. The scheme ensures equity in education provision among different ethnic groups. An endowment fund was established with a capital sum of S$1 billion to be topped up yearly up to S$5 billion. Government recurrent expenditure on education per student increased from S$2,013 per primary student in 1991 to S$3,541 in 2005 and S$2,843 per secondary student in 1991 to S$5,390 in 2005 (Ministry of Education 2005, 49).

At the teacher-training level, Singapore is perhaps one of the few countries in the world that provides a generous employment package to retain teachers and maintain a high-quality teaching force. Besides remunerations that are compatible with (or even better than) beginning lawyers, engineers, and medical doctors in the government service, all teachers are entitled to fully subsidized 100 hours of professional training per teacher per year. In this way, teachers are given in-service opportunities to maintain and increase their "intellectual capital," while the country benefits in terms of a teaching cadre whose training does not become obsolete. A *Connect Plan* was also introduced that provided a monetary reward for teachers who stayed in service after a certain number of years. In the spirit of lifelong education, school leaders and teachers are encouraged to take sabbatical leave to acquire new knowledge and skills—and not necessarily in an education institution but in other sectors, such as the hospitality industry.

It was also during this period that information and communication technology (ICT) "took off" in Singapore's schools and tertiary institutions. In the first Master Plan of 1997, the underlying rationale was that ICT could be integrated in the "thinking curriculum" to motivate students to be creative and independent learners. Funding of S$2 billion (for the period 1997–2002) was set aside to introduce ICT in the schools and to have pupils spend 30 percent of curriculum time learning with, or through, computers. Principals were given the funds to equip the schools, pupils, and teachers with the necessary infrastructure and training programs. The Second Master Plan continued this rationale of adopting ICT as a key enabler in making student-centered learning and assessment a reality, and in helping to reach the objectives of ability-driven education and the vision of TSLN. The Second Master Plan adopts a systematic and holistic approach by integrating all the key components in the education system—curriculum, assessment, pedagogy, professional training, and culture.

CONCLUSION

As in OECD countries, Singapore enters what Robert Reich describes as the "Age of Terrific Deal," where choices are almost limitless and it is easy to switch to something better (Reich 2001, 13). Social and economic forces are exerting strongly on education change, the outcomes of which, in turn, affect every aspect of the Singapore society. Pragmatic Singaporeans are becoming better educated and well traveled. But income disparities are widening. As the stakes in getting a good education continue to rise and with meritocracy consistently emphasized in the Singapore society, wealthier and more ambitious parents aggressively resort to "school sorting" and seek the best education they can afford for their children. At the other end of the spectrum are families who are socially and economically disadvantaged and likely to have children who form the bulk of school dropouts.

In the years ahead, the Singapore government will be constantly planning and reviewing education policies and changes that are aimed to achieve the following:

• Prepare young Singaporeans for the KBE and, in the process, sustain Singapore's world competitiveness standing.
• Strengthen national identity, values, and social cohesion and, in the process, sustain Singapore's society regardless of race, language, or religion.

The task at hand is not just to deal directly with pupils, teachers, and schools. More significant, a proactive approach toward engaging parents and the community as "Partners in Education" will be adopted.

Education provides the city-state of Singapore the strong fundamentals it needs to sustain competitiveness. With no natural resources to exploit, the development of the country's manpower resources through a sound and robust education system is crucial. Singapore's case study has shown that strong political leadership and will has guided overall education development and has produced a structure and system that is relevant and responsive to the ever-changing economic and social landscape. Singapore inherited a colonial legacy of a fragmented education system consisting of English and vernacular schools. In the 1950s and 1960s, in the midst of social and political turbulence (largely arising from ethnic tension), the government adopted measures to do away with vernacular schools. Without any natural resources, it recognized the importance of education and the urgent need for a national system of running schools. Singapore wasted no time in devising policies to integrate the various ethnic races.

The Singapore government invests heavily in education, especially at the secondary level, and in the lifelong training of its labor force. Besides defense, the education sector receives the largest share (about 4 percent) of the GDP each year. The overall objective is to sustain the nation's world economic competitiveness. A key learning point is that, as in constructing a house, it is essential to build a strong foundation before adding the whole structure. Singapore developed its primary and secondary education base before expanding its vocational and technical education and tertiary sectors. And when the "quantity" component was being worked on, attention was also given to the "quality" aspect. Many developing countries, including the African nations, may not follow the same path as Singapore (or OECD countries in general), nor will they go through the same stages of development. Basic lessons from the Singapore experience, however, can be relevant to policy makers in education in developing countries.

Singapore's education since 1965 exemplifies the general rule that the development of widespread basic education is necessary, though not sufficient, for sustaining economic growth. During the early phases of growth (in the 1960s and early 1970s), the government's priority was to create jobs so that the people and the country could survive. It attempted to quickly expand accessibility to primary education for all Singaporeans. This effort would at least create a young labor force with basic education to support the labor-intensive factories provided for by largely foreign companies. Additionally, rapid construction of schools would also provide employment opportunities. Once the drive toward universal primary education had been embraced to meet the surging demand for education, the target was quickly achieved through rapid construction of schools and training of teachers. Resources, including free textbooks to those who could not afford them, and funds were fully supplied by the government. The government ensured that a sufficient number of secondary schools could cater to the increased size of primary cohorts. Up to the late 1970s, however, education wastage was high and, although the attainment of universal primary and secondary education was achieved, the quality of education was highly uneven and unsatisfactory in parts. On the economic front, the labor shortage was severe, productivity of the Singapore worker was low, and largely as a consequence of being heavily dependent on MNCs for technology, the indigenous technology base was poorly developed. Urgent measures were taken by the education planners to upgrade the quality of the education system and to reduce education wastage in the 1980s. At the tertiary level, a substantial expansion of engineering and technical enrollment was achieved.

The rising education level of the populace was crucial for the Singapore economy as it made the transition from a labor-intensive strategy to a high value added, technology-intensive industrial strategy in the 1990s. Singapore's economic strategy for the new millennium hinges strongly on raising the technological literacy of its people. This can be achieved largely through the education system. Besides its emphasis on science, mathematics, and computer education, technical and vocational education forms a core component of Singapore's education system. Although it has its fair share of problems, the government persisted in modernizing and uplifting the status of technical and vocational training. Today, Singapore's ITE plays a vital role in preparing young Singaporeans with the technical knowledge and skills they need to service a wide range of industries. This bias toward a technical rather than a purely academic stream of learning is important for Singapore as a global city. The majority of the workforce has to be technically proficient to sustain the manufacturing and services sector.

The new economic paradigm of the new century has led to sweeping reforms of the education system, such as the initiatives to instill innovation, problem-solving skills, creativity, and entrepreneurship in young Singaporeans, while at the same time, maintaining a strong emphasis on content mastery and good values. The school curriculum is constantly revisited and revised, whenever necessary, to ensure its appropriateness in the context of Singapore's overall economic and social development. Emphasis was placed on literacy, numeracy, bilingualism, science and mathematics, the arts, and moral education. Schools were encouraged to be innovative, take greater ownership of their programs and resources, and be more accountable to all stakeholders. This is a significant departure from the top-down approach taken by the Ministry of Education for several decades. School leaders and teachers are trained to respond to change and to initiate change. This "top-down support for ground-up initiatives" approach encourages schools to make decisions and exercise greater autonomy. With greater autonomy comes greater accountability. Education planners in developing countries should recognize that teachers and principals are the key to the successful transformation of school governance and pedagogy. They are the ones who will nurture and train tomorrow's workforce. Singapore's teachers and principals enjoy high status recognition, ample opportunities for professional development, good career advancement, and employment packages.

One sacrosanct feature of Singapore's education structure is bilingualism. It was crucial for the government to introduce a main language of instruction (in this case, the English language) throughout the education system. During the early years after independence, English had been portrayed by the Chinese educated as colonial and thus antinational. Indeed, there were strong and violent protests. However, measures were in place to ensure that the mother-tongue languages (Chinese, Tamil, and Malay) were preserved and taught as second languages. Hence, bilingualism became a main component of Singapore's education once the city-state gained full independence in 1965. The use of English as the medium of instruction allows young Singaporeans to meet the challenges of the global economy, but the mother tongue is also important as a cultural ballast and as a way to inculcate Asian values.

Many developing countries have learned and some have attempted to transfer aspects of Singapore's education model into their respective systems. In the case of Singapore, however, behind the mechanisms and processes of education change is the force that drives them all—the political leadership of Singapore. The few that were entrusted by the populace at the time of independence to lead the small island city-state proved to be equal to the challenge of establishing stability, having both the capacity to make sound social and macroeconomic policies and the political will to make changes. Education was (and is) seen as the key to a good life and, since the early years after independence, the political leadership worked hard to provide education for all. Singaporeans recognized the importance of a good education in order to enjoy economic independence and good standards of living. It must be reiterated, however, that this drive toward attaining good education is sustainable because the nation possesses the economic and social environment that would allow its citizens to reap the full benefits of their investments in education pursuits. For Singapore, the human resources are seen as the most fundamental element in the nation-building process, and, as such, education and training are at the heart of the nation's wider economic plans. For developing countries, this is perhaps one of the most significant challenges in the new millennium.

NOTES

1. In the 1950s, frequent clashes and demonstrations against the government were held by Communist-infiltrated trade unions and Chinese schools. The British soon decided that the best political weapon against the Communist insurgency would be to grant national independence to Singapore. This would deprive the Communists of their role as champions

of antifreedom movements and, hence, the justification for insurrection against the government. Therefore, the stage was set for the first democratic election of a self-governing Singapore in May 1959. The People's Action Party, under the leadership of Lee Kuan Yew, won convincingly. Lee became the first prime minister and, at the same time, the state flag and national anthem "Majulah Singapura" were inaugurated. About four years later, in September 1963, Singapore became part of Malaysia. But political differences soon reached an intolerable level. On August 9, 1965, under the leadership of Lee Kuan Yew, the island of Singapore was formally separated from Malaysia and became a sovereign, democratic, and independent city-state.

2. The Colony of Singapore's Report of the Industrial Resources Study Groups, appears in Andrew Gilmour's Official Letters, 1931–1956. Andrew Gilmour was the Chief Planning Officer in Singapore during the 1950s.

3. The Malays were (and are) considered to be the indigenous people living in Singapore at the time when the British founded Singapore in 1819. Hence, the Malay language became Singapore's national language. Singapore's national anthem is sung in the Malay language.

4. Readers may wonder how the various investments in school construction, teacher recruitment, and free textbooks were made under an education budget that was consistently 20 to 25 percent of the government's budget. The explanation lies in Singapore's steadily rising economic growth rate during this period, which enabled a fairly constant slice of a growing budgetary pie to steadily increase in size.

5. Vocational training and employer-based training constituted the twin strategies of skill-level manpower development. In this respect, the Skills Development Fund (SDF), administered by the Economic Development Board, was an invaluable source of funding for companies to promote employer-based training. This training includes custom training to meet production, restructuring, and specific development needs, undertaken directly by employers as a part of their investment in manpower resources. The SDF worked closely with VITB to promote vocational skill-level training and awarded grants to employers to sponsor (up to 90 percent) employees for VITB's skill courses and apprentices.

6. Objectively, the resignation rates of 1.7 to 2.2 percent for this period were not particularly high. The rates today remain more or less in the same range as they were in the 1970s.

7. Since the 1950s, more and more parents have sent their children to English-stream schools. In 1960, 49 percent of all students were registered for the English stream, and by 1970, it reached 66 percent. In 1982, the figure went up to 90 percent. The reason behind this trend was an economic one. Singapore's economy was inextricably tied to the outside world, particularly industrial nations where the international language for business and trade is English. Moreover, all MNCs (where employment was highly sought) in Singapore used the English language.

8. Dr. Albert Winsemius was the leader of a United Nations Industry Survey Mission to Singapore in 1961. The Winsemius Report, as it became known, convinced the Singapore leaders that the traditional dependence on entrepôt trade would not ensure the future economic survival of the small nation.

9. These statements reflected the optimism of a young but fast-developing nation. In fact, Goh's comments made in 1970 raised several significant, closely related issues concerning Singapore's quest for technological excellence in the 1980s and 1990s—including the transfer and diffusion of technology and skill from the MNCs, the lack of a critical mass,

the brain-drain of local expertise, the weak university-industry link, the lack of a well-planned science and technology policy, and the painfully slow development of research and development in Singapore's indigenous firms. Compared with the newly industrializing countries in East Asia and Japan, Singapore in the 1970s suffered from low labor productivity. Between 1973 and 1978, "real productivity growth in Singapore averaged about 3 percent per annum, compared to an average of 7 percent for Hong Kong, Taiwan and South Korea" (Goh 1978).

These labor-intensive industries do not require professional scientists or engineers; they only need to have experienced foremen or plant supervisors and imported managers. Even within the larger MNCs, transfer and diffusion of technology and skill was rare. See also the "Speech by the Minister of Trade and Industry" quoted in Lim Joo-Jock (1980, 279).

10. Eventually, on April 1, 1981, 12 years after it was formed, the Ministry was dissolved. As explained by Goh Chok Tong (the former prime minister and now Singapore's senior minister), "the defunct Ministry of Science and Technology had only a budget of $100,000 to disburse as research grants. . . . We did not have a research and development policy until now [1991], because research and development was not critical to our economic growth strategy in the last decade" (*Straits Times* February 18, 1981).

11. In Singapore's context, a work permit is a work pass issued to a skilled or unskilled foreigner earning a certain maximum monthly salary to work in Singapore. Currently, the monthly basic salary stands at not more than S$1,800.

12. The impact of an expanding manufacturing base through foreign enterprises on the general managerial and technical skill levels of the workforce was not easily seen. Local industrial establishments in Singapore during this period were characterized by their small size, low capital input, and simple use of technology. In 1969, 70 percent of manufacturing enterprises employed 10 to 39 workers, whereas only 10 percent had more than 100 to 300 workers. Although foreign investors were quick to take advantage of Singapore's open-door policy and the many incentives offered by the government, they were also rational in their technological choice and organization of work. Besides other factors, the small domestic market and the scarcity of local managerial and technical know-how and expertise imposed a limit to the size of the foreign firm. Therefore, apart from the shipbuilding and repairing industry and the chemical-petroleum industry, industrial firms in Singapore were largely labor-intensive, low-wage, and low-productivity enterprises, requiring the mere repetition of simple operations along the assembly and production line.

13. In view of Singapore's growing economy during the 1980s, the declining share represented by private contributions does not necessarily imply a reduction in the absolute levels of private contributions.

14. In Singapore's context, "nongraduate teachers" are trained teachers who do not possess university degrees. Teachers who have a bachelor's degree are "graduate" teachers.

15. Each year, about 400 out of the 3,500 ITE graduates join the polytechnics for a diploma course. For a comprehensive understanding of the development of technical education in Singapore, see Chiang (1998).

16. As a matter of comparison with some OECD countries, the Netherlands's enrollment in the higher education sector increased by 13 percent from 1980 to 1988; in Japan, university undergraduate enrollment rose by about 9 percent between 1978 and 1989; and in Norway, the corresponding figure was 10 percent between 1979 and 1986. The main reason for increased enrollment is the stronger presence of women within the student population (see OECD 1992, 137).

17. This important prerequisite for technological self-reliance was mentioned by Hayashi in his analysis of Japan's experience in absorbing foreign technology.

> Foreign engineers and technologists can and should play only a supplementary role . . . in spite of the diachronic, trans-cultural nature of technology, it cannot function independently of the society and culture in which it is expected to function. Only members of that society can make the best use of a technology. In other words, only native engineers can adapt a foreign technology to their country's climate and history, can intermediate, stabilize, disseminate, and finally, root it firmly in their country (see Hayashi 1990).

18. This visionary initiative is described in: Koh, Thiam Seng, and Sai Choo Koh. 2008. "Digital Skills and Education: Singapore's ICT Master Planning for the School Sector." In *Toward a Better Future: Education and Training for Economic Development in Singapore since 1965*, ed. Lee, Sing Kong, Goh Chor Boon, Birger Fredriksen, and Jee Peng Tan. Washington, DC: World Bank.

19. The TSLN concept or vision was launched by then-Prime Minister Goh Chok Tong on June 2, 1997 (see also Sharpe and Gopinathan 2002). Although the paradigm shift is timed at 1997, rethinking the merits of the efficiency-driven system actually began in the mid-1980s. The *Towards Excellence in Schools* report of 1987 led to the first decentralization moves and the establishment of independent and later autonomous schools.

20. In line with these changes, the National Institute of Education (NIE) reviewed its teacher-training curriculum to meet the objectives of TSLN. NIE ensured that its pre-service training curriculum and professional development programs would stay relevant and responsive. One key factor for its successful role is the close and strong tripartite relationship between the Ministry of Education, schools, and the institution.

21. Many African countries have infrastructure and equipment for technical and vocational training that, for the most part, are obsolete and inadequate to cater to the needs of industries. The problem is compounded by the high costs of importing new equipment.

CHAPTER 4

Education in Vietnam: Development History, Challenges, and Solutions

NGUYEN Quang Kinh and NGUYEN Quoc Chi

INTRODUCTION

Vietnam is an S-shaped country, stretching from $8°02'$ to $23°23'$ north of the equator. It borders China in the north, the Lao People's Democratic Republic and Cambodia in the west, and the Pacific Ocean in the east. Its surface area is approximately 331,000 square kilometers. The population is more than 83 million persons[1] and includes 54 ethnic groups. The Vietnamese majority group accounts for 90 percent of the population. Vietnamese is the common language for the ethnic group community. Regarding administration, Vietnam is divided into 64 centrally managed provinces and cities; 659 districts, towns, and provincially managed cities; and 10,732 communes, quarters, and towns.[2]

Despite being a poor country, Vietnam has made significant achievements in increasing the value of its gross national product, raising its export turnover, controlling the population growth rate, raising living standards, and reducing poverty in rural areas. In the education sector, Vietnam has obtained impressive results compared with those countries that have similar economic development: more than 90 percent of the working-age population is literate; more than 98 percent of children of primary school age attend schools; and the enrollment rates for boys and girls are more or less similar.

To share the country's experiences with policy makers from six African countries during their study tour organized by the World Bank,[3] this chapter provides a brief history of Vietnamese education development over the last decades. The chapter highlights efforts made to overcome different challenges and to reach the current level of achievement. At the same time, it endeavors to clearly present challenges to Vietnam to achieve the Education for All (EFA) goals by 2015 and to enhance education development with a view toward meeting the requirements of industrialization and modernization in the context of globalization and the development of information and communication technology.

HISTORY OF EDUCATION DEVELOPMENT

EDUCATION IN VIETNAM DURING FEUDAL AND COLONIAL PERIODS

The promotion of learning and respect for teachers are traditional values of the Vietnamese people. In olden times, the perception among intellectuals in Vietnamese society was that the position of a teacher was higher than that of parents and lower only than that of the king. Ordinary people believed that they should give their children opportunities to learn to know how to be good citizens. In many communes and villages, rich people invited teachers to stay in their houses to teach their own children and those from other families. The selection of mandarins (civil administrators) during the historic dynasties required a candidate to have excellent learning achievements and to have gained high marks in competitive exams to become a leader. The first such exam for civil administrators was conducted in 1075.

For nearly one thousand years, the Vietnamese people learned Chinese characters and used them for writing, but pronounced them in a Vietnamese way. This learning, combined with the preservation and strengthening of an awareness of national independence, ensured that the Chinese did not assimilate the Vietnamese people. As well as using Chinese characters, the Vietnamese people adapted such characters to provide an ancient Vietnamese script for writing and expressions. Thanks to this adaptation, a number of valuable works of literature and history in ancient Vietnamese script have been preserved for future generations.

At the end of the nineteenth and into the first half of the twentieth centuries, the French forcibly colonized Vietnam and all of Indochina. The traditional Confucian-oriented education, which had been built and maintained by the Vietnamese people, was replaced by French-Vietnamese education, which was aimed mainly at training people to serve the colonial apparatus. During the most prosperous period of French-colonial Indochina, Vietnam had only 2,322 elementary schools (for the first three years of primary education) with an average of one elementary school for every three villages. The total number of students accounted for only 2 percent of the total population: Vietnam had 638 primary schools (for the last years of primary education), with the number of students making up 0.4 percent of the total population; 16 primary colleges (for four years of postprimary education), with students accounting for 0.05 percent of the population; and six secondary schools of which three were public with only 0.019 percent of the total population as secondary students. The whole of French-colonial Indochina had only three universities (law, medicine/pharmacy, and sciences) located in Hanoi with 834 students, of which 628 were Vietnamese. Under the French-Vietnamese education system,

French was the dominant language and was the language of instruction at the higher education level (Tran et al. 1995). With such an education system, 95 percent of Vietnamese people were illiterate.

FROM INDEPENDENCE DAY TO THE VICTORY OF THE FIRST RESISTANCE WAR, 1945–54

After taking control and declaring the country's independence, during the first session of the government, President Hochiminh identified "fighting against poverty, illiteracy and invaders" as the three key tasks of the Vietnamese government and people (*The Works of Ho Chi Minh* 1984). On December 6, 1945, the president sent an open letter to students on the occasion of the opening of the 1945–46 school year, confirming the birth of a new education system with its mission to preserve independence and rehabilitate the country.

Starting from the philosophy that "an illiterate nation is a powerless one," on December 8, 1945, the government issued important legal documents, including Decree No. 17-SL: "Everyone in the country has to be literate"; Decree No. 19-SL: "For the entire country, there will be literacy classes established for farmers and workers to attend at night"; and Decree No. 20-SL: "While waiting for the establishment of compulsory primary education, from now on teaching the national language will be compulsory and free for everyone" (*The Education Law of the Socialist Republic of Vietnam* 2005).[4] In October 1945, President Hochiminh issued the "Call for Literacy." In response to these government policies and President Hochiminh's call, within less than one year, 75,000 literacy classes had been instituted with nearly 96,000 teachers to help some 2.5 million people escape illiteracy.

Thus, with the establishment of the democratic republic, literacy and improvement of people's learning qualifications became the national policy. Learning how to read, write, and calculate was seen as a criterion for demonstrating a person's education. Since then, Vietnam has, for a number of decades, been committed to literacy and improvement of people's learning qualifications. This commitment explains Vietnam's quick response to the World EFA Declaration (1990), active implementation of the Jomtien Action Plan, and strong commitment to the achievement of the Dakar goals.

In 1946, in its emphasis on fighting against the war plans of the colonialist forces, Vietnam tried to establish the legal framework for its education policies by issuing two decrees—namely, Decrees No. 146-SL and No. 147-SL—with the following contents:

Statement: the new education system is built on three fundamental principles: *national, scientific, and popular,* and aimed at serving the *national ideals and democracy.*

Structure of the new educational system: after the pre-school level, there are three levels of education:

First level, i.e., the basic education level, of 4 years.

Second level, with two subsectors: (a) general, including two sub-levels of 4-year general education and 3-year specialized education; and (b) specialization, including two sublevels of 1-year experiment and 1 to 3-year vocational education (depending on each stream).

Third level, with universities (including literature, science, law, and so on) and specialized colleges of at least 3 years. Next to universities were "research institutes."

In parallel with three levels of education, three levels of pedagogy (teacher education) were put in place, namely elementary, intermediate, and advanced.

Establishment of legal provisions: for the basic levels of education all children from 7 to 13 years old could attend schools on a free basis, and from 1950, the basic education level would be compulsory. As for universities, all subjects would be taught in Vietnamese beginning in 1950 (the latter a somewhat rash decision which showed the national spirit of then Vietnamese intellectuals, as French had been used as the language of instruction in all universities for a long period).[5]

During the resistance war (1946–54), schools continued to operate in demilitarized areas. To prepare skilled human resources to contribute to the resistance war and the country's development after victory, the government officially passed an *education reform* project in 1950. It defined the training objective for schools as educating and fostering the younger generation to become future citizens, loyal to the people's democratic regime, and competent to serve society and the resistance war. In accordance with the war effort, the main contents of the reform were to adjust the structure of general education (with a reduced number of years) and the relationship among various components of the education system to ensure consistency with such a transformation. Accordingly, general education included three levels: four years of primary education (exclusive of Vietnamese language reading and writing class); three years of lower-secondary education; and three years of upper-secondary education. In respect of teaching content, several subjects were suspended (such as foreign languages, music, drawing, and housework), and other subjects were added (current affairs, policy, citizenship, and production). Because of the temporarily condensed general education curriculum, students had to complete pre-university courses upon completion of grade nine (initially two years but subsequently one year) before entering universities. At the same time, the literacy and professional education system also changed (following general literacy programs, primary and secondary programs were added). Medical/pharmacy and science (mainly literature and mathematics) universities continued to operate.

In temporarily occupied areas, schools taught a 12-year curriculum, which was based on one that had been adjusted by several patriotic scholars at the beginning of 1945 when French-administered Indochina was invaded by the Japanese.[6] In such temporarily occupied areas, the education system was characterized by a reduction in the domination of colonial education emphasis. Vietnamese language was used in schools to replace French, and a number of national elements were included in school curriculum. The curriculum used in the temporarily occupied areas was still heavily influenced by French education.

YEARS OF TEMPORARY SEPARATION, 1955–75[7]

Once peace was achieved in the North, the Vietnamese government took over the education system in the newly liberated areas. It actively prepared for a new education reform in the context of economic rehabilitation, building the North, and continuing the fight to reunify the whole country. Under this second education reform, the purpose of education was identified as training and fostering young people to become "persons with all-round development in all aspects, who were good citizens and officials" (*The Education Law of the Socialist Republic of Vietnam* 2005). To achieve this goal, education content was made comprehensive (with an emphasis on moral, intellectual, physical, and aesthetic aspects) and highlighted the government's motto of creating "linkages between theory and practice, and school and social life" (*The Education Law of the Socialist Republic of Vietnam* 2005). From a methodological perspective, this reform abolished the command education system, began a more equitable relationship between teachers and students, brought into play the usefulness of extracurricular activities, and gradually introduced production activities into schools as an important way to shape personalities. Through the second education reform, the 9- and 12-year general education systems in newly liberated and freedom areas were combined into a 10-year system (four years of primary education, three years of lower-secondary education, and three years of upper-secondary education).[8] This system was somewhat similar to the Soviet Union's education system.

To meet people's demand for learning, the government planned "to make use of all resources for the development of general education" (*The Education Law of the Socialist Republic of Vietnam* 2005). At the end of the five-year plan cycle (1961–65), the school network was expanded—most communes now had primary schools, every two or three communes had one lower-secondary school, and most districts had upper-secondary schools. Schools that provided both academic and technical education were established, for example, industrial schools in cities, agricultural schools in rural areas, and boarding schools in mountainous provinces. In response to the government's policies, School Protection Committees were established in most communes in the North. These committees were tasked with mobilizing human and financial resources for construction of primary and lower-secondary schools, nominating local people as teachers, and determining contribution norms for salary payments to teachers. These activities resulted in the emergence of people-founded schools. The government determined that teachers working in people-founded and public schools should enjoy similar incentives and policies, the only difference being that local authorities would fund salary expenditures for teachers in people-founded establishments with reasonable support from the state.

During this same period, new universities—in addition to the existing medical/pharmacy, pedagogy, and science institutions—were established in fields such as agriculture and forestry, polytechnics, and economics. The higher education system was further strengthened to train the new pool of intellectuals. Professional secondary and vocational schools were established, with special importance placed on vocational classes attached to enterprises. This contributed to the provision of human resources to develop the northern region, provide fatherland protection, and pursue country reunification.

In parallel with the reform of general education, the government created the "Central Steering Committee on the Elimination of Illiteracy," which identified popular education as an integral part of the state plan (Circular No. 114/TTg, March 27, 1957) and launched a three-year plan to eliminate illiteracy (1956–58). As a result, 2,161,362 people escaped illiteracy, most residents in delta provinces learned to read and write, and the percentage of literate people in the 12 to 50 age-group increased to 93.4 percent. Such literacy achievements, however, like those gained in other periods, were not sustained because of various reasons—the most common of which was the "do-it-only-once" perception.

Based on the literacy achievements, the popular education system moved its emphasis to improving the education levels of adults of working age. This was called, in parallel with general education, the complementary education system. Together with the development of complementary education, the government permitted industrial and agricultural complementary schools to open, which provided additional learning opportunities for workers. A number of graduates from these schools were accepted to study in domestic and foreign universities. Some of them went on to become well-known intellectuals and local and national leaders.

During U.S. Air Force attacks on the North (1965–72), schools were bombing targets.[9] In the context of this violent war, the government identified the goals of continuing education development, ensuring the safety of students, and strengthening links between school and real life, as well as between production and fighting activities. General schools, vocational schools, and higher education institutions were evacuated from cities, towns, key transportation points, and large residential areas to allow teaching and learning activities to continue. The biggest success during this period was that schools and institutions at all levels continued to educate and produce a generation of young people who were ready and willing to fulfill their obligations as citizens, making contributions to the establishment of a values system that emphasized patriotism, national pride, and confidence in national independence and socialism.

In the South during 1954–75, within the Saigon government–controlled and subsequently liberated areas, education activities attended to people's learning needs and fulfilled responsibility of training human resources. The education activities in these two areas had different, even opposing, characteristics.

First, in Saigon government–controlled areas, education gradually changed from European and French-influenced education to North American–dominated education. General education experienced several changes with the components of primary education (five years), lower-secondary education (four years), and upper-secondary education (three years), including academic and practically oriented streams. Higher education was more academic than practically oriented with an emphasis on fundamental sciences, law, economics, and administration. Universities of engineering, technology, and agriculture and forestry followed slower development. During the time when the Saigon government controlled the Southern urban areas, despite the impact and influence of North American education, young people still maintained a spirit of resistance.

After the Provisional Revolutionary Government of Southern Vietnam was established in liberated areas, students followed a 12-year curriculum with textbooks that demonstrated a patriotic and resistance spirit. These textbooks were significantly different from those used in temporarily occupied areas.

10 YEARS OF PREREFORM, 1975–85

In April 1975, the Vietnamese people's resistance war to protect independence and reunify the country achieved complete success. After the victory day, the government focused on two tasks for the education sector in southern provinces: (a) removal of influences from the old education system, and (b) implementation of literacy activities for people in the 12- to 50-year age-group.

For the first task, the Ministry of Education quickly developed and issued a new 12-year curriculum, and developed and printed 20 million copies of new textbooks to replace the ones previously used in the South. Most of the teachers working under the old regime were rehired. At the same time, the nationalization of private schools,[10] removal of schools from religious influence, and unification of private schools under state management also took place.

For the second task, the government planned, as a first priority, to quickly eliminate illiteracy and strengthen complementary education. Once again, literacy activities were seen as a patriotic symbol, and thus attracted millions of people to participate in teaching, learning, and helping others learn. At the beginning of 1978, all southern cities and provinces basically eliminated illiteracy. Out of 1,405,870 people who had been identified as being illiterate, 1,323,670 people were helped to escape from illiteracy, achieving 94.14 percent of the plan.

While carrying out these urgent intermediate tasks, the government prepared an education reform to establish a unified national education system appropriate to the national reconstruction strategies and development of the country.

The third education reform[11] started during the 1981–82 school year. The important characteristics of this reform were as follows:

- Education objectives were redefined as the provision of care and education for the younger generation from early childhood to adulthood with an aim of laying the foundations for well-rounded human development; implementing universal education to facilitate changes in productive relationships, science and technology, and culture and ideology; and training and promoting—in line with the personnel requirements—an increase in the size of the working staff.
- For education content, focus was placed on "Improving the quality of comprehensive education, and producing a new type of worker who are masters and able to shoulder the cause of the construction of people's socialism."
- Education principles included learning together with practice, education, and work, and strengthened connections between school and society.
- The structure of the education system was revised: the 12-year system in the South and the 10-year system in the North were replaced by a new 12-year general education structure, in which primary and lower-secondary schools were combined and preparation was made for streaming in upper-secondary schools. A number of specialized universities were established and developed.

The replacement of textbooks at all schools—the most important task in the third education reform and completed in 1996—brought consistency to general education across the nation. As for education content alone, the reformed curriculum included modern elements that resulted in preconditions for the improvement of education quality. This reform faced a number of challenges, however, and revealed several limitations during implementation. The main limitations were unrealistic goals and nonfeasible solutions. Examples of unrealistic goals included a large expansion in the size of the system for rapid universalization and the provision of education subsidies for all—both of which were to be achieved during a time when adequate resources were lacking because of the border war and economic recession. An example of an unfeasible solution, a reflection of centralized planning, was the combination of primary and lower-secondary schools (because of inappropriate conditions—weak and poor teachers and education managers, insufficient equipment—these combined schools were separated again at a later stage). Another unrealistic solution was the expectation that large contributions and education welfare support would be forthcoming from all people and, as a result of this expectation, only a small proportion in the state budget in comparison with other sectors was spent on education. The people, however, thought that their children's education, even vocational or higher education, should have been subsidized. The government's expectations of people's contributions and the people's expectations of state subsidies were inappropriate in a poor and developing country like Vietnam, especially in the context of a postwar period and economic crisis, and the shortfall in resources led to the underdevelopment of education.

20 YEARS OF REFORM, 1986–2005

The biggest challenge faced by Vietnamese education in the early 1980s was that the state was unable to provide financial resources while it dismantled the importance of the collective command economy. Consequently, education, like other social sectors, was faced with a serious shortage of resources. Schools had little or no operating funds, and finances for teacher salaries were insufficient. As a result, both teachers and students left schools, and the size of the education system and its quality declined. Universities, colleges, and professional secondary schools did not have sufficient minimum budgets to maintain their regular activities. Graduates could not find employment. Lecturers had to supplement their meager income with inappropriate jobs. Universities, colleges, and professional secondary schools had no autonomy within a bureaucratic system.

In 1986, to overcome the national economic crisis, Vietnamese leaders planned for a major national economic and social reform to move from the centralized planning system to a socialist-oriented market mechanism.[12] A direct consequence of this major change in overall national policy was that the education sector also needed to reform. The content and scope of this education reform were broad. One fundamental issue was to change the inappropriate perceptions and solutions of the past, and instead to actively propose and implement new solutions that could halt the recession, stabilize and strengthen the system, and generate a situation with the resources needed for continued development. To meet this objective, changes were required in the socialization, democratization, diversification, and mobilization of social, family, and school resources for the younger generation. The education sector made efforts to maintain, enhance, and develop the national education system, and emphasized the need to improve the material and intellectual lives of teachers and education managers—that is, those with a decisive role in achieving better education quality and efficiency.

For general education, the reform orientations were (a) to continue to make modifications to curricula objectives and content, textbooks, and education-related perceptions; (b) to gradually achieve comprehensive quality in a manner appropriate to each type of student, teacher, school, and locality; (c) to link general education with vocational education; (d) to continue to strongly affirm the state's responsibilities; and (e) to implement education socialization.[13] And while implementing socialization activities, it was important to avoid any unrealistic expectation of public subsidies.

In its approach to reform general education the government allowed the collection of tuition fees at all levels (with the exception of primary education because this subsector had a target of universalization). Additionally, permission was given to open private preschool classes and schools, and semipublic and people-founded classes and schools at all levels. The education sector classified learning activities according to levels of student abilities; it established specialized schools at lower- and upper-secondary levels for gifted students; and it established selective classes for excellent students in teacher-education lower- and upper-secondary schools (specialized schools and selective classes were not proposed at the primary level to avoid any overload that might compromise children's development). The reform strengthened the pilot work to stream the upper-secondary curriculum, and it prepared for an expansion of the streamed curriculum to classify learning activities according to student's abilities and expectations and to provide different pathways. Work and vocational skills were provided through links between general and vocational education. At the primary education level, together with the gradual finalization of the ongoing reformed curriculum, various programs were developed for ethnic minority children and disadvantaged children to introduce more flexible classes. Drawing on the experience in previous literacy campaigns, the government established the National Committee on Literacy and attached the literacy task to primary education universalization.

For vocational education, reform orientations were designed to transform human resources training, which previously had been oriented toward the state-owned and collective sector, to training oriented toward the needs of the market economy. The reform adjusted the structure of training disciplines and areas according to labor market needs with a view toward meeting the requirements of a labor structure that was appropriate for the economic transition. The reform also aimed to raise training quality to better fulfill the requirements for skilled human resources and sought to create competitiveness within the economic relationships in domestic and international markets.

Some of the approaches used in the reform of vocational education included asking for student contributions through tuition fees and covering the costs of practical sessions. The state budget was used to maintain the existing professional secondary and vocational schools, to build infrastructure, and to cover teacher-training activities. Permission was given for the establishment of semipublic-, private-, and people-founded vocational institutions. Technical teaching activities were organized for students to provide vocational skills for young people and to establish a technical education system in the society. A model for a vocational secondary school was adopted that combined general and vocational education.

A pilot training scheme for highly skilled technicians in the fields of post and telecommunications, light industry, transportation, mine engineering, chemicals, and culture and the arts was launched to replace those with secondary qualifications. Training was to be conducted on the basis of vocational "skill modules," which classified a vocational skills system into various skill components that were equivalent to those required for certain jobs. The training for a specific job would require an accumulation of various skill components. Because various skills were required by different jobs, links among various training areas were achieved.

For higher education, the reform orientations were that, instead of training for public organizations and parts of the collectives, training was provided for various economic components and designed to meet the diverse learning needs of the society. Instead of relying on the state budget, all possible financial sources were to be mobilized and used. Instead of implementing the plan targets set by the state, other nonstate targets were also set and fulfilled. And instead of rigid training programs, various flexible and diverse training programs were developed to create employment opportunities and identify employment in the market economy with many job-related changes.

Approaches used in the reform of higher education included managing the organization and quantity of the minimum knowledge required and escaping from the perception that higher education was just one form of professional training. The reform aimed to renovate the training process with broad disciplines and it divided learning at the higher education level into two stages—replacing year-based courses with modular credit-based training. It aimed to improve monitoring, assessment, and testing procedures; to delegate authority for entrance examinations to be organized by the higher education institutions; and to allow a candidate to sit for such exams in several institutions. The reform aimed to renovate management activities and to strengthen state management functions with laws and regulations, to decentralize and reduce professional activities undertaken by the Ministry, to increase autonomy for higher education institutions, and to give a green light to institutions to set and fulfill their own targets to meet socioeconomic development requirements. It required that higher education institutions expand their student intakes, carry out continuous monitoring during the learning process, and provide accurate evaluation of outputs. It encouraged and facilitated connections between research institutes and enterprises in training, research, and application activities. It aimed to renovate the higher education organization model and restructure the institutional network to overcome the "patchwork" or "piecemeal" problem, establishing new types of higher education institutions (for example, universities with various institutional members, open universities, community colleges, and semipublic, private, and people-founded universities).

Thanks to such sound directions, after 10 years of this reform, the education sector experienced positive development and gained considerable achievements.

In the 1993–94 school year, the size of the education and training system at all levels from preschool and general education to vocational education and higher education had expanded and surpassed the most successful year during the prereform period. For the primary level alone, the dropout rate decreased from 12.7 percent in 1989–90 to 6.58 percent[14] and the repetition rate fell from 10.6 percent in 1989–90 to 6.18 percent. In the mid-1990s, the numbers of primary, lower-secondary, and upper-secondary students totaled more than 10 million, 3.7 million, and 860,000, respectively. After five years, localities mobilized more than 1.7 million out-of-school children to attend schools, of which 200,000 children fulfilled primary education universalization requirements and hundreds of thousands of them returned to school. Additionally, more than 1.2 million adults were provided opportunities to attend literacy classes, of which nearly a half million could read at the equivalent level of grade three.[15] The school textbook production system was revised with (a) the introduction of competitive bidding for printing (book manufacture) to keep down the cost of textbooks; (b) the realignment of the central government's subsidy of textbooks from the Education Publishing House, the national textbook agency (the producer), to provincial education departments (the consumers); and (c) a pilot scheme of textbook lending was introduced in disadvantaged areas.

As for vocational education, the number of those following short training courses increased from 95,500 (1993) to 128,700 (1994). Vocational secondary programs were organized by 50 schools and many graduates found work in economic units.[16] The biggest challenge was the organization of the training process (shortage of teachers, teachers required to teach multiple subjects, and so on). Laboratory units were insufficient for various subjects, leading to the inadequate training quality. MES training was conducted in 15 training areas and disciplines, and sets of MES-based teaching and learning materials for five areas were developed and published for wide application. Several vocational schools with longer-term programs in the fields of construction and post and telecommunications also started to offer module-based training programs.

As for higher education, these institutions gradually stabilized and expanded their size, with their lecturers getting better income through their own professional activities. Within the higher education institution network, five major multidisciplined universities were established in Hanoi, Ho Chi Minh City, Thai-Nguyen, Hue, and Danang. Additional nonpublic universities were also established. International relations were expanded with opportunities for leaders, professors, and lecturers to have academic exchanges with their international colleagues.

Although serious challenges were addressed at the beginning of this reform period, some of the abovementioned solutions were difficult to implement, not fully effective, or faced distortions and required adjustments. At the end of 1996, Vietnamese leaders conducted a 10-year review of education reform that identified strategic orientations for the education development required for industrialization and modernization, and the tasks for the education sector in the last years of the twentieth century.[17] Several of the initial solutions adopted in the reform were adjusted, such as the discontinuation of selective classes in general schools and specialized schools at the lower-secondary level; abolishment of rigid and widespread regulations on the two stages and the transition exam between the two stages in higher education; improved preparation for school curriculum and textbook reforms, particularly the streamed upper-secondary curriculum; and discontinuation of vocational secondary education.

In the most recent 10 years, the size of the education system has continued to expand with an increase of the total number of students from 20 million (in 1996) to 23 million (in 2005). The universalization of primary education at the correct age and lower-secondary education universalization activities are positive achievements. In the 2004–05 school year, the participation rate of primary school-age children was 98 percent; the transition rate from primary (graduates) to lower-secondary (grade six) levels was 98.5 percent; the participation rate of lower-secondary school-age children was 84 percent; and the transition rate from lower-secondary (graduates) to upper-secondary (grade 10) levels was 77.1 percent. The school network has continued to expand and basically now meets children's learning needs at primary and lower-secondary schools. Growth in enrollments, however, has not been uniform at different levels of the education system; instead, it has followed the government's priorities and the demographic shift.[18]

The new school curriculum and textbooks were introduced in the 2002–03 school year and should become universal by the 2008–09 school year, thus laying the groundwork for improved education quality. And in the most recent five years, 5.3 million people were trained in vocational training institutions, of which two-thirds followed the longer courses. The average rate of enrollment growth was 14.7 percent per year in professional secondary education. As for higher education, the number of students increased from 760,000 to more than 1.3 million during the 1998–2004 period with an average increase of 6.4 percent per year. Nonformal education was strengthened with a network of continuing education centers covering all districts nationwide. Community learning centers were established in more than half of the nation's communes. Together with this significant growth of the system, important progress was made in the equity of education opportunities. The gaps in education access across ethnic groups were narrowed. The average increase rates in the number of ethnic minority children attending lower-secondary and upper-secondary schools were 7.3 percent per year and 26.1 percent per year, respectively (National Institute for Educational Strategy and Curriculum 2001–05, paragraph 30).

Parallel with these achievements, however, the Vietnamese education system still faces a number of weaknesses and mismatches such as low education quality and efficiency, especially in vocational and higher education. Several negative cases and slow progress are causing social concern. Therefore, education has become a hot topic of discussion in the media and at conferences, workshops, seminars, and the National Assembly's Congresses. Given today's significant developments in science and technology and socioeconomic fields, and considering globalization and the requirements for the development of a knowledge-based economy, both the Vietnamese leaders and people are not satisfied with the current situation and are calling for stronger reform in the education sector.

THE CURRENT EDUCATION SYSTEM: ISSUES, POLICIES, AND EXPERIENCE

SYSTEM STRUCTURE—SCHOOL NETWORK

The Vietnamese education system includes formal and continuing education. In terms of different subsectors and training qualifications the system includes the following:

- Early Childhood Care and Education (ECCE), comprising kindergartens and preschools.
- General education, comprising three levels: primary, lower secondary, and upper secondary.
- Vocational education of three stages: basic, intermediate, and college level.
- Higher education: college, undergraduate, master's degree, and doctoral levels.
- Continuing education.[19]

In terms of curricula and programs, some are structured on the basis of education levels and training qualifications as stated above, while other programs are not directly equivalent to an education level or training qualification (such as continuing education programs or professional training, in-service training, updating knowledge and skills, and so on). Education institutions include schools, colleges, universities, institutes, and education centers. Vietnam is making efforts to offer distance learning and education through the media.

As for the school and classroom network, the principle of schools that are "close to people" is followed, and education institutions are present in all residential areas nationwide. More specifically:

- Each commune, quarter, or town has at least one preschool unit, a primary school, a lower-secondary school, or a combined primary and lower-secondary school (this type of school only exists in socioeconomically disadvantaged areas); most communes have community learning centers.

- In addition, each district, town, or provincially managed city has one or more upper-secondary schools and a district-level continuing education center. Towns, urban districts, and many rural districts have comprehensive technical and career orientation centers. Each mountainous and island district has a lower-secondary boarding school for ethnic minority students and a general school with different levels.
- Furthermore, each province and centrally managed city has a specialized upper-secondary school for excellent (gifted) students, a normal or pedagogical training school or a junior college, and a provincial continuing education center. Mountainous provinces and those provinces with a large proportion of mountainous districts have an upper-secondary boarding school for ethnic minority students. Some provinces and centrally managed cities even have art and sports/physical education schools for students gifted in these areas, as well as schools for those with disabilities.
- Colleges and universities are concentrated in Hanoi, Ho Chi Minh City, and some other cities such as Haiphong, Thai-Nguyen, Hue, Danang, and Cantho.

IMPLEMENTATION OF CHILDREN'S RIGHTS

ECCE in Vietnam provides nurturing, caring, and learning services for children from three months to six years old. Crèches accept infants from three months to three years of age. Kindergartens accept children from three to five years of age. In the 2004–05 school year, 2,754,094 children were attending 47,906 ECCE units, of which 37,520 were crèches with 421,436 infants, and 10,386 were kindergartens with 2,332,658 children.

The Vietnamese government's policy toward children in ECCE institutions is to ensure all children's rights as stipulated by the Education Law and the Law on Child Protection and Care. More specifically:

- Children are provided with nurturing, care, and education for the comprehensive physical, emotional, intellectual, and aesthetic development that is appropriate to their age psychology.
- Children are provided with free primary health care, medical examination, and treatment in public medical units.
- Children are provided with a fee reduction for entertainment and play activities.

The establishment of kindergartens helps mothers by providing them with a place that can take care of their children while they are working or participating in social activities. This service contributes to the fulfillment of gender equity by providing mothers with wider opportunities.

According to the Education Law, ECCE units in Vietnam are established under the authority of the District People's Committee (for public units), communities (for people-founded units), or individuals (for private units).

- The establishment of public ECCE units is only allowed in socioeconomically disadvantaged or poor communes and ethnic minority areas.
- People-founded ECCE units are mainly located in rural areas. Residents in the community make their contributions to the creation of the unit, the purchase of equipment, and the operating costs; local authorities are responsible for providing resource-related assistance.
- The government encourages individuals to open private ECCE units. These units enjoy special treatment, such as being provided with space or rental land or physical facilities, and given tax or credit preferences.

Vietnam's ECCE objectives for the period up to 2010 are as follows:

- To improve the quality of care of children before they reach the age of six.
- To reduce the child malnutrition rate to less than 15 percent in ECCE units.[20]
- To expand the system of crèches and kindergartens in all types of residential areas, especially in rural and disadvantaged areas, to attract 18 percent and 67 percent of under three and three- to five-year-old children, respectively. As for five-year-old children alone, 95 percent[21] will be mobilized to prepare them for entering grade one of primary education.
- To strengthen the dissemination of knowledge and advisory activities for grandparents and parents in relation to children's development, nurturing, and education.

PRIMARY EDUCATION

Primary education in Vietnam consists of five grades, starting with six-year-old children. Therefore, children will, without repeating, complete primary schools by the age of 11. In the current primary school curriculum, children in grades one through three should study six subjects: the Vietnamese language, mathematics, natural and social sciences, moral education (civics), physical education, and arts. Although only Vietnamese language and mathematics have textbooks (for student's use), the remaining subjects have teacher's guides (for teacher's use). Children in grades four through five learn seven subjects: the Vietnamese language, mathematics, history and geography, sciences, moral education (civics), physical education, and arts. In these grades the four subjects of Vietnamese language, mathematics, history and geography, and sciences have student textbooks, whereas the remaining subjects only have teacher's guides. The earlier reforms in textbook printing and production[22] have maintained the low textbook costs and helped their affordability for most families.

In the 2004–05 school year, Vietnam had 14,518 primary schools and 1,034 combined primary and lower-secondary schools. The total number of primary students in the 2004–05 school year was 7,773,484. In recent years, the number of primary students has continued to decline.[23] Analysts believe that this phenomenon is due to the decreasing population growth rate, which has led to a declining number of the 6- to 11-year-old population, and the achievement of correct-age enrollment (previously, with pupil repetition and late entry or overage pupils, the number of students in primary schools was larger than the 6- to 11-year-old population). To fulfill the regulations stipulated in the Primary Education Universalization Law in 1991 (that is, every child must complete primary school by the age of 14 at the latest), for the past 10 years, September 5 has been chosen as the *"Day for bringing children to schools,"* with the aim of encouraging all families with six-year-old children to enroll their child in grade one. In 2000, the enrollment rate for 6 to 11 year olds was 95 percent; this figure was more than 98 percent in the 2004–05 school year.[24]

For the period up to 2010, the objectives for primary education are as follows: (a) to achieve the goal of universalization of primary education with students of the correct age (attracting 99 percent of the children to enroll in schools and reducing the repetition and dropout rates); (b) to improve the quality and efficiency of such schooling, moving toward full-day schooling; (c) to introduce foreign languages to students starting with grade three; (d) to encourage the use of information technology in teaching and learning; and (e) to reduce the student-to-teacher ratio and class size.

SECONDARY EDUCATION

Secondary education in Vietnam is divided into two levels: lower and upper secondary. Lower-secondary education consists of four grades (grades six to nine). Upper-secondary education includes three grades (grades 10 to 12). Because the lower-secondary level is universal, every primary student who completes primary school is allowed to enter grade six. At the upper-secondary level, all lower-secondary students have to be successful in a selection examination to continue on to upper-secondary school. The selection can be made in three ways—either through an exam, through consideration based on grade-nine learning achievements, or through a combination of both. The decision on which selection method should be used in a particular province or centrally managed city is made by the provincial or city People's Committee.

In the 2004–05 school year, Vietnam had 10,075 lower-secondary schools (of which 1,034 were combined lower-secondary and primary schools) with

6,670,714 students; 2,224 upper-secondary schools (of which 396 were combined lower- and upper-secondary schools) with 2,802,101 students. In provinces with a high proportion of ethnic minorities (that is, mountainous provinces and those with many mountainous districts), there are some lower- and upper-secondary boarding schools. The total number of boarding schools for ethnic minority children is 325, of which 11 are central-level schools with 4,400 students; 48 are provincial-level (upper-secondary) schools with about 20,000 students; and 266 are district-level (lower-secondary) schools with some 60,000 students.

Implementation of a streamed upper-secondary curriculum is one of the important parts of the education reform. During the 2006–07 school year, the upper-secondary curriculum will be divided into three streams: (a) basic, (b) natural sciences and mathematics, and (c) social sciences and foreign languages. All three streams include the following subjects: literature, history, geography, mathematics, physics, chemistry, biology, foreign languages, politics and citizenship, and physical education/sports. The requirements for the three key streams are knowledge and skill standards (that is, minimum and essential requirements) in all subjects in the curriculum. The natural sciences stream requires achieving an advanced level for four subjects: mathematics, physics, chemistry, and biology. The social sciences and foreign languages stream requires achieving an advanced level for four subjects: literature, history, geography, and foreign languages. For a school, the principal or school council can make a choice on how many streams and which stream(s) the school should offer after reporting and obtaining approval from the director of the Provincial Department of Education and Training. Schools operating the basic stream may also teach advanced subjects in the two other streams of natural sciences/mathematics and social sciences/foreign languages to widen the choice of subject options available to their students.

For the period up to 2010, the objectives for secondary education are as follows: (a) to achieve universal lower-secondary education; (b) to attract 99 percent of children between the ages of 11 and 15 and 50 percent of those between the ages of 15 and 18 to attend lower- and upper-secondary education, respectively; (c) to reduce the repetition and dropout rates; and (d) to ensure that all students are provided with the opportunity to continuously study a foreign language from grades 6 to 12.

VOCATIONAL EDUCATION

Vietnam's vocational education subsector aims to train workers and help them to find jobs or further their professional and technical skills and qualifications. According to the new Education Law, vocational training itself has three stages: basic, intermediate, and college. Training is delivered by specialized secondary, postsecondary, and college institutions through basic vocational courses of less than one year and by intermediate and college-level training courses of between one and three years, depending on the profession's characteristics and require-ments, and the student's qualifications.

Vocational institutions include professional secondary schools under the man-agement of the Ministry of Education and Training (MOET) and vocational training schools and centers under the management of the Ministry of Labor, War Invalids and Social Affairs (MOLISA). According to the Education Law, the voca-tional training system under the responsibility of MOLISA will provide training at all three stages—basic, intermediate, and college.

In the last five years (2001–05), the vocational education network (under MOLISA's management) has been rigorously strengthened and developed. At pres-ent, 1,688 vocational training institutions are distributed nationwide across all provinces. These include 236 vocational schools (doubled in comparison with the number in 1998), 404 vocational centers, and more than 1,000 vocational train-ing classes (National Institute for Educational Strategy and Curriculum 2001–05). In the vocational institution system, there are public, private, and foreign-funded schools as well as schools for the army to train demobilized soldiers. As for pro-fessional secondary schools (under MOET management), in the last five years, the number of these schools has increased despite the fact that some of the stronger schools were upgraded to become colleges. Specifically, there were 253 schools in the 2000–01 academic year and 285 schools in the 2004–05 academic year with 283,335 students. Of these, 238 were public schools and 47 were private estab-lishments. These were ministry and locally managed schools, with an average of three to five schools in each province (excluding three newly established provinces).[25]

Some shortcomings need to be addressed for the vocational training institution net-work. For example, although vocational schools and centers are distributed evenly across provinces, some lower-level localities still do not have a center. In 2004, only about 100 out of more than 600 districts had vocational centers (16.6 percent). Meanwhile, the objective for the period up to 2010 is that 100 percent of districts would have vocational training centers. With such a narrow vocational training institution network, it is difficult to meet the training demands in all localities, especially in rural areas. In addition, the demand for skilled human resources, especially for foreign-funded enterprises, is becoming increasingly pressing. Despite this pressing need, the training capacities of Vietnamese vocational train-ing institutions are still quite limited.

For the period up to 2010, the objectives for vocational education are as follows: (a) to establish a practical technical training system that meets the demands of socioeconomic development; (b) to pay attention to short-term vocational train-ing of skilled workers, technicians, and professional staff at the college level on the basis of upper-secondary or intermediate levels; and (c) to attract 30 percent of students who complete lower-secondary education and 10 percent of students who complete upper-secondary education to attend vocational schools at the intermediate and college levels, respectively.

HIGHER EDUCATION

Higher education in Vietnam includes four levels: college, undergraduate, master's, and doctorate. Access to higher education is achieved through institution-specific competitive entry examinations that candidates normally take after successful completion of their secondary education. The four levels of higher education are as follows:

- College-level training over two- to three-year courses is available for upper-secondary or professional and vocational secondary graduates; or over one- to two-year courses for graduates in the same training area or discipline.
- Undergraduate-level training over four- to six-year courses is available for upper-secondary or professional and vocational secondary graduates; or over two-and-a-half- to four-year courses for graduates from the same training area or discipline at the secondary level; or even one-and-a-half- to two-year courses for graduates in the same training area or discipline at the college level.
- Master's-level training courses of one to two years are available for university graduates.
- Doctorate-level training over four years is available for university graduates; and over two to three years for master's degree holders.

Higher education institutions in Vietnam include the following:

- Junior colleges.
- Colleges and universities, including those with different university institutional members and others with only faculties, academies.
- Universities and research institutes that may provide master's and doctoral training if they have a sufficient pool of professors and associate professors, physical facilities, equipment, and experience in the responsibilities of conducting state-level scientific research.

In the 2004–05 academic year, Vietnam had 230 colleges and universities with 1,319,754 students, and 122 postgraduate training units with 34,789 master's degree students and research students.[26] In 2005, the proportion of students per 10,000 population was 140.

In the last 20 years of reform, Vietnam's higher education has experienced significant development, expansion of enrollments, extension of training objectives, and diversification of ownership and resources for investment. As for the enrollment growth during the 2001–02 to 2004–05 academic years alone, the number of college students increased by 29.7 percent; university students increased by 37.1 percent; and master's and doctoral degree students increased by 62.4 percent. Managers, scientists, teachers, social workers, businesspersons, and civil servants—most of whom were trained in Vietnam with university and postgraduate degrees—have actively and efficiently made their contributions to the reform.

Despite these successes, Vietnam's higher education still faces mismatches in fulfilling the needs for industrialization, modernization, and international economic integration, and it does not yet satisfy people's demand for tertiary learning. Universities and research institutes have lacked connections to reality; training quality and efficiency have been poor; teaching and learning methods have been out of date; resources have been limited and resource utilization has been inefficient; and institutional autonomy and accountability have not been fully used. These shortcomings and mismatches require further strengthening of the higher education reforms. The government's introduction of Decree 10 (Decree 10/2002/ND-CP) provides service delivery units (schools, colleges, universities, hospitals, and so on) with greater autonomy in the management of their expenditures and the setting and collection of user fees. Given the strong incentives to generate revenues that arise from Decree 10, many training centers and universities are expected to introduce reforms and new training programs with linked charges.

CONTINUING EDUCATION

For a long time, Vietnam has been consistent in its determination to achieve the goals of literacy and development of adult education (initially with literacy classes, then through complementary education and currently with continuing education). As a result, tens of millions of people have escaped illiteracy. Millions of people, through complementary and in-service training classes, have expanded their knowledge and understanding.

At present, continuing education helps people to work and study at the same time, achieve lifelong learning, improve their personal characteristics, and expand their knowledge. Through continuing education, people should raise their knowledge levels and professionalism, improve their quality of life, gain better self-employment and job creation opportunities, and improve their contributions to society.

Continuing education includes the following:

• Literacy and postliteracy programs.
• Tailor-made programs to update knowledge and skills and technology transfer.

- Programs for in-service training, retraining, and upgrading professional qualifications.
- Education degree-granting programs in the national education system.

The organization of the continuing education network consists of provincial and district continuing education centers and community learning centers. In parallel, general education schools and vocational and higher education institutions are also involved in providing continuing education programs. In the 2004–05 academic year, there were 61 provincial continuing education centers, 517 district continuing education centers, 29 complementary schools, 478 informatics and foreign language training in cities, and 5,383 community learning centers (in communes in rural areas).

For the period up to 2010–15, the objectives for continuing education are as follows: (a) to improve literacy achievements and the literacy rate among the population age 15 to 35; (b) to expand learning opportunities for adults and workers, helping them access and benefit from training programs to improve their knowledge, working abilities, and quality of life; and (c) to establish continuing education units in all locations nationally.

CHALLENGES TO EDUCATION AND KEY SOLUTIONS

REFORM OF GENERAL EDUCATION CURRICULA

The renovation of the general education curricula in Vietnam officially began in 2000.[27] From then up until 2006, new curricula and textbooks were introduced and used for teaching and learning in all grades at primary and lower-secondary schools. Streamed upper-secondary curriculum and textbooks were introduced in the 2006–07 school year.

To produce the new curricula and textbooks, a collective of distinguished teachers and scientists conducted a tight research and development process with two to five years of pilot testing before expansion nationwide. The number of pilot schools was 450 primary schools, 159 lower-secondary schools, and 48 upper-secondary schools, which were spread across different locations in more than 10 provinces. As for textbooks, the draft manuscripts followed a two-stage appraisal process before they were printed for pilot trials and administrative use. The pilot trial was subject to further review and comments before books were issued for generalized classroom use.

Overall, this renovation of the general education curricula has met the objectives and requirements of education content and methodology at different levels as specified in the Education Law. The revised curricula has improved consistency in learning, and has facilitated continuation and development among levels; it has enhanced links across general, vocational, and higher education; and it has provided the basis for creating pathways in the national education system. The revised curricula have made for better harmonization between a subject's content and the teaching and learning methodology, and it has improved connections among the curriculum, textbooks, and teaching tools. It has strengthened practical components and lightened theoretical elements; and it has recognized social and humanity sciences, as well as science and technology achievements, that are appropriate to each student's cognitive abilities.

Although streamed upper-secondary curriculum is not a new concept, it has taken more than 10 years of pilot tests, debate, and modifications to reach a final decision. The main constraint has been hesitation between two choices: on the one hand, a single comprehensive curriculum, and on the other, a streamed curriculum that provides more options to students. Despite such encouraging progress, Vietnam's general education curricula have not yet fully escaped from the classical difficulties that maintain distinct separations between various subjects (literature, history, geography, mathematics, physics, chemistry, and so on). Consequently, the expected integration of different specializations has not yet been achieved.

The biggest challenge to curriculum renovation is that curriculum specialists and textbook writers want students to follow the same path that they experienced. Most curriculum specialists and textbook writers have been unable to go beyond their established perceptions or the approaches that traditionally divide subject specializations. Objectively speaking, the current school management capacities and teacher qualifications cannot yet meet the requirements of renovated curricula. Nevertheless, the learning content provided by schools cannot be allowed to fall behind the scientific and technology discoveries constantly and rapidly emerging in today's world. The question of "what should secondary schools teach students today?" is still a challenge to Vietnamese policy makers in the education sector. Moreover, this is not a question only for Vietnam.[28]

REFORM OF HIGHER EDUCATION

To enhance the national intellectual capacity, the competitiveness of human resources, and the country's economy, the government tasked the MOET to develop the World Bank–supported Higher Education Renovation Project for 2006–20. The overall objectives of the renovation of higher education over the next 15 years are to make fundamental changes in the quality and size of higher education; improve institutional and system competitiveness; and make higher education institutions responsive to, and operate efficiently within, the socialist-oriented market mechanism. On that basis, higher education should better fulfill its mission of training highly qualified human resources that meet Vietnam's socioeconomic development requirements and its people's learning needs.

To achieve the above objectives, universities, colleges, and the entire higher education subsector will need to address the following *specific objectives*:

- Complete the national network of higher education institutions with distinct organizational tiers (national, regional, provincial, and so on) that are in line with the country's socioeconomic development plan.
- Refine the division of training programs into two categories: research and career application. Shift to a system of credit-based courses. Finalize the higher education quality assurance and accreditation system; coordinate certifications with other countries in the region and elsewhere; and consequently establish several international-level universities.
- Expand enrollments to meet the target of 200 students per 10,000 population by 2010 and 450 students per 10,000 population by 2020, of which 70 to 80 percent of the students will follow career-application programs and 40 percent of students will attend nonpublic institutions.
- Ensure that by 2010 at least 40 percent and 25 percent of academic and lecture staff have master's and doctoral degrees, respectively; ensure that the student-to-lecturer ratio in higher education institutions will not exceed 20.
- Use modern management methods and technology, especially information technology and media in higher education institutions; establish a national database center for training and scientific research, and an "e-library" system.
- Significantly improve the scope and efficiency of science and technology-related activities within higher education institutions. Major universities will need to become strong national scientific research centers. Income from scientific research, technology transfer, production, and services taking place in institutions should account for about 15 percent of their total revenue.[29] More than 1 percent of the state budget will be allocated for universities to conduct scientific research tasks.
- Ensure greater institutional autonomy and accountability, the latter by making sure that the state management and the society's monitoring and evaluation roles oversee the activities of higher education institutions.[30]

Higher education renovation will be implemented in three phases:

- In the period 2006–10, a detailed higher education renovation program should be finalized. Emphasis will be placed on several of the abovementioned approaches, such as renewal of training content and methods, and renovation of management and resource mobilization mechanisms to bring about quality improvements.

- During 2011–15, the renovation should concentrate on strengthening achievements gained during the first phase. Timely implementation of solutions should focus on improved efficiency of human resource utilization, and provision of sufficient—in both quantity and quality terms—lecturing staff and higher education managers. The renovation should strive for significant improvements in quality to come closer to regional and international standards.
- In the 2016–20 period, the renovation should ensure the establishment of a modern higher education system with an appropriate qualification structure and network. This system will be equal to that of other countries in the region and basically meet the demands for highly qualified human resources for industrialization and modernization.

UNIVERSALIZATION OF EDUCATION

The implementation of universal education in Vietnam has the following notable features:

Encouragement without Sanctions. Although primary education is compulsory as stipulated in the Universal Primary Education Law of 1991, and in the Education Laws of 1998 and 2005, no sanctions apply to parents who do not follow these laws. The difference between compulsory and noncompulsory levels is that students in public schools at a compulsory level do not pay any tuition fees.

Enrollment at the Correct Age. Correct-age enrollment can be fulfilled on a phased basis. For primary education, the universalization process is divided into two phases:

- Before 2000, the objective was that most 14-year-old children would complete primary school.
- From 2000 onward, the objective is that most 14-year-old children will complete primary schools at the right age, that is, *correct-age universalization.*

After universal primary education, universal lower-secondary education has been implemented without following the model of cumulatively increasing the number (that is, five then six and seven) of compulsory years like other countries.

Evaluation and Recognition of Achievements. Such recognition should be made by each administrative unit. Specifically, the National Assembly established the certification criteria for universal education at commune, district, and provincial levels. As regulated by the government, the MOET and local authorities will undertake evaluation and certification at different levels.

Criteria for the certification of universal lower-secondary education are set by the National Assembly (Resolution No. 41/2000/QH10) for each administrative unit as follows:

Communes, quarters, and district towns should—

- Maintain, strengthen, and consolidate the achievements of universal primary education.
- Ensure that the annual transfer rate of primary school graduates to lower-secondary schools is 95 percent (80 percent or more in socioeconomically disadvantaged communes).
- Improve education quality at the lower-secondary level by reducing the repetition and dropout rates and making sure that the annual lower-secondary completion rate is 90 percent or more (75 percent or more in socioeconomically disadvantaged communes).
- Ensure that the proportion of young people in the 15- to 18-year-old age group with lower-secondary education is 80 percent or more (70 percent or more in socioeconomically disadvantaged communes).

Districts, provincial towns, and provincially managed cities should—

- Achieve universal lower-secondary education objectives in 90 percent of their communes, quarters, and district-towns.

Provinces and centrally managed cities should—

- Achieve universal lower-secondary education objectives in 100 percent of their districts, provincial towns, and provincially managed cities.

The responsibilities for checking and certifying universal lower-secondary education results for each administrative unit are regulated by the government (Decree No. 88/2001/ND-CP) as follows:

- The Central Steering Committee, chaired by the MOET with participation from relevant ministries and agencies, is responsible for providing evaluation and certification for provinces.
- The people's committees of provinces and centrally managed cities establish provincial-level steering committees to provide evaluation and certification for districts, provincial towns, and provincially managed cities.
- The people's committees of districts, provincial towns, and provincially managed cities establish district-level steering committees to provide evaluation and certification for communes, quarters, and district towns.

By 2010, Vietnam's target for universal lower-secondary education and correct-age primary education is for all provinces to meet the national universalization standards. By March 2006, 35 provinces and centrally managed cities were certified by the MOET as meeting the national standards on universal correct-age primary education and 32 met the national standard on lower-secondary education. Among these provinces and centrally managed cities, some were certified as achieving universal lower-secondary education but not universal correct-age primary education, and others were certified as having achieved the opposite.

The lessons drawn from the successes and shortcomings faced during the drive for universal literacy and primary education are being applied to universal lower-secondary education activities. They include the following:

To achieve lasting success, the *development of a minimum knowledge foundation for the entire population* must be carried out in three ways simultaneously: (a) to facilitate universal education for children, adult illiteracy must be eliminated; (b) universal education for children must be achieved to prevent new illiterate people; and (c) nonformal education models should be used to maintain and promote literacy and universal education achievements, and to prevent people falling back into illiteracy. Among these three aspects, the establishment, maintenance, and development of the school network according to the "school-close-to-local-people" principle is a decisive factor.

Government officials and policy makers should closely link the development of the basic or minimum knowledge foundations of the entire population with key national tasks. This link should be part of the goal of nation building, socioeconomic development and growth, and the preservation of national independence. With the national spirit and citizen awareness, all stakeholders from teaching staff, to learners, to sponsors can recognize the social importance of their activities.

Socialization is the most important lesson drawn from the first literacy campaign (1945–46), and has been continually strengthened during the education development process. The success of the literacy and the universal primary education campaigns in Vietnam is due to the combination of efforts made by tens of millions of people, including teachers, learners, and organizers. In addition, this success is also the result of active participation by mass organizations and support and assistance from other sectors.

The establishment of an enabling cultural environment that promotes and maintains all of the achievements gained to date is an integral part of the development of a minimum knowledge foundation for the entire population. In addition to dissemination, culture agencies, publishing houses, media, television, and radio all play important roles in the introduction of appropriate materials, further contributing to improving people's knowledge and skills. Moreover, such dissemination helps people access knowledge treasured in a developing society and continually use this media for their lifelong learning process, thereby helping them apply what they have learned in real life.

EFA GOALS: BUILDING A LEARNING SOCIETY

In response to the Dakar commitment, the government of Vietnam provided guidance for drafting the Learning Society Building Project for the 2005–10 period, and on May 18, 2005, the prime minister approved this project.

The overall objectives as stated in the project document are to enable people of different ages and education levels to conduct regular and lifelong learning, and to promote the development of (and links between) both formal and continuing education, in which continuing education is the precondition for building a learning society.

The specific objectives up to 2010 are as follows:

- Enhance literacy achievements; increase the proportion of literate people in the age 15- to 35-year-old age group from 94 percent to 99 percent with an emphasis on ethnic minority areas and remove differences and create gender equity in all literacy activities.
- Ensure that 80 percent of officials at commune, quarter, and district levels have opportunities for learning and updating their knowledge and skills on management, law, economy, and social affairs; 100 percent of civil servants in state agencies are provided with professional training and upgrading in terms of management, politics, informatics, and foreign languages; and 85 percent of workers in the fields of agriculture, forestry, and fishery can access and benefit from programs to improve their knowledge and working abilities, and their resulting quality of life.
- Ensure that 100 percent of provinces and centrally managed cities and 100 percent of districts and provincial towns have continuing education centers; and 80 percent of commune and quarters nationwide are able to establish community learning centers.

To achieve the abovementioned objectives, the intermediate tasks for Vietnam's education sector are as follows:

- Strengthen and *develop continuing education* as part of the national education system; refine continuing education and community learning center networks; make the activities of continuing education and community learning centers relevant in content, lively in format, and appropriate to learners' needs, and ensure that they provide learners with the knowledge and problem-solving skills needed for their daily lives.
- *Finalize degree-granting programs of continuing education*; develop education programs that meet the learning demands of the entire population.
- Develop and *improve the quality of teaching staff and managers of continuing education*; implement measures to attract teachers, scientists, and social workers to

participate in teaching at continuing education and community learning centers. Education management bodies should actively cooperate with local Learning Promotion Associations to conduct training and provide mentoring for key staff members who are responsible for the development and operation of community learning centers.

• *Renovate the continuing education management mechanism*; strengthen the links and coordination among various sectors; implement socialization activities so that continuing education makes considerable contributions to building learning societies.

SOCIAL EQUITY IN EDUCATION AND EQUITY IN OPPORTUNITIES FOR ACCESS TO EDUCATION

Social equity in education and equity in opportunities for access to education are major challenges for poor countries such as Vietnam. Since the day of independence, the government of Vietnam and its people have been working to overcome this challenge. Within the context of a socialist-oriented market economy, implementation of social equity in education and equity in education access is the underlying principle of the Vietnamese national education system.

According to Vietnam's Education Law, every citizen has equal learning opportunities, regardless of ethnicity, religion, gender, family background, social status, and economic conditions. To achieve social equity in education, the government of Vietnam creates learning conditions for everyone—with priorities given to ethnic minorities, children from socioeconomically disadvantaged families, and people with disabilities—to implement their learning rights and obligations. The affordability of primary textbooks, in part because of low manufacturing costs obtained through competitive bidding, ensures that well over 80 percent of all parents can afford to purchase textbooks for their children—average private costs for textbooks per primary pupil are 38,600 Vietnamese dong per year.

For ethnic minorities, children from socioeconomically disadvantaged and poor families, and people with disabilities, the government has policies for social subsidies, scholarships, and fee exemptions or reductions. For primary and lower-secondary students in disadvantaged communes, the government has schemes for the provision and distribution of free textbooks and learning materials.[31] An important step to achieve social equity in education is that, in the near future, the government will provide financial support so that private schools will be able to apply the fee exemption and reduction policy to these children.[32]

To develop the human resources of the ethnic minorities, the government established 4 pre-university institutions, 11 central-level boarding schools,

48 provincial-level boarding schools, 266 district-level boarding schools, and 680 semiboarding schools. These institutions provide learning places for nearly 300,000 ethnic minority students. Students in these schools receive scholarships, free textbooks, and learning materials. At the same time, the government uses a "nomination" model to select ethnic minority students (most are upper-secondary boarding school graduates) for training in universities without having to sit for the entrance exam. Other children from ethnic minority groups, socioeconomically disadvantaged families, and rural areas benefit from slightly lower entrance requirements (less than three marks, two marks, and one mark, respectively) than other students in the university selection process.

Two important indicators that illustrate the equity in learning opportunities are the proportions of females and ethnic minority students in the total student population. Past efforts to achieve gender equity are clearly reflected in the current teaching force. The proportions of female teachers and lecturers in education are high: nearly 100 percent of teachers at ECCEs are women, 78 percent of primary school teachers are women, and 70 percent of teachers in lower-secondary schools are women, as are 55 percent of teachers in upper-secondary schools, and 40 percent of teachers in professional secondary schools. In colleges, 47 percent of the teaching staff are women, and 36 percent of university lecturers are women (National Institute for Educational Strategy and Curriculum 2001–05). This high proportion of women teachers has been built on gender equity in enrollments in the student population. In the 2004–05 school year, the proportion of female students was 47 percent, 47 percent, and 49 percent in primary, lower-secondary, and upper-secondary schools, respectively. This figure was even higher in professional secondary schools, that is, 58 percent. In university entrance exams, the newly enrolled female students accounted for 48 percent.

The gaps in access to education among different ethnic groups have been narrowed. In the last five years (2001–05), the number of ethnic minority students has experienced significant increases, for example, by 7.3 percent per year and 26.1 percent per year at lower- and upper-secondary schools, respectively. In 2004–05, the percentages of ethnic minority students out of total enrollments were 15.7 percent, 18.5 percent, 13.7 percent, and 9.4 percent in general, primary, lower-secondary, and upper-secondary schools, respectively. In university entrance exams, however, the newly enrolled ethnic minority students accounted for less than 4 percent of entering students. Therefore, although ethnic minorities make up some 10 percent of the total population, the proportions of ethnic minority students (9.4 percent) in upper-secondary schools and newly enrolled ethnic minority students (4 percent) in higher education institutions are relatively low and need improvement. The government has asked the MOET to investigate and draft a decree that revises the nomination model to better facilitate ethnic minorities' access to higher education programs.

The government has paid special attention to education for children with disabilities. Currently, Vietnam has approximately 1 million children with disabilities, and many of the children are victims of Agent Orange used by the American army during wartime. Because of many difficulties in the provision of care and education for these children with disabilities, the enrollment rate is only 24.2 percent for these children, of whom 3 percent attend special schools and 97 percent attend inclusive classes in regular schools. Regarding training teachers for children with disabilities, four universities and three colleges have established faculties or sections to address special education. But challenges, in relation to the provision of care and education for children with disabilities, persist because of misconceptions, lack of physical facilities, and shortage of specialized teachers.

PRESERVATION OF ETHNIC MINORITY LANGUAGES

In the community of 54 ethnic groups in Vietnam, each group has its own spoken language. Except for the ethnic Vietnamese (the Kinh), however, only about 10 of the more than 50 ethnic minority groups (for example, Chinese, Cham, Khmer, Thai, Tay, Hmong, Nung, Ede, Giarai, Bana, Xedang, K'Ho, and so on) have written scripts. The government's language policy is to enable ethnic minorities to learn their spoken languages and scripts with a view toward maintaining and promoting national cultural diversity.

For those ethnic minorities with written scripts, their languages are, in parallel with the Vietnamese language, taught as a separate subject and used in literacy and complementary classes. Teaching ethnic minority languages in primary schools is carried out according to the following principles:

- For those languages with the script in Latin characters, the teaching of such languages starts from grade three to avoid the burden of learning two systems of Latin characters (that is, Vietnamese and mother-tongue languages) at the same time
- For those languages with the script in traditional (non-Latin) characters, the teaching of such languages starts from grade one

Regardless of starting from grade one or three, all schools are required to ensure that their students will be good at reading and writing their mother tongues.[33] Generally speaking, ethnic minority languages are taught in ECCE units, helping children use their mother tongues and understand Vietnamese before entering grade one. To help ethnic minority children easily acquire knowledge, the government plans, in parallel with teaching the mother tongue, to encourage parents to send their five-year-old children to schools and learn Vietnamese before entering grade one at the age of six.

For foreign languages, in most Vietnamese lower- and upper-secondary schools, students can learn one of four foreign languages (English, Russian, Chinese, and French) as a compulsory subject. In several large cities, the foreign language is considered an optional subject in some primary schools. In some specialized schools, the foreign language is considered a specialized subject for training gifted students. And for French alone, a handful of localities have implemented a project that uses French as the primary language of instruction. Because of a shortage of experienced foreign language teachers, the organization of foreign language instruction in Vietnam faces difficulties such as limited instruction time and low quality. Despite being compulsory, foreign language has only recently been made an examination subject for graduation at upper-secondary schools. Initially students could choose between foreign language and another subject in the examinations, but foreign language later became a compulsory subject. In the 2001–02 school year, the number of examination candidates taking foreign language tests accounted for more than 90 percent.

To meet the needs of socioeconomic, scientific, and technological development, as well as international economic integration, the government of Vietnam has asked the MOET to prepare for a project on the improvement of foreign language teaching. Under the proposed project, instruction time will be increased starting from grade six (grade three in advantaged locations). Together with strengthened foreign language teaching, in several training disciplines under some international projects, the use of English or French as the language of instruction has been followed in some universities. In the near future, foreign languages (primarily English) as the medium of instruction will be encouraged in various universities.

DEVELOPMENT OF TEACHING STAFF AND EDUCATION MANAGERS

To produce sufficient teachers for the growth of the education system, Vietnam has made many efforts to develop its teacher training system, and it has operated intensive teacher training courses (9+3, 12+1, and so on, where 9 or 12 is the number of years of general schooling and 3 or 1 relates to the teacher training professional courses). As of the 2004–05 school year, Vietnam had 986,604 teaching staff, representing an increase of 213,644 compared to the 1998–99 school year. Among the total number of teaching staff in the 2004–05 school year, there were more than 7,000 vocational trainers,[34] 155,699 preschool teachers, 360,624 primary teachers, 295,056 lower-secondary teachers, 106,586 upper-secondary teachers, 13,937 professional secondary trainers, 13,677 college lecturers, and 33,969 university lecturers. Notably, the number of teachers continues to rise at the primary level even though the number of primary students is declining because of demographic changes. In the future, this will also occur at the lower-secondary level. These changing demographics provide an opportunity to reduce the student-to-teacher ratio, which is an important factor for quality improvement. It also presents a challenge for education management, however, because some staff may need to be redeployed.

In terms of qualifications of teaching and lecturing staff, the Education Law states that preschool and primary teachers must possess an upper-secondary pedagogical diploma; lower-secondary teachers must possess college diplomas; upper-secondary and professional secondary teachers must possess a pedagogical university degree (or university degree plus a certificate of pedagogy training); college and university lecturers must possess a university degree or higher and a certificate of pedagogy training; a master's degree or higher for teaching specialized subjects or supervising a master's thesis; and a doctoral degree for teaching specialized subjects or supervising a doctoral thesis. Because of the proportion of unqualified teachers, however, the upgrading of staff (through in-service training courses) remains a critical requirement of the education sector. In the 2004–05 school year, the percentage of qualified teachers was as follows: 75.8 percent in the ECCE subsector; 82 percent at the primary level, of which about 10 percent were holding higher (college or university) qualifications;[35] 93 percent at the lower-secondary level, of which about 20 percent were holding higher (undergraduate or postgraduate) qualifications; 97 percent at the upper-secondary level, of which about 3 percent were holding higher (postgraduate) qualifications; and 68.7 percent and 75.3 percent in vocational and professional secondary schools, respectively.

To improve education quality, Vietnamese education policy makers and managers feel that the *human factor*—teaching staff and education managers—plays a decisive role. Therefore, Vietnam is trying to overcome weaknesses in pre-service and in-service training, deployment, organization, and utilization of teachers. The aim is to develop a sufficient pool of teaching staff that is organized in an appropriate structure and that meets the moral and professional requirements of the education renovation. At the same time, it is important to support education managers with increased professionalism and standardized management capacities and qualifications. Within the current context, Vietnam pays special attention to the enhanced professional ethics and knowledge of its teachers and education managers. To protect the reputation of schools and education bodies, the government addresses all cases of dishonesty and mistreatment of students. In addition, teaching staff and education managers are increasingly faced with a requirement for computer skills and improved foreign language skills, primarily in English.

Regarding teacher incentives and policies, the Education Law states that, in addition to salary, teachers shall receive allowances and other preferential rewards while working in areas with extreme socioeconomic difficulties, specialized schools, schools for gifted students, boarding schools for ethnic minorities, and schools for people with disabilities. Teachers nominated to attend professional and pedagogical enhancement programs will receive full salary and subsidies. Trainees at teacher-training institutions are exempted from tuition fees and given scholarship priorities. If system expansion occurs through nonpublic institutions, the trend will be toward achieving equity in teacher rewards and responsibilities with no distinction between teachers working in public and nonpublic schools, and those who are permanent and contracted.

In training the human resources needed for the education system, Vietnam's pedagogical institutions have focused only on training teachers and have paid little attention to other skills (such as curriculum developers, education planners, and so on). The college for training education managers mainly focuses on in-service training and does not have a scientific pre-service manager-training program. Therefore, the development of a system that is similar to that of other countries remains a challenge to be addressed.

In the short term, to improve education quality, the MOET requires teacher-training institutions and the education manager-training college to strongly renew teaching and learning methodologies. Such institutions should actively apply information technology to teaching, learning, and management and use this technology to achieve breakthroughs in the renewal of these areas.

MOBILIZATION OF ALL RESOURCES FOR EDUCATION DEVELOPMENT

The biggest challenge faced by the Vietnamese education system during the entire development process is the *contradiction between goals (system expansion and continual quality improvement) and limited resources*. During the long prereform period, the education system relied on the state budget for its resources. In making the transition from the centrally planned command economy to the socialist-oriented market economy, the government wished to mobilize all possible resources in the society for education development. Past evidence proves the efficiency of this policy. According to the Education Law, financial sources of investment for education include the following:

- The State budget;
- Charges and Fees: tuition fees; admission fees; income from consulting work, technology transfer, production, and business and service activities of educational institutions; investments from domestic and international institutions; educational development registration fees; and other funding from domestic and international organizations and individuals as regulated by law.

In recent years, Vietnam has achieved a high and stable growth rate of gross domestic product (GDP). In the period from 2000–03, the annual rate of growth of GDP was 7 percent. In real terms, public expenditure has almost doubled over the 10 years from 1994 to 2003. Thus, budget resources have grown considerably. Together with people's contributions, especially from wealthy families and those in economically developed areas, the government has continually increased the budget share for education over the recent reform years. The share of GDP spent on education has increased from 3.5 percent in 1994 to 4.3 percent in 2004. Compared with other sectors, education has been given priority—for example, education spending as a proportion of total public expenditure increased from 14 percent in 1994 to 17 percent in 2004. Vietnam's objective is to continue to increase education spending as a proportion of total public expenditure to 20 percent, thus contributing toward improved education quality and efficiency, and the achievement of national goals.[36]

With the education sector's increased share in the growing budget, the public expenditure structure for different levels and subsectors has changed with an increased percentage for general education and ECCE (called the education or schooling subsector), and a decreased percentage for vocational and higher education (called the training subsector). This demonstrates the government's policy of giving priority to basic education and education in socioeconomic disadvantaged and ethnic minority areas. Specifically, in 1998, the public expenditure spending shares were 73.3 percent for schooling and 26.7 percent for training, respectively. By 2002, the figures had moved to 77.7 percent for schooling and 22.3 percent for training. During this period, the share of public spending for higher education declined from 12.4 to 9.7 percent, because at the higher education level, cost-sharing was obtained from student and family contributions.

The ratio of recurrent and capital expenditure components of public expenditure in education and training did not significantly change during 1999–2002, with 73 percent allocated for recurrent expenditures and 27 percent for capital spending. In terms of absolute figures, capital expenditures doubled from 2,418 thousand billion dong in 1999 to 4,375 thousand billion dong in 2002. The current challenge is that spending on the schooling subsector for the purchase of fixed assets and small repairs (including pedagogical and teaching equipment) is a low 10 percent, while overall spending on salaries remains high. In 2002, spending on salaries and allowances in the schooling subsector accounted for 71.3 percent of total expenditures, whereas spending on salaries and allowances in the training subsector (vocational and higher education) was only 27.4 percent. Since 1999, the spending on teacher salaries per student has increased at all education levels (in line with general civil service pay increases),[37] but primary-level salary spending per student has experienced the sharpest increase, doubling in the last four years (from 263,023 dong per student in 1999 to 516,023 dong per student in 2002). This increase reflects the priorities and incentives given to teachers (a decisive factor in the education quality improvement process), the decline in the primary-school-age population, and the resulting fall in the pupil-to-teacher ratio.

In response to the national policy of socialization in the education sector (cost-sharing and financial participation from users and their families), nonpublic education has been considerably expanded since 1994. This expansion has been strongest at ECCE and upper-secondary levels. The number of nonpublic preschools increased from 30 percent in 1994 to 58 percent in 2004. Similarly, the number of nonpublic upper-secondary schools increased from 20 percent in 1994 to 32 percent in 2004.

Two types of parent contributions are made: compulsory and voluntary. According to government regulations, parent's compulsory contributions include fees for tuition, examinations, and construction. These contributions are considered state budget revenues that are collected and retained by the school to finance education activities. In line with their better incomes, parent's average spending on their children's learning went up to 627,000 dong per student in 2002 (a 14.6 percent increase in comparison with the 1997–98 period). Although parents increased their spending on primary pupils, the state budget spending increased even faster. Thus, as parents spent more on their children's education, between 1993 and 2002, the parents' share of total spending on primary students declined from 55 to 27 percent because the state budget spending on education increased substantially. The share of the state budget in total spending on pupils at the lower levels of education is greater than that at the upper levels of education. For example, in 2002 the state budget's share in spending for primary, lower-secondary, and upper-secondary education levels was 73 percent, 59 percent, and 52 percent, respectively. These figures once again demonstrate the government's efforts to give priority to the schooling subsector and to foster equity in education. They also demonstrate the commitment of families to education and the important levels of cost-sharing and cost-recovery that underpin the government's socialization policy in the education sector.

In the coming years, education socialization and mobilization of people's contributions, especially from wealthy families and those in advantaged areas, will continue. In 2002, with a view toward more efficient and effective use of public expenditures and increased contributions from society, the government introduced Decree 10/2002/ND-CP. This decree gave revenue-producing service delivery units (such as schools, colleges, universities, hospitals, and so on) greater autonomy in the management of their expenditures and the collection of user fees. This increased financial autonomy provides strong incentives to training centers and universities to generate revenues with new programs and linked charges and thus offers valuable opportunities for service improvement.

Another objective posed for the education sector is to continue increasing the state's budget for education toward its target of 20 percent of public expenditure. Based on that assumption, the structure of state budget spending will be adjusted with greater focus and priority being given to the development of education in disadvantaged, ethnic minority areas. These adjustments will provide support for poor families and those who benefit from special policies, regardless of whether they live in urban or rural areas or study in public or private schools. In parallel with the refinement of support policies for students from poor families and those with special benefits, the government's Comprehensive Poverty Reduction and Growth Strategy and sector strategies have set targets for the abolition of fees and charges in primary and lower-secondary education. Vietnamese education policy makers and managers believe that only if the abovementioned solutions are systematically addressed, can the societal gaps and differences in access and benefits among various areas be narrowed quickly.

COOPERATION AND INTERNATIONAL INTEGRATION IN EDUCATION

In response to the government's policies on open international relations, over the last five years the MOET has diversified patterns of international cooperation and established international relationships with an increasing number of partners. Presently, the MOET has formed partnerships with nearly 60 countries and with 36 international, intergovernmental, and nongovernmental organizations. It has signed 14 official documents to strengthen and expand its relationships with 12 countries.

Through international activities, Vietnam's achievements and experience in the education sector have been shared with its international partners. Thanks to these activities, the number of overseas students who have studied and conducted research in Vietnam (under bilateral cooperation agreements and at their own cost) has significantly increased. Moreover, the number of scholarships provided for Vietnam has also increased, providing opportunities for 4,000 Vietnamese students to study overseas in the last five years. To encourage and facilitate overseas studies by Vietnamese students, the Vietnamese government spends about 100 billion dong per year to send 350 to 400 students overseas. These students study advanced skill areas that Vietnam needs but is not yet capable of training. The government also provides subsistence allowance support to Vietnamese students to study in 13 countries, as well as other support to motivate student's studies.

In parallel with student exchanges, Vietnam has actively exploited various sources of aid to supplement its education budget. The total funding of aid and loan projects signed in the last five years is US$217.8 million, in which the share of grants is significantly increasing. Part of this funding has been disbursed, and the remaining amount will be spent over the next five years.[38] In general, these projects have contributed to improved education quality and efficiency, enhanced education access to disadvantaged children, strengthened capacities of teaching staff and education managers, and improved the quality of physical facilities and equipment for education institutions, especially those in disadvantaged areas.

A number of Vietnamese universities have taken advantage of international funding sources to establish high-tech science centers to improve the quality of training and research. Those centers emphasize science and technology in such priority areas as biotechnology, new material sciences, information technology, and automation. Despite different sizes, these centers have been provided with modern and up-to-date equipment.

Vietnam's active participation in the activities led by regional and international organizations—for example, the United Nations Educational, Scientific, and Cultural Organization; United Nations Children's Fund; United Nations Development Programme; Agence Intergouvernementale de la Francophonie, Agence Universitaire de la Francophonie, Association of Southeast Asian Nations +1,2,3; Gang and Mekong Rivers Cooperation; and Southeast Asian Ministers of Education Organisation—is part of a major effort to achieve regional and international integration in the education sector. Annually, hundreds of lecturers, researchers, and education managers participate in conferences and seminars. Additionally, long- and short-term training courses are organized by various countries and international organizations to exchange and share experience and expertise with foreign colleagues.

In response to the Vietnamese government's policies, a relatively large number of foreign partners have come to Vietnam and established 100 percent foreign-funded education institutions or have cooperated with Vietnamese counterpart institutions to provide undergraduate training, vocational training, distance education, and short-term training courses. With their high-quality infrastructure, advanced training programs, and selected teaching staff, foreign education institutions in Vietnam have contributed to the training of high-quality human resources who are highly sought after in the labor market.

Through joint training programs, Vietnamese education institutions are able to access training methodologies initiated by developed countries that can be used to renew content, programs, and instructional methods. This is helping Vietnamese education institutions develop and implement their own programs to meet international standards. By adopting the model of joint training programs or 100 percent foreign-funded education institutions, Vietnamese students now have more opportunities to "study overseas in Vietnam" and choose the most appropriate type of studies. Through this approach, the education sector can mobilize parent and other resources and reduce the high costs of sending students overseas.

The management, oversight, and evaluation of the operations of foreign-related education institutions present challenges when the government's regulations are not strictly followed. The breaches made by some of these institutions include operating without following registered activities, condensing the training curriculum and programs, and failing to meet the required quality standards and conditions. Some foreign-funded education institutions have not been certified as meeting the quality standards required by their own countries. In addition, because of the absence of a legal framework that defines profit or nonprofit institutions, the majority of foreign investors have labeled themselves as nonprofit organizations to avoid paying taxes or duties. To address this issue, Vietnam needs to refine its legislation and, at the same time, accredit foreign-funded education institutions operating in Vietnam, thus protecting student rights and interests and avoiding the import of foreign-made—but low-quality—programs.

EDUCATION MANAGEMENT: DECENTRALIZATION, INCREASED AUTONOMY, AND ACCOUNTABILITY[39]

In Vietnam, the concept of management includes two components: state management and professional management. State management at a macro level includes developing and guiding the implementation of strategies, plans, and education policies; issuing and overseeing the implementation of education-related legal documents; and inspection and evaluation of the application of education-related laws, decrees, and regulations. According to the Government Organization Law, the Education Law, and the government's assignment, the MOET is responsible for providing the state management of ECCE, general education, higher education, and a portion of vocational education (professional secondary education). The MOLISA manages vocational education (excluding professional secondary education). According to the People's Council and the Committee Law, the Education Law, and the assignment made by the government, people's committees at different education levels provide state management, confirm the quality of the teaching staff, ensure appropriate financing, and verify the condition of the physical facilities and the teaching and learning equipment in public schools. People's committees should meet the requirements of education quality and efficiency improvement in their own localities, and at the same time, control the fulfillment of regulations by nonpublic schools.

The education management responsibilities of provincial and district people's committees are divided as follows. Provincial people's committees provide management of upper-secondary schools, professional secondary and vocational schools, and provincial-level colleges and continuing education centers. District people's committees provide management of primary and lower-secondary schools, district comprehensive career orientation and technical centers, district continuing education centers, and district vocational training centers. The provincial department of education and training is the technical body that provides education sector management support to the provincial people's committees. The district bureau of education and training is the technical body that provides education sector management support to the district people's committees.

Education management activities have contributed to the achievement of success in the sector; however, because of their shortcomings, these activities have also been an important source of constraints and weaknesses. Therefore, Vietnamese education policy makers and managers are emphasizing a renewal of education management activities in the hopes of bringing about fundamental changes in education development.

The intermediate task for the renewal of education management is to direct education institutions by following the public administration approach, and to ensure the effectiveness and efficiency of the socialist-based regulations in the education sector. Following the National Assembly's approval of the Education Law, the MOET and MOLISA are actively preparing to submit, during this and the next term of the National Assembly, a Vocational Education Law, a Teachers' Law, a Higher Education Law, and a Continuing Education Law to complete the legal framework for education and training activities.

In the short-term, the MOET and MOLISA will finalize the education management mechanism with clear and strong decentralization of functions, responsibilities, and rights across ministries, subsectors, and localities. The increased institutional autonomy and accountability will be coordinated with strengthened oversight and inspection. Democracy will be enhanced in the development, implementation, and monitoring of the implementation of education-related policies, guidelines, and incentives; and transparency and equity in the mobilization and use of resources for education will be ensured through publicity.

A key task is to address the perception that quality management is part of education management. Vietnam's education management bodies are investigating and learning from the experience of developed countries to renovate education management activities and to understand modern quality management methods that are appropriate to Vietnam's level of economic development and its cultural and social characteristics. According to authorized officials, the decisive action will be to establish and finalize a *national education standards system*, which will form the basis for monitoring, overseeing, and conducting assessments and quality assurance of all chains in the education process across all various learning models.

As school teaching and the learning experience are key factors for quality, the school is the true reflection of education management effectiveness and efficiency. Vietnamese education officials believe that education management bodies are, on the basis of increased school autonomy and accountability, responsible for making education management activities realistic and for listening to the voices of teachers, parents, and society to make accurate, suitable, and feasible decisions. One of the current requirements is to quickly modernize and computerize management activities so that a reliable two-way information exchange channel will be established between education management bodies and schools, families, and society, as well as among schools, teachers, parents, and students.

CONCLUSION

LESSONS LEARNED: PROSPECTS FOR VIETNAMESE EDUCATION

The first lesson learned from the actual development of Vietnamese education, especially over the last 20 years of reforms, is that the government should always be determined and consistent in its actions and perceptions, and that it should constantly *regard education and training—together with science and technology—as one of the country's top national priorities.* This position should be demonstrated publicly through a series of important decisions ranging from the establishment of the necessary legal environment (education sector laws, decrees, and regulations) to the strengthening of the operational conditions required by the education system (policies relating to finance, teaching staff, school physical facilities, and so on) and the regular evaluation of education activities. Such measures are fundamental to ensuring that the education system is fully responsive to national socioeconomic development. Starting from this position, public awareness of the importance of education has been increased, and education development has become an important goal of both the Vietnamese state and its people.

The second lesson is that, for its development, the Vietnamese education system must be fundamentally and comprehensively renewed in the directions of increased *democratization, socialization, diversification, standardization, and modernization.*

In respect to *democratization,* Vietnam has made continual efforts to build an education system that is *of the people, by the people, and for the people.* It has transformed from a command system to a more open democratic style with a learner-centered approach to education. It continues to complete and refine the legal system to ensure the rights and interests of students, teachers, and parents; gradually increase institutional autonomy and accountability; and decentralize the management of education in an appropriate manner.

In respect to *socialization* (direct support from students and their families), the resourcing of the Vietnamese education system has gone through fundamental changes. Support has been mobilized from all social sources, and nonformal education has experienced strong growth. Many nonpublic institutions have been established and different education models are now used to meet people's diverse learning needs. At present, the human resource needs for industrialization, modernization, and the knowledge economy require the Vietnamese education system to strengthen the socialization process even more, bringing into play the strengths of the state and the peoples' cooperation, and thus facilitating lifelong learning and the building of a *learning society*.

In respect to *diversification*, Vietnamese education has been transformed from a monotonous system that lacked a distinction between consistency and uniqueness into a system with diverse organizational and operational models and styles. This has facilitated an expansion of learning opportunities and increased the system's responsiveness to people's learning needs.

In respect to *standardization*, the Vietnamese education system is trying to shift from a system based on following general regulations to one with more specific and detailed regulations. In the context of continuing quantitative expansion, this shift will facilitate accurate and regular measurement of qualitative performance to underpin quality assurance. This effort began with the development of a *national standards system* in the education sector and the concurrent establishment of curriculum and program *accreditation* standards as well as the creation of quality assurance conditions throughout the education sector. The Vietnamese education policy makers expect that through standardization and quality assurance the Vietnamese education system will achieve *consistency with diversification* and accelerate the process of integration, cooperation, and competition with other advanced education systems regionally and internationally.

In respect to *modernization*, Vietnamese education policy makers expect to bring the national education system to regional and international levels. This requires high standards in the national education standards system. Within the context of a poor country like Vietnam, this is a significant challenge that requires educators to actively seek ways to rapidly narrow the gaps with various advanced education systems in the world.

The third lesson is that Vietnamese education policy makers and managers believe that it is important to *renew and change the way of thinking*. To bring about fundamental and comprehensive changes to the Vietnamese education system that reflect the goals of standardization, modernization, socialization, and democratization, requires escaping from the so-called traditional ways of thinking and operating and avoiding a piecemeal management style. The most challenging task while renovating the current way of thinking in education is to establish an *overall vision* for education that is relevant to the country's socioeconomic development in the context of globalization and a knowledge economy. At the same time, a *new working style*—with a focus on quality and efficiency as the basis for assessment—needs to be established for all teaching staff and education managers. Moreover, as education is a sensitive area, *renovating the way of thinking of education policy makers and managers must be translated into renovating the way of thinking of the entire society*. To achieve this, all changes must come from real needs and serve the long-term interests and benefits of the people. Hence, publicity and transparency must be considered as the most important elements in education policy making and management styles. Here, a major challenge to be addressed is the relationship between *renovation and stability*. With a view toward maintaining the necessary stability in the education system, all changes must follow an appropriate pathway, one that is well understood by all teaching staff and education managers and agreed on by parents and society, and one that leads to the preservation of order in the education reform process.

An important goal for Vietnam's socioeconomic development in the coming years is to "... *lay the foundations for accelerating industrialization, modernization and development of [a] knowledge economy*" (Central Committee of Vietnamese Communist Party 2006). This development requires that the country continually increase the *knowledge content* in all its socioeconomic development activities and bring about *fundamental changes in education and training*. From the reality of the country and lessons learned from other countries, many Vietnamese education policy makers and managers believe that the education system that Vietnam now requires must be an *open* education system that is accessible to everyone, that is, an education system that nurtures and promotes the creativity of young people, with education institutions— primarily universities—acting as cradles of science and technological innovation. This underlines the need for an education system closely linked with science and technological progress, especially information technology and connectivity, a system that can *continuously renovate but preserve stability*, and an education system that promotes *competition* among various education institutions to improve *quality* and to gradually raise—through cooperation and competition with foreign education institutions—Vietnam's regional and international *status*. Moving toward such an education system is not only a challenge but also an opportunity for Vietnam. Future success will depend on the policy makers' sensitivity to new factors and the capacity for implementing renovation within the current context, as well as to efforts made by teaching staff, education managers, parents, students, and the entire society.

NOTES

1. Estimates for 2005 are as follows: age distribution is 0–14 years: 27.9 percent, 15–64 years: 66.4 percent, 65 years and over: 5.8 percent. The population growth rate is 1.04 percent (2005 estimate).

2. As of April 1, 2004.

3. Including Cameroon, Ethiopia, Ghana, Lesotho, Madagascar, and Mozambique.

4. The person who signed these Decrees, on behalf of President Hochiminh, was General Vo Nguyen Giap, who was the minister of internal affairs of the provisional government of the Democratic Republic of Vietnam.

5. In preparation for the use of Vietnamese as the language of instruction in universities, Vietnamese scientists had to make great efforts to develop terminologies in the Vietnamese language for a number of subjects. Excellent examples are "Nouns for Math, Physics and Chemistry" (Hoang Xuan Han), "Nouns for Natural Sciences" (Dao Van Tien), "Nouns for Medical Sciences" (Le Khac Thien), and "Nouns for Agricultural Sciences" (Le Van Can and Nguyen Huu Quan).

6. The curriculum developed by the patriotic scholar Hoang Xuan Han.

7. According to the Geneva Convention (reestablishment of peace in Indochina), from 1955, Vietnam was temporarily separated into two regions: namely, a northern region managed by the government of the Democratic Republic of Vietnam and a southern region managed by a pro-French government. It was planned to achieve the reunification of the country through a general election in 1957. The Americans took the place of the French, built a pro-American government, gradually sent the U.S. army to Vietnam, and, through its air force, expanded the war into the North. The Vietnamese people's second resistance war lasted 15 years and ended with victory on April 30, 1975, bringing liberation to the South and reunification of the country.

8. In essence, the general education programs included reading and writing classes before entering grade one.

9. According to "Escalade de guerre et du crime par Nixon au Vietnam," in the first four years of U.S. Air Force attacks, 1,558 schools and institutions were destroyed (1,334 primary schools, 179 lower-secondary schools, 38 upper-secondary schools, and 7 universities).

10. In the old regime, there were 2,500 private schools, half of which were operated by religious organizations.

11. Principle orientations for this education reform were outlined in Resolution No. 14-NQ/TW dated 1979 by the Politburo, Central Committee of the Vietnamese Communist Party (Term 3).

12. This important decision on the historic reform was approved in the 6th Congress of the Vietnamese Communist Party (December 1986).

13. Socialization in the Vietnamese context implies society's participation in the sector through cost-sharing and cost recovery.

14. In 2004, the repetition rate at primary level was 1.01 percent, lower secondary was 0.83 percent, and upper secondary was 1.34 percent.

15. In early 1990, there were about 2.1 million out-of-school children in the 6- to 14-year-old age group, and 2 million illiterate adults in the 15- to 35-year-old age group.

16. The biggest challenge to this type of vocational program was that it was only advantageous when academic and technical knowledge and skills were taught in parallel with academic theory and vocational practice that were structured in integrated ways, rather than as a simple combination of complementary and vocational training components. Because of the failure to address this challenge and the lack of physical facilities and equipment, the vocational secondary programs could not be maintained.

17. According to the Resolution of the Second Conference of the Vietnamese Communist Party Central Committee, Term VIII (December 1996).

18. For example, as the participation rate of primary-school-age children edged toward the national target, the absolute number of primary pupils declined from its peak of 10.2 million in 1998–99 to 7.8 million in 2004–05 in line with a fall in the primary school-age

population. Meanwhile, at the lower-secondary level the absolute number of pupils continued to increase (from 5.6 million in 1998–99 to 6.6 million in 2003–04) in line with the steady rise in the participation rate to 84 percent.

19. Since 1945, adult education in the form of nonformal education (initially literacy classes, subsequently "complementary" education, and currently "continuing education") has existed in the Vietnamese education system. At the end of twentieth century, however, some education policy makers and researchers saw continuing education as only a delivery mode and not a part of the structure of the education system. The Education Law of 1998 showed some hesitation to nonformal education, by stating, "Non-formal education units consist of continuing education centers. . . ." In the Education Law of 2005, however, this regulation was modified to read as follows: "The national education system consists of formal education and continuing education." Therefore, it should now be understood that continuing education is not just a delivery mode but also a part of the overall system.

20. Twenty percent in 2005.

21. These were 15 percent, 58 percent, and 85 percent, respectively, in 2005.

22. Competitive bidding for textbook manufacturing with large-scale production.

23. In the 2001–02 school year, the number of primary students was 9,311,010. Therefore, there has been an annual average decrease of nearly 400,000 to 500,000 students.

24. The state provides free primary education for half-day instruction and many primary schools operate a shift system. An increasing proportion of primary pupils (approximately 30 percent) mainly in urban areas follow "full-day" instruction for which their families pay for the additional afternoon session.

25. In 2004, there were 286 schools, of which 246 were public schools and 40 were nonpublic. From a management responsibility perspective, 211 schools were managed by localities and central agencies and 75 schools by ministries.

26. Those trained to hold a master's degree and those trained to hold a doctoral degree.

27. Some people perceived this as the fourth education reform.

28. France, a country considered to have a perfect secondary education system, also has concerns with this question (see Le defi XXI 2005).

29. Income from nonstate budgetary resources (tuition fees, contract work, other charges, donation grants, and so on) has played an increasingly important role in the financing of higher education.

30. The implementation of Decree 10 in the higher education subsector provides greater financial autonomy for service delivery units such as colleges and universities by decentralizing responsibility for the management of expenditures and the collection of user fees and related charges.

31. The pilot textbook "lending" scheme and about 25 percent of the MOET's budget-based National Target Program supports the provision of free textbooks to minorities and disadvantaged areas. Presently about 13 percent of pupils in primary education, mainly those from ethnic minorities, receive free textbooks.

32. According to the Education Law of 2005.

33. According to Circular No. 01/GDDT dated February 3, 1997, by the MOET on the instructions on teaching ethnic minority spoken languages and scripts.

34. There were 7,056 vocational trainers in the 2003–04 school year.

35. The MOET is trying, with success, to upgrade primary teachers to meet a standard that requires postsecondary professional training (that is, 12+2 or better).

36. The evolution of GDP, public expenditure, and state spending on education is as follows:

	Trillion Vietnamese dong (1994 price base)		
	1994	1998	2002
GDP	170.3	244.7	312.9
Public expenditure	42.8	49.7	78.0
Education sector	6.0	8.6	13.3

37. The ratio of primary teachers' salaries and wages to GDP per capita in Vietnam has risen gradually from 1.7 in 1998 to 2.4 in 2003 (the same as the Asian mean of 2.4).

38. Official development assistance provides approximately 10 percent of the total education expenditure in Vietnam, substantially less than nonstate resources (families and so on) and domestic public expenditure on education.

39. The management of the education sector in Vietnam must be placed in the broad context of the national economic and social reform (Doi-Moi) that began in 1986 and moved the country from a centralized planning system and economy to a socialist-oriented market mechanism. To this must be added the government's more recent public administration reforms and its revision of the budget processes and the 2003 public finance law. These changes increased decentralization and required substantial changes in the roles and responsibilities of ministries, provincial level managers, and service delivery units. The policy analysis, strategy formulation, governance, oversight, and quality assurance tasks of the ministry have been increased considerably, while its implementation and service delivery roles have been passed to provincial education departments, universities, colleges, and schools.

CHAPTER 5

Education in the Republic of Korea: Approaches, Achievements, and Current Challenges

Chong Jae LEE

INTRODUCTION

This paper seeks to elucidate the unique process of education development that the Republic of Korea has undergone and the new challenges that have emerged in the process of becoming a knowledge-based society. The remarkable economic growth of Korea merited worldwide attention; the rapid process of industrial development and political development toward democratization provided a model after which other developing countries could pattern themselves. Its economic success is illustrated by the contrasts between per capita income in the early 1960s, which stood at US$100, and that of US$15,000 for 2005. Although Korean exports in the 1970s were worth just US$1 billion, the figure leaped to US$250 billion in 2005. Notwithstanding this high economic growth, Korea is known for having achieved a relatively balanced distribution of income compared with other rapidly developing countries (World Bank 2004).

Education is thought to have been one of the most important contributing factors to Korean economic development (OECD 2001a). In the context of education development and its contribution to economic growth, many questions were raised. How did Korea achieve its education expansion in such a short period of time? How was Korea able to expand access to education under economically poor conditions? How has Korean education contributed to economic development? How did technical and vocational education and training (TVET) develop in the process of economic development? How did Korean students score so high at Programme for International Student Achievement (PISA) and Trends in International Mathematics and Science Study (TIMSS), and what are the implications of their high achievement to the quality of Korean education? What challenges is Korean education facing today considering the achievements of the last

60 years? Does Korean education development offer any lessons to other developing countries?

Each of these questions demands intensive study. This chapter attempts to identify the Korean approach to education development and provides an overview of the major challenges and policy choices made at key stages of its education development. This chapter was prepared as a paper presented at "The Asia Study Tour for Senior African Education Policy Makers," which was organized by the World Bank in Singapore in June 2006. Since this chapter examines some characteristics inherent in the education development of Korea, it does not intend to conduct an analytical study on each stage of development. Rather, it focuses on policy choices in coping with challenges that emerged during each stage of education development. To save space in the body of this chapter, statistical data and figures are included in the annex.

DEVELOPMENT STAGES OF EDUCATION DEVELOPMENT

THE BEGINNINGS OF MODERN KOREAN EDUCATION[1]

Education under U.S Military Governance. The conclusion of World War II in 1945 liberated Korea from the yoke of Japanese colonial rule, but the Korean peninsula was occupied by the two forces of the United States and the then Soviet Union. The Republic of Korea was placed under U.S. military governance from 1945 to 1948. Under this military governance, the Choson Educational Committee (Korean Education Committee) was instated to provide policy advice and technical support as partner to the military governance. According to a survey, the population age 13 years old and above was estimated at 15 million and 53 percent of that population (8 million) was illiterate. Those who received at least secondary education or more accounted for 12.6 percent of the population. The military government launched education programs to deal with illiteracy, develop a new school system, and expand education opportunities. During this period, Seoul National University became the first national university transformed from the KyungSung Imperial University.

The Republic of Korea. A U.N. supervised general election was held in the Republic of Korea in 1948, and the Republic of Korea was proclaimed on August 15, 1948. Among the urgent tasks confronting the fledgling government was the need to establish a new school system and expand the enrollment capacities of elementary schools to accommodate the burgeoning demand for school education. From this point, a restless struggle with the burgeoning demand for education set in.

The Establishment of a School System. A new school system that had been conceptualized by the Korean Education Committee was adopted. The ideal educated person was defined as "Hong Ik In Gan," which literally meant a person devoted to the welfare of people. The Education Committee recommended three guidelines to develop the new school system. First, the education system should provide easy access to education for all aspirants for education. Second, the education system should provide relevant education opportunities to meet the diverse needs for education. Third, the new education system should be compatible with those of other countries by accommodating the worldwide trends of education practice. Having defined the education ideals and the education system, the Education Law was enacted in 1950 to guide the operation of the system.

Six principles guided the development of the new education system. They were as follows:

- Six years of free elementary education were made compulsory.
- Secondary education was divided into middle school and high school levels to reduce the number of dropouts from schools and improve the relevance of secondary education.
- In principle, secondary education was to follow a single track. For high schools, the single track would branch into various streams of study in such a way that facilitated the transfer of students between the streams. Vocational education was diversified with the provision of occupational training courses.
- Higher education was provided by a variety of institutes, which varied in program content and duration in response to various social demands.
- Teacher education institutes were divided into the preparation of elementary school teachers and secondary school teachers. The former was the responsibility of teacher training at the high school level and the latter was the responsibility of colleges or universities.
- To provide adult education, civic schools were established.

The 6-3-3-4 School System. The school system is developed with four basic school ladders: (a) six years of elementary education, (b) three years of middle school education, (c) another three years of high school education, and (d) four years of higher education. Within this framework, remedial education reforms have been made over the last 60 years. A significant reform was to upgrade teaching qualifications for elementary school teachers. These qualifications were upgraded from high school graduation to the completion of two years at a junior teachers' college. Later, they were upgraded to require the completion of four years at a teachers' college. The institutes of higher education were divided into universities and junior colleges. The expansion of education opportunities at the secondary level resulted in the elimination of the civic schools for adults who missed opportunities to attend school.

The War-Ravaged Schools. The Korean War had resulted in damage to about 68 percent of the school buildings and makeshift barracks that were substituted

Figure 5.1   The Current School System

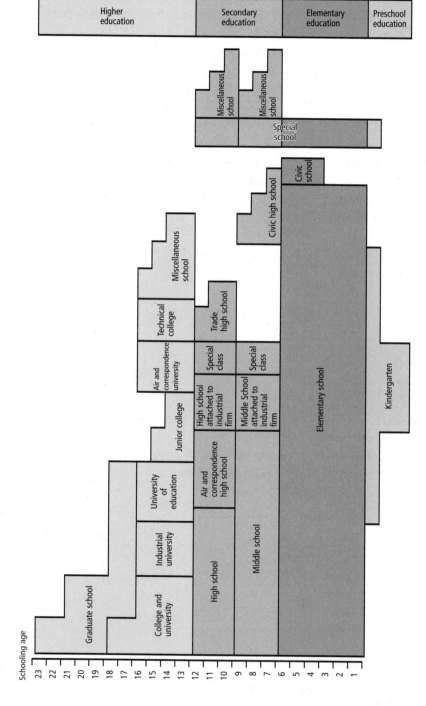

Source: Lee 2004a.

for the damaged schools. To continue university education, the "war-time joint universities" accommodated students from different universities in Pusan city. It was after the ceasefire in 1953 that the Six-Year Compulsory Education Plan was put forward and implemented. This plan marked the beginning of the expansion of access to education that was to follow in the Republic of Korea.

THE DEVELOPMENT STAGES OF EDUCATION AND UNFOLDING MAJOR POLICY CHOICE

Development Stages. The process of education development can be categorized into several stages. To explicate the relationship between education development and economic growth, it is necessary to compare the relationship between the stages of economic development and those of education development. The Korean Development Institute (KDI), the most influential economic policy research institute, offered a conceptualization of three stages of economic development (KDI 1997). To this KDI model, this chapter adds the present stage, which is a transition stage into a knowledge-based structure (World Bank 2000c).

- Economic disruption and recovery (1945–60).
- Export-oriented, high-growth strategy under the Park administration (1961–79).
- Structural adjustment and stabilized growth (1980–2000).
- Transition into a knowledge-based society (2001–present).

Key Issues of Education by Stage. Along with the various stages of economic development, the stages of education development were defined. Challenges to each stage of education development were defined as the tasks required for that stage of education development. The trends in enrollment growth patterns highlight some challenges for education development. The period before the 1960s,

Table 5.1 Major Economic Indicators

	Population (1,000 persons)	Employees (1,000 persons)	GDP (billion won)	Per capita GDP (US$)	Exports (US$ billion)
1945	25,120	—	—	—	—
1960	24,989	—	243	80.0	—
1970	31,435	9,617	2,764	257.6	0.84
1980	37,407	13,683	38,775	1,705.6	17.50
1990	43,390	18,085	186,691	6,077.4	65.00
2000	45,985	21,156	578,665	11,129.6	172.30
2005	47,279	22,856	806,622	16,656.4	284.40

Source: For 1945 data, Korea Education Publishing Committee 1960; for 1960 and later data, National Statistical Office (Korea).
Note: — = not available. The 1945 population is taken from 1944 data.

for instance, reflects the expansion of education opportunities for elementary education when the country was confronted with an explosive growth in the elementary-school-age population. The challenge of education expansion was transferred from elementary to secondary education in the 1960–80s. After the 1980s, stabilized enrollment allowed the administration to address the qualitative improvement of education. Coincidental to the transformation of the Korean economy toward a knowledge-based economy, Korean education was confronted with new challenges. Following are the challenges for education development by stage:

- 1945–60: Reconstruction and enrollment expansion of elementary education
- 1961–80: Quantitative growth of secondary education and development of TVET
- 1981–2000: Qualitative improvement of education and expansion of opportunities for higher education

Table 5.2 Stages of Korean Education Development

Focus by period	1945–1960 Reconstruction	1961–1980 Education for economic growth	1981–2000 Search for new paradigm of educational development	2001–Present Restructuring
Callenges to education	• Compulsory education	• Secondary education for all • Supply for technical manpower	• Universalization of higher education	• Lifelong learning • HRD
Major concerns	• Access to opportunity	• Growth of quantity, efficiency, and control	• Quality • Autonomy • Accountability	• Competitiveness in globalization knowledge-society

Polity choice	• Universal compulsory education
	• Reconstruction of educational infrastructure
		• Expansion and equalization of secondary education
		• Technical vocational education and training
			• Decentralized local autonomy of education
			• Expansion of higher education
			• Quality improvement
				• Restructuring higher education
				  −Support research productivity
				  −Regional development
				  −HRD, L-L
				• Quality improvement of public schools
				• Coordinated approach to HRD

Resources or tools	• Using foreign assistance	• 5 Years planning long-term planning • Law of local education financing fund established • Foreign loans to support TVET	• PCER: Presidential Commission for Education Reform • Education reform (1995)	• Educational and financial support for higher eduation (BK, Nuri, Post BK)

Source: Lee 2006a.
Note: HRD = human resources development; NURI = New University for Regional Innovation; BK = "Brain Korea;"
  L−L = lifelong learning.

- 2001–present: Development of human resources to bolster transition into a knowledge-based society (the relevancy of student achievement, development of core competency, restructuring education institutions).

EDUCATION RECONSTRUCTION, 1945–60

Recovery of Destroyed Schools. This period highlights efforts to eliminate the remains of colonial education and recover the war-ravaged schools. The elimination of colonial education led to the institutionalization of a new education system. Achieving the targeted enrollment of the whole elementary-school-age population was the first priority. The United Nations Korea Reconstruction Agency (UNKRA) greatly assisted this effort (Kim 1989).

The Six-Year Compulsory Education Plan. This plan laid out specific education activities to be conducted on a yearly basis that would help the country realize universal enrollment of the elementary-school-age population. Started in 1954, the plan aimed to achieve the targeted 90 percent enrollment or higher by 1959. Because of limited financial resources, the capacity to accommodate more students was constrained. In some urban schools, the number of children per class exceeded 100. The expansion of elementary school enrollment set the stage for future expansion of secondary school enrollment.

EDUCATION IN THE ECONOMIC GROWTH PERIOD, 1961–80

Rapid Economic Growth. The rapid economic growth of the Republic of Korea was the result of implementing a series of Five-Year Economic Development Programs. Starting with the first Five-Year Economic Development Plan in 1962, the successive four plans were implemented by 1976. The higher growth rate of the economy was accompanied by high population growth, massive migration toward cities, and a marked increase in social demand for education. In the earlier stage of development, export-oriented industries flourished by virtue of intensive government support, and the policy emphasis shifted to capital-intensive heavy and chemical industries in the 1970s. The 1973 oil shock interrupted the sustained growth of the economy for some time, and the government's education financing suffered a setback during this period. As part of the overall effort to reduce the disparity in income between urban and rural areas, the New Community Development Movement (Saemaul Undong) was launched to benefit rural needs. In the 1970s, the government began to establish national research and development (R&D) institutes to support national development tasks. The KDI was the first national institute founded.

For Economic Development. To sharpen the development edge of education, technical-vocational education was expanded and upgraded in quality. First, the

Table 5.3 Social and Economic Index of the Economic Growth Period

	City population rate to total (percent)	Per capita GNP (US$)	Industrial origin of GDP (percent)		
			Mining and agriculture	Manufacturing, electricity, and construction	Services
1961	28.0 (1960)	82	48.8	12.3	38.9
1965	—	105	44.5	16.4	39.1
1970	41.1	254	32.4	27.1	40.5
1975	48.4	602	26.4	32.1	41.1
1979	57.2	1,676	16.2	40.1	44.1

Source: National Statistical Office (Korea).
Note: GNP = gross national product.

vocational high schools were expanded in enrollment capacity from the early 1960s, and the government's support for science and technology education increased substantially. Second, the rapid expansion of the elementary school enrollment resulted in a situation of overcrowded classrooms, leading to the double or triple shift in lower grades. Therefore, the expansion of education facilities for elementary education continued to be a priority. During the first Five-Year Economic Development Program, education funds were allocated to the "Special Account for Education in Economic Development." The elementary education's share of this budget during the Five-Year Economic Development Plan was 73.4 percent, totaling 46.2 billion won.

Meeting the Target for Secondary School Enrollment. The increase in elementary education enrollment in the 1950s caused an increase in demand for secondary education. This, in turn, made middle school entrance highly competitive. Parents felt forced to rely on private tutoring to prepare their children for the entrance examination to middle schools. To relieve parents of the burden of private tutoring and to keep school education from being driven into examination preparation, the entrance examinations to middle schools and high schools, which had been administered by individual schools, were abolished in 1969 and in 1974, respectively. Applicants to lower schools and high schools were assigned by lottery to one of the secondary schools in their district of residence. The abolition of these entrance examinations improved the percentage of those who advanced to middle schools to 90 percent. If universalized admission is defined as admission of 90 percent or higher of graduates from one level of education to the next level then middle school admission was universalized in 1979 and high school admission was universalized in 1985.

The Legally Stipulated Share of Education Financing (Chung et al. 2004). Legislative actions secured a fixed percentage of education resources during this

Table 5.4 Qualitative Improvement of Education by School

	Elementary		Middle		High	
	Students per class	Students per teacher	Students per class	Students per teacher	Students per class	Students per teacher
1962	62.9	60.0	60.1	40.5	55.8	27.3
1965	65.4	65.4	60.7	39.4	57.0	30.2
1970	62.1	56.9	62.1	42.3	58.1	29.7
1975	56.7	51.8	64.5	43.2	58.6	31.4
1979	52.2	48.0	65.6	45.3	59.4	32.8

Source: Ministry of Education and Human Resource Development 1960–2005.

period. According to the law, 12.98 percent of domestic tax revenue was set aside for elementary and secondary education in the name of local education grants. The increased financial resources for education attendant to the economic growth resulted in the quantitative expansion and qualitative improvement of education at the elementary and secondary levels. In terms of the numbers of students, schools, and recruited teachers, education expansion during this period was most remarkable. By linking the number of students per class and per teacher to the education conditions, this period saw remarkable improvement of education conditions.

EXPLORATION OF THE QUALITATIVE IMPROVEMENT OF EDUCATION: 1981–2000

Political Democratization. In the earlier part of the 1980s, Korean society was seething at the relapse of political leadership into military governance. However, the continued outcry for democracy forced the military government to accept society's popular political demands in 1987. An important bridge was laid during this period to set the stage for a series of democratic governments to follow in the 1990s.

The July 30 Educational Reform. In the 1980s, the entrance to higher education became increasingly competitive and was characterized by "the feverish pursuit" of private tutoring (Chung 1991). The ever-widening income gap was manifested in the accessibility to private tutoring. In 1980, the new military government formulated the July 30 Educational Reform to eradicate private tutoring and relieve students from the burden of competitive examinations. This action brought the need for expanded university enrollment. The government maintained control of university enrollment, but the July 30 Educational Reform lifted that control. The sudden increase of students, however, caused the conditions of higher education to deteriorate. The problem was less serious for private universities that were able to use the additional income from tuition to expand facilities.

Local Autonomy of Education Administration and the Teachers Union. The authoritarian control of the central government was challenged and demands for democratization in education were made. In 1995, the government gave autonomy to the local government in the provinces[2] and to special metropolitan units like Seoul and Pusan. Accordingly, provincial board members of education were elected by school council members. Teachers organized a union allegedly to protect their rights and promote their welfare. The organization of a teachers union was highly sensitized with special reference to the legitimacy of the new entity. The government declared it illegal, and in one instance, teachers were dismissed en mass (Chung 1991).

New Demands on the Relevance and Accountability of Education Emerged. Distinctive from the quantitative expansion period, policy attention shifted from efficiency to relevance and from bureaucratic control to accountability during the third stage of quality improvement. Efforts were made to search for a new system of education. With the exception of higher education enrollment, the quantitative growth of total enrollment reached its height in the 1980s. Regarding numbers of students, enrollment of elementary schools hit a record high in 1971 and middle and high school enrollments reached their heights in 1985 and 1989, respectively. Since then, enrollment size has decreased, except for that of higher education. The 1990s marked the beginning of new challenges to improve qualitative relevance and accountability in education.

A New Vision for the Education System. To set forth new directions for education development, the Presidential Committee for Educational Reform (PCER) was instated in 1995. The PCER formulated a new direction and envisioned that education development would feature the following characteristics:

• Emphasis was placed on learner-centered education, diversification of education programs, autonomy and accountability of school operations, and a new information system
• A new evaluation mechanism was implemented to assess the results of school education

Table 5.5 Net Changes in the Number of Students
(unit: thousand persons)

	Elementary	Middle	High	Tertiary	Total
1945–60	+2,247	+449	+198	+93	+2,987
1960–80	+2,037	+1,943	+1,424	+501	+5,905
1980–2000	−1,638	−611	+374	+2,532	+657
2000–05	+3	+150	−308	+415	+260

Source: Derived from annex table A5.6.

Figure 5.2   The Changing Pattern of Enrollment Growth by School Level

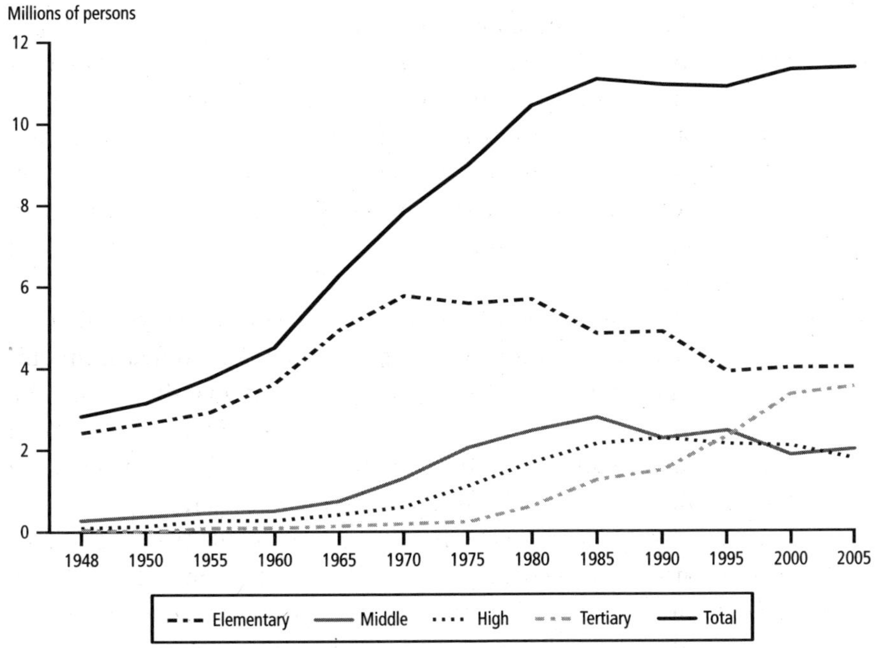

Source: Derived from annex table A5.6.

The 1995 framework for a new education system provided a blueprint for future education reforms to be undertaken by the two succeeding government administrations under Kim Dae Jung and Roh Moo Hyun. In the process of implementation, however, the proposed reforms lost sight of their direction, strategic approach, and core values.

RESTRUCTURING PERIOD, 2001–PRESENT

Financial Crisis. The Korean economy faced financial crisis in 1997. This is the period during which the nation renewed its effort to overcome financial difficulties and restructured the economic system in anticipation of new challenges (World Bank 2000c). The economic recovery coincided with the transfer of power from the ruling to the opposition party. It was also during this period that the Teachers Union was formally legalized.

Restructuring the Education System for Manpower Development. Globalization saddled Korean education with two challenges. One was to support the nation's competitiveness in the international market and the other was to align the education system to meet the challenges of human resource development (HRD). To address both education and HRD, the Ministry of Education was upgraded to the Ministry of Education and Human Resource Development, and the minister was promoted to deputy prime minister. This structural realignment was intended to revitalize the role of education in HRD (Ministry of Education and Human Resource Development 2003).

Reform of Higher Education. The first priority of the government during the restructuring period was to reform higher education in a way that enhanced its relevance and the international competitiveness of the universities. A new research project, Brain Korea 21 (BK 21), supported research-oriented graduate programs in selected universities. The New University for Regional Innovation (NURI) project was designed to support universities in their efforts to enhance HRD for regional community development (Ministry of Education and Human Resource Development 2001).

Lifelong Education. In improving the nation's competitiveness and in preparation for the advent of becoming a knowledge-based society, lifelong learning was considered an integral part of the education system. To this effect, the Ministry of Education has promoted specific policy measures to promote lifelong education on the basis of the formal education system. To link lifelong learning to the attainment of formal education, a "credit bank" was established. Additionally, encouragement and support have been given to corporations for education services to provide corporate college programs. Universities began to play more important roles in providing lifelong learning programs. Many universities established "Life-Long Learning Centers," which offer many courses for credit.

A Shadow Education System. The number of students who participated in extracurricular activities has increased not only to prepare them for the competitive higher education entrance, but also to enrich them through exposure to a variety of education programs while they are in elementary and secondary schools. In some instances, the extracurricular activities have developed into an alternative system to the existing school education. Foreign language training was gaining popularity among youngsters, which led to the trend of students leaving for overseas study at earlier ages. As the credibility of school education has been impaired among the parents, extracurricular activities are being developed as a shadow education system (Bray 1999).

Upgrading Public Education. Korean education is confronted with the challenge of improving the quality of its school education. The most important policy goals for elementary and secondary levels are to upgrade the quality of school education and to reduce the degree of parental reliance on private tutoring. The government has been concerned about the negative effects of private tutoring, which increases the financial burden on parents and the inequality of education among social levels and regions. This is a serious transgression of equality, which is the fundamental principle of democracy. The negative effect of private education was the direct motive for the articulation of education reform measures (Ministry of Education 2002a, 2004).

SYNOPSIS

Korea has registered impressive economic growth and education development since the end of World War II. When the Republic of Korea was established in 1948, more than half of the population was illiterate. Education was given high priority by the new government, but it suffered a major setback during the Korean War in which two-thirds of all schools were destroyed or damaged. Subsequent education development has passed through four main phases to date. During the economic disruption and recovery period (1945–60), the principal education concern was to expand access to primary education and eradicate illiteracy. This phase was followed by export-oriented high economic growth during which time the education emphasis shifted to the development of secondary education and TVET in support of the strengthening economy. The following two decades featured economic consolidation, stabilization, and structural adjustment wherein education policies focused on improving the quality of basic education and expanding enrollments in higher education. With the advent of the twenty-first century, the transition to a knowledge-based economy and society began (and has continued). Education efforts now target curriculum reforms; institutional restructuring; strengthened correspondence between student skills, graduate output, and labor market demand; lifelong learning; and new partnerships uniting government, education institutions, and private enterprises in common efforts to boost national competitiveness.

Over half a century, sustained attention to sequenced education development and continuous system adjustment in response to changing circumstances contributed to a 20-fold increase in per capita income between 1960 and 1980, and a further tenfold rise in per capita income from 1980 to 2005. In the process, the education sector demonstrated a constant concern for equity, most notably, in its initiatives to manage private tutoring within a competitive education environment. It has also worked to adapt to democratization as rising local government autonomy brought the decentralization of education administration, and a more open political environment gave birth to a national teachers union and a growing voice to various education stakeholders. As these events have circumscribed the strong central planning approach that characterized Korea's earlier phases of education development, education policy makers have compensated by creating a wide range of institutional types for education system support and performance monitoring, and by developing new skills in public communications and stakeholder negotiation.

THE KOREAN APPROACH TO THE DEVELOPMENT OF EDUCATION

THE EXPANSION OF EDUCATION OPPORTUNITIES AND A QUANTITATIVE GROWTH STRATEGY

Universal Enrollment Achieved in 50 Years. Under the Japanese colonial rule, education opportunities were severely limited for Koreans. At the end of the colonial rule, 64.0 percent of the elementary-school-age children were enrolled, and this percentage drastically dropped to 3.2 percent for secondary education and 0.18 percent for higher education. Defining universal enrollment as attaining a 90 percent enrollment rate, Korea achieved universal elementary education by 1957, middle school education by 1990, and high school education by 1999. Several years after universal enrollment was achieved at one level, more than 90 percent of the graduates of that level entered the next level of education. In 1979, entry of graduates from elementary education to middle school hit 90 percent, and the entry of middle school graduates to high school reached this level in 1985. In 1995, more than 50 percent of high school graduates entered into higher education. Universal enrollment of elementary and secondary schools was achieved within 50 years of liberation from colonial control in 1945.

Eight Key Factors in the Quantitative Expansion. The quantitative expansion of Korean education has certain characteristics. These are considered to be contributing factors.

- The achievement of *universal access* to elementary education in the beginning stage of education expansion
- A *sequential bottom-up approach* that expanded elementary education, which was followed by middle school and high school education
- A *low-cost approach* was implemented to expand access to education at the cost of quality conditions of education
- *Private schools* contributed to the expansion of access to secondary education to achieve targeted enrollment

Table 5.6 The Years of Attainment of Universal Enrollment

Year 90 percent entered school of a higher level		Year of 90 percent enrollment rate	
		Elementary	1957
Elementary to middle	1979	Middle	1990
Middle to high	1985	High	1999
High to tertiary[a]	1995	Tertiary	2000

Source: Ministry of Education (Korea) 1980, Research of Korean Educational Policy 1953–65, and National Statistical Office (Korea) 1965–2005.
a. In tertiary education, an enrollment rate of 50 percent is applied.

- *Egalitarian approach* to expand the access to education was implemented with the Abolition of Entrance Examination to Middle Schools and the High School Equalization Policy (HEP). The affirmative action programs were also applied to financing and providing free textbooks.
- Legal provision was made to *secure funding* for education. The "Law of Grants for Local Education Financing" set aside 12.98 percent of total domestic tax revenue for elementary and secondary education.
- Parents' *strong aspirations* for their children's education success built up strong demand for education even in the period of low per capita income.
- Korean education owes much of its rapid expansion to *economic growth,* which provided the financial resources and job opportunities for graduates.

In retrospect, the elementary education enrollment expansion to a universal level in less than five years after the Korean War, laid a foundation for enrollment growth in secondary education. In the following discussion of the Korean approach to the expansion of education opportunities and quantitative growth, special attention is given to the expansion of elementary education, the low-cost approach, and the egalitarian approach as key factors for this quantitative expansion.

THE EXPANSION OF COMPULSORY ELEMENTARY EDUCATION

At the time of the liberation in 1945, enrollment in elementary education was 64 percent. The U.S military governance and the Republic of Korea set the expansion of elementary education as their top priority for education development, as 68 percent of the school buildings were destroyed during the Korean War.

The Six-Year Compulsory Education Plan (1954–59). This plan, beginning in the year following the ceasefire, set a target of 96 percent enrollment to be achieved by 1959. It projected the yearly demands for teachers and financial requirements. During this period, the government stipulated that 80 percent of the education

Table 5.7   Development of Elementary Education Enrollment, 1945–57

	Schools	Teachers	Students	Enrollment rate (percent)
1945 (at liberation)	2,807	27,847	1,572,046	64.0
1948 (founding of the Republic of Korea)	3,400	41,335	2,405,301	74.8
1951 (outbreak of the Korean War)	3,917	32,371	2,073,844	69.8
1954	4,053	41,857	2,678,374	82.5
1957	4,369	56,705	3,170,982	91.1

Source: Kim 1989, 108.

Table 5.8   Quality Index of Elementary Education

	Students (1,000 persons)	Students per class (person)	Students per teacher (person)
1965	4,941	65.4	62.4
1970	5,749	62.1	56.9
1975	5,599	56.7	51.8
1980	5,658	51.5	47.5
1985	4,857	44.7	38.3
1990	4,869	41.4	35.6
1995	3,905	36.4	28.2
2000	4,020	35.8	28.7
2005	4,023	31.8	25.1

Source: Ministry of Education and Human Resource Development 1960–2005.

budget be spent on elementary and secondary education. The implementation of this plan led to a phenomenal expansion of elementary education enrollment. Because elementary education was made compulsory and provided free of charge by the Education Law, schools were not allowed to reject any children in their school zone. This compulsory situation marked the introduction of a low-cost approach to education in Korea. Parents bore the cost of textbooks and recurring payments to the schools in the name of school promotion funds.

LOW-COST APPROACH

An approach that brings quantitative expansion in education at the expense of qualitative conditions is defined in this chapter as a "low-cost approach." The expansion of elementary education was made possible through this low-cost approach. Through compulsory elementary education, the implementation of the low-cost approach was an inevitable policy choice. The forced expansion of enrollment in elementary education resulted in large class sizes and double or triple shifts in classroom use. In the large cities to which people were migrating, class sizes exceeded 90 in some schools. During the implementation periods of the Six-Year Compulsory Education Expansion Plans, some 40 percent of all classrooms practiced such double or triple shifts.

Changes in the Number of Elementary School Children. Elementary school enrollment increased from 1.37 million in 1949 to a peak of 5.75 million in 1970. Reflecting the decreasing birth rate, the number is expected to decrease to 2.6 million in 2020. With the government's continued and intensive financial support that aimed to improve school conditions and address the declining school-age population, school conditions began to improve beginning in 1965. As noted in

Figure 5.3 The Enrollment and Quality Index of Elementary School

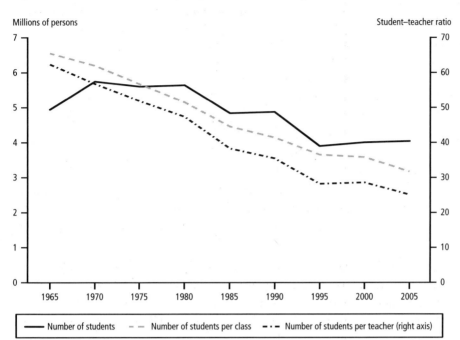

Source: Ministry of Education and Human Resource Development 1960–2005.

table 5.8, the number of students per class significantly decreased from 65.4 in 1965 to 31.8 in 2005. The number of students per teacher showed a similar decrease.

EGALITARIAN APPROACH

Egalitarian Policy Framework. In the process of expanding the access to education, the government implemented an equity-oriented policy framework. This equity-oriented policy framework is called the egalitarian approach for its policy orientation. This policy aimed at reducing gaps in the enrollment ratio, improving school quality conditions, and improving student achievement between regions and family backgrounds by supporting the least favored areas and social classes. It set out to achieve the following:

- Abolish entrance examinations to middle schools and high schools in urban areas and replace them with lottery assignment of students to schools within school districts.
- Allocate more resources to the schools in those regions with poor school conditions.
- Implement programs for low-income areas and families free of charge, covering the cost of textbooks and tuition fees.

The Abolition of Entrance Examinations to Middle Schools was devised to reduce the inequality caused by private tutoring to prepare for entrance examinations to selective middle schools and high schools and to free lower-level schools from the pressure to prepare the exams. The abolition of entrance examinations contributed to liberating elementary education from exam-oriented instruction and increasing the enrollment of middle school education.

Middle school enrollment increased from 1 million in 1968 to 2.8 million at its peak in 1985 (it since dropped to 2 million in 2005). As the government increased public school capacities to accommodate more students, the share of private school enrollment shows a declining trend from 50.3 percent in 1968 to 31.8 percent in 1985 and down to 18.9 percent in 2005. As occurred in the elementary schools, the rapid increase of enrollment caused deterioration in school conditions. The average class size rose from 60 before the new entrance system to 65.7 at its peak in 1979. But soon class size began to fall, declining to 50 in 1990 and 35 in 2005. The enrollment increase of middle schools created a situation of fierce competition in the entrance examination to high schools. This gave rise to a new policy aimed to equalize high school education.

Figure 5.4 The Enrollment and Quality Index of Middle School

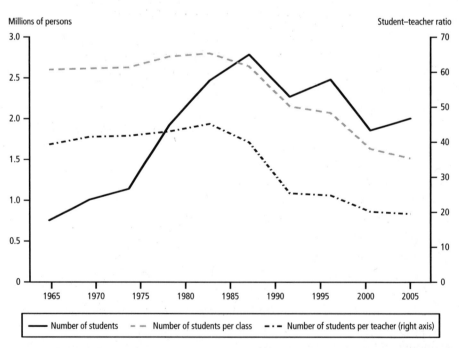

Millions of persons

Student–teacher ratio

Legend: —— Number of students   – – Number of students per class   – • – Number of students per teacher (right axis)

Source: Annex table A5.6 for number of students, annex table A5.8 for students per class, and annex table A5.9 for number of students per teacher.

Implementation of Free Programs. By 1979, the entrance ratio of elementary school graduates to middle school had already surpassed 90 percent. This achievement set the stage for extending the implementation of free compulsory education to the middle school level. The government implemented "free of charge programs" covering the cost of textbooks, tuition, and school supporting fees, starting with remote and insular areas in 1985 and extending nationwide by 1997 (Ministry of Education 1998).

THE HIGH SCHOOL EQUALIZATION POLICY

The quality of high school education differed from school to school and this acted as an open invitation to overheated competition for entrance to high schools. The equalization of high school education was considered to free middle school students from extreme examination stress.

By abolishing the entrance examinations that had been administered by individual high schools, candidates were placed by lottery into one of the high schools in their respective residential area. The equalization program was not universally applied; districts better conditioned to implement the new scheme were distinguished from those less prepared. "Better conditioned" districts were defined as the districts in which all of the high schools provided the same or similar quality of education.

The disparity in education quality between high schools was also attributed to the differing teacher quality. In the case of district public high schools subject to the equalization policy, teachers were rotated among schools. In these districts, private high schools were subsidized by the government so that they would accept assigned students at the same tuition rate as public schools.

The number of high schools subject to the equalization policy increased progressively to account for 57.2 percent in 2004. The proportion of students affected by the equalization policy was 69.6 percent. The share of private schools subject to the new system was larger than the share of middle schools, because most of the private schools were located in urban areas.

HEP Critique. From the beginning of its application, the equalization policy was a hot issue with pros and cons equally divided (Kang 2006). Views expressed about the HEP may be summarized as follows:

- **Positive effects:** The immediate effect of the new policy was manifested in a sudden upsurge of students who advanced from middle to high school. By 1995, the share of these students had already surpassed 90 percent. The equalization policy eliminated the need for private tutoring and middle school students were liberated from the burden of preparing for the competitive examination. This allowed the middle schools to normalize education. High school disparities in quality and conditions were greatly reduced as a result of the equalization policy. These effects were expected by the equalization of high schools.

- **Negative effects:** Criticism was leveled against the equalization policy, including the fact that students were limited in their choice of high school and that heterogeneous grouping made it difficult to provide focused instruction. The equalization policy deprived both the schools and children of positive competition. Schools lost the opportunity to develop their unique identities and the autonomous capacity to run the system themselves.

The progression of enrollments and two quality indicators (students per teacher and students per class) between 1955 and 2005 are shown in figure 5.5.

THE JULY 30 EDUCATIONAL REFORM IN 1980

By abolishing entrance examinations, competition to gain entrance to the best schools moved from middle schools to high schools and then to selective universities. Because of the widespread belief that private tutoring was an added insurance to pass competitive examinations, parents were under heavy pressure to pay

Figure 5.5   The Enrollments and Quality Index of High School

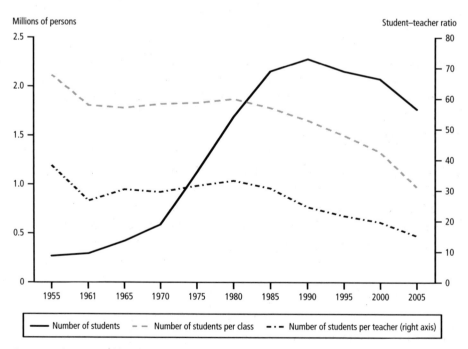

Source: Based on annex tables A5.6, A5.8, and A5.9.

for private tutoring. The resolute and bold decision to ban the practice of private tutoring was taken in 1980 amid the political maelstrom that gave rise to a new military regime. The July 30 Educational Reform highlighted the following:

- Entrance examinations administered by individual universities were abolished and replaced with the national entrance examination to university administered by the state. The selection of candidates was determined by each university based on a student's high school record and national examination score.
- University enrollment quotas were determined by new graduation quotas. This measure was taken to encourage intensive study following admission. Admission quotas were to be 30 percent higher than graduation quotas,[3] but those admitted were able to graduate within the graduation quota. This measure shifted the intensity of learning away from the high school level and improved the attention given to university study.
- The enrollment capacity of higher education institutes was enlarged. As a result, the number of students increased from 400,000 in 1980 to 930,000 in 1985. Enrollment of junior colleges followed suit. During this period, the junior teacher's college program was upgraded to a four-year program.
- The July 30 Educational Reform declared the pursuit of private tutoring illegal. The Educational Broadcasting Station (EBS), an education television channel, began to broadcast education programs as a substitute for private tutoring.

Doors Open to Higher Education. Education reform met strong opposition from university students who forced the repeal of the principle of using graduation quotas to determine enrollment levels. As a result, university enrollment rose, paving the way for the popularization of higher education. This was not a policy choice; rather it was a conclusion dictated by the evolving situation.

The Achievement of Universal Access to Education. The sustained expansion of education opportunities led to universal enrollment. If universal access to education is defined as the achievement of 90 percent enrollment or a 90 percent rate of entrance to the next level of education, elementary education was universalized in 1957, middle school education in 1979, and high school education in 1985. Since 1995, the entrance rate from high schools to higher education has exceeded 50 percent. As noted in table 5.7, the average number of years spent in the education system rose from five years in 1965 to 10.6 years in 2001 (Song 2003).

ENLARGED ACCESS TO EDUCATION AND ECONOMIC GROWTH

Human Capital Perspective. Widening access to education contributed to the enhancement of human capital and helped elevate earnings. In relation to economic growth, education's role is to produce human capital to meet different

Figure 5.6 The Enrollment and Quality Index of Tertiary Education

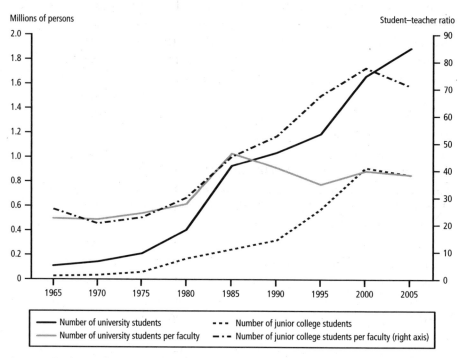

Source: National Center for Education Statistics and Information.

Table 5.9 Social Indicators for Korea, 1965–2001

Education	1965	1970	1980	1991	2001
Average education (years)	5.0	5.7	7.6	9.5	10.6
Total students (in thousands)	6,694	7,986	10,568	10,825	10,819
Student/population ratio (%)	22.1	25.4	27.7	24.5	22.9
High school graduates entering higher education (%)	—	26.9	27.2	33.2	70.5

Source: Song 2003.
Note: — = not available.

manpower needs required by the economy in its various stages of development. The sequential expansion of access to education from elementary education to higher education corresponded well to these evolving industrial needs.

In this chapter, the sequential expansion of access to education from elementary education to higher education is named the "sequential bottom-up approach." In retrospect, the low-cost approach, the egalitarian approach, and continued high economic growth combined to enable successful implementation of the sequential bottom-up approach. Economic growth benefits education by increasing education investment and the education share of the government budget.

Cooperation between Education and Economy. The rapid growth of the Republic of Korea's economy was the result of economic development planning, starting with the first Five-Year Economic Development Program in 1962. Education development after the 1960s reflects the national development strategies for supporting economic development. Accordingly, education was considered a major factor in manpower development in support of the targeted economic growth. Economic development planning corresponded with education development.

Young Hwa Kim (1997) identified a consistent line of interaction between industrial manpower needs and the supply of manpower from the education sector. In the 1960s when economic policy threw its full weight behind developing export-oriented labor-intensive light industries, free elementary education had already been made compulsory, and the expansion of secondary education had just taken off. In the second phase of the development program, emphasis shifted to the development of heavy and chemical industries, and the education system realigned itself to respond to these manpower needs. During this period, the equalization of high schools was implemented, and vocational high school programs were specialized in accordance to technical manpower needs. Coming into the 1980s, a new industrial transition was made in anticipation of the age of the information industry and the establishment of Korea as a knowledge-based society. It was during this period that opportunities for higher education expanded.

The Preconditions for Economic Growth. Thinking about the preconditions for economic growth, attention is readily drawn to the universalization of elementary education and the expansion of secondary education, which took place before economic takeoff and growth. There was a strong relationship between economic growth and education development. The Korean model features a progressive development moving in sequence from the low-cost approach, to quantitative egalitarian growth, to the sequential bottom-up approach. This model can be compared with a quality approach, which focuses on limited quantitative expansion of selective higher education and secondary education. The former reflects the Asian model, including Korea, and the latter seems to represent the model adopted by some African countries.

Mutually Reinforcing Effects between Education and Economic Growth. One can see the contribution that Korean education made to economic growth by the way it responded to the demand for specific manpower skills. Conversely, the expansion of education opportunities at all school levels was supported by the increasing revenue provided by the state, which in turn depended on economic growth. Economic growth provided the policy makers with the confidence to designate a legally stipulated share of state resources to education, thus supporting the expansion of education facilities and improvement of education conditions. By securing 12.98 percent of domestic tax revenue, it was possible to create the needed infrastructure for education development.

TECHNICAL AND VOCATIONAL EDUCATION AND TRAINING

The system of TVET is a dual system including technical and vocational education on the one hand and occupational training on the other. The former is the responsibility of vocational high schools, junior technical colleges,[4] and the open-technical university, and falls under the supervision of the Ministry of Education. Occupational training is aimed at developing the specific skills necessary for industrial workers to accomplish their job tasks. Such training activities are provided to employed workers outside the formal education system. Compared to formal TVET education, occupational training requires less time, but its programs are more varied in terms of clientele and more specific in content. Occupational training is offered by the Central Occupational Training Institute and its subordinate institutes. All occupational training programs offered by public institutes were placed under the Ministry of Labor Affairs. These two components of the system will be discussed in turn.

DEVELOPMENT OF TECHNICAL-VOCATIONAL EDUCATION, 1960–79

The importance of vocational education has been stressed since the establishment of the Republic of Korea. Vocational education suffered from a lack of public attention, however, when graduates of vocational high schools found it hard to obtain decent jobs. The importance of vocational education was recognized in the context of HRD, including occupational training, which was included in the series of Five-Year Economic Development Plans.

In the early 1960s, the system of vocational education and occupational training was streamlined to sharpen its developmental edge by producing the necessary manpower to bolster the development of labor-intensive light industry.

Table 5.10 Status of Vocational High Schools, 1945–2005

Year	No. of schools	Percent to total h.s.	No. of students	Rate to total h.s.	No. of classes	Rate to total h.s.	No. of teachers	Rate to total h.s.
1945	58	—	24,942	—	442	—	1,093	—
1955	249	43.1%	98,452	36.7%	1,857	47.0%	2,997	42.5%
1965	312	44.4%	172,436	40.4%	3,225	43.1%	6,214	44.0%
1975	479	41.6%	474,868	48.4%	8,327	43.4%	15,340	42.9%
1985	635	39.6%	885,962	41.1%	15,820	41.8%	29,506	42.4%
1995	762	41.6%	911,453	42.2%	19,034	42.3%	42,656	43.0%
2005	713	34.0%	503,104	28.5%	17,539	30.9%	37,253	32.0%

Sources: Korea Education Publishing Committee 1960; Ministry of Education and Human Resource Development 1960–2005.
Note: h.s. = high schools; — = not available.

Into the 1970s, vocational education shifted gear to address the manpower needed for the development of heavy-chemical industries. During this period, the problem of supplying qualified teachers and the failure to acquire the necessary facilities for practical-centered education contradicted efforts to upgrade vocational education.

Support for Vocational Education. The Act of Vocational Education Support was enacted in 1963, which held central and local governments responsible for financing vocational education. The act was considered a timely response to securing the legal basis for supporting vocational education.

During the second Five-Year Economic Development Plan (1967–71), vocational education was treated as an integral part of the education projects for economic development. According to this program, the government increased enrollment for science and engineering programs. During this period, the vocational and science education share of the Ministry of Education budget increased from 0.8 to 3 percent.

Support for Vocational and Technical Education. During the third (1972–76) and fourth (1977–81) Five-Year Economic Development Plans, the government expanded the enrollment of vocational and technical education and implemented programs for quality improvement. The following highlights the policy measures implemented to support vocational and technical education:

- Technical high schools were functionally specialized to supply the necessary skilled manpower for the development of heavy and chemical industries (1973).
- To ensure the relevance of technical education to industrial needs, internship programs were made an integral part of education programs. This system required students to work at industrial sites for a certain period of time before graduation.
- The national skill qualification system was put into effect in 1974. This certification system was introduced by the government to recognize a skill grade obtained by individuals and to improve the social status of those with skill certificates. The required financing of the technical education was supplemented by foreign loans (see the discussion of foreign assistance earlier in this chapter).

TECHNICAL-VOCATIONAL EDUCATION IN THE 1980s

Science and Technology Education Emphasized. International competitiveness in the manufacturing industry in the 1980s and problems introducing advanced technology necessitated an emphasis on science and technology education.[5] In shifting the emphasis, vocational high schools had to find a new identity in terms of their role in developing technical manpower. Various kinds of technical schools were upgraded to junior technical college level providing two to three-year technical education programs. The government increased support for science and technology education in elementary and secondary education and began to establish specialized "science high schools," The effort to develop high-level human resources in science and technology laid the cornerstone for new HRD programs such as BK 21 and NURI[6] projects in the 1990s.

The Diminishing Demand for Vocationally Trained Manpower. The technical and vocational education in high schools made a marked contribution to the economic development of Korea in the 1970s. In the 1980s, however, economic transition toward technology-intensive industries led to a decrease in demand for vocationally trained graduates from high schools, forcing vocational schools to seek a new means of survival.

Some technical high schools, for instance, specialized to meet industrial needs. Some agricultural high schools were driven to developing programs for self-managed farm householders. Commercial high schools followed suit. By and large, however, job opportunities for graduates from technical-vocational high schools (TVHS) decreased, and vocational high schools faced problems recruiting enough students to meet their enrollment capacities.

Improving the Status of Technical Postsecondary Schools. In response to the increased demand for technically trained middle-level labor, various technical postsecondary schools were upgraded to the level of junior technical college with two- and three-year programs. These junior technical colleges aimed to develop technician-level manpower, while technical high schools intended to develop skilled manpower.

The Open-Technical Colleges. A new kind of institute was established to meet the continuing education needs of those who were already working. The open-technical colleges are four-year technical education institutes for high school graduates with at least one year of experience in industry. Six open-technical colleges were established in 1982.

TECHNICAL-VOCATIONAL EDUCATION IN THE 1990s

As globalization intensified the need for Korean industries to be internationally competitive, the HRD program was reviewed. The axis of technical-vocational education shifted from the technical high schools to the junior technical colleges. Education was no longer limited to a certain period of schooling and perspectives on technical and vocational learning expanded into lifelong learning and competency development.

Structural Change of Enrollment to Technical High Schools. In the course of defining a new identity for technical high schools, the government tried to expand the enrollment of technical education in high school education to relocate the demand for higher education. Earlier vocational high schools accounted for 35.5 percent of total students in high schools, and by restructuring high school enrollment, the government hoped to increase the vocational share to 50 percent. The vocational share increased to 42.2 percent in 2002 but has since dropped to the same level as at its implementation.

The implementation of restructuring enrollment led to an expansion of technical education, but resulted in a poor quality education. To compensate for this decline in quality the "2+1 system" was introduced. The 2+1 system offered two years of instruction at school and one year of work experience in industry. The relevance of the one year work experience depended on the quality of onsite training within the industry. These two structural changes failed to reap the expected results. First, the restructuring expanded technical-vocational school enrollment at a time when its identity was not clear and the demand for graduates was decreasing. Second, the 2+1 system weakened the effectiveness of the technical high schools.

The Market Control of Junior Technical Colleges. Although junior technical colleges have displayed variety in their quality, their relevance has been continually enhanced by the market control mechanism. Graduates are evaluated by the industry, and the reputation of the program affects applications to the colleges. This mechanism has contributed to an 80 percent graduate employment rate—which exceeds the university graduate employment rate. The junior technical colleges enjoyed a higher degree of operational autonomy and pursued close college-industry cooperation. The junior technical colleges tried to tailor their programs to meet industrial needs and they provided a flexible semester system for faculty and students. The possibility to upgrade diplomas to baccalaureate degrees was an added incentive for student recruitment.

Legal Support for the Technical-Vocational Education System. The government passed two laws to support technical-vocational education. One was the Technical and Vocational Education and Training Promotion Law (TVETPL) and the other was the Skill Certification Law (SCL). The TVETPL had two components: (a) it defined the qualifications needed to get training and (b) it defined the government's responsibilities. The SCL stipulated the grading and certification systems of various levels of skills acquired. Skill certification meant that people who mastered a certain level of technical training received social recognition. The government established and funded the Korean Research Institute for Vocational Education and Training (KRIVET) to provide research and development on TVET.

THE PROBLEMS AND TASKS OF TECHNICAL-VOCATIONAL EDUCATION[7]

Perspectives on Technical-Vocation Education. Korean society has traditionally encouraged the study of humanities over mastering technical competency. This tradition-bound value had been a major impediment to the promotion of vocational education. It has been well accepted that measures are needed to improve the social and economic value of technical-vocational education.

The qualitative improvement of technical-vocational education requires sustained efforts in the broader context of lifelong learning for HRD. In recent years, a new trend has emerged among youngsters who are now seeking high-quality vocational education in institutes of world renown (Dong-a Il bo International Department 2006). High-quality vocational education seems to be an attractive alternative career development option for youngsters.

School-Industry Cooperation. Keeping technical and vocational education close to industry was supposed to ensure the relevance of technical-vocational education. The school-industry cooperation system was designed with a view toward developing custom programs to provide human resources and making the best use of the industrial facilities to develop technical competency. Policy efforts are being made to extend school-industry cooperation into the cooperative networks of the central and provincial government and to utilize schools and industries as the innovation cluster for regional development.

Identity Problems of TVHS. As Korean industries demanded better technically trained human resources; junior technical colleges became the central focus for technical-vocational education. The shifting orientation of vocational education drove the vocational high schools to the brink of crisis (Jang 1999). TVHS found it difficult to recruit students. This difficulty was related to the perception among the younger generation that vocational education offered no prospect for raising socioeconomic status. The TVHS are not highly rated by the corporate sector, resulting in a vicious circle of low prospects for good jobs, low levels of academic competency, low quality of instruction, and low quality of technical competency. This trend is illustrated by an increase in the number of TVHS graduates going on to higher education, from 6.5 percent in 1975 to 67.6 percent in 2005, the majority of them continuing in the same field of study at junior colleges.

Two Models for the Development of TVHS. The critical review of TVHS suggested two development models regarding the relevance and competitiveness of the education offered. These two models are under policy discussion. The first, the program specialization model, would make TVHS functionally specialized (Jang 1999). The technical-vocational education system of Switzerland was considered an alternative (Metzger 2005). This model would expect to develop high-level technical competence and self-learning capacities for further development. It assumes that the technical-vocational education track is a separate vocational track at the high school level, and it reflects the perspective that TVHS may have to be reinvented to adapt their programs to industry needs. Any TVHS that did not sharpen its competitive edge would be considered for conversion into an academic high school. The second model would develop a basic type of TVHS that would orient vocations and foundational courses toward the development of core technical competence and learning capabilities. This model of TVHS would offer high school education to those who do not go on to junior technical college.

DEVELOPMENT OF OCCUPATIONAL TRAINING[8]

The System of Occupational Training. In contrast to TVET, occupational training aims at developing the specific skills necessary for industrial workers to accomplish their job tasks. Such training activities are conducted outside the formal TVET system as a way to upgrade the skills of employed workers. Occupational training requires less time, but its programs are more varied in terms of clientele and content.

The Beginning of Occupational Training. Occupational training dates back to 1967 when the Law for the Promotion of Occupational Training was enacted. Upon the completion of the first Five-Year Economic Development Plan, skilled manpower development emerged as an important need to support economic development programs. In addition to TVHS, the government established public occupational training centers that largely targeted middle school graduates or high school dropouts. Upon successful implementation of the first and second Five-Year Economic Development Plans in the 1970s, occupational training was directed toward producing a labor force for the heavy and chemical industries.

The Expansion of and Stipulated Financial Contribution to Occupational Training. This expansion was a characteristic of the 1970s and was linked to the third and fourth Five-Year Economic Development Plans. During this time, the development of heavy and chemical industries was activated. Because of the Middle East construction boom in the 1970s, the economic growth rate hit a record high of 10 percent per year, resulting in a shortage of skilled workers. To address this shortage, the government's Law for the Promotion of Occupational Training obligated corporations that employed more than 500 workers to offer occupational training. If employers could not implement occupational training, the law obligated them to pay a stipulated share of occupational training costs.

Occupational training was conducted by public and private institutes. Government-led training offered programs for teacher training and skilled workers. Private institutes mainly offered on-the-job training for the employed. The government provided subsidies to private training institutes.

STREAMLINING OCCUPATIONAL TRAINING, 1980–90s

The Advent of a New Perspective. This new perspective promoted job competence of the employed and supported the efforts of the private sector. The structural change of the industry in the 1980s generated new demands for occupational training, such as the demand for multitask-performing technical competencies rather than simple skilled workers, as production patterns changed from mass production of a few products to diversified small-quantity production. As the access to secondary education expanded, the potential target group for occupational training—that is, non–high school graduates—decreased significantly. A new perspective on occupational training was needed. A new demand for specialized, high-quality occupational training emerged, which targeted on-the-job training to upgrade the competency of workers. The government policy for occupational training shifted from government-led training programs to supporting private sector–led occupational training programs. Developments under this new perspective can be summarized as follows:

- **Establishment of the Korean Occupational Training Management Corporation (KOTMC):** On behalf of the government, KOTMC was established to incorporate all public training institutes, including occupational training centers, research institutes, technical colleges, and the Korean Skill Certification Corporation. By placing them under a unitary purview, the new corporation was designed to improve the administrative and managerial efficiency of all training programs. In 1998, KOTMC was renamed the Korean Industrial Manpower Development Corporation with a structural change to strengthen its training function. The existing one-year program was diversified into programs of various durations.
- **Transition of some occupational training centers into technical colleges:** In response to the increasing demand for professional technicians, some training centers were upgraded into two-year junior technical colleges and the graduates were awarded junior technical degrees.
- **Establishment of technical education colleges:** Before 1971, the Central Occupational Training Institute offered a two-year program to train teachers in industrial technology. As industrial technology advanced, this institute was upgraded in 1992 to a Technical Education College, the equivalent of a four-year postsecondary education program. Its programs offered onsite practice with theoretical learning. Corporate employees placed a high value on graduates of this college.
- **Implementation of legislative action:** The institutionalization of employment insurance created a fund to support laid-off industrial workers with unemployment compensation and the promotion of occupational training programs. The employment insurance system was applied to companies that employed more than 70 workers. The insurance fee was set at 0.05 percent of annual salaries paid. The Law of Occupational Training, which was passed in the 1960s and obligated companies to provide occupational training, was replaced in 1997

with the Law for Promotion of Occupational Training. This law encouraged company participation in occupational training and worker initiative to participate in training programs that meet their needs. After the 1990s, the need for in-service training was greater than occupational training for unskilled workers.

A NEW PERSPECTIVE ON OCCUPATIONAL TRAINING

The Development of Job Competency with Lifelong Learning. In the earlier stage of occupational training, occupational training targeted the production of skilled workers. This pattern was changed to developing job competency from the perspective of lifelong learning and career development. Accordingly, training programs have been diversified in terms of content, method, and clientele. After the financial crisis of 1997, employer and employee appreciation for job-competency development grew. Many companies began to support lifelong learning for competency development by forming training organizations within companies.

Encouragement and support is needed to upgrade on-the-job training and, depending on the situation, a consortium of small- and medium-size companies to implement the occupational training programs may be considered as an alternative. Public financing of occupational training accounts for 40 percent of total training expenditures. In addition to funds from the employment insurance system, ways to expand the government's support for public and private occupational training are being explored.

SYNOPSIS

The defining characteristics of what may be called the "Korean approach to education development" include the following: (a) a sequential bottom-up strategy of progressively addressing the main needs of the education sector, beginning with primary education and continuing through secondary to technical-vocational education and ultimately to tertiary education; (b) a consistent emphasis on quantitative (enrollment) goals over qualitative concerns (class size and teacher-to-student ratios), but with a capacity to address education quality problems once expansion targets are largely achieved; (c) encouragement of private provision at the levels of secondary and tertiary education to complement the government's own enrollment expansion efforts; (d) an unwavering concern for egalitarian approaches to issues of socioeconomic class and geographic distribution within the education system, evidenced most notably by the decision to abolish entrance examinations for middle schools and high schools, and by the HEP; (e) stable and politically sheltered funding for primary and secondary education in the form of an earmarked 12.98 percent of tax revenues; and (f) compatibility, if not coordination, between economic and education policies.

By making education both free and compulsory, the Korean approach enabled the country to achieve universal primary enrollment within five years, universal middle school (junior secondary) enrollment 20 years later, and universal high school (senior secondary) enrollment a decade after that. A 50 percent enrollment in tertiary education was achieved by 2000. In the process, a strong role was accorded to TVET, as well as to occupational training. Schools were functionally specialized in response to industry skill needs, systematic efforts were made to improve the status of TVET in the public's eyes, relevance was enhanced through student attachment programs with industry, and a national qualifications framework was established. At the tertiary level, various financial incentive schemes steered enrollments toward science and technology and expanded applied research activities within the universities.

DEVELOPMENT OF QUALITY AND INSTITUTIONAL FACTORS

Many factors determine the quality of education. For the simplicity of explanation, they are divided into quality factors and institutional factors. The quality factors have an immediate influence on the effectiveness of the learning-instruction process, including (a) the tradeoff between quantitative and qualitative development, (b) the teacher education system, (c) the development and supply of textbooks, (d) the examination and assessment system, and (e) the role of information and communication technology (ICT). The institutional factors refer to (a) the financing of education, (b) political leadership, (c) the emerging political dynamics of stake holders, and (d) the role of foreign assistances.

QUALITY FACTORS

The Tradeoff between Quantitative Expansion and Qualitative Improvement. Competition for limited resources demands a policy choice that strikes an optimum tradeoff between quantitative expansion and qualitative improvement. Policy choices in favor of quantitative expansion over qualitative improvement were made three times in the process of expanding access to education. They were as follows:

- To realize free and compulsory education.
- To expand access to middle school education.
- To open the door to higher education after the July 30, 1980, Educational Reform.

These three instances were discussed above (see section "The Expansion of Education Opportunities and a Quantitative Growth Strategy"). The proquantity expansion policy choice followed the low-cost approach.

Low-Cost Structure for Education Expansion. The quantitative expansion of education in its earlier stage followed a low-cost approach. Under financial constraints, the low-cost approach resulted in expanding the capacities to accommodate more students. In addition to overcrowded classrooms, exceeding 60 students per classroom and requiring double classroom shifts in some urban areas, low salaries for teachers and minimum cost school operations were important components of the low-cost approach.

TEACHER-TRAINING PROGRAMS

Teacher-Training Institutes. The major teacher education institutes are teacher's colleges and colleges of education. The teacher's colleges prepare elementary school teachers and colleges of education prepare secondary school teachers. Until the 1960s, education for elementary school teachers was the responsibility of the high schools, which were upgraded to junior teacher's colleges in 1962 and to teacher's colleges offering four years of post–high school education in 1982. The colleges of education produced three times more graduates with teaching certificates than the numbers demanded.

Improving the Teacher Education Program for Elementary School Teachers. As noted in table 5.5, by 1960, the number of students in elementary and middle school education had increased by 2.7 million. From 1960 to 1980, students at both levels increased by 4 million. The sudden increase of students further aggravated the problem of recruiting qualified teachers. This period coincided with a high economic growth period that led an increasing number of teachers leaving school to favor more highly remunerated occupations. Additionally, teachers enjoyed a longer tenure until they were 65 years old. In 1998, the government reduced the retirement age from 65 years to 62 years. This caused a sudden increase in departure of teachers around 2000 (see table 5.11). The transition of teacher preparation institutes to four-year colleges occurred after enrollment levels peaked. Upgrading teacher preparation institutes and subsequently improving remuneration levels made teaching more attractive (see table 5.12).

THE DEVELOPMENT AND SUPPLY OF TEXTBOOKS

Textbook-Approval System. Textbooks provide criteria and content for a teacher's instruction and a student's learning. Within the framework of the government-promulgated curriculum, textbooks were compiled by the Ministry of Education (state-compiled textbooks) or written by individual authors subject to approval by the Ministry of Education (state-approved textbooks). Until 1980, state-compiled textbooks accounted for a larger share of textbooks published, but the share of state-approved textbooks has been increasing since then. This trend has reduced

Table 5.11   Departure Rate of Teachers
(unit: percent)

Year	Elementary school	Middle school	High school General	High school Vocational	Tertiary
1965	2.3	5.2		5.1	4.0
1970	7.0	10.8	9.8	10.3	6.1
1975	2.3	7.1	7.9	6.5	5.5
1980	3.7	9.3	8.0	9.4	2.7
1985	1.4	3.8	4.5	4.5	8.8
1990	1.7	2.7	3.5	2.8	10.7
1995	2.5	2.0	2.3	2.2	11.7
2000	7.4	6.3	5.1	5.8	3.9
2005	1.2	1.2	1.3	1.4	4.2

Source: Ministry of Education and Human Resource Development 1960–2005.
Note: Departures include teachers leaving employment because of illness, death, retirement, or voluntary resignation.

Table 5.12   International Comparison of Teacher Salaries, 1995
(US$)

Country	Elementary school teacher First year	Elementary school teacher 15 year	Middle school teacher First year	Middle school teacher 15 year
Korea	19,630	33,490	19,720	33,580
France	18,910	25,540	21,580	28,210
United States	23,430	31,630	22,930	30,460
Germany	26,820	34,070	29,450	37,060
OECD	19,140	25,910	20,260	27,660

Source: OECD 1997.
Note: OECD = Organisation for Economic Co-operation and Development.

the review and approval role of the Ministry of Education. The adoption of textbooks is consigned to the free choice of the individual schools. This trend is shown in table 5.13.

Instructional Materials. Textbooks are just one example of instructional materials. Textbooks have limited space for content and the need for other reference materials has been increasing. Commercial publishers have designed workbooks and exercise books to support textbooks, and these essential materials have dominated in the market. Internet sites provide access to additional reference materials.

UNKRA's Support for Textbooks. During the postwar period, UNKRA's financial support enabled the government to publish and provide textbooks for elementary education. Although elementary education was made compulsory, parents had to pay for textbooks and a supplementary fee for the operation of the school. The 1968 nonexamination entrance system set the stage for the extension of compulsory

Table 5.13   Number of Titles and Volumes of Published Textbooks

Year	Kindergarten No. of titles	Kindergarten No. of copies (millions)	Elementary school No of titles	Elementary school No. of copies (millions)	Middle school No. of titles	Middle school No. of copies (millions)	High school No. of titles	High school No. of copies (millions)	Special education No. of titles	Special education No. of copies (millions)	Total No. of titles	Total No. of copies (millions)
1975	—	—	91	70.6	226	20.6	957	11.4	—	—	1,074	102.6
1980	—	—	91	88.1	72	38.0	555	21.9	—	—	718	148.0
1985	—	—	71	55.8	190	35.6	1,083	24.0	—	—	1,344	115.5
1990	—	—	217	117.5	250	29.6	1,239	29.1	—	—	1,706	178.3
1995	281	0.12	155	107.2	182	34.7	770	26.2	—	—	1,388	168.4
2000	12	0,12	365	88.6	488	26.7	1,099	21.8	475	0.26	2,439	137.6
2005	12	0.21	244	100.1	761	34.4	1,458	22.3	269	0.21	2,744	157.1

Sources: Data for 1975–80 is from Daehan Printing and Publishing Company (1988); data for later years is from the National Center for Education Statistics and Information (Korea) 1985–2005 and Chong (2001).
Note: — = not available.

education to middle school education. Under this plan to extend compulsory education, the government implemented a financial support policy to free families from the burden of supplementary tuition and the cost of textbooks, starting with remote rural and fishing regions and for low-income families. This policy is part of the egalitarian policy discussed earlier in this chapter. Because of the gradual implementation of the policy, the cost of textbooks was never a serious impediment to education development.

THE EXAMINATION AND ASSESSMENT SYSTEM

Evaluation and Assessment System. Evaluation is targeted at student achievement and such an evaluation was pervasive in public education. Because these evaluations are made within the school setting, they are labeled "internal assessments." The assessment of student achievement in high schools provides data for selecting applicants to higher education. Performance evaluations of teachers and schools have been excluded from the domain of evaluation. Notably, the government's introduction of pilot performance evaluations for teachers and schools has been met with strong opposition from teacher organizations.

External Assessment of Student Achievement. In addition to the internal assessments, external institutes have conducted assessments of student achievement. External assessment is divided into domestic and overseas assessment depending on by whom it is conducted. The quality of school education has been evaluated by the Korea Institute for Curriculum and Evaluation (KICE). Only national and regional average achievement scores are open to the public, based on the fear that regional disparity in student achievement may develop into a political issue. Various teacher organizations are opposed to revealing the results in school level or regional details. Because of these limitations, the potential evaluative function of the evaluation and assessment system has not fully been utilized.

The Organisation for Economic Co-Operation and Development-coordinated PISA and TIMSS recently published international comparisons of student achievement. According to the 2000 and 2003 evaluations, Korea ranked within the top five countries. The achievement of Korean students showed characteristics of high average scores, smaller variance in the scores, and less influence of family background on the achievement. Figure 5.7 illustrates Korea's position in performance level and the impact of family background.

The Impact of the Entrance Examinations on the Quality of Public Education. Over the past 60 years of education development, Korean education has seen that entrance examinations have had a determining impact on the content and mode

Figure 5.7   Performance in Mathematics and the Impact of Socioeconomic Background

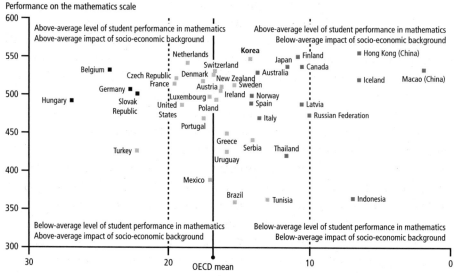

Source: OECD 2004b.
Note: The OECD mean used in this figure is the arithmetic average of all OECD countries.

of teaching and learning in public education. Exam-oriented school education has been blamed for producing fragmented and low-level knowledge development in students. The competition caused by entrance examinations encourages private tutoring, which results in the inequality of education opportunities.

This problematic situation resulted in the sequential abolition of entrance examinations to middle and high school. Tension and conflict surrounding the selection systems for admission to college and university intensified. Universities now place greater importance on high school evaluation and the performance of students in a variety of fields, rather than simply rely on the written exam scores and the national Scholastic Achievement Test (SAT) scores.

ROLE OF ICT

Education Information Support System. From the latter part of the 1990s, ICT in the Republic of Korea entered a new level of development. ICT has been widely used for school management and instructional program development. In the education sector, the education information support system made its greatest contribution to school education with the establishment of (a) the National Educational Information System (NEIS), (b) the Korean Educational Research Information Services (KERIS), (c) Web-based instruction in the classroom, (d) the EBS e-learning system, and (e) learning sites operated by private education institutes.

NEIS. The NEIS has been in operation since 2003 and unites all administrative authorities and schools under one information network. This network allows the agencies concerned to share information about students, administration, academic affairs, school management, and education financing. This system faced strong opposition from the Teachers Union in particular, however, because of the possibility of exposing the privacy of individual students. This area of public sensitivity was excluded and the system has since benefited school operations and administration through the sharing of information.

KERIS. In 1999 the government established KERIS, which is a government-supported R&D institute for education information services. KERIS developed "edunet," a Web site that provides education materials for use in the classroom. Connected to this, each provincial board of education is operating the education information center as a local center. KERIS provides information network services that link major sources of academic information for research.

EBS. The EBS television channel was established in the 1980s to broadcast education programs that are directly linked to instruction at the elementary and middle school levels. Between 1980 and 1995, as private tutoring developed into a social problem, EBS began to provide supplementary tutoring programs as alternatives to private tutoring. EBS offered these television programs as a low-cost substitute. In 2004, when private tutoring became a social program again, EBS provided supplementary programs that were connected to the Internet. This marked the beginning of a system that made ICT available nationwide. The private education sector has developed e-learning systems that offer tutoring. Mega-study is the front runner in developing e-learning systems that offer private tutoring on the Internet (see www.megastudy.net). Vocational education and training is another benefici-ary of the e-learning system. Credue's programs are gaining in popularity as well (see www.credue.com).

INSTITUTIONAL FACTORS

EDUCATIONAL FINANCING SYSTEM

Classification and Structure of Education Costs. The education financing system is a determining institutional factor for the quantitative expansion and quality improvement of education. The public cost of education is composed of two parts. One is the public cost borne by the government budget. The other is borne by the private sector in the form of tuition and fees. The private costs that households pay are excluded from the public cost of education.

The total public cost of education in 2005 accounted for 6.2 percent of GDP. Earlier, the Korean government set a goal to bring the public share up to 5 percent of GDP. The government covered 3.5 percent of this amount and the private sec-tor covered 2.7 percent. The private sector share of total costs was therefore 43 per-cent. Table 5.14 indicates the government's contribution to the total public cost of education.

The 2005 Public Expenditure. To break down expenditures by school level, ele-mentary education took the lion's share of 80 percent in the 1950s, although this share has declined and now stands at 30 percent. The same trend can be observed in secondary education, maintaining the public share at 36 percent. Meanwhile, the share of public expenditure on tertiary education has been increasing.

The Source of Education Financing. The government has paid special policy atten-tion to developing a system for securing public revenue for education. Beginning in the 1950s, the government passed a law to secure public revenue for education. The first to be instated in 1962 was the Law of Grants for Compulsory Education, accompanied by the Law of Grants for Local Education. These laws, put together, were called the Law of Grants for Financing Local Education. This law guaranteed that 12.98 percent of total domestic tax revenue would be set aside for the financ-ing of local education. After the 1974 oil shock, the government suspended the legal effects of the law to relieve the government of the heavy financial burden. In 1982, the education tax was instated to make up for the loss of education revenues by the suspension, which was effective until 1986. As it came close to expiration, the law was extended to remain effective until 1991. Later, the law was replaced by

Table 5.14   Ministry of Education Budget as a Share of GDP and Total Government Budget
(100 million won)

Year	GDP (A)	Government budget (B)	MOE budget (C)	C/A (percent)	C/B (percent)	Total public education expenditures (D)	D/A (percent)
1950	—	2	0.1	—	5.7	—	—
1955	1,131	281	26	2.3	9.3	—	—
1960	2,431	420	64	2.6	15.2	—	—
1965	7,981	947	153	1.9	16.2	—	—
1970	27,639	4,463	785	2.8	17.5	—	—
1975	103,861	15,869	2,279	2.2	14.3	—	—
1980	387,749	58,041	10,992	2.8	18.9	27,320	7.0
1985	840,610	122,524	24,923	3.0	19.9	46,000	5.5
1990	1,866,909	226,894	50,624	2.7	22.3	85,240	4.6
1995	3,988,377	548,450	124,958	3.1	22.8	192,150	4.8
2000	5,786,645	939,371	191,720	3.3	20.4	310,870	5.4
2005	8,066,219	1,343,704	279,820	3.5	20.8	495,250	6.2

Source: Compiled from various sources.
Notes: C/A = MOE budget as percent of GDP; C/B = MOE budget as percent of total government budget; D/A = total public education expenditures as percent of GDP; MOE = Ministry of Education.

Table 5.15   Sources of Revenues for the Local Education Special Account

Year	Central government Total	Local government Total	Tuition	Transferred income
1965	13,656	10,975 (80.4)	2,681 (19.6)	16.4	3.2
1970	80,989	67,354 (83.2)	13,635 (16.8)	14.3	2.5
1975	220,073	163,788 (74.4)	56,284 (25.6)	22.7	2.9
1980	1,074,163	845,271 (78.7)	228,892 (21.3)	18.9	2.4
1985	2,644,861	1,949,389 (73.7)	695,472 (26.3)	24.2	2.1
1990	5,023,490	3,797,099 (75.6)	1,226,391 (24.4)	17.7	6.7
1995	12,251,423	10,269,367 (83.8)	1,982,057 (16.2)	10.6	5.6
2000	19,318,097	14,513,794 (75.1)	4,804,304 (24.9)	19.1	5.8
2005	30,637,008	21,568,424 (70.4)	9,068,584 (29.6)	9.8	19.8

Source: Ministry of Education and Human Resource Development 1960–2005.

another called the Law of Local Educational Tax, which constituted an added revenue to fund local education.

Local Education Financing. The total revenue for local education comes from two sources. One source of revenue comes from the tax laws, and this portion constitutes 70 to 80 percent of the Ministry of Education budget. This revenue is transferred to the budget of the Provincial Board of Education as a grant. The

Table 5.16 Per Capita Expenditure on Public Education: Korea and Some OECD Countries (US$, in PPP)

Year	Level	Korea	United States	United Kingdom	Japan	Finland
1997	Elementary	3,308	5,718	3,206	5,202	4,639
	Secondary	3,518	7,230	4,609	5,917	5,065
	Higher	6,844	17,466	8,169	10,157	7,145
1999	Elementary	2,838	6,582	3,627	5,240	4,183
	Secondary	3,419	8,157	5,608	6,039	5,863
	Higher	5,356	19,220	9,554	10,278	8,114
2001	Elementary	3,714	7,560	4,415	5,771	4,708
	Secondary	5,159	8,779	5,933	6,534	6,537
	Higher	6,618	22,234	10,753	11,164	10,981

Source: Kang et al. 2005.
Note: PPP = purchasing power parity.

remaining 20 to 30 percent is revenue from tuition and fees and transferred revenue from local government. The share of the grants slipped back to 70 percent in 2005, whereas the shares of tuition and transfer from the local government were maintained at 9.8 percent and 19.8 percent, respectively.

An International Comparison of Public Expenditure on Education. As shown in table 5.16, public expenditure on education by education level in the Republic of Korea falls short of that in some OECD countries, although not by much. Table 5.16 indicates per capita public expenditure on education.

THE IMPACT OF THE EDUCATION FINANCING SYSTEM ON THE DEVELOPMENT OF EDUCATION

Revenues for Education Provided by Law. The financial resources secured by law made it possible to expand enrollment in compulsory and secondary education between 1960 and 1980. The Law of Grants for financing local education provided a steady flow of resources, at 12.98 percent of total domestic tax revenue every year. The passing of this law coincided with the takeoff stage of the series of Five-Year Economic Development Plans and it bolstered the quantitative expansion of Korean education in parallel with economic growth.

Parental Burden of Tuition and Expansion of Private Schools. Despite the increases in government support for the quantitative expansion of elementary and secondary education, the parents' tuition payment made an important contribution. It made up about 20 to 25 percent in total local education expenditure during the enrollment expansion period of 1965–85 (see table 5.15). It was possible for private schools to accommodate more students because of parental payment of tuition. Korean education owes its development in large measure to the private schools and parents willing to bear the burden of financing education.

Financial Difficulties for Higher Education. The underfinancing of higher education in the earlier stages of development was attributed to being given low priority amid the overriding policy concern to expand compulsory elementary and secondary education. The larger proportion of private universities also contributed to the lack of attention paid to financing higher education. Education investment in higher education largely depended on tuition. Any measures to increase tuition encountered persistent resistance by students.

Beginning in the 1990s, policy attention was given to research and HRD in higher education. Research grants were strong incentives to activate research and improve education quality. BK 21 was a new grant scheme to activate research and HRD in research-based universities. The NURI Project was another attempt to improve HRD at provincial universities to spur regional development.

A Higher-Cost Structure of Public Education. Beginning in 1985, a continued effort to reduce the average number of students per classroom and to upgrade the remuneration of teachers increased the public cost of education. The low-cost approach gave way to a high-cost approach. This transition heightened policy concern about how to upgrade the quality of teachers. Interestingly, reducing class size increased the per capita public cost of education more than the increased remuneration for teachers.

Figure 5.8   Teacher Remuneration, per Capita GNI, and Number of Primary Students per Class and per Teacher

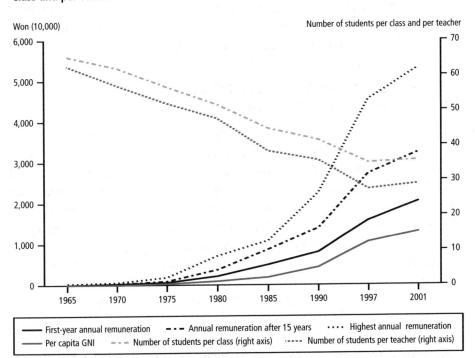

Sources: GNI per capita is from the National Statistical Office (Korea) 1965–2005; number of primary students per class is from annex table 8 in this chapter; all other data is from Lee et al. (2000).
Note: GNI = gross national income.

Table 5.17 International Comparison of Elementary School Teacher's Salary against per Capita GDP, 1996
(US$ in PPP)

Country	First-year teacher's salary (A) (minimum)	15-year teacher's salary (B) (minimum)	Teacher's highest salary (minimum)	A/ per capita GDP	B/ per capita GDP
Korea, Rep. of	23,675	42,311	67,353	1.7	3.1
Australia	19,166	34,897	34,897	0.9	1.7
France	19,474	26,298	36,409	0.9	1.3
Germany	28,384	35,885	38,703	1.3	1.7
United States	24,090	32,533	40,398	0.9	1.2
United Kingdom	19,434	29,948	29,948	1.0	1.6
Norway	17,328	21,127	21,416	0.7	0.9
Finland	17,664	23,384	24,057	0.9	1.2
OECD average	18,486	25,360	31,186	1.0	1.4

Source: Lee et al. 2000.
Note: PPP = purchasing power parity.

POLITICAL LEADERSHIP

The Political Leadership of the Late President Park Chung Hee. Political leadership has played an important role in the process of education development in the Republic of Korea. The leadership of President Park Chung Hee deserves special attention for his role in the remarkable economic growth, which, in turn, provided resources for education development. President Park is credited with improving the per capita GDP of the Republic of Korea from $82 to $10,000 in a 30-year time span. He exemplified the political leadership of the government-led economic development model. His leadership was characterized by pragmatism, coordination and consensus building, strategic concentration on key goals, and service to national interest (Oh 2006).

Education Tasks for National Goals. The national goals of President Park's government were national defense and economic development. Major education development projects were framed in the context of education's contribution to the national tasks. Special attention was made to enact laws to secure the financing of education development.

President Park was educated to teach at an elementary school as a graduate of a normal high school. His concern for education was manifested in the articulation of strategic planning for education development to support economic development. Specific policy measures implemented under his leadership are as follows:

- **Betterment of elementary school conditions:** Although the enrollment goal was achieved, school conditions for elementary education had deteriorated by maximizing enrollment. Improving conditions for elementary education was made the priority task in the education sector as part of the first Five-Year Economic Development Plan.

- **Expansion of vocational high schools:** In the context of prioritizing national security and economic development, President Park supported technical–vocational education and training. The expansion of vocational education was made an integral part of the education sector plan for economic development. He also supported vocational training in the public sector. The Office of Labor Affairs was upgraded to the Ministry of Labor Affairs to assume new tasks related to vocational training.

- **Enlarged education opportunities for working youngsters:** President Park was sympathetic to the career development of employed youngsters. He supported measures to provide learning opportunities for these youth. Administrative and financial support was made for industrial companies to establish company-attached schools or education programs, which enabled young workers to continue their education. A new "working and learning model" was developed in the 1970s.

- **Sequential extension of compulsory education to middle school education:** The Democratic Republic of Korea proclaimed in 1971 that the children in the north were enjoying 11-year compulsory education, encompassing one year of preschool education, four years of people's school, and six years in secondary education. At that time, the Republic of Korea lagged behind the Democratic Republic of Korea economically, industrially, and even in per capita income. By 1975, the Republic of Korea surpassed the Democratic Republic of Korea in these domains. The world was polarized into two ideological camps and Korea was in the dark shadow of the cold war. In confrontation with the Democratic Republic of Korea, President Park directed education policy to extend compulsory education up to middle school education after providing education free of charge in rural areas and for low-income families.

- **Views against increasing the enrollment of higher education:** The expansion of enrollment in higher education was considered in the context of its link to manpower needs. Some feared that the open-door policy would result in an unemployed surplus of higher education graduates, which might lead to political instability. Park's government was characterized by strict control, a major impediment to the expansion of higher education. It was after his demise that the doors to universities were opened by the July 30 Educational Reform in 1980.

Government-Funded R&D Institutes. President Park appreciated the need for national think tanks for national development. From the latter part of the 1960s, the government began to establish national R&D institutes. The Korea Institute of

Table 5.18. Education-Related R&D Institutes

R&D institute	Web site
KIST (Korea Institute of Science and Technology)	http://www.kist.re.kr
KDI (Korea Development Institute)	http://www.kdi.re.kr
KEDI (Korean Educational Development Institute)	http://www.kedi.re.kr
KICE (Korea Institute for Curriculum and Evaluation)	http://www.kice.re.kr
KRIVET (Korea Research Institute for Vocational Education and Training)	http://www.krivet.re.kr
KERIS (Korea Education Research Information Service)	http://www.keris.or.kr

Source: Author's compilation.

Science and Technology (KIST) was established in 1964. Then, KDI and the Korean Educational Development Institute (KEDI) followed. The number of R&D institutes increased to 43, and these institutes have played important roles. The German Max Plank Institute stands as a reminder of the pioneering role these institutes played in R&D. The 1990s witnessed the establishment of another three major education-related R&D institutes: KICE, KRIVET, and KERIS. KICE, as its name suggests, is responsible for curriculum development and evaluation of student achievement. The National Test of Academic Achievement, which is responsible for entrance to universities and is the Korean equivalent of the SAT in the United States, was developed by KICE. KRIVET engages in R&D related to the development of occupational skills and HRD. KERIS develops education information support systems. Each of these organizations has played an important role in the improvement and development of Korean education.

EMERGING POLITICAL DYNAMICS

Political Impact of Nongovernmental Organizations (NGOs) and Teacher Organizations. NGOs and teacher organizations grew in number and began to affect policy choice and implementation in various ways. The Korea Federation of Teachers Associations (KFTA) was the first to come into being to promote teacher's rights and professionalism. The Teachers Union was formed more recently. The wind of political democratization that gained political power in the 1980s stimulated a segment of teachers to organize a union illegally. In August 1989, 1,500 teachers were fired for their participation in the allegedly illegal organization. Ten years later, the Teachers Union was granted legal approval as a legitimate organization.

Veto Power Group. The Teachers Union has consistently opposed government policies to upgrade the quality of education. Although government policy initiatives are undertaken, their implementation is often hampered by the Union's persistent resistance to these policies (for example, the NEIS) on the grounds that it invades the privacy of individual learners. Nor has the Union's opposition been limited to education issues. Its public education activities for its members are ideologically inclined in favor of the Democratic Republic of Korea. To obtain consent in the process of negotiation, the government has more often than not made concessions to reach compromises with the Teachers Union. It appears that the Teachers Union has found its raison d'etre as a veto power group.

Public Skepticism on the Political Line of the Teachers Union. At the outset, the Teachers Union used the catchwords "for true education," "education democratization," and "teacher-directed innovations." In the process of fighting for these causes, these teachers have shown a posture of standing for the sake of opposing the government. Furthermore, they opposed the evaluation of teacher performance and schools and the idea of differentiated instruction of learners. Their opposition was not limited to education issues: education programs for its constituents were ideologically inclined in favor of the Democratic Republic of Korea. Their positions regarding national defense, north-south relationships, and the Korea-United States Free Trade Agreement attested to their anti-American posture. The public is increasingly skeptical of the Teachers Union's ideologically driven posture.

ROLE OF FOREIGN ASSISTANCE

In the process of education development in the Republic of Korea, foreign assistance has made an enormous contribution. While the Korean War was raging, Korean education was highly dependent on foreign assistance, predominantly in the form of grant-in-aid, which consisted largely of U.N. and U.S. donations. Starting in the 1960s, education loans replaced grant-in-aid.

Table 5.19. Foreign Assistance in the Postliberation Period
(US$ millions)

Assistance name	Period	Total assistance
Government Appropriation for Relief in Occupied Area (GARIOA)	1945–48	409.3
OFIC	1947	24.9
Assistance by Economic Cooperation Act (ECA)	1949–53	201.8
Civil Relief in Korea (CRIK)	1950–56	457.3
Assistance by U.S Public Law 480 (PL480)	1955–58	269.9
Loan by Development Loan Fund (DLF)	1957	18.8
United Nations Korea Reconstruction Agency (UNKRA)	1951–60	122.8

Source: Korea Education Publishing Committee (1960) and Kim et al. (1996).

Table 5.20 Foreign Loans and Donors
(US$ thousands)

Donor	Total loan	Ratio
Export Import Bank of the United States (EXIM)	98,685	9.2
Export Credits Guarantee Department (ECGD)	34,967	3.3
Asian Development Bank (ADB)	57,538	5.4
Overseas Economic Cooperation Fund (OECF)	251,584	23.5
International Development Association of the World Bank (IDA)	35,005	3.3
International Bank for Reconstruction and Development (World Bank) (IBRD)	592,112	55.3
Total	1,069,891	100.0

Source: Han 2001b.

Education Loans (Han 2001a). To make up for the underfinancing of education development, the government sought foreign loans totaling US$1 billion during the period of 1969–99 to finance 21 projects. The flow of education loans came to an end in 1999. The major donors of foreign assistance were the International Development Association (IDA), the International Bank for Reconstruction and Development (IBRD), the Overseas Economic Cooperation Fund (OECF), the Asian Development Bank (ADB), the Export Credits Guarantee Department (ECGD), and the Export Import Bank of the United States (EXIM). As noted in table 5.20, some 80 percent of total foreign loans came from IBRD and OECF.

IBRD and IDA Loans. For 30 years from 1969 to 1999, 11 foreign loans were brought into the Republic of Korea. The foreign loans were channeled to support the vocational high schools and junior technical colleges to expand their shop and lab facilities, teacher training, research projects, development of skilled manpower, and basic science. The foreign loans reflect the time-specific needs for education development. The fact that 80 percent of the total education loan was intended for costly lab and shop equipment attests to the utility of these resources for lab and shop participants. Most people in the country have a positive view about the impact of foreign loans.

Because of economic growth and since the Republic of Korea has become a member of OECD, loans from the World Bank are no longer anticipated. The Republic of Korea has matured to the point that it can consider ways, based on its own experience, to contribute its resources and experiences to other transitional countries.

SYNOPSIS

As near universal enrollment was successively achieved at the various levels of education, the government increasingly turned its attention to festering issues of quality. The emphasis on expansion had forced compromises in education quality, which took the form of large class sizes, double classroom shifts, low teacher salaries, and limited operational expenses. These were addressed in turn. As the economy grew, teacher remuneration was progressively improved. Teacher quality was upgraded by raising teacher qualifications from a high school diploma to a college diploma and then to a university degree. The supply and range of textbooks and learning materials steadily expanded, which was achieved in part by setting standards for commercial publishers and enabling them to augment the Ministry of Education's own publication capacities. In recent years, emphasis has been placed on the use of ICT for both institutional management and instructional learning.

Procedures for monitoring learning achievements were progressively introduced. These first took place through in-school examinations, but they were later complemented by national examinations administered by KICE and then international examinations coordinated by the OECD (PISA and TIMSS). Notably, Korea now scores in the top five countries on these tests.

At the same time, institutional capacities were constructed to support and guide the education system. Stable and predictable sector financing arrangements were introduced in the form of a law requiring 12.98 percent of tax revenues to be used for primary and secondary education. Strong political commitment and leadership were demonstrated at the highest level. A series of government-funded R&D institutes (now numbering 43) were established to attract diaspora scholars in support of regional and national development. KICE monitored student achievement and maintained curriculum relevance. KRIVET provided targeted support to the technical education subsector. KERIS promoted the expansion and integration of ICT capabilities, including the creation of "edunet" for Web-based learning. As Korea continued to develop, civil society organizations appeared to represent particular stakeholder interests (for example, KFTA and the Teachers Union).

Foreign development assistance was employed by the Korean government to accelerate the process of education development. To augment the government's financial resources for education, a total of US$1 billion was borrowed over the 1969–99 period. These resources were used for capital investments, mainly in the TVET subsector, for workshops, laboratories, equipment, teacher training, applied research, and science education.

NEW CHALLENGES AND EMERGING ISSUES

NEW APPROACHES TO QUALITY EDUCATION: INCONGRUENT MATCH IN THE 1990s

New Challenges for Democracy and Quality in Education. The 1980s brought new challenges for Korean education. The voice for education democracy found its manifestation in the autonomy of local education. That is, departure from the control of the central authorities. Cries for improvement in the quality of education were heard louder. These voices called for a radically different approach from the one adopted for quantitative development.

Limits of the Approach to Quantitative Expansion. New challenges rendered the characteristic elements of the approach to quantitative expansion obsolete. First, the low-cost approach was replaced by a high-cost approach. Second, the enrollment expansion reached its peak in secondary and higher education. The quantitative expansion no longer held valid and attention refocused on the relevance of education and the autonomy of operation. Third, the egalitarian concern for education was translated into policy measures aimed to reduce individual, regional, and class gaps in access to quality education. Socially and economically deprived people and regions were given priority in access to quality education. The relevance of education and accountability of school education emerged as important concerns. In this context, the relevance of HEP has been questioned. Private tutoring seemed to have the most negative impact on the egalitarian concerns. These questions and concerns suggest the need for an alternative approach. Fourth, the administrative system, which had supported the quantitative expansion of education, is expected to be incompatible with new requirements that favor the diversification of education programs and the quality of education.

New Approach to Quality Education. Confronted with these new challenges, it is not easy to establish a viable system to support the qualitative improvement of education. Since the 1990s, a variety of approaches have been attempted. They are as follows:

- **Presidential Council for Educational Reform:** Since the promulgation of the 30 July Educational Reform in 1980, the PCER has been in operation to discuss education problems with wider participation and expertise. By virtue of its direct link to the president, this model appeared to be effective in winning presidential support and giving a powerful drive for the implementation of reform proposals. In 1995, "The Framework for New Educational Systems" was adopted as the basic guideline for education reform. It presented a new education system model for moving toward becoming a knowledge-based society. The education reforms framework continued to hold true by providing a blue print for further education development under the succeeding governments of Kim Dae Jung and Roh Moo Hyun (Seo 2002). The rhetoric of education reform seemed to remain. However, the coherence of the reform and strategies are not sufficiently clear to make a difference.
- **Administrative model for quality education:** Since the 1990s, various kinds of evaluation models have been applied to the evaluation of education programs. Universities, provincial boards of education, and schools are evaluated by the administrative authority. These bodies formed an evaluation committee, which

assesses the data and processes against the arbitrarily established criteria. This practice is to provide an administrative evaluation and control model. The administrative system should be built with an evaluation mechanism that continually monitors the outcomes and feeds information into the input process.

- **Keeping the egalitarian model:** The egalitarian model considers the equality of education opportunities as its most important policy goal. It considers the effects of family background on the competition to enter selective schools or universities as a major hindrance to the equality of education opportunities. Therefore, the egalitarian policy orientation does not favor quality differences among schools and competition, and efforts including private tutoring. Public opinion seems to be evenly divided on these issues. The government has maintained a pro-egalitarian policy. In this context, the HEP has survived since its implementation in 1974.

Korean parents find themselves engaged in "a game of crimes" (Lee 2003). Education in Korea does not provide hope for the future; rather it heralds a painful burden (Hahn 2003) to be shouldered whether one wants it or not. In policy formulation, any measure that would lead to the revival of private education is something to be guarded against by all means. Built against this warning, the government laid out a plan to normalize public education in a way that will progressively reduce the cost of private education (Ministry of Education and Human Resource Development 2002). The possibility of intensifying private tutoring becomes a policy criterion to evaluate the relevance and effectiveness of any education policy.

EMERGING CHALLENGES

The previous section highlighted the incongruent match between the new challenges and responses to them. Korean education seems to be facing new challenges presented by globalization and efforts to become a knowledge-based society.

New Challenges to HRD. The twenty-first century confronts Korean education with a host of new challenges, calling for a change in approach. Korean education has to prepare students with different skill sets so that they can perform well in the emerging knowledge-based society and global economy (World Bank 2000c). Politically, the sustained confrontation between the North and South has blurred the national identity. In this vein, civic education is receiving special attention for its potential contribution. The political and economic identities of Koreans are premised on liberal democracy and the market economy, as stipulated by the Constitution. The Republic of Korea is a sovereign state built on the philosophical ideals that respects human dignity and individual freedom and creativity based on good-will competition (Kim 1998). Socially, a low birth rate and larger proportion of elderly among the population add new dimensions to be grappled with in policy articulation (Park 2005). These issues all suggest new roles and responsibilities for education in HRD, and do so in a way that improves the nation's global competitiveness.

Quality Improvement of Korean Education. The above challenges require us to consider four tasks in the Korean context:

- **Relevance:** In the first 25 years, education development was made through quantitative expansion. The quality dimension of Korean education is now the domain in which special efforts have to be made. The relevance of education is improved by education programs being varied enough to complement different types of learners. Quality education, therefore, means to "provide access to a meaningful and suitable education" and is accompanied by the development of diversified programs that allow individual learners to choose their own level and pace. The quality of education, comparable to an attribute by its nature, requires the function of "caring" (Beck 1994) and the improvement of education conditions. In terms of class size, Korean education has been approaching the OECD level. Now, what remains to be done is to improve the quality of education with diversity, choices, and caring.

- **Monitoring results:** The results of education may be measured against the achievement indexes. Monitoring results is an important function. As discussed in the section on examination and assessment systems in "quality factors" earlier in this chapter, a consistent monitoring system of the education results has yet to be established (Lee 2006b).

- **Search for a new management system:** What management system would be appropriate for quality management? The bureaucratic control model used for quantitative expansion has shown its limitation for quality control. New attention is given to the model of allowing schools to have more autonomy and accountability. Along these lines, discussion is under way to introduce a market control model that incorporates the choices by parents and students of education programs (World Bank 2000c).

- **Innovations in teacher training and the appointment system (Ministry of Education and Human Resource Development 2008):** Teacher training and the appointment and promotion system of teachers are other factors behind the quality of education. As school conditions and the remuneration of teachers have continually improved, the cost of public education has increased. An appointment and promotion system is needed to bring about more effective teaching. The government has conducted studies into a better system, but its efforts have been met by opposition. The Teachers Union, in particular, appeared to have a strong influence on the process of decision making related to the public concern for education quality development. The public hearings to discuss the policy issues were made difficult by their persistent refusal to participate.

Reliance on Private Tutoring. Korean parents feel as though they are forced into paying for private tutoring. Private tutoring is considered the most important factor in gaining entrance to higher education (Lee 2004b). Student achievement is found to be seriously affected by the amount of exposure to private tutoring. Thus, the financial ability of parents has a profound impact on the education opportunities for students. In selecting applicants for admission to university, most universities consider (a) high school academic achievement with the school's recommendation, (b) the scores made in the National Examination (the Korean version of the SAT), and (c) entrance essays and interviews held by the universities. Any effort to improve the university admission systems must consider reducing the impact of private tutoring associated with overheated competition. The policy needs to be formed between two policy spectrums: (a) the random assignment model based on the high school records and (b) the selection of applicants based on test scores without paying attention to the effects of private tutoring. A successful model to intensify private tutoring or select the right candidates in accordance with the purpose of the university has not emerged.

Restructuring Higher Education. Since the 1990s, higher education in the Republic of Korea has faced new challenges. The first challenge comes from the need to develop high-caliber professionals who are viable in the knowledge-based society and to improve research capacities that can keep up with the rapidly advancing frontiers of science and technology. The industrial needs for science and technology development saddles the universities with another role as R&D centers. The institutes of higher education in the Republic of Korea have already been drawn into competition one way or another at home and abroad. This requires the universities to develop high-level human resources. BK 21 and NURI are direct responses to this need to activate government support for research into high technology and represent an innovative role for the regional communities. These programs were an open invitation for higher education institutes to competitively bid for financial support for their research proposals. These higher education institutes have to develop themselves more competitively in research capabilities and HRD. This task requires the institutes to reorganize their academic and research programs and the government to restructure higher education continually (Lee 2005).

The Politics of Teacher Unions and NGOs in Policy Formulation. Teachers unions and NGOs have increased in number and have a strong influence on the process of policy formulation. On many occasions, the government has found itself torn between the Teachers Union and other NGOs, including parental groups. These two camps are often in conflict on key education issues. Of all the groups, the Teachers Union appears to be a formidable power group opposed to the government. The government keeps the channel of communication open and provides for the process of negotiation to strike compromises. Confronted by this strong opposition group, the government has often failed to reap the benefits of negotiation. From inception, the Teachers Union has advocated "true education" (or authentic education), education democratization, and teacher-led innovations. Its stance against the NEIS, on the grounds that it may intervene with the private domain of individual learners, became particularly notorious.

Public Opposition to the Teachers Union. In reaction to the persistent stance of the Teachers Union against all government-led innovations, various parental groups have emerged to oppose this union. There was widespread apprehension among the populace about "the conscious education," because this was taken to reflect an ideological proclivity in favor of the Democratic Republic of Korea against the United States. Amid the political movement toward education democratization, the Teachers Union attempted to take full advantage of a leadership hiatus and grasp full control of the decision-making process. Their concerns have been not so much for the reform of the present system but toward one that would benefit the welfare of its members. In the recent election of board members to the provincial board of education, most candidates who were nominated by the Teachers Union failed to get elected. The time is coming to develop more mature politics of education that might lead to reasonable policy discussion and decision making based on wider participation and negotiation.

CONCLUSION

Korean education has achieved remarkable success in terms of quantitative expansion and qualitative improvement. Compulsory education was universally implemented sequentially from elementary education to secondary education and then to tertiary education. The qualitative improvement of schools followed. Education development contributed to economic growth through timely expansion of enrollment in response to emerging manpower needs.

The new millennium brought new challenges to Korean education, namely, those of quality improvement and increasing competitiveness in the global environment. These challenges are not limited to Korean education and are drawing global attention. Based on past experience, Koreans are drawing up a new education road map and fresh strategies to cope with the new challenges.

The qualitative attributes of education need to be made more relevant through greater diversity in education programs supported by better education conditions and qualified teachers. We are looking for a kind of "ecology of education" that will allow individual students and education institutes to define their identity and grow. This ecology of education will enable education to maximize individual potential. Korean education has passed the threshold of low-cost structure and is now a high-cost structure. With more resources put toward education, education productivity becomes a matter of priority concern. These concerns direct our attention to a new evaluation scheme that places a greater emphasis on the assessment of education results in terms of their relevance to the needs of potential users.

Education is no longer the sole responsibility of the schools. Education is a concerted effort that necessarily involves schools, universities, industry, local community people, and local government. We need to develop education communities that respect the administrative autonomy that draws on local initiatives, creativity, and accountability.

In dealing with private tutoring and possible improvements of university admission selection systems, past experience indicates the need to ensure that universities and high schools cooperate with each other and break loose from the vicious cycle of competitive examinations and reliance on private tutoring. We can find such a model in the project of the "KEDI Eight Years Study" (Chung et al. 2004).

NOTES

1. This section draws on Oh (1964) and Korean Education Publishing Committee (1960).

2. The province is the largest local government unit, which is similar to a state government in the United States.

3. By this, it is understood that admissions were linked to graduation numbers, and then set at a level 30 percent above these.

4. Junior technical college is a two- to three-year college-level technical education institute that follows high school education. The open-technical university is a four-year adult technical education institute for those who are employed.

5. Technology education means higher-level technical education at a postsecondary-level educational institute.

6. BK 21 is a government-supported grants project for graduate education in research universities. NURI is a government-supported grants project for graduate programs in universities located in the provinces.

7. This section draws on Jung (2006).

8. This section draws on Chung (2006).

ANNEX: STATISTICAL TABLES AND FIGURES

Table A5.1 Quantitative Growth of Elementary Schools, 1945–2005

Year	Elementary school			
	Schools	Students	Classes	Teachers
1945	3,037	1,372,883	25,315	13,064
1950	3,942	2,658,420	—	47,248
1955	4,205	2,947,436	47,020	47,020
1960	4,496	3,621,269	—	61,749
1965	5,125	4,941,345	75,603	79,164
1970	5,961	5,749,301	92,596	101,095
1975	6,367	5,599,074	98,684	108,126
1980	6,487	5,658,002	109,855	119,064
1985	6,519	4,856,752	108,753	126,785
1990	6,335	4,868,520	117,538	136,800
1995	5,772	3,905,163	107,183	138,369
2000	5,267	4,019,991	112,437	140,000
2005	5,646	4,022,801	126,326	160,143

Source: Korea Education Publishing Committee 1960 and Ministry of Education and Human Resource Development, 1960–2005.
Note: — = not available.

Table A5.2 Quantitative Growth of Middle Schools, 1945–2005

Year	Middle school			
	Schools	Students	Classes	Teachers
1945	297	79,846	—	1,225
1950	395	380,829	—	9,100
1955	949	480,295	7,554	10,594
1960	1,053	528,593	—	13,053
1965	1,208	751,341	12,374	19,067
1970	1,608	1,318,808	21,253	31,207
1975	1,967	2,026,823	31,441	46,917
1980	2,100	2,471,997	37,741	54,858
1985	2,371	2,782,173	45,082	69,553
1990	2,474	2,275,751	45,310	89,719
1995	2,683	2,481,848	51,523	99,931
2000	2,731	1,860,539	48,946	92,589
2005	2,935	2,010,704	56,968	103,835

Source: Korea Education Publishing Committee 1960 and Ministry of Education and Human Resource Development, 1960–2005.
Note: — = not available.

Table A5.3   Quantitative Growth of High Schools, 1945–2005

Year	High school Schools	Students	Classes	Teachers
1945	—	—	—	—
1950	279	130,000	—	2,269
1955	578	267,915	3,953	7,049
1960	645	273,434	—	10,022
1965	701	426,531	7,473	14,108
1970	889	590,382	10,150	19,854
1975	1,152	1,123,017	19,167	35,755
1980	1,353	1,696,792	28,392	50,948
1985	1,602	2,152,802	37,808	69,546
1990	1,683	2,283,806	43,233	92,683
1995	1,830	2,157,880	45,003	99,067
2000	1,957	2,071,468	48,694	104,351
2005	2,095	1,762,896	56,795	116,411

Source: Korea Education Publishing Committee 1960 and Ministry of Education and Human Resource Development, 1960–2005.
Note: — = not available.

Table A5.4   Quantitative Growth of Tertiary Education, 1945–2005

Year	Tertiary education[a] Schools	Students	Teachers
1945	21	5,260	628
1950	55	11,358	1,100
1955	74	84,996	2,626
1960	85	101,041	3,803
1965	199	141,636	8,609
1970	206	177,996	9,265
1975	198	238,719	11,416
1980	357	601,989	20,900
1985	456	1,277,825	33,895
1990	556	1,490,809	41,920
1995	327	2,343,984	58,977
2000	372	3,363,549	56,903
2005	419	3,548,728	66,862

Source: Korea Education Publishing Committee 1960 and Ministry of Education and Human Resource Development, 1960–2005.
Note: — = not available.
a. Tertiary Education = College, Teacher's College, University, Graduate School, Air and Correspondence University, Industrial University, and miscellaneous schools.

Table A5.5   Quantitative Growth of General and Vocational High Schools, 1945–2005

Year	General high				Vocational high			
	Schools	Students	Classes	Teachers	Schools	Students	Classes	Teachers
1952	166	59,448	1,707	1,428	160 (49%)	64,206 (52%)	1,390 (45%)	1,827 (56%)
1955	311	101,251	2,096	3,672	249 (44%)	98,452 (49%)	1,857 (47%)	2,997 (45%)
1962	338	199,352	3,371	6,315	283 (45%)	124,341 (38%)	2,430 (42%)	4,750 (43%)
1965	389	254,095	4,248	7,894	312 (44%)	172,436 (40%)	3,225 (42%)	6,214 (44%)
1970	408	315,367	5,251	9,845	481 (54%)	275,015 (46%)	4,899 (48%)	10,009 (50%)
1975	673	648,149	10,840	20,415	479 (41%)	474,868 (42%)	8,327 (43%)	15,340 (43%)
1980	749	932,605	15,533	27,480	606 (45%)	764,187 (45%)	12,815 (45%)	23,468 (46%)
1985	967	1,266,840	21,850	40,040	635 (40%)	885,962 (41%)	15,820 (42%)	29,506 (42%)
1990	1,096	1,473,155	27,496	58,074	587 (35%)	810,651 (35%)	15,737 (36%)	34,609 (37%)
1995	1,068	1,246,427	25,969	56,411	762 (42%)	911,453 (42%)	19,034 (42%)	42,656 (46%)
2000	1,193	1,324,482	30,416	63,374	764 (39%)	746,986 (36%)	18,278 (37%)	40,977 (39%)
2005	1,382	1,259,792	39,436	79,158	713 (34%)	503,104 (28%)	17,539 (30%)	37,253 (32%)

Sources: Korea Education Publishing Committee 1960; Kim et al. 1996; and National Statistical Office (Korea) 1965–2005.

Table A5.6   Changing Trends in the Number of Students, 1945–2005
(person)

Year	Elementary	Middle	General high	Vocational high	High school	Tertiary[a]
1945	1,372,883	80,828	50,343	24,942	75,285	7,819
1950	2,658,420	380,829	—	—	130,000	11,358
1955	2,947,436	480,295	141,702	112,009	253,711	78,649
1960	3,621,269	528,593	—	—	273,434	101,041
1965	4,941,345	751,341	254,095	172,436	426,531	141,636
1970	5,749,301	1,318,808	315,367	275,015	590,382	177,996
1975	5,599,074	2,026,823	648,149	474,868	1,123,017	318,683
1980	5,658,002	2,471,997	932,605	764,187	1,696,792	601,989
1985	4,856,752	2,782,173	1,266,840	885,962	2,152,802	1,451,294
1990	4,868,520	2,275,751	1,473,155	810,651	2,283,806	1,490,809
1995	3,905,163	2,481,848	1,246,427	911,453	2,157,880	2,343,894
2000	4,019,991	1,860,539	1,324,482	746,986	2,071,486	3,134,112
2005	4,022,801	2,010,704	1,259,792	503,104	1,762,896	3,548,728

Sources: Korea Education Publishing Committee 1960 and National Statistical Office (Korea) 1965–2005.
Note: — = not available.
a. Tertiary = College, Teacher's College, University, Graduate School, Air and Correspondence University, Industrial University, and miscellaneous schools.

Figure A5.1 Trends in Number of Students by Level of Education, 1945–2005

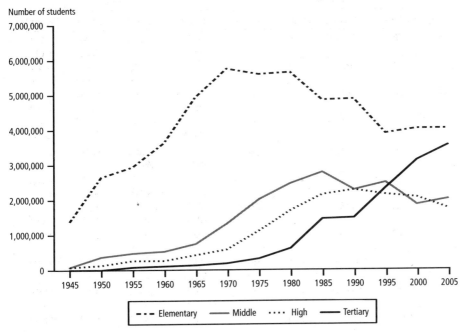

Number of students

Sources: Calculated from data in table A5.6 of this chapter (Ministry of Education [Korea] 1980, Research of Korean Educational Policy 1953–65, and National Statistical Office [Korea] 1965–2005).

Table A5.7 Changing Trend in Number of Teachers, 1945–2005
(person)

Year	Elementary	Middle	General high	Vocational high	Total high	Tertiary
1945	13,064	1,225	1,810	1,057	2,867	1,490
1950	47,248	9,100	—	—	2,269	1,100
1955	47,020	10,594	3,672	2,997	6,669	2,626
1960	61,749	13,053	—	—	10,022	3,803
1965	79,164	19,067	7,894	6,214	14,108	6,966
1970	101,095	31,207	9,845	10,009	19,854	9,265
1975	108,126	46,917	20,415	15,340	35,755	13,981
1980	119,064	54,858	27,480	23,468	50,948	20,900
1985	126,785	69,553	40,040	29,506	69,546	33,895
1990	136,800	89,719	58,074	34,609	92,683	41,920
1995	138,369	99,631	56,411	42,656	99,067	58,977
2000	140,000	92,589	63,374	40,977	104,351	56,780
2005	160,143	103,835	79,158	37,253	116,411	66,520

Sources: Korea Education Publishing Committee 1960 and National Statistical Office (Korea) 1965–2005.
Note: — = not available.

Figure A5.2   Trends in Number of Teachers by Level of Education, 1945–2005

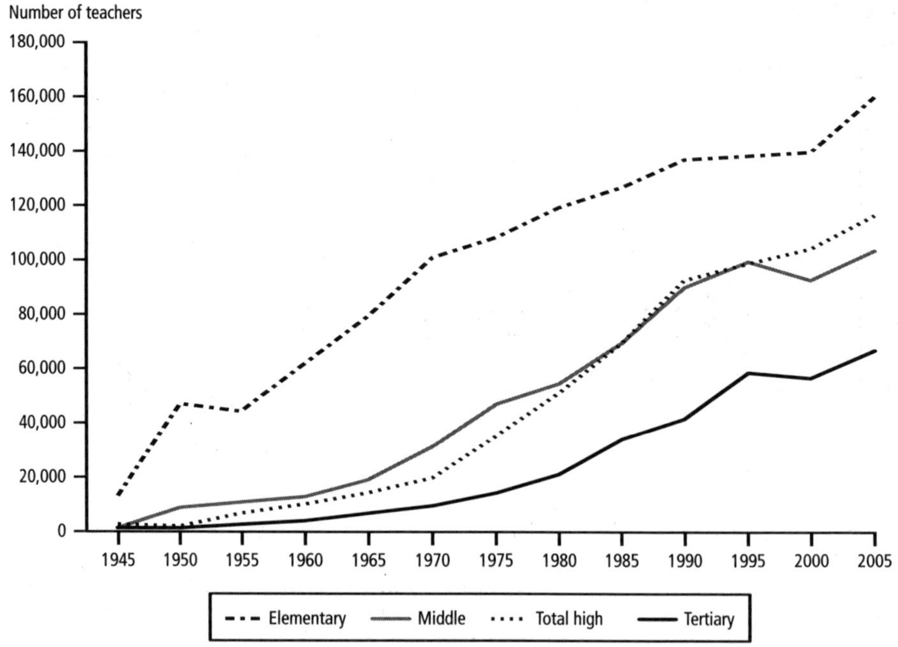

Number of teachers

Source: Calculated from data in table A5.7 of this chapter (Kim 1989).

Table A5.8   Number of Students per Class, 1945–2005
(a person)

Year	Elementary	Middle	General high	Vocational high
1945	54.2	—	—	—
1952	126.2	83.2	34.8	46.2
1955	62.7	62.9	67.6	60.3
1962	62.9	60.1	59.1	51.1
1965	65.4	60.7	59.8	53.4
1970	62.1	62.1	60.1	56.1
1975	56.7	64.5	59.8	57.0
1980	51.5	65.5	59.9	59.6
1985	44.7	61.7	58.0	55.5
1990	41.4	50.2	53.6	51.5
1995	36.4	48.2	48.0	47.9
2000	35.8	38.0	44.1	40.3
2005	31.8	35.3	33.9	30.0

Note: — = not available.

Figure A5.3 Trends in Number of Students per Class by Level of Education, 1945–2005

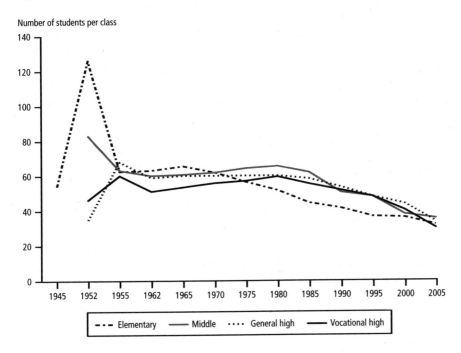

Table A5.9 Number of Students per Teacher, 1945–2005
(a person)

Year	Elementary	Middle	General high	Vocational high
1945	105.0	68.1	27.8	23.5
1952	66.5	41.2	41.6	35.1
1955	62.7	44.8	38.5	29.9
1962	60.0	40.5	31.5	26.2
1965	65.4	39.4	32.1	20.3
1970	56.9	42.3	32.0	27.5
1975	51.8	43.2	31.4	22.7
1980	47.5	45.1	33.9	32.6
1985	38.3	40.0	31.0	30.0
1990	35.6	25.4	25.4	23.4
1995	28.2	24.8	21.8	21.3
2000	28.7	20.1	20.9	18.2
2005	25.1	19.3	15.9	13.5

Source: Calculated on basis of tables A5.6 and A5.7.

Figure A5.4 Number of Students per Teacher, 1945–2005

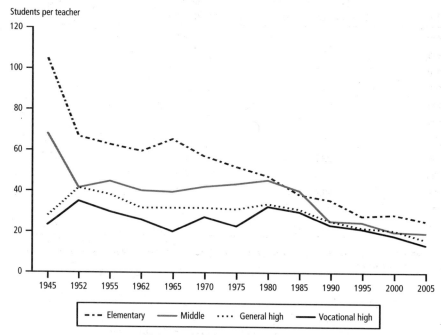

Source: Calculated from data in table A5.9 of this chapter (Song 2003).

Table A5.10 Enrollment Rates of Each School Level, 1945–2005

Year	Elementary	Middle	High	Tertiary
1945	64.0	—	—	—
1951	69.8	—	—	—
1955	89.5	28.9	17.3	5.0
1960	95.3	32.2	20.0	6.4
1965	95.1	39.4	27.0	6.9
1970	97.0	53.3	29.3	9.2
1975	97.8	74.0	40.5	9.3
1980	97.7	73.3	48.8	11.1
1985	99.0	82.0	64.2	22.6
1990	100.5	91.6	79.4	22.9
1995	98.5	93.5	82.9	35.9
2000	97.2	95.0	89.4	50.2
2005	98.8	94.3	92.2	62.3

Sources: Ministry of Education (Korea) 1980, Research of Korean Educational Policy 1953–65, and National Statistical Office (Korea) 1965–2005.
Note: — = not available.

Table A5.11   Ratio of Students Entering Upper Level Education, 1950–2005

Year	Elementary (advance to middle)	Middle (middle to high)	High (high to tertiary)
1950	26.1	64.5	—
1955	42.8	83.7	—
1960	39.7	75.9	—
1965	54.3	69.1	—
1970	66.0	70.1	—
1975	77.2	74.7	—
1980	96.8	84.5	23.7
1985	99.2	90.7	36.4
1990	99.8	95.7	33.2
1995	99.9	98.5	51.4
2000	99.9	99.6	68.0
2005	99.9	99.7	82.1

Sources: Ministry of Education (Korea) 1980, 384; and National Statistical Office (Korea) 1965–2005.
Note: — = not available.

Table A5.12   Dropout Ratio of Teachers at Each School Level, 1965–2005
(percent)

Year	Elementary school	Middle school	High school General	High school Vocational	Tertiary
1965	2.3	5.2	5.1		4.0
1970	7.0	10.8	9.8	10.3	6.1
1975	2.3	7.1	7.9	6.5	5.5
1980	3.7	9.3	8.0	9.4	2.7
1985	1.4	3.8	4.5	4.5	8.8
1990	1.7	2.7	3.5	2.8	10.7
1995	2.5	2.0	2.3	2.2	11.7
2000	7.4	6.3	5.1	5.8	3.9
2005	1.2	1.2	1.3	1.4	4.2

Source: Ministry of Education and Human Resource Development 1960–2005.
Note: Dropout rate = the number of resignations this year/total number of teachers last year × 100. Resignation includes sickness, death, retirement, marriage, discipline, voluntary resignations, and change of occupation.

Table A5.13 Teacher Wage Comparison with Principal Countries, 1998–2004
(indicated in purchasing power parity)

A5.13a Entrance Wage of Elementary School Teachers
(US$)

Year	Korea	Germany	United States	United Kingdom	Italy	Japan	France	Finland
1998	24,150	28,564	25,165	22,393	19,444	21,899	20,080	19,983
1999	23,759	29,679	25,707	19,999	19,188	—	19,761	18,110
2000	26,300	31,213	27,631	22,428	20,927	22,670	20,199	18,489
2001	25,177	38,412	28,681	23,297	23,537	22,800	21,702	19,835
2002	26,983	36,934	29,513	25,403	22,915	23,493	22,688	26,647
2003	27,214	38,216	30,339	28,608	23,751	24,514	23,106	27,023
2004	28,569	37,718	32,703	—	23,753	24,469	23,112	27,922

Source: Kang 2006.
Note: — = not available.

A5.13b Entrance Wage of Middle School Teachers
(US$)

Year	Korea	Germany	United States	United Kingdom	Italy	Japan	France	Finland
1998	24,150	32,769	24,624	22,661	21,108	21,899	22,579	20,660
1999	23,613	33,196	25,155	19,999	20,822	—	21,918	20,394
2000	26,148	34,891	27,643	22,428	22,657	22,670	22,358	20,720
2001	25,045	39,853	28,693	23,297	25,400	22,800	24,016	22,320
2002	26,852	38,319	29,525	25,403	24,710	23,493	25,101	30,514
2003	27,092	39,650	30,352	28,608	25,602	24,514	25,564	30,336
2004	28,449	39,132	31,439	—	25,595	24,469	25,570	32,407

Source: Kang 2006.
Note: — = not available.

A5.13c Entrance Wage of High School Teachers
(US$)

Year	Korea	Germany	United States	United Kingdom	Italy	Japan	France	Finland
1998	24,150	35,177	24,869	22,661	21,108	21,899	22,579	—
1999	23,613	35,096	35,546	19,999	20,822	—	21,918	21,047
2000	26,148	37,394	27,751	22,428	22,657	22,670	22,358	21,517
2001	25,045	43,100	28,806	23,297	25,400	22,800	24,016	23,104
2002	26,852	41,441	29,641	25,403	24,710	23,493	25,563	32,136
2003	27,092	42,881	30,471	28,608	25,602	24,514	26,035	34,374
2004	28,449	42,321	31,578	—	25,595	24,469	25,928	34,825

Source: Kang 2006.
Note: — = not available.

A5.13d Elementary School Teacher's Wage after 15 Years
(US$)

Year	Korea	Germany	United States	United Kingdom	Italy	Japan	France	Finland
1998	39,921	38,138	33,973	34,087	23,468	41,201	27,116	23,539
1999	39,411	26,046	34,705	33,540	23,137	—	26,599	24,799
2000	43,952	37,905	40,072	35,487	25,115	42,820	27,172	25,183
2001	42,845	46,459	41,595	36,864	28,483	43,043	29,193	27,175
2002	46,400	44,617	42,801	39,350	27,726	44,345	30,519	31,687
2003	46,640	46,223	43,999	41,807	28,731	45,515	31,082	31,785
2004	48,875	46,935	39,740	—	28,731	45,753	31,090	32,541

Source: Kang 2006.
Note: — = not available.

A5.13e Middle School Teacher's Wage after 15 Years
(US$)

Year	Korea	Germany	United States	United Kingdom	Italy	Japan	France	Finland
1998	39,921	38,640	32,713	38,010	25,773	41,201	29,615	27,942
1999	39,265	38,596	33,418	33,540	25,397	—	28,757	28,225
2000	43,800	40,561	40,072	35,487	27,507	42,820	29,331	28,690
2001	42,713	49,053	41,595	36,864	31,072	43,043	31,507	30,945
2002	46,269	47,165	42,801	39,350	30,220	44,345	32,933	36,552
2003	46,518	48,804	43,999	41,807	31,304	45,515	33,540	36,444
2004	48,754	48,167	40,088	—	31,291	45,753	33,548	38,318

Source: Kang 2006.
Note: — = not available.

A5.13f High School Teacher's Wage after 15 Years
(US$)

Year	Korea	Germany	United States	United Kingdom	Italy	Japan	France	Finland
1998	39,921	43,307	35,455	38,010	25,773	41,225	29,615	29,127
1999	39,265	39,265	41,745	33,540	26,175	—	28,757	29,530
2000	43,800	43,881	40,181	35,487	28,329	42,845	39,331	30,124
2001	42,713	52,839	41,708	36,894	31,959	43,069	31,507	32,429
2002	46,269	50,805	42,918	39,350	31,073	44,372	33,394	40,482
2003	46,518	52,570	44,120	41,807	32,186	45,543	34,010	42,139
2004	48,754	51,883	40,043	—	32,168	45,761	33,906	43,526

Source: Kang 2006.
Note: — = not available.

6

Education in Thailand: Improving Secondary Education*

Luis BENVENISTE

This paper was not originally prepared for the Asia study tour undertaken by education policy makers from Africa. Although the study tour included an informative presentation on secondary education in Thailand by a senior Thai policy maker, this took the form of a PowerPoint presentation rather than a background document. Thus, the present paper was identified later for inclusion in this volume principally because the development of secondary education in Thailand over the past 15–20 years is very relevant to the challenges currently faced by many Sub-Saharan African countries.

INTRODUCTION

Secondary education has the potential to serve as a pathway for student progress and advancement. It can offer skills development to produce a workforce with expertise that matches the needs of the labor market. Indeed, investment in secondary education reaps great rewards when it serves as the critical link between basic education and higher education or the labor market. Yet secondary education can also act as the main bottleneck preventing the equitable expansion of

*This paper benefited from the overall guidance of Ian Porter (country director), Christopher Thomas (sector manager), and Tamar Manuelyan Atinc (acting sector director). The team especially thanks Khunying Kasama Varavarn and the Ministry of Education staff for their input and invaluable comments. The team benefited from background papers prepared by Dilip Parajuli and Deon Filmer, Niels-Hugo Blunch, and Ana Revenga and Chaiyuth Punyasawatsut. The team also extends its appreciation to the peer reviewers, Ernesto Cuadra, Daniel Mont, Carmen de Paz Nieves, Omporn Regel, Kaspar Richter, Norbert Schady, Christopher Wheeler, Charlotte Vuyiswa McClain-Nhlapo, and Birger Fredriksen for their insights and suggestions to strengthen this study. Finally, the team thanks Keiko Inoue, Achariya Kohtbantau, Rachadawan Pasugswad, and Juliana Williams for excellent research and administrative assistance.

education opportunities. Thailand's secondary education is currently at a crossroads, with the potential to improve opportunities for young people or become a binding constraint to greater economic growth and competitiveness. It is thus an opportune time to take stock of recent accomplishments in the advancement of Thailand's secondary education and to consider the challenges ahead.

This chapter elucidates the importance of developing the Thai secondary education system, first by considering its distinct historical development. Education reform efforts since 1932 are considered to explore the trajectory that Thailand's secondary education system followed. Next, the potential for secondary education to serve as the key bridging point between primary schooling, tertiary education institutions, and the labor market is considered. The advancement of secondary schooling is then discussed with respect to its links to the alleviation of poverty and income inequality. Finally, an international comparison places the current state of Thai secondary education in the context of the accomplishments of comparable countries.

EDUCATION REFORM IN THAILAND: HISTORICAL CONTEXT

Since Thailand shifted from an absolute to a constitutional monarchy in 1932, education policy has been regarded as an integral component of national development planning. The first National Education Development Scheme (NEDS) was devised the same year, formally recognizing every individual's education ability. During the 1960–76 NEDS, the Royal Thai Government (RTG) pledged compulsory primary education, with special provisions made for children with disabilities. The primary school dropout rate was as high as 60 percent in the 1960s, and secondary enrollment was only 2 percent of the age-group (World Bank 1998). The NEDS of 1977–91 changed the structure of the education system from 4+3+3+2 (four years lower primary, three years upper primary, three years lower secondary, and two years upper secondary) to 6+3+3, whereby six years of compulsory primary education is followed by three years each of lower- and upper-secondary schooling. The subsequent NEDS of 1992–2001 oversaw the passing of a new Constitution in 1997, which ensures the "equal right to receive fundamental education for the duration of not less than twelve years which shall be provided by the State thoroughly, of quality, and without charge," paving the way for universal access to 12 years of quality education for all Thai children.

In 1999, the National Education Act (NEA) was promulgated to serve as the cornerstone of education provision and administration. The NEA raised compulsory education from six to nine years, ensuring that parents enroll their children in schools until they graduate from the lower-secondary level. In particular, the NEA recognizes children with special education needs. Those with physical, mental, intellectual, emotional, social, communication, or learning deficiencies (as well as economically or legally disadvantaged groups) are fully entitled to government education services and basic education is to be specially provided.

Under the NEA, the Thai education system was divided into formal, nonformal, and informal sectors.[1] All education institutions, regardless of the type of education provided, are expected to allow the transfer of credits both within and across different types of institutions so that students are able to transition smoothly between school levels and academic tracks, as necessary. This eases the transition for students who drop out of the formal education system but elect to continue their learning through community-based or nonformal programs. The policy also allows students to reenter the formal education system at a later date. This section of the NEA spurred the building of additional schools for special programs and learning centers to enhance informal education. Use of the credit transfer across different types of education institutions has remained limited to date.

The NEA calls for major reforms in all aspects of the Thai education system. Among them are three priority areas: (a) learning reform, (b) teacher reform, and (c) education quality assurance. Learning reforms developed a more targeted core curriculum responding to capabilities and interests of different groups of learners. The new basic education curriculum was implemented country-wide in 2001. A primary goal is for teaching to be more learner oriented and encourage a thirst for knowledge that leads to lifelong learning.

Teacher reform focused on improvements in the quality of pre-service and in-service teacher training, professional standardization, and personnel administration. A five-year university program to prepare new teachers has been executed. During the 2003–06 period, the Ministry of Education (MOE) set a target to produce teachers and school managers with postgraduate qualifications (higher than a bachelor's degree). The results of these reform efforts will be interesting to assess. Although support for in-service teacher development has become more available, training programs have tended to be conventionally provided through short-term workshops. A cascade model predominates where ministry officials train Education Service Area (ESA) supervisors who subsequently train teachers. Training sessions generally provide little time for teachers to practice what they are learning and seldom is any follow-up support provided when they return to their classrooms to implement what they have learned. There is limited evidence that these training programs are demand driven or fully responsive to teachers' needs. Nor is there evidence that the current approach to teacher professional development leads to improved teaching practices and improved student learning. The ongoing decentralization process has hindered teacher development activities and it remains unclear whether the MOE or ESAs should play a leading role in this arena. Moreover, delays in the development of professional standards and enactment of legislation related to decentralized personnel administration have had an unfavorable effect on teacher reform as a whole.

The quality of education provision must be monitored through internal and external quality assurance mechanisms. The NEA requires that internal evaluations for secondary education be conducted annually by individual institutions on the basis of the MOE's standards. These evaluations must be made available to the public. External evaluations are conducted by an independent agency—the Office for National Education Standards and Quality Assessment (ONESQA). For the most part, it appears that the internal and external quality assurance process to date has been largely procedural. There is limited demand for information on school quality, and the formative evaluation process has not translated yet into a reflective exercise that improves school development planning or fosters accountability to education sector stakeholders regarding the quality of service delivery.

Most recently, the National Education Plan 2002–16 has advanced a vision of education that embraces human-centered development and a holistic scheme integrating education, religion, art, and culture. It is hoped that the National Education Plan will "(1) lead to a knowledge-based society, (2) promote continuous learning, and (3) involve all segments of society in designing and decision-making concerning public activities" (Bhangananda 2003). The goals outlined in the National Education Plan reflect an ongoing debate in Thailand about the balance between education development for the sake of promoting economic competitiveness and for preserving "cultural self-reliance" (Witte 2000). This debate has intensified during the years following the Asian Crisis, as Thailand attempts to navigate the tides and pressures of economic globalization.

Considerable structural change has been introduced in recent years. The agencies mainly responsible for education provision, namely, the MOE, the Ministry of University Affairs, and the Office of National Education Commission (ONEC), were reorganized into a single ministry (the MOE). Some 175 ESAs have been established to handle education management at a decentralized level. These ESAs have different capacities to absorb service delivery functions transferred to them because of variations in coverage area, the number of qualified personnel, and endowed resources. Sustained technical assistance will be needed to build local-level institutional capacity for efficient service provision.

The 1997 Constitution ensures the right of local administration organizations to participate in the provision of education to improve outcomes through increased community participation. The decentralization initiative requires local government organizations (LGOs) to assume greater responsibility in school management. LGOs began taking on some functions in late 2004, including the monitoring of child development centers, developing appropriate activities for preprimary schools, overseeing subdistrict libraries and village reading centers, and providing school milk and lunches. The transfer of secondary school management to LGOs, however, has been more complex. A study conducted by the Office of Inspection and Evaluation found that around 78 percent of LGOs were ready to assume transferred functions in primary education, but only 11 percent of these LGOs were ready to take responsibility for secondary schools. Further evaluation is needed to assess the readiness of school administration capacities before this transfer occurs at the secondary level. Currently, the Cabinet has agreed to slow down the transfer process and has requested that the MOE work closely with related stakeholders to ensure a smooth transition. In addition, teachers have raised concerns about transferring administrative responsibility for secondary schools to LGOs, fearing that this could lead to political interference in education issues such as teacher job security, curriculum, and classroom pedagogy as well as possible recruitment of teachers for electoral purposes.

In addition to recent reforms, the RTG currently allocates more than 20 percent of its total budget to the education sector, reflecting its strong commitment to education development. The emphasis on the importance of education comes at a crucial time for Thailand. Emerging from the Asian Crisis, the country has revived and projected itself toward being a competitive nation in the global marketplace. Four national priorities have been outlined, all of which require better quality of education and knowledge management: (1) increasing competitiveness, (2) reducing poverty and inequality, (3) developing social capital, and (4) managing natural resources. Furthermore, as economic growth picked up speed after the crisis, exports have grown from US$50,000 million in 1998 to almost US$111,000 million in 2005. Foreign direct investment (FDI) rose from US$6,900 million to US$9,800 million over the same period. The trend in economic growth and FDI has placed pressure on local firms to be more competitive, as well as stimulate technological progress, and hence has heightened the demand for a better skilled and more highly educated workforce.

BRIDGING FROM BASIC EDUCATION TO TERTIARY EDUCATION AND THE LABOR MARKET

At a global level, limited investments in secondary education have been an outcome of several factors. No comprehensive initiatives have been pursued for secondary education, such as Education for All and the Fast Track Initiative pursued at the primary level. Although advocates tend to push for the expansion of primary and tertiary institutions at the country level, secondary schooling tends to be neglected. Finally, reaching political consensus for secondary expansion and reform has been more difficult than for primary or tertiary education, making secondary school policy choices more ambiguous, risky, and complex (Moreno 2005). Increasingly, however, secondary education has been recognized as the bridging point between primary schooling, higher education, and the labor market. Below, the link between primary expansion and secondary schooling in Thailand is outlined. Subsequently, the importance of secondary education in connecting young people to tertiary education and the labor market is discussed.

During the 1980s, the RTG promoted universal primary education and reduced the adult illiteracy rate through the heavy expansion of primary education. In this period, the government built at least one primary school with extension classes up to lower-secondary levels for every two villages throughout the country (Suwansathit 2002). In addition, the change in the format of the education system from 4+3+3+2 to 6+3+3 ensured that children stayed in school longer. Through this effort, universal primary education, measured in terms of the gross enrollment ratio (GER) was successfully achieved (104 percent in 2003). Household survey data largely confirm official statistics, showing a rising trend toward universal primary completion. School participation rates (SPRs)—that is, the proportion of children 6 to 11 years of age who enroll in school regardless of their schooling level—have demonstrated impressive outcomes. In 2003, the transition rate from the primary to lower-secondary level was 93 percent, the retention rate at the primary level was 90 percent, and the literacy rate was 96 percent (Thailand Ministry of Education 2004).

Such achievements at the primary education level were experienced across the Thai population, regardless of income, geographic location, or gender. Especially across income groups, recent trends between 1994 and 2002 show that the primary SPR for the poorest quintile has risen continually over time, reflecting the successful inclusion of poor households (see figure 6.1).

An analysis of public expenditure in 2000 supports this finding. A calculation based on the number of students enrolled in public schools and the fixed unit cost show that at the preprimary and primary education level, about 31 percent of public expenditure was allocated to the poorest quintile, whereas only 8 percent went to the richest quintile (see table 6.1).

As the RTG intensified efforts to achieve universal primary education in the 1980s, it also focused on boosting access to tertiary education. This resulted in almost universal access to primary education and a rapid expansion of tertiary education, while secondary enrollments stagnated through this period. Main obstacles have been poverty and the high direct and opportunity cost of education (World Bank 1998). Such factors resulted in a sluggish secondary GER of around 30 percent with almost half of all children finishing primary education dropping out of the formal education system.

In a recent World Bank study titled *Closing the Gap in Education and Technology*, de Ferranti, et al. (2003) found that most member countries of the Organisation for Economic Co-operation and Development (OECD) and many East Asian countries followed an education transition trajectory that resembles a pyramid: primary education was universalized first, followed by an expansion of the secondary system, and finally broader access to universities. Thailand took a different path. In the 1980s, after a decade of successful expansion at the primary level, the focus shifted toward tertiary education, leapfrogging the expansion of secondary education. Consequently, only a small number of secondary graduates constituted the

Figure 6.1 Primary School Participation Rate by Income Quintile, 1994–2002

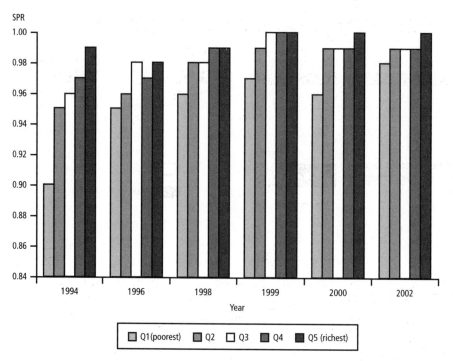

Source: National Statistics Office 1994–2002.
Note: SPR = school participation rate.

Table 6.1 Incidence of Public Spending for Primary Education by Income Quintile, 2000

Level of income	Public school enrollment (thousands)	Enrollment fixed unit cost	Expenditure incidence (percent share)
Q1 (poorest)	2,118	29,755	31
Q2	1,739	24,425	25
Q3	1,463	20,549	21
Q4	1,050	14,754	15
Q5 (richest)	548	7,704	8

Source: National Statistics Office 2000.

pool of recruits entering the skilled labor force and the middle income bracket. In other words, the distribution of education attainment in Thailand was "squeezed from the middle," where the base got thinner and the top wider, while the middle remained relatively unaffected. The distribution looked more like an anvil than a pyramid, with the majority of the population having only primary education or less, but more individuals with tertiary education than secondary education (see figure 6.2).

Figure 6.2 Education Transition Patterns

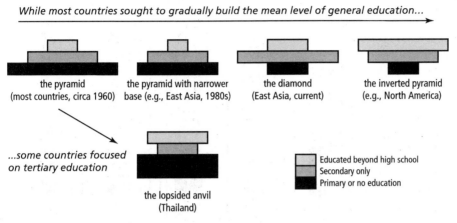

While most countries sought to gradually build the mean level of general education...

the pyramid
(most countries, circa 1960)

the pyramid with narrower
base (e.g., East Asia, 1980s)

the diamond
(East Asia, current)

the inverted pyramid
(e.g., North America)

*...some countries focused
on tertiary education*

the lopsided anvil
(Thailand)

Educated beyond high school
Secondary only
Primary or no education

Source: de Ferranti et al. 2003.

The achievement of universal primary education eventually led to increasing pressure on the government to expand compulsory education to cover the lower-secondary level. Direct subsidies were introduced in 1987 covering free textbooks and uniforms, low-cost dormitories, health and nutrition programs, and school fee exemptions. Approximately 50 percent of all rural secondary students benefited from these subsidy programs. Poverty and the cost of schooling, however, have continued to be a constraint for expanding secondary schooling and reaching universal coverage.

Country comparisons show that Thailand's secondary GER was stagnant until around 1990 and then picked up dramatically. In contrast, other Asian countries started with higher secondary GERs and continued to grow at a more modest pace during the same period (see figure 6.3).

Low levels of investment at the secondary level through the 1980s led to a relatively low-skilled workforce in Thailand. In 1997, 70 percent of the total labor force had only received an elementary education or less, while 17 percent had obtained a secondary education and 8 percent had a university degree. But investments in secondary education in the 1990s began to pay off. By 2004, the labor force with more than a primary education reached close to 40 percent. Secondary GERs had jumped from 68 percent in 1994 to 77 percent in 2002.

But disaggregating by household per capita quintile reveals large differences in secondary school enrollment between the poorest and the richest population groups. These differences have remained quite substantial over time. The gap in SPRs between the wealthiest and poorest population quintiles in 1994 was 24 percent (85 percent versus 61 percent) and stood at 17 percent in 2002 (93 percent versus 76 percent). Although it is clear that secondary schooling opportunities for

Figure 6.3   Comparison of Secondary GER Trends, 1970–2000

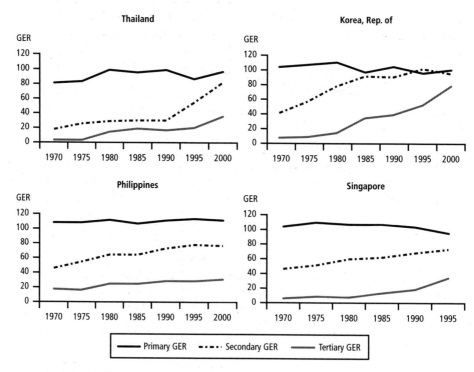

Source: World Bank 2005.

the poorest children still have much room for improvement, Thailand had accomplished an impressive rate of expansion nonetheless (see figure 6.4).

The incidence of public expenditure for secondary education shows that spending is distributed almost equally across quintiles (see table 6.2). This is a difficult and thus laudable achievement. Such spending patterns partially explain why the gap in secondary achievement between the richest and the poorest quintile has remained relatively stable over time. Enrollment rates are higher in Bangkok than in other parts of the country, higher in urban than in rural areas, and lower in those districts in which ethnic groups account for a high percentage of the population. The challenge facing the government is how to continue to expand basic education to disadvantaged groups while maintaining universal access to and ensuring good quality of primary education.

Mandatory education under the 1999 NEA only includes up to lower-secondary schooling. Students who want to continue their education beyond the lower level have an option between three years of upper-secondary education or three years of lower-vocational (technical) education. Most students who choose upper-secondary education aim to go to university. Those who choose lower-vocational

Figure 6.4   Secondary Participation Trends by Income Quintile, 1994–2002

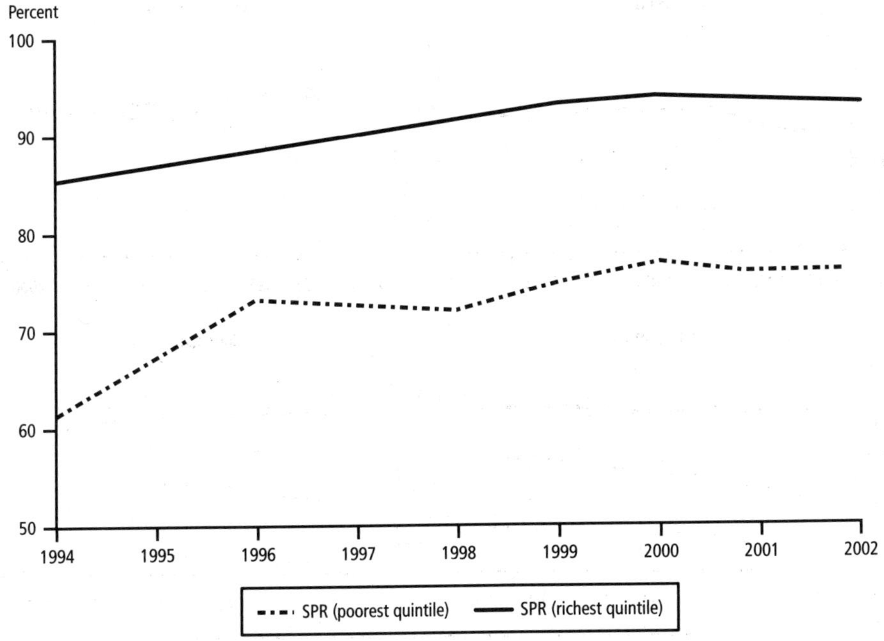

Source: National Statistics Office 1994–2002.

Table 6.2   Incidence of Public Spending for Secondary Education by Income Quintile, 2000

Level of income	Public school enrollment (thousands)	Enrollments fixed unit cost	Expenditure incidence (percent share)
Q1 (poorest)	843	11,829	19
Q2	987	13,846	23
Q3	967	13,575	22
Q4	885	12,412	20
Q5 (richest)	646	9,064	15

Source: National Statistics Office 2000.

education tend to continue their education at the upper-vocational level. Students with a diploma or upper-vocational education can continue to a university degree by continuing with two more years of schooling at a university.

Enrollment estimates at lower- and upper-secondary levels indicate that growth trends and between-group gaps are much larger in the higher grades, probably as a result that in upper-secondary education there has been greater room for improvement. For example, the average SPR for lower secondary (12- to 14-year-old age-group) increased from 88 percent in 1994 to 94 percent in 2002, while at the upper-secondary level (15- to 17-year-old age-group), it increased from 57 percent in 1994 to 77 percent in 2002. The absolute (and relative) gains were larger in the poorest quintile—from 31 percent to 56 percent at the upper-secondary level.

In an effort to continue to expand secondary education, Thailand faces two critical challenges: developing an effective strategy for further broadening access to upper-secondary education and finding an appropriate balance between the academic and vocational tracks. Thailand's ability to address these issues will affect its ability to open up the pipeline from secondary to tertiary education as well as to the labor market.

A recent external quality evaluation done by ONESQA indicates that vocational education in Thailand calls for urgent attention, particularly in terms of quality improvement. Although employers or business operations are moderately satisfied with overall quality of vocational graduates, students and teachers themselves are not satisfied with their learning and teaching inputs. The education equipment they use represents a low standard of quality (with the exception that those of private vocational schools are of high quality). The shortage of teachers is prevalent, particularly in agricultural schools and private vocational schools. Regarding teacher qualification, teachers are not sufficiently qualified throughout the vocational institutions. Simultaneously, many of their qualifications are not related to the academic subjects they teach. Research and innovation done by vocational teachers is accomplished only at a minimum level, less than one research project per teacher per year. Academic services to society and community are also low, receiving less than 1 percent of the annual operational budget.

Furthermore, Thailand's reform program focuses not only on access, but also on enhancement of quality and market relevance. Anticipating the needs of the new knowledge-based economy will prove key. The "new general skills" needed for such an economy go beyond reading and writing and mathematics to include such things as the ability to work in a team, to approach new problems creatively, to know how to use a computer, and at least to understand English, if not speak it fluently (World Bank 2001b). The Thai secondary education system will act as the bridging point to a changing labor market only to the extent that graduates attain such skills and their talents and creativity are harnessed into the economy.

A KEY TOOL FOR CLOSING EQUALITY AND EQUITY GAPS

Secondary education is a key tool for alleviating poverty in Thailand. A recent report on *Poverty and Public Policy* (World Bank 2001a) finds that in 1998–99, individuals with upper-secondary education and vocational and technical qualifications improved their standard of living. In contrast, those with secondary or lower levels of schooling suffered real income declines. Education also had a powerful effect on reducing rural poverty. The risk of poverty declined from 66 percent to

74 percent when the highest educated adult in the household had primary or secondary education, as compared with no education. Finally, the less-educated population was at greater risk of increased poverty during times of crises. Between 1996 and 1999, poverty incidence increased from 21 to 24 percent for households headed by an illiterate person and from 12 to 19 percent among those headed by a primary-educated person. In contrast, the rate did not change appreciably among households headed by persons with vocational and postsecondary education.

Secondary education is an important vehicle for bringing about broader income equality and social equity in Thailand, particularly because the country has one of the highest Gini coefficients in the region (0.51 in 2002, contrasted with the regional average of 0.38). Furthermore, Thailand was estimated to have the fifth-worst income distribution among developing countries in the 1990s (Phongpaichit and Sarntisart 2000). Income inequality in Thailand worsened steadily from the 1960s to 1992, improved marginally over 1992–98, and then lost all those gains over one year in the Asian economic crisis. Evidence from Thailand, as well as other countries such as Turkey, Chile, and the Russian Federation, shows that differences in the education attainment of the household head contribute to lingering inequality in income distribution (see table 6.3). Additionally, differences in education attainment alone account for at least one-fifth of total overall inequality and for an even larger fraction for within-region inequality. In particular, inequality in access to secondary education may adversely affect the extent of inequality in income distribution (Phongpaichit and Sarntisart 2000). Evidence suggests that as secondary education is expanded, and as the supply of literacy and other skills is distributed among more youth, income inequality begins to diminish (UNESCO 2003a).

Apart from private rates of return, which are realized through higher earnings of individuals, an increase in education attainment contributes to higher social returns to investment in education, particularly with respect to health benefits. Social returns, for example, may come in the form of a better-educated mother who heads a family that is more health conscious, better nourished, and has the prospect of realizing the importance of education for the next generation.

Table 6.3 Differences in Education Attainment of Household Head, Gini Coefficient by Country and Share

Country	Gini coefficient	Percent of total income inequality due to education
Thailand (1999)	0.53	19
Turkey (1994)	0.45	22
Chile (1999)	0.51	26
Russian Federation (1995)	0.47	5

Source: World Bank 2000b and 2001a.

Evidence from 45 demographic and health surveys across countries show that children of mothers with secondary schooling have a mortality rate that is 36 percent lower than those whose mothers only have primary schooling (Filmer and Prichett 1997). Additional years of schooling serve as an effective prevention scheme against the spread of HIV/AIDS, an epidemic that is increasingly of concern in Thailand and the region (World Bank 2002). Finally, children residing in households headed by an educated individual have an increased chance of continuing with additional years of schooling.

Secondary education attainment is also a contributing factor to nonmarket public benefits. In general, better-educated citizens tend to participate more in public affairs in the form of increased voting rates and staying abreast of current events in politics. Additionally, better-educated citizens tend to have less association with crime. One study shows a decreasing likelihood of youths engaging in criminal activities when they attend school and work (Witte and Tauchen 1994). Increased years of schooling, usually associated with higher earnings, can reduce the reliance on welfare and public assistance programs.

The NEA paved the way for a new stage in the enhancement of Thailand's education system. The most recent National Education Plan has the potential to further advance the system with strategies currently in place through 2016. In particular, efforts to balance economic competitiveness and human-centered development mark a distinct phase in the thinking that frames Thailand's future education advancement. Although recent trends in secondary education expansion show improving results, much remains to be done to promote access and quality as well as the efficiency of the secondary education system.

The next section reviews the current state of the Thai secondary education system as a whole and across different groups of the population. Additionally, comparisons are offered across regions. Based on these results, an analysis of the demand side of secondary education is presented, including effects of household decision making in sending children to school. This analysis is followed by an examination of the issue of the quality of secondary education in Thailand and suggestions for improving it. Options to enhance efficiency in the utilization of financial resources are investigated next. Finally, policy recommendations are suggested that consider the goals of the RTG and the distinct historical evolution of its education system.

ACCESS TO AND EQUITY IN SECONDARY EDUCATION

The RTG recently intensified its efforts to expand access to secondary education, particularly in rural areas, where an additional 500 schools have been constructed. Its commitment is mirrored in the 1997 Constitution that guarantees access to 12 years of education for all Thai children. Greater commitment is reflected in the

1999 NEA, which extended compulsory education from six to nine years. To translate these commitments into action, the RTG has set a target to achieve universal lower-secondary education by 2006 and universal upper-secondary education by 2015.[2]

Currently, lower-secondary education is within reach for most children. Compared with enrollment rates in 1994, access to secondary schooling has notably expanded for all socioeconomic groups. By 2005, the GER for lower-secondary education had reached 82.9 percent. This is a result of a concerted effort from the RTG to redress inequities in education participation. Despite important gains, much work remains to be done. Although 98.6 percent of children were estimated to complete primary school in 2002, only 88 percent transferred to lower secondary and 69 percent continued to upper secondary. Poor and rural children are at the greatest disadvantage. One of the challenges for the RTG in developing appropriate policies and strategies to enroll and keep disadvantaged children in secondary school is to continue to promote equitable development and growth opportunities. Thus, this section offers an in-depth look at secondary education attainment, disaggregated along the lines of gender, rural-urban divide, region, and income groups.

The analyses in this chapter are largely based on two data sources: (1) administrative data collected by the MOE and (2) a national survey of representative households, called the Household Socio-Economic Survey or SES[3] (National Statistics Office 1994–2002). The MOE administrative data are considered to be census-based, but errors caused by inconsistency and data manipulation exist. The SES has been recognized as a credible source of data. Its reliability, however, is limited because of its small sample size—45,000 households for most of the analyses in this chapter, but even smaller when focusing on the secondary-school-age population (between 12 and 17 years). A snapshot of data from these two sources is not always consistent, but it reflects similar trends over time.

ACCESS TO SECONDARY EDUCATION

The average number of years of education attainment for the Thai population age 15 and over has risen gradually but consistently. For the population age between 15 and 21, in particular, average years of schooling is nearly 10 years. This suggests that most children have at least completed lower-secondary education, which is the minimum compulsory level.

Education attainment profiles for ages 16 to 19 show a notable improvement over time. Based on the SES, the number of youth between 16 and 19 years old who completed primary education (grade six) and lower-secondary education (grade nine) rose continuously since 1994 (see figure 6.5). By 2002, about 95 percent of the 16- to 19-year-old population completed at least grade six, indicating an

Figure 6.5   Thailand Education Attainment Profiles for Ages 16 to 19, 1994–2002

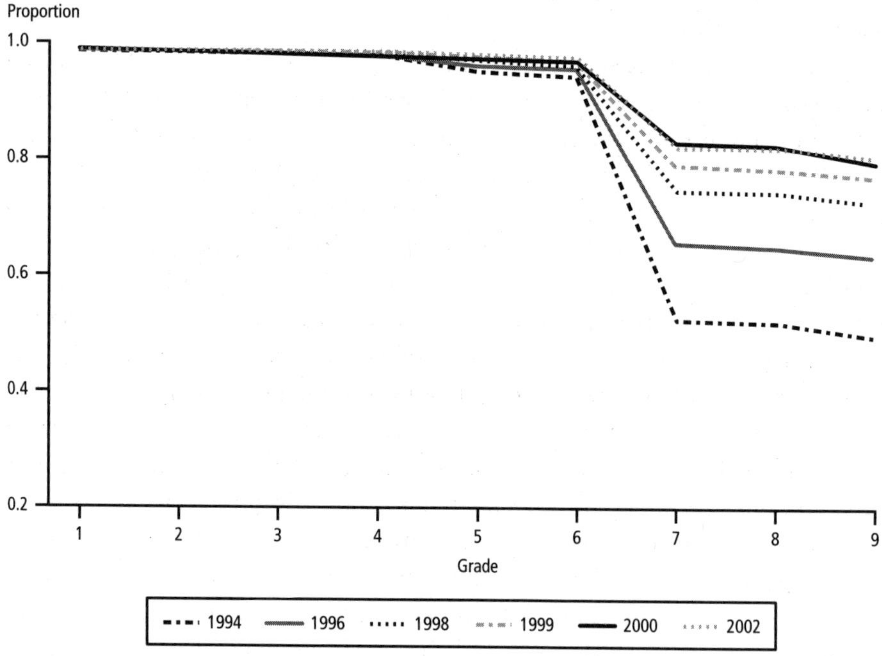

Proportion

Grade

- - - 1994   —— 1996   ····· 1998   —·— 1999   —— 2000   ····· 2002

Source: National Statistics Office 1994–2002.

impressive primary school completion rate. Moreover, 80 percent of the population between 16 and 19 years old had completed lower-secondary education in 2002, which is a significant increase compared with 50 percent in 1994. A closer review, however, shows that most of the gains in education attainment took place before 1998.

Overall, secondary education enrollment has improved after a period of stagnation before the 1990s. Even through the financial crisis in the late 1990s, enrollment growth remained relatively constant. GER rose from 68 to 77 percent between 1994 and 2002, while the net enrollment rate (NER) also rose from 68 to 74 percent. Both GER and NER have risen at a decreasing rate in recent years.

Table 6.4   Average Years of Education Attainment, 1999–2003

Age	1999	2000	2001	2002	2003
15 and over	7.1	7.2	7.4	7.6	7.8
15–21	9.4	9.5	9.6	9.7	9.8
15–59	7.7	7.8	7.7	7.8	7.9
60 and over	3.5	3.6	3.7	3.8	3.9

Source: Office of Education Council 2004a.

The challenge of maintaining a constant growth rate over time, which is known as the "ceiling effect," is common among countries as they approach universal access to schooling.

Various measures have helped to expand secondary enrollments. Most important, secondary education was reconceptualized as basic education for the general public and labor force instead of just preparation for university professionals. In addition, lower-secondary education classes were established in rural primary schools along with free tuition in 1987. Within eight years, these extended primary schools increased to 6,600 schools (22 percent of the total) and accommodated 21 percent of students in lower-secondary education. Special schools were set up to welcome students with disabilities. Presently, some 43 specialized schools serve more than 15,000 students in all areas of disability. An additional 4,000 integrated schools bring 150,000 disabled students into mainstream education. Furthermore, the government supports 45 welfare schools where 40,000 marginalized children receive a fully subsidized education. These students include certain ethnic minorities, street children, children living with HIV, and others in difficult circumstances. Alternative forms of education have been promoted to provide equivalent secondary education at these schools, which now graduate a half million students annually. These programs include procedures that recognize graduates from nonformal education, Buddhist education, Islamic education, home schools, and distance education.

Disparities between gross and net enrollment rates in Thailand are minimal, suggesting little age mismatch. Unlike countries such as Brazil, where the ratio of gross to net enrollment rate is high (1.63 for primary and 1.24 for lower secondary), Thailand's ratio at the secondary level is around 1.1 (Larach 2001). The gap between secondary NER and GER reflects the extent of over- and underage students in the education system. For most grades, less than one-third of children attend school at the grade corresponding to their age, but the vast majority of children are within one year of their expected official grade level (see table 6.5). This

Table 6.5 Age Distribution by Grade, 2002
(percent)

Grade	Age	12	13	14	15	16	17	18	19
Grade 7	12	**36.46**	55.02	6.81	1.23	0.47			
Grade 8	13	3.92	**33.48**	54.78	6.59	1.23			
Grade 9	14	1.10	3.46	**34.59**	53.84	7.02			
Grade 10	15				**29.81**	59.22	8.74	1.65	0.59
Grade 11	16				3.77	**27.77**	58.73	8.08	1.64
Grade 12	17				1.60s	3.79	**28.33**	57.49	8.80

Source: Education Management Information System, Ministry of Education 2002 (personal communication).

is good news for Thailand. Students who are significantly overage often run a higher risk of dropping out of school for reasons including the rise in the opportunity cost of education to foregone income from labor as a child grows older.

Education participation for teenage children has expanded, but there is still room for improvement. The SPR of the cohort ages 12 to 17 years increased from 75 to 86 percent between 1994 and 2002. This reveals an improvement in general access to and permanence within the education system, because SPR measures the school participation level of children in a particular age-group, regardless of the grade attended. Given that about 5.8 million children were in the 12- to 17-year-old cohort in 2002, about 800,000 children were excluded from the education system. The challenge for the RTG lies in reaching the last 14 percent of the 12- to 17-year-old cohort and successfully bringing them into the formal education system. To achieve universal secondary education, it will be crucial to formulate appropriate strategies for reaching out-of-school youth and to target interventions that address the obstacles these youth face in attending secondary school.

Repetition is a minor problem. MOE data from 2002 show that while there was a slight repetition rate (1 to 2 percent) at the primary level, there was none for

Figure 6.6   Transition of Three Cohorts from Grades 1 to 12, 2001–03

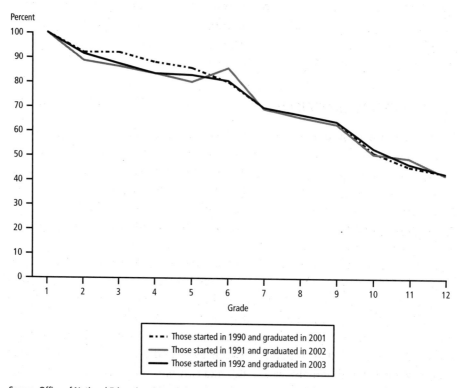

Source: Office of National Education Commission 2001, 2002, 2003.

secondary education. Dropout is a source of greater concern. An analysis of school dropouts in 1999, which sampled 1,157 schools and included grades 1 to 12, found that only 2 percent of students dropped out of school. Examining data that follow three cohorts from grades 1 through 12, however, it is clear that students primarily drop out of the education system when they transition from one level to another (for example, from grade 6 to 7, and grade 9 to 10). Once students start grade one, they tend to stay on through grade six. From grades six to seven, some students drop out of the system while those who continue tend to stay on through grade nine.

The vast majority of secondary school students are enrolled in traditional general academic programs. A review of secondary students in 2004 using MOE data shows that out of approximately 5.8 million youth between 12 and 17 years old, around 74 percent are enrolled in the formal education system. About 84 percent of all students attend a school administered by the MOE. For the upper-secondary level, approximately 63 percent of students pursue an academic track while 37 percent pursue a vocational track. Less than 1 percent of students attend welfare schools (provided for those in need of financial assistance) and less than 1 percent of secondary students attend schools for the disabled or with special programs. The private sector plays a small role in general secondary education, accounting for 11 percent of student enrollments in lower-secondary and 20 percent in upper-secondary education. The highest proportion of private enrollments is found in the vocational education track at the upper-secondary level, accounting for approximately 38 percent of students enrolled in 2004.

EQUITY IN SECONDARY EDUCATION

Equity in access to secondary education has improved. Participation rates in secondary education demonstrate that access across gender, rural-urban divide, region, and income groups has expanded, benefiting all groups in some measure. Although the income and rural-urban gaps have grown smaller, on average, the gender gap has grown significantly larger *and to the benefit of girls*. In contrast to many other developing nations, a different equity challenge—keeping boys in school—has arisen.

Girls outperform boys in secondary school participation and completion. NER for girls in 1994 was 63 percent, contrasted with 61 percent for boys. In 2002, NER for girls was 72 percent and 64 percent for boys. Thus, while enrollment for both girls and boys is on the rise, girls outperform their male counterparts, and this gap has grown over time (see figure 6.7). In addition, the grade-nine completion rate for females overtook that of males between 1994 and 2002. In 1994, about half of the cohort for both females and males had completed grade nine, but by 2002, the completion rate was 84 percent for females and 76 percent for males.

Figure 6.7 School Participation Rates, Gross Enrollment Rates, and Net Enrollment Rates by Gender and Gains, 1994–2002

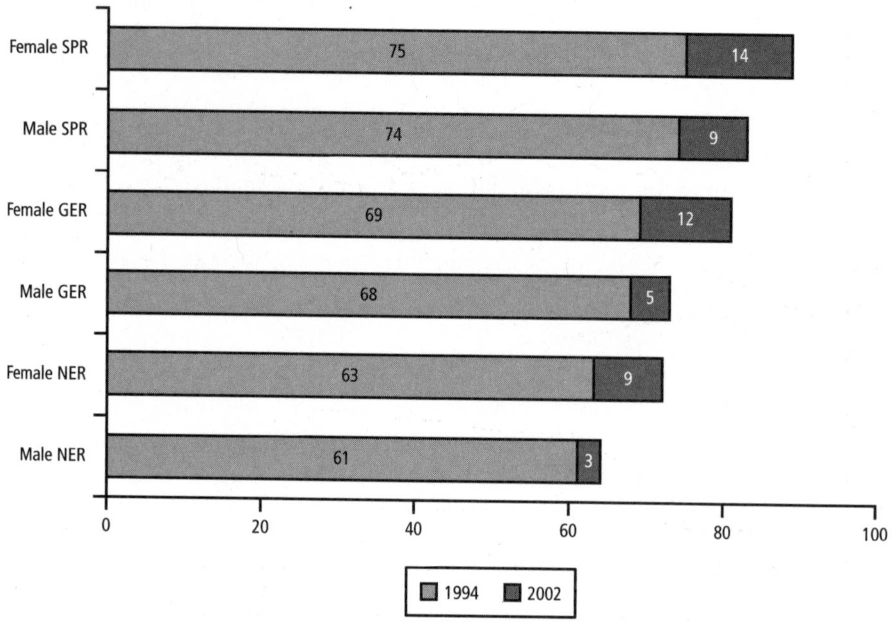

Source: National Statistics Office 1994–2002.
Notes: SPR = school participation rate; GER = gross enrollment rate; NER = net enrollment rate.

Coverage has expanded to rural areas. With respect to the rural-urban divide, net enrollment and school participation rates in nonmunicipal, or rural, areas parallel rates in municipal areas, and in some cases even exceed rates of their urban counterparts. The gradual rise in both SPR and NER reflects improvement in access to secondary education for rural children, following massive expansion of schools to remote locations in the early 1980s. Similarly, the urban-rural gap for grade completion has decreased from 25 percent in 1994 to only 8 percent in 2002.

The poorest region in Thailand (the northeast), is catching up with other regions. In the 1980s, there was great concern about lagging enrollment rates in the most impoverished regions in Thailand, particularly the northeast. SES data show that by 1994, NER for the northeast was higher than other regions and continued to maintain that position through 2002 (see figure 6.8). More striking is the NER trend in Bangkok, where the NER fell between 1994 and 1998, even though rates in other regions continued to climb.

Disparities exist across provinces, especially among the richest and the poorest provinces. Based on data collected by the MOE, most provinces achieved secondary GERs around 60 to 70 percent by 2002, reflecting notable improvements but also extensive room for further expansion. Grouping provinces into five quintiles according to provincial per capita income, school participation rates are relatively

Figure 6.8   Secondary Net Enrollment Rates by Region, 1994–2002

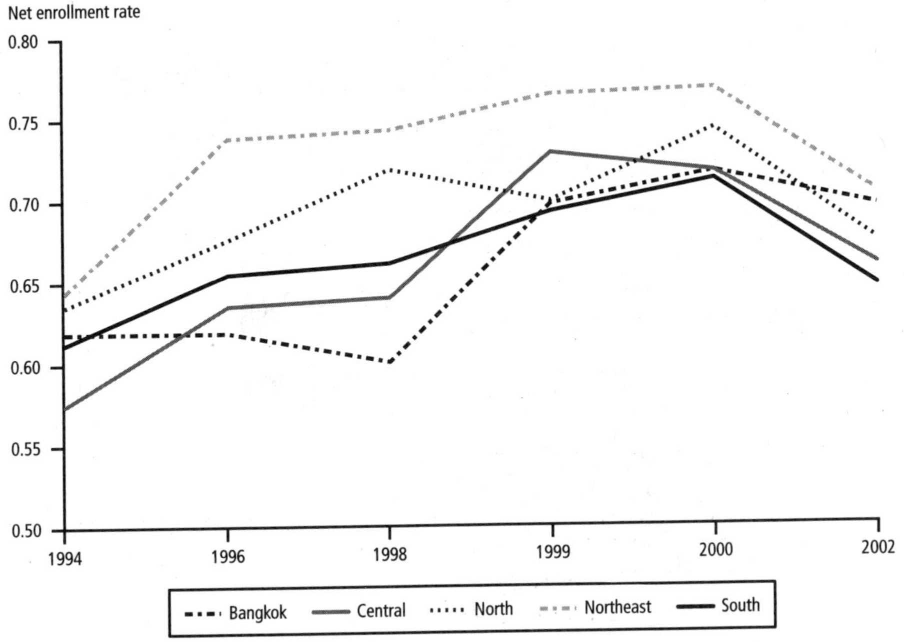

Source: National Statistics Office 1994–2002.

Table 6.6   School Participation Rate by Income Quintile and Provincial per Capita Income, 2002

Quintile	12–14 years old (percent)	15–17 years old (percent)	12–17 years old (percent)
Q1 (poorest)	51.73	36.47	44.03
Q2	51.84	35.40	43.58
Q3	55.49	35.81	45.59
Q4	55.04	36.69	45.74
Q5 (richest)	66.36	41.21	53.91

Source: Author's estimation using data from the Ministry of Education and Ministry of Interior.

consistent among the bottom four quintiles (see table 6.6). However, the provinces in the wealthiest quintile achieved higher rates than those in the bottom quintiles, across all age-groups.

Figure 6.9 shows survival curves for all children in the 6- to 15-year-old age-group in 1994 and 2002, both overall and disaggregated by wealth quintile. Over-all survival probabilities through grade six were already high in 1994, and were more than 98 percent for 2002. In both years, the transition between primary and secondary school is where attainment dropped off. Nevertheless, by 2002, overall grade-seven completion was more than 90 percent. This average masks significant

Figure 6.9 Survival Curve Estimates for Ages 6 to 15 in Thailand, 1994 and 2002

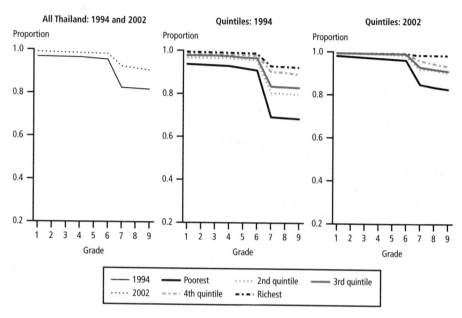

Source: National Statistics Office 1994–2002.

differences by quintile. In 1994, the completion rate gap between the poorest quintile and other groups was less than 5 percent through grade four, and then widened progressively: 6 to 10 percent for grades five and six, 20 to 50 percent for grades seven to nine. By 2002, the gap between the richest and the poorest quintiles' completion rates had narrowed, but persisted, despite improvements in absolute levels for both quintiles. The richest quintile's survival rate was almost 100 percent for grade nine, but it was only slightly above 80 percent for the poorest group. These survival estimates confirm that, overall, the problem of retention is more pronounced in the transition between primary and lower secondary and only minor across each grade within these levels.

Urbanicity is a relatively minor factor in explaining inequities of survival and completion. Survival probabilities to grade six of urban and rural children were largely similar in 1994 and more so in 2002. Urban-rural differences grow larger across the lower-secondary grades, albeit less pronounced now than a decade ago.

International comparisons show that Thailand made dramatic improvements over the past two decades. Data from the *World Development Indicators* (World Bank 2003) confirm that Thailand started out in the late 1980s with one of the lowest secondary GERs in the region, but subsequently picked up the pace in later decades to position itself in the top tier because of a concerted government effort to expand access (see figure 6.10).

Figure 6.10   Trends in Secondary GERs across Asian Countries, 1980–2003

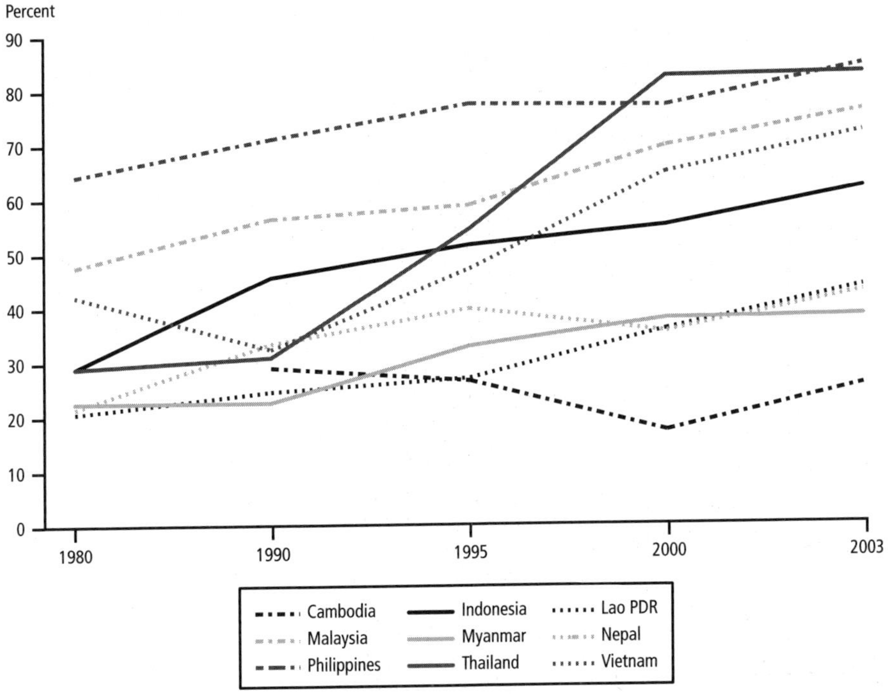

Source: World Bank 2006c.
Note: Data for Thailand and Philippines in 2000 are from *World Development Indicators 2003.*

GERs for the upper-secondary level have also experienced a notable increase. The share of upper-secondary school graduates to the population has steadily increased, reaching 59 percent in 2003. Thailand performs comparatively better than other regional neighbors such as Indonesia, China, and India in this realm (OECD 2005b). Furthermore, Thailand's share of secondary school graduates was largely on par or better than countries with a higher gross domestic product (GDP) per capita, such as the Philippines, Argentina, or Mexico (see figure 6.11).

REACHING OUT TO THE EXCLUDED

Thailand's recent expansion of secondary education is a success story, but many children still remain excluded from sharing in the benefits of school participation. For Thailand to achieve its commitment of universal secondary education by 2015, it is necessary to tease out the supply- and demand-side constraints to education faced by the remaining 14 percent of the school-age population outside the formal education system. On the one hand, several socioeconomic factors determine family decision making regarding the demand for secondary education and the

Figure 6.11 Percentage of Upper-Secondary Graduates in the Population, 2003

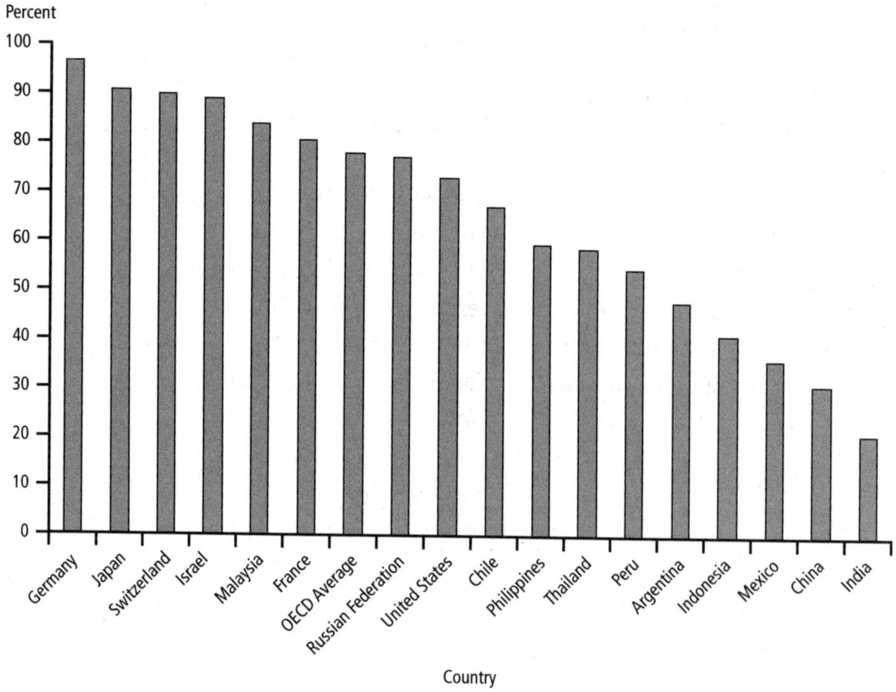

Percent

Country

Source: OECD 2005a.

level of investment in human capital. On the other hand, supply-side variables affect access to secondary education. Understanding the interplay between these variables will allow the RTG to develop appropriate strategies that better target out-of-school children, broadening coverage even further and achieving universal participation objectives.

Children with disabilities have been largely neglected from efforts to universalize basic education. The MOE manages 43 specialized basic education schools for children with disabilities throughout Thailand that serve approximately 15,000 students. In addition, the MOE has generally espoused an inclusive policy of mainstreaming children with disabilities within the regular education system that could encompass an additional 150,000 students. But this policy has not been clearly articulated, and children with disabilities traditionally have not been emphasized as a priority target group to reach Education for All targets. Thus, they have remained largely excluded from education participation. According to national statistics, in 2004, only 175,000 children with disabilities were enrolled in preprimary through upper-secondary school. The total population between 3 and 17 years old in 2004 was 13,774,909. Thus, the share of children with disabilities enrolled in school was approximately 1.3 percent. Estimates from other

BOX 6.1   THE PATH TO UNIVERSAL SECONDARY EDUCATION IN THE REPUBLIC OF KOREA

The Republic of Korea achieved nearly universal primary and secondary education in just four decades, following the end of the Korean War in 1953. Education expansion in Korea was accompanied by a declining Gini coefficient, indicating that equality gaps were narrowed during the same time period. Korean students are among the top performers in both mathematics and science in OECD countries, as illustrated by recent Programme for International Student Achievement (PISA) and Trends in International Mathematics and Science Study (TIMSS) results.

According to a case study on Korea's path to universal secondary education in *Expanding Opportunities and Building Competencies for Young People: A New Agenda for Secondary Education* (World Bank 2005), several factors played a key role. First, Korea included strategies for a strengthened and broadened education system in its national development plan as early as the late 1950s. Education was identified as a top priority area in the 1960s and a focus on secondary education was established in the 1970s, followed by the tertiary level in the 1980s. Second, Korea included equality and equity considerations in its education expansion strategies. In 1968, the government abolished entrance examinations for middle schools and introduced a lottery system for student placement, which was intended to democratize access at this level. The High School Equalization Policy was passed in 1974, which was intended to equalize school inputs such as operating expenditures, student intake, class size, and education facilities. As a result, there is no discernible quality difference across public schools or between private and public institutions. Third, government expenditure on education has increased steadily since the 1950s. Education expenditure as a percentage of GDP increased from 2.9 percent in 1970 to nearly 5 percent in 2003. Fourth, private school participation has played a significant role in sustaining expansion. Although providers of secondary education were greatly supported by government tax incentives, fees, family contributions, and foreign aid at first, government revenues have been reinvested in education following the introduction of school-leveling policies.

Source: World Bank 2005.

Table 6.7   Number of Disabled and Special Students by Type and Gender, Academic Year 2004

Type	Male	Female	Total
Seeing impaired	5,898	5,445	11,343
Hearing impaired	3,578	3,302	6,880
Mentally impaired	15,302	14,125	29,427
Physically impaired	8,343	7,701	16,044
Students with learning difficulties	39,478	36,442	75,920
Speaking impaired	5,994	5,532	11,526
Students with autism	1,965	1,814	3,779
Students with behavioral or emotional problems	5,001	4,617	9,618
Students with more than one characteristic of disability	5,518	5,094	10,612
Total	**91,077**	**84,072**	**175,149**

Source: Office of Education Council 2005.

middle-income countries suggest that the share of children with disabilities tend to oscillate between 4 and 5 percent, suggesting that a few hundred thousand children with disabilities in Thailand are likely to be outside the school system.

Another group that has remained at the margins of inclusive education policies is composed of children of non-Thai families currently living in Thailand. According to MOE and Ministry of Interior regulations, non-Thai children have a right to receive basic education with financial support from the RTG. This policy has been irregularly implemented. Demand-side constraints keep a large share of non-Thai children out of school. Language of instruction has also been a problem as alien children may not be fluent in Thai. Efforts to reach immigrant out-of-school youth have been small in scope and mostly led by specialized nongovernmental organizations. Furthermore, schools that do enroll non-Thai children often do not claim their entitled government per capita funding for these students because of their ignorance of existing policies or they may fail to receive their entitled allocation. At present, approximately 45,000 noncitizens in Thai schools are receiving budgetary per capita entitlements. A study of the Office of Education Council (OEC) covering 250 children of immigrant workers in Samut Sakhon province shows that the provision of free education has resulted in a 46 percent decline in the number of school dropouts and child labor abuse cases. Yet nearly half of the schools that were providing free education for alien children have not received state subsidies.

MOE data indicate that while financial constraints are often identified as the main obstacle keeping students out of schools, another important factor is student relocation (without transfer to a new school) (see figure 6.12). Financial

Figure 6.12   Reasons Cited for Dropping Out, Grades 7–12, 2004

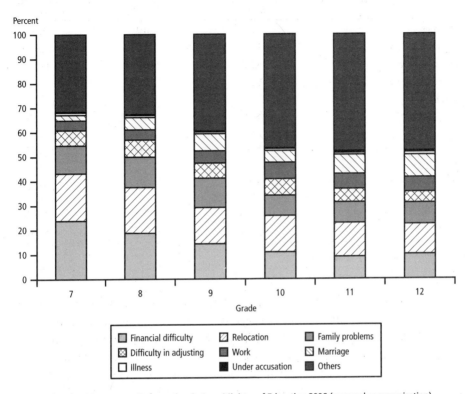

Source: Education Management Information System, Ministry of Education 2006 (personal communication).

constraints tend to lessen as students progress to higher grades, although relocation grows in relative significance into the upper-secondary level. Nevertheless, relocation shows a diminishing impact when moving along the higher grades. The "other" category in this survey probably captures lack of knowledge about the reasons for dropout because of an inability to track students outside the formal system.

A multivariate analysis model was constructed to determine how demand-side indicators affect school participation rates of children ages 12 to 17 years old. Children with educated parents tend to achieve higher secondary school participation rates. The education attainment of adult males and females are positively associated with children's participation in secondary school. The higher the education attainment of the adult in a household, the likelier it is the children in that particular household will participate in school. This effect is even stronger with females. The marginal effect of adult education attainment has increased over time between 1994 (2.5 percent) and 2002 (3.5 percent).

The relationship between school enrollment and household expenditures has remained strong. Relative to children from the poorest quintile, children from the second, third, forth, and fifth (the richest) quintiles had higher probabilities of

Table 6.8 Private Expenditure Estimates on Education by Income Quintile, 1994–2002 (real baht)

Quintile	1994	1996	1998	1999	2000	2002
Overall						
Primary	1,308	1,233	1,447	1,631	1,569	1,701
Secondary	2,053	2,160	1,909	2,202	2,194	2,353
Tertiary	9,465	13,429	15,839	17,010	17,344	19,203
Poorest quintile						
Primary	414	502	477	500	471	469
Secondary	967	1,175	1,175	1,053	1,081	864
Tertiary	2,583	2,417	2,392	3,303	3,143	1,864
Quintile 2						
Primary	658	721	646	676	733	717
Secondary	1,425	1,501	1,551	1,682	1,599	1,492
Tertiary	3,467	3,058	4,237	3,549	3,231	5,888
Quintile 3						
Primary	898	1,081	1,176	1,291	1,064	1,318
Secondary	2,032	2,143	1,929	1,935	2,242	2,180
Tertiary	4,117	3,908	4,350	5,731	4,795	6,044
Quintile 4						
Primary	1,772	1,915	2,240	2,588	2,541	2,876
Secondary	2,399	2,898	2,874	2,864	2,908	2,963
Tertiary	5,866	6,233	7,142	7,082	8,095	9,403
Richest quintile						
Primary	5,604	4,850	6,735	8,702	7,144	8,380
Secondary	4,336	4,394	5,244	6,566	5,687	6,889
Tertiary	11,759	18,560	21,584	22,698	22,615	22,821

Source: National Statistics Office 1994–2002.
Note: Prices are deflated by regional and yearly CPIs (base region = Bangkok, base year = 2002). Yearly CPIs: 1994 = 75.0, 1996 = 84.1, 1998 = 96.0, 1999 = 96.3, 2000 = 97.8, 2002 = 100. SES data does not disaggregate household education spending by levels, therefore, the above figures are estimated using OLS regression of education expenditure on the number of students at each level of schooling and reading off the appropriate coefficients.

school participation of 7.3, 11.9, 17.0, and 18.3 percentage points, respectively, in 1994. Effects have decreased over the years (standing at 5.5, 8.0, 8.8, and 9.9, respectively, in 2002), but they remain statistically significant.

Direct costs of education act as a barrier to access to secondary schooling. The transition from one level of education to another is heavily influenced by financial considerations. According to the Children and Youth Survey (CYS), regularly conducted by the NSO, inability to pay is overwhelmingly the prime reason for children who are completing an education cycle not to progress to the next level. Other reasons include having to work, traveling greater distances to school, and having insufficient knowledge for the work required.

The gap between the rich and the poor for household expenditures in secondary education is widening. Average household spending on education was 3,449 baht per year in 2002 with vast differences across quintiles—from 840 baht in the poorest quintile to more than 7,870 baht in the richest quintile—and across regions—from about 1,750 baht in the northeast to more than 9,585 baht in Bangkok. Poor households allocate on the order of 1.5 percent of total expenditures to education, whereas richer households allocate 2 or 3 percent.

"Free" education for all does not truly meet the needs of poor households. While the RTG committed to provide 12 years of free education for all under the 1997 Constitution, tuition covers only a small part of total expenditure that households must bear in association with education. Data from the CYS show that, in 2002, school tuition and textbooks represented only 19 to 25 percent of the total cost of sending a child to the lower- or upper-secondary level (see figure 6.13). Meals and transportation costs combined represented about 65 percent of total education-related expenditures. A recent study from the National Human Rights

Figure 6.13 Average Annual Expenditure on Education per Person by Education Levels, 2002

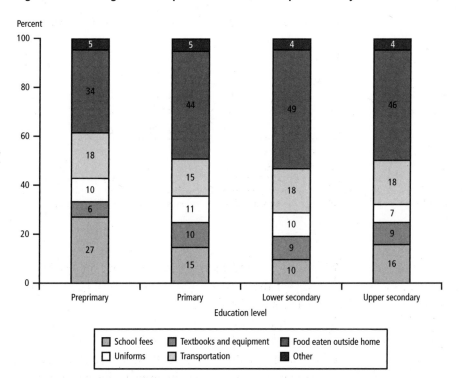

Source: National Statistics Office 2002.
Note: Average annual expenditure for upper-secondary level includes both academic and vocational streams.

Commission also indicates that students often had to pay "hidden fees" to utilize libraries, access computers, and sit for examinations. Other students report being charged for school landscaping or afterschool tuition classes (Mass Communications Organization of Thailand 2006).

Opportunity costs may hinder households from sending children to school. A large number of rural children, especially in poor households, contribute financially to their families by working inside or outside the home. By sending these children to school, households forego these financial benefits. Opportunity costs relate to how households perceive the impact of income foregone, which is often affected by conditions in the labor market. For the poorest households, this indirect cost may be substantial, with seasonal variations relating to the demand for agricultural and other labor. In Thailand, this is a problem for only a small fraction of children at the lower-secondary level. Data from the CYS confirm that only a small minority of out-of-school youth cite having to work as a reason not to enter lower-secondary education. According to the SES, children become involved in productive work when they are around 15 years old (see figure 6.14). Thus, work begins to compete with schooling by precluding school attendance at a higher rate in the upper-secondary level. In 2002, 17 percent of 16 year olds were engaged in productive work and 14 percent of children in grade nine cited work as a reason to stop their education at the lower-secondary level.

Figure 6.14 Share of Children and Youth at School or Work by Age, 2002

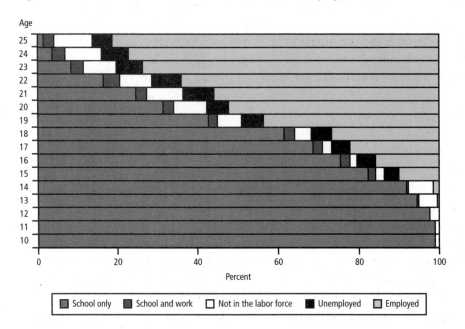

Source: di Gropello 2006.

But to achieve universal secondary education, it is crucial to ensure that there is not only strong demand for, but also a sufficient supply of, education services. In the early 1990s, a school infrastructure development program was pushed forward by the Department of General Education. There were on average 18 public secondary schools in every province. In addition, the Office of National Primary Education Commission expanded existing rural primary schools under its jurisdiction to cover lower-secondary education. Expanding schools into the rural areas enabled students to attend schools by reducing transportation costs for households. With such heavy expansion, the enrollment gap between children in urban and rural areas was dramatically reduced. But while secondary schools have grown over time, a simple analysis shows that there may still be room for expansion. Comparing the number of students in the official secondary-level age-group between 12 and 17 years old and the number of secondary classrooms available by province, it is clear that more classrooms may be needed. The student-to-classroom average ratio ranges from 27:1 in Pattani to 42:1 in Nontaburi and Samutprakarn. For many provinces, if all students in the respective age-group decided to attend secondary school, there would not be enough classrooms to hold them.

INTERVENTIONS TO STIMULATE EQUITABLE SECONDARY SCHOOL EXPANSION

So what accounts for the extraordinary growth in secondary school enrollments in the 1990s? As noted immediately above, the expansion of the schooling network, either through a new infrastructure program or with the addition of lower-secondary grades to existing primary schools, is credited with dramatically opening new education opportunities for children throughout Thailand. Studies conducted in rural areas provide evidence that parents saw secondary education as a means to break the cycle of poverty for their children or open up greater job opportunities in the expanding labor market. Bringing schools closer to the point of demand reduced the costs associated with schooling and minimized concerns about their children falling into bad company. The use of excess physical facilities and teachers in primary schools, resulting from the declining primary-school-age population, facilitated the transition to lower-secondary education. The primary schools prioritized for expansion had to be (a) successful in teaching vocational programs in which students could earn income while studying, (b) staffed by an adequate number of teachers, and (c) located in areas with low continuation rates as a result of poverty (Jones 2003). The number of primary schools supplying secondary education increased from 119 in 1990 to 2,688 in 1992, 4,081 in 1994, and 6,281 in 1997. Despite this dramatic expansion, as the rough estimations already provided suggest, Thailand may still face a supply-side shortage to offer adequate opportunities for all children.

Financial incentives were introduced to reduce the cost burden on families. Although the government has expanded its school network and committed to provide free tuition for grades 1 to 12, expenditures for school-related costs such as uniforms, textbooks, and transportation are large and significant. To address demand-side constraints, the RTG launched a comprehensive set of programs to assist poor children in response to the evidence that lack of financial support is a significant constraint to secondary school participation. The main features of these programs are described in box 6.2. Among the government-initiated programs, the Student Loan Program, established in 1996, receives more than 185 billion baht and is the largest education-related intervention. More than 2 million students have received loans to attend upper-secondary and tertiary schools to date.

Diverse government financial incentives are now well established, but their impact could be improved. In 2000, about a quarter of students at the upper-secondary level (general and vocational) received student loans (including 40 percent of students enrolled in private vocational upper secondary). Yet the loan program itself did not produce the expected boost in overall upper-secondary education enrollments. An in-depth study of the Student Loan Scheme shows that over the period 1996–2000, upper-secondary education evidenced a declining overall share in terms of number of borrowers and total size of loan disbursements (from 63 to 47 percent and 46 to 21 percent, respectively). In 1999, the loan scheme covered approximately 453,000 children or 33 percent of poor students enrolled—that is, two-thirds of eligible poor students enrolled in upper-secondary schools that year did not receive any assistance and an additional 600,000 poor youth were out of school (Ziderman 2003). Furthermore, more recent evidence suggests that loans do not seem to reach their intended beneficiaries—that is, students who would be unable to attend school in the absence of a loan. Interview data show that only 30 percent of borrowers would drop out if the loan was terminated. According to a recent study by Chulalongkorn University's education faculty, 58 percent of secondary school recipients did not need financial assistance to stay in school, while 21 percent of rejected applicants at all education levels were actually worse off than scholarship recipients (*Bangkok Post* 2006b). In addition, there is a problem with slow repayment and low recovery rates. In relation to other Asian countries, Thailand has the lowest repayment rate (21 percent), compared with 55 percent in the Republic of Korea and 79 percent in China. Moreover, the recovery rate, which includes default and administrative costs, is considered to be low at 8 percent, compared with 53 percent in China (Ziderman 2004). To ensure that the student loan program functions as an effective intervention, the RTG clearly needs to improve its outreach and targeting to the poorest students.

Scholarships may act as a stronger incentive for poor families to send their children to secondary school, while cutting down related administrative costs of the

BOX 6.2   SUMMARY OF GOVERNMENT-INITIATED INTERVENTIONS

Policy intervention	Target population	Target level	Total budget
School Lunch Program *Objective:* The fund, established in 1992, aims to ensure sufficient nutrition for preprimary and primary students across countries, including preprimary children in mosque and temple schools. Each student receives 6 baht per day for 200 days in each school year, totaling 1,200 baht per person per school year. This program has been replicated independently with community contributions across the nation.	Children with nutritional problems, in Rachaprachan-ukrao, in border police schools, from hill tribes, and the poor, which account for 30 percent of all children.	Preprimary and primary levels	Around 4,000 million baht in FY 2005

Responsible agency: Ministry of Education

Current situation: In 2005, more than 2 million students received free school lunches.

| **Scholarships for Poor Children from Essay Writing** *Objective:* Scholarships for poor children using government revenue from lottery ticket sales. Scholarships are granted to children who have submitted an essay describing hardships they face. Scholarships are awarded after verifying attendance with schools and teachers. | Poor students | All levels | |

Responsible agencies: Ministry of Education (Office of Basic Education Commission, Office of Vocational Education Commission, Commission on Higher Education) tracks students and monitors project outcomes.

Policy intervention	Target population	Target level	Total budget
Current situation: Currently, around 250,000 children have received a scholarship with 150,000 applications being processed. In total, the program is currently using about 67 percent of its allocated resources.			
Scholarships for Poor Students Whose Parents are Dedicated to Social Activities *Objective:* The project aims to help poor students whose parents have devoted their time and efforts to government and social activities. *Responsible agencies:* Ministry of Education, Office of Lottery Service *Current situation:* The project started in 2004. There were 66,560 scholarships granted.	Poor children of government officials and permanent employees of every ministry, volunteers on special taskforces (public health, antidrug), junior police officials	All levels	
Bicycle Lending Project *Objective:* Beginning in 2003, students who live in remote areas at least 3 kilometers away from schools and whose annual family income is less than 300,000 baht can borrow a bicycle to travel to school. The borrowed bicycles are returned to the project upon graduation. *Responsible agencies:* Ministry of Education and Ministry of Industry	Poor students who have to travel long distances to school	Primary and secondary levels	Around 500 million baht has been allocated

Policy intervention	Target population	Target level	Total budget
Current situation: 426,734,545 baht have been allocated and 75,900 bicycles have been loaned to students.			
Student Loan Scheme *Objective:* Established in 1996, the fund aims to provide financial assistance to children from poor families who wish to continue to the upper-secondary or tertiary level on both general and vocational tracks. This also includes students in nonformal education programs who wish to further their studies beyond lower secondary. The loan provides 55,400 baht per year for upper-secondary study and 100,000 baht for bachelor's degree study.	Children from poor households whose annual family income is less than 150,000 baht (for recipients before 1998 their annual household income could be no more than 300,000 baht)	Upper-secondary and tertiary levels	26,045 million baht in FY 2004
Responsible agencies: Ministry of Education is responsible for loan recipients. Ministry of Finance is responsible for allocation of loans while Krung Thai Public Company Limited is responsible for debt repayment from students after graduation.			
Current situation: In 2004, around 880,000 students were recipients, using around 26 billion baht of student loan funds.			
One District One Scholarship Program *Objective:* The project aims to address issues of equal access to quality education for Thai students. Scholarship applicants are poor students whose	Poor students whose family income is less than 100,000 baht per year	Tertiary level both in-country and overseas	Allocation of 1 billion baht on an annual basis

Policy intervention	Target population	Target level	Total budget

family income does not exceed 100,000 baht per year. In addition, these students are required to have a minimum 3.00 grade point average, pass the general test (on mathematics, science, and social science), pass an English writing test, and complete an interview.

Responsible agencies: Office of Lottery Service and Ministry of Education

Current situation: In 2005, the first year of the program, 921 students received scholarships, out of which 740 studied abroad and 181 have attended universities within the country.

Source: NESDB Web site, http://www.nesdb.go.th, and Ministry of Education Web site, http://www.moe.go.th.

scheme. Indeed, the government has announced an intention to replace loans for upper-secondary students by grants and use an Income Contingent Loan (ICL) for tertiary education. The ICL was introduced in 2006. Student loans for upper-secondary students are expected to be gradually phased out and replaced by student grants for grade 10 students.

There are no prominent schemes to assist poor students at the lower-secondary level. Official assistance programs targeting lower-secondary students in need are relatively small and unfocused. For instance, the bicycle lending program, which does not specify an education level, tends to overwhelmingly support students at the primary level. Lower-secondary students account for 25 percent of recipients in this scheme and upper-secondary students account for only 5 percent. Thus, while many of the programs do target poor households, some interventions could be better directed or specifically earmarked for at-risk lower-secondary school students to redress the notable drop in enrollments in the transition beyond primary schooling.

Increasing the role of alternative education service delivery programs may provide further opportunities for rural and poor students. At present, Non-Formal Education (NFE) programs are prohibited to serve children under the age of 16, unless they are referred by an ESA. The NEA encourages schools to organize flexible classes for out-of-school children and youth, but this practice is not widespread. In 2002, more than 4 million children were enrolled in NFE institutions at all education levels. Most of these students attended schools under the jurisdiction of the MOE; hence, they are included in counts of participation and gross and net enrollment rates collected by the MOE as well as the SES. Unfortunately, data on specific age-groups are not available at the moment. It is thus difficult to estimate how many children between 12 and 17 years old enroll in alternative education programs. Data from ONEC indicate that approximately 1.8 million out of 4 million students were enrolled at the secondary education level. Alternative education pathways provide opportunities for those who cannot attend schools during regular hours, and such students tend to come from disadvantaged families. The Vocational Education Certificate Course involves a community-based curriculum over a three-year period. An evaluation conducted in 2000 showed that only 30,000 students per year opted for this option (Jones 2003). Increasing the role of credible alternative education programs may provide enhanced opportunities for children from poor households and further strengthen the equity dimension of the education system.

Promoting private sector involvement may alleviate some of the education expenditure demands on the government. The expansion of public schools places an additional burden on government resources, especially when the government is committed to providing 12 years of free education for all students. Promoting the expansion of private schools, especially in urban areas, could potentially alleviate pressures on government expenditure on education, allowing the government to redirect additional resources to rural areas or better target out-of-school children. At the lower-secondary school level, more than 90 percent of students attend public schools (see figure 6.15). Public sector provision of upper-secondary education grew from around 72 percent of the student population in 1992 to 85 percent by 2002. In other words, the private sector share in secondary education has either remained stagnant or diminished over the past decade, suggesting that there is room for improvement.

Education reforms have stimulated private partnerships. Currently, various schemes have been put in place to promote private partnerships in the education system. For example, any individual or organization that establishes a school or institution is permitted to deduct 30 percent of the profits from the operation on a tax-free basis. Additionally, incentives such as tax rebates or exemptions are provided for contributions from nonprofit organizations. A Revolving Fund for Developing Private Higher Education Institutions was launched in 1999 to provide loans

Figure 6.15 Ratio of Number of Students Attending Public to Private Schools at Secondary Level, 1992–2003

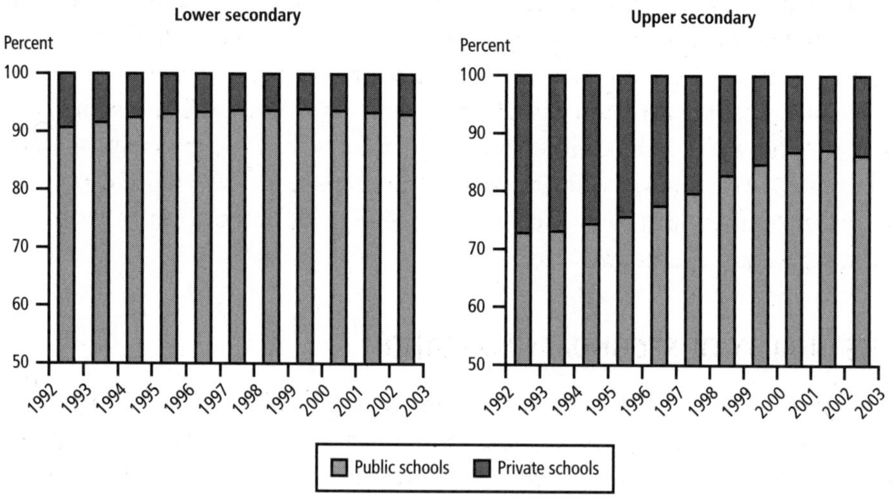

Source: Ministry of Education Statistics, http://www.moe.go.th/data_stat.

to private sector agents. A closer analysis of the impact of these measures would be desirable to assess their possible utility in expanding education opportunities.

Thailand could draw lessons from several financing mechanisms implemented in other countries. Programs such as the Programa Nacional De Educación, Salud y Alimentación (PROGRESA) in Mexico or Bolsa Escola in Brazil have proven to be effective mechanisms to stimulate demand for education and to encourage households to send children to school. They are expected to produce higher school attendance rates while lowering school dropout rates. The most comprehensive programs, such as PROGRESA in Mexico, resulted in a reduction of child labor, increased education attainment, and improved health and nutrition of the most impoverished. This particular program targets the poorest population in rural areas and provides monetary assistance to each child under 18 years old who enrolls in school between grades 3 and 9. Each year, the grant amounts increase as the student progresses to the next level. This grant compensates for a household's foregone income as their children attend school instead of working and contributing to the family income. More than 97 percent of eligible families choose to participate in the program.

Special groups of children also require additional resources. Although children who have a physical or intellectual disability are small in number, they often require support as well as additional resources and tailored services.[4] Schools have been given incentives to attract and serve children with disabilities by providing increased per capita expenditures in addition to allocations for the general student body under the NEA. Additionally, mainstreaming strategies for inclusive education within the existing curriculum and teacher-training programs have provided teachers, principals, and administrators with some basic tools to support children with disabilities and strive toward an inclusive school system. These have been important first steps in the right direction, but a more comprehensive and clearly articulated policy to mainstream children with disabilities will be required to achieve Education for All targets. Other barriers to education access include inaccessible school infrastructure to accommodate children with disabilities and negative social perceptions about disability that tend to keep these children at home or in segregated institutions.

THE QUALITY OF SECONDARY EDUCATION

Accurately capturing and evaluating the various facets of education quality is difficult. Education quality encompasses multiple areas of learning, ranging from content knowledge of both external and local or indigenous subjects; skills to apply what is learned in the larger society and labor market; qualities to build more cohesive, peaceful, and equitable societies; and opportunities to develop personally. Unfortunately, many of these areas of education quality are difficult to assess, measure, or compare. Because of this, most research is confined to the more conventional area of content knowledge.

International assessments are attempting to ameliorate this weakness, at least partially, by testing skills and practical applications of content rather than content alone. One of the principal international assessments, the OECD Programme for International Student Assessment (PISA), does this by measuring content "literacy," a concept that encompasses how 15-year-old students apply knowledge and skills; how they identify, solve, and interpret problems; and how they analyze, reason, and communicate. Another international assessment, Trends in International Mathematics and Science Study (TIMSS), is a curriculum-based test for mathematics and science administered to eighth-grade students (typically 14 to 15 years old). Together, these tests have proven to be valuable and reliable instruments for measuring education quality comparatively across countries and to explore the reasons that affect student performance (see box 6.3). Thailand participated in TIMSS assessments in 1995 and 1999 and in PISA assessments in 2000 and 2003.

The RTG has recognized the importance of education quality in realizing the potential of all young children and maintaining long-term economic competitiveness. Thus, it has placed improving the quality of education at the top of its list of priorities. Thailand has adopted several national mechanisms to monitor student learning and assessing progress in education achievement. First, every Thai student must take a school-based midyear examination at the end of

BOX 6.3   MEASURING THE QUALITY OF EDUCATION ACROSS COUNTRIES

In the late 1950s, the International Association for the Evaluation of Educational Achievement (IEA) was formed. It initiated what would become a
major set of studies aiming to measure cognitive achievement at various
levels of education in several countries and to identify the main causes of
differences in outcomes. Twelve countries joined its first mathematics
study. By 2000, some 50 countries were participating in surveys covering
mathematics and science (now called the Trends in International Mathematics and Science Study), reading (the Progress in International Reading
Literacy Study), and other subjects. Strongly influenced by the IEA experience, several other such studies, usually regionally focused, have since
been established. They include the Programme for International Student
Assessment, set up by the OECD in 1998 and now covering 59 mainly
industrial and middle income countries; the Southern and Eastern African
Consortium for Monitoring Educational Quality, which since its first survey in Zimbabwe in 1991 has expanded to 15 African countries; the Latin
American Laboratory for the Assessment of Quality in Education, which
began in 1997 and covers 16 countries; and the survey in French-speaking
Africa known as the Programme d'analyse des systemes educatifs de la
CONFEMEN. At present, both the United Nations Children's Fund and
the World Bank are sponsoring separate East Asian regional training programs with selected countries to strengthen national capacity to regularly
monitor and assess student achievement.

Source: Compiled by the author.

the first semester and a final examination at the end of the school year to pass
on to the next grade. Second, standardized national tests at the end of primary,
lower-secondary, and upper-secondary levels were introduced in the year 2000
by the Office of Education Assessment and Testing Services, under the Department of Curriculum and Instruction Development, and were conducted until
2003. These tests were comparable in measuring student performance within
and across provinces. At present, the National Institute of Education Testing
Services (NIETS), founded in 2004, is responsible for the evaluation and testing of Thai education at all levels, including secondary education. In academic
year 2006, NIETS introduced the Ordinary National Educational Test and the
Advanced National Educational Test at grade 12. These tests are required for
university admission.

Figure 6.16   PISA 2003 Test Score Results in Mathematics by Income Group

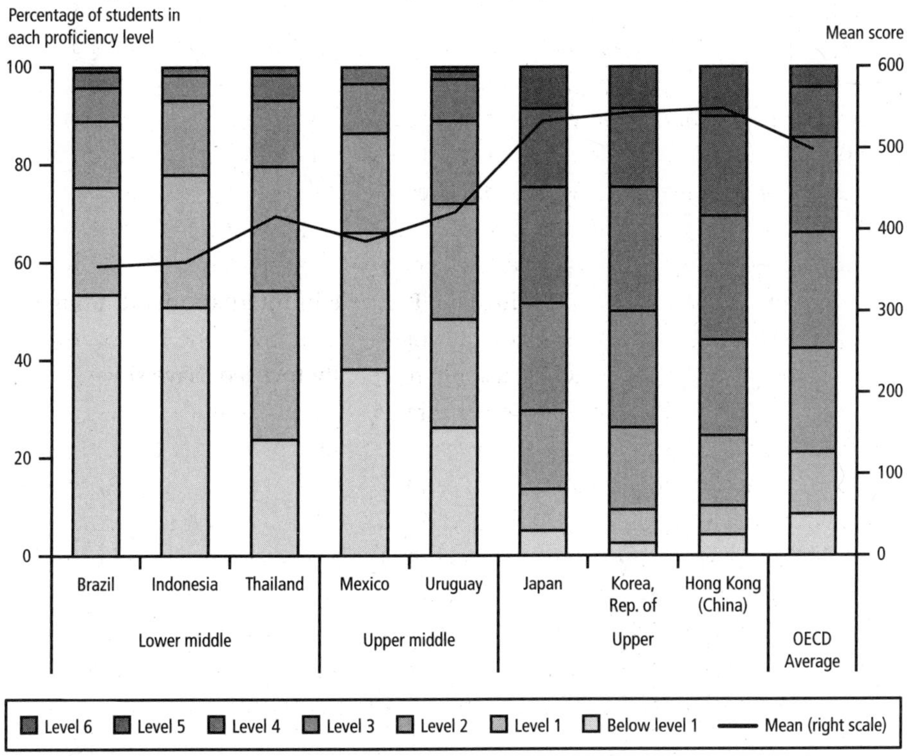

Source: di Gropello 2006.

QUALITY OF THAI EDUCATION: LESSONS FROM INTERNATIONAL DATA

This section uses international assessments to analyze education quality in Thailand compared with other countries in East Asia and Latin America. An important conclusion stands out from benchmarking the performance of Thai students internationally: *Thailand has higher scores than other countries at similar income levels, suggesting that it has been generally successful at providing education services of certain quality equitably.*

The bars in figure 6.16 show the proportion of students in participating East Asian and Latin American countries divided into PISA's six proficiency levels for the PISA 2003 exam in mathematics. The line running through the figure shows the mean test score for each country. The countries are grouped according to the World Bank's income groupings. Figure 6.17 shows the same information for the PISA 2000 exam in reading literacy. In this case, student scores were divided into five rather than six proficiency levels.

Figure 6.17 PISA 2000 Test Score Results in Reading Literacy by Income Group

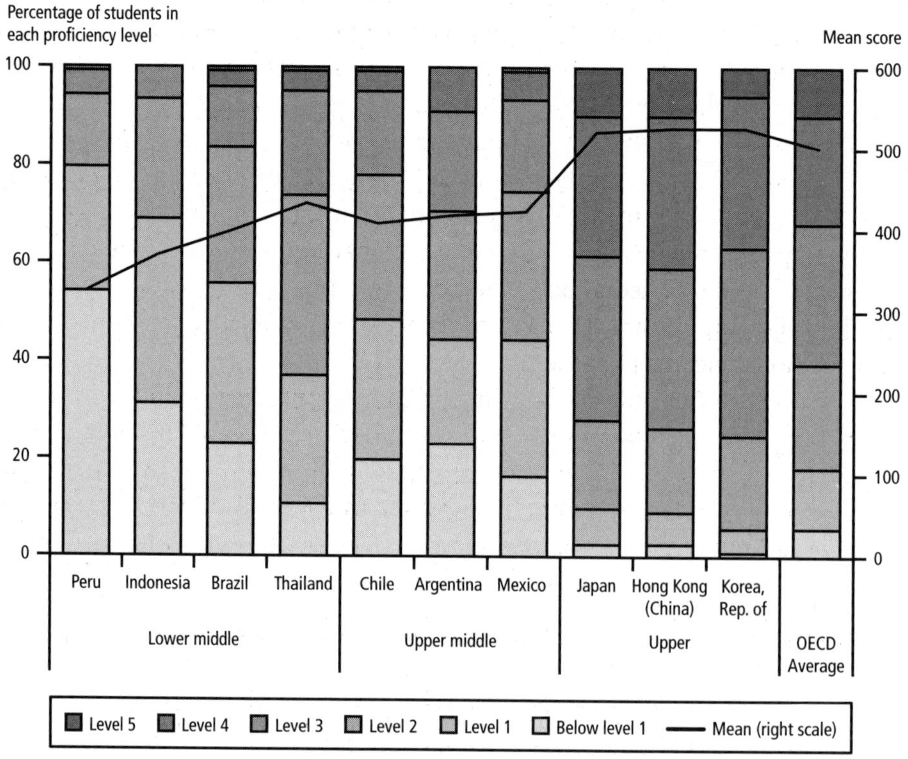

Percentage of students in
each proficiency level   Mean score

Level 5 ■ Level 4 ■ Level 3 ■ Level 2 ■ Level 1 ■ Below level 1 ── Mean (right scale)

Source: di Gropello 2006.

In both years and in both subjects a clear trend of lower-income countries scoring below higher-income countries is seen. Thus, Thailand trails significantly behind its wealthier Asian counterparts: Japan, Hong Kong (China), and Korea. This is not surprising. The average 2003 PISA mathematics test score for lower-middle-income countries (381) is more than 150 points below that of upper-income countries (542). This indicates a quality gap between wealthier countries, such as Japan and Korea, and developing countries, like Thailand and Indonesia. The same pattern holds for 2000 PISA Reading Literacy, where the average test score for lower-middle-income countries (385) is 139 points below that of upper-income countries (524).

When analyzing the performance of Thailand against other lower-middle-income countries, such as Indonesia or Brazil, however, Thailand performs better than its peers both in terms of mean test scores and proficiency level distribution. In fact, Thailand performed more than 50 points above the other countries in its income grouping in the 2003 mathematics test. Although 20 percent of Thai students scored at or above proficiency level three, notably fewer Brazilian,

Indonesian, or Mexican students reached that benchmark. A similar phenomenon can be observed in the 2000 reading literacy exam. This substantial congruence in the results of both tests over time suggests that Thailand has been more successful at producing better student outcomes—at least as is measured by the skills and contents of the PISA exam—than other countries at similar income levels.

The results of the 1999 TIMSS study show a similar pattern to the PISA results. Thailand ranked 27th in mathematics and 24th in science among 38 participating countries (statistically equal to the international average), among the bottom tier of participating countries. Yet, relative to national income levels, Thailand's performance could be rated as adequate (see figure 6.18 and figure 6.19). In both mathematics and science, Thailand ranks above the trend line for its per capita gross national income (GNI) level.

Not only do Thai students perform well, on average, relative to their peers in other countries at similar income levels, but the distribution of knowledge across Thailand is fairly equitably distributed. Figure 6.20 graphs the performance in mathematics of individuals from different wealth quintiles in PISA 2000, but the basic results hold for other subjects and years. The wealth variable is based on an

Figure 6.18   Trend Line of TIMSS Mathematics Scores against 2003 GNI per Capita

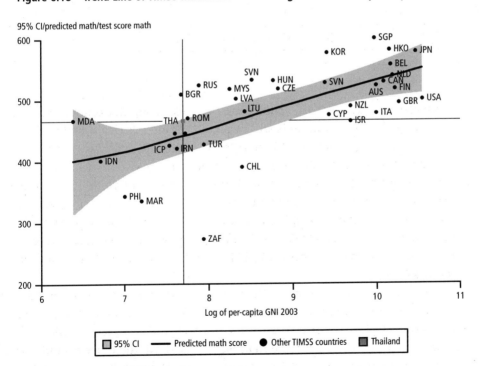

Source: Richter 2006.
Note: TIMSS = Trends in International Mathematics and Science Study.

Figure 6.19   Trend Line of TIMSS Science Scores against 2003 GNI per Capita

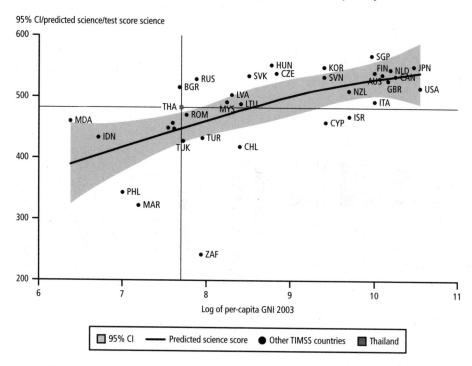

Source: Richter 2006.
Note: TIMSS = Trends in International Mathematics and Science Study.

index of several household asset-ownership and housing condition variables.[5] As expected, there are statistically significant differences in test scores across wealth quintiles in all countries. Individuals from wealthier households perform better than individuals from poorer households. But in the case of Thailand, these differences are less sharply marked than in other countries such as Argentina, Brazil, and Chile. Wealth accounts for a modest share of the total variation in Thai mathematics scores overall.

Although PISA and TIMSS results suggest that Thailand's performance is acceptable given its income level and is rather fairly distributed, they also point to underlying problems. First, few children score in the top proficiency levels. For PISA, less than 10 percent of students scored beyond level four in mathematics or reading. This is in stark contrast to all three participating East Asian upper-income countries, where roughly 50 percent of students in mathematics and 40 percent in reading scored above this level. The same holds true for TIMSS. Only 16 percent of students in Thailand reached the upper-quarter proficiency benchmark in the mathematics test, whereas in Singapore, Chinese Taipei, Korea, Hong Kong (China), and Japan at least 64 percent of students performed at this level.

Figure 6.20 Average Mathematics Performance by Wealth, 2000

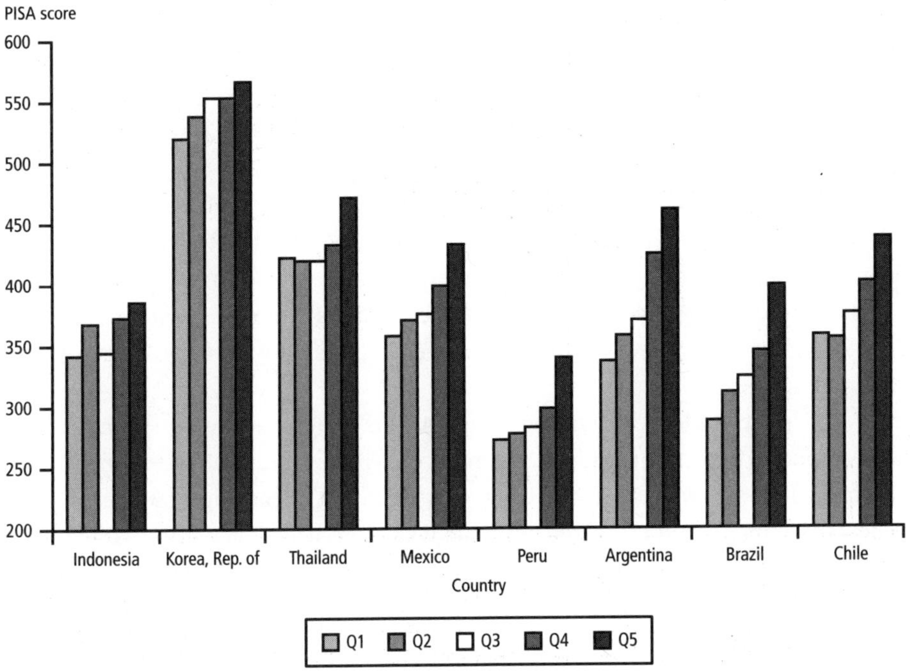

PISA score

Source: di Gropello 2006.
Note: Q1 refers to the poorest quintile and Q5 refers to the richest quintile.

Furthermore, a large portion of students is performing below acceptable proficiency levels. Thailand had roughly 40 percent of students performing at or below the PISA level one in literacy and more than 50 percent of students performing at or below the PISA level one in mathematics. This contrasts sharply with the upper-income countries where only around 10 percent of students score at or below level one. A sizeable proportion of students are functioning at or below the most basic level of language, mathematics, and science ability.

FACTORS AFFECTING QUALITY OF EDUCATION IN THAILAND

What do we know about school inputs that affect education outcomes? In the sections below, selected education input variables are discussed to better understand which factors positively affect education outcomes in the Thai context. International assessments have collected extensive background data to appraise the relationship between various education inputs and outcomes. We now turn our attention to the contributions of teacher, school, and household characteristics to student learning and performance.

Teacher Characteristics. Teacher quality is considered one of the most important contributing factors to improving student achievement (Rice 2003; Rivkin, Hanushek, and Kain 2005). In 2005, about 87 percent of secondary school teachers under the Office of Basic Education Commission had earned at least a bachelor's degree. Only a small minority of teachers in lower- and upper-secondary schools possessed a master's degree or above—about 4 and 11 percent, respectively. The Bangkok Metropolitan Region (BMR) and northern provinces tended to have a greater concentration of teachers with a master's degree or higher (see table 6.9), whereas teachers from other regions tended to have comparatively less education. The distribution of teachers with higher education degrees is more heavily biased toward schools that cater to children of higher-income brackets, whereas schools that serve lower income populations have teaching staff with fewer years of professional training.

What is the evidence regarding Thai teachers' contributions to student learning? About 80 percent of students interviewed by the PISA 2003 test reported that their teachers showed an interest in every student's learning, gave extra help when students needed it, helped students with their learning, continued teaching until students understand, and gave students the opportunity to express opinions (OECD 2004b). These are subjective perceptions of teacher performance, rather than an accurate description of teacher attitudes and classroom practices. Nonetheless, they portray an overall positive general classroom environment in which student learning can be adequately nurtured.

On the basis of data from questionnaires completed by school principals, however, an index of teacher adequacy was constructed reflecting perceptions about the extent to which teacher supply hindered student learning. Thailand was among the countries where principals reported shortages or inadequacy of teachers. For instance, 37 percent of students had principals who believed instruction in mathematics was hampered by teacher inadequacy and 24 percent reported lack of experienced teachers (OECD 2004b). Moreover, poor students' perception of teacher-student relations—that is, students who disagree that most teachers are

Table 6.9   Percent of Teachers with Master's Degree or Higher, 2002

Region	Lower secondary	Upper secondary
BMR	5.9	18.6
North	5.4	15.5
Northeast	2.6	8.4
Central	3.3	9.7
South	3.3	7.3
Whole kingdom	**3.8**	**11.0**

Source: Office of National Education Commission (2003).
Note: BMR = Bangkok Metropolitan Region.

interested in their well-being, treat them fairly, or provide help when needed—had on average a strong and significant negative correlation on mathematics performance (OECD 2004b).

TIMSS constructed an index based on teacher perceptions of their own ability to teach various topics (for example, properties of geometric figures, solving linear equations, earth's features, chemical reactivity). In 1999, 55 percent of students were taught by instructors who felt less than adequately prepared in mathematics and 58 percent of students were taught by instructors who felt less than adequately prepared in science. Only 13 and 18 percent of students were taught by instructors who felt confident in their abilities in science and mathematics, respectively. Higher levels of teacher confidence were associated with superior student scores.

Traditionally, Thai secondary classrooms have relied on a teacher lecture format, rather than on child-centered pedagogical methodologies or active learning environments. On average, Thai students spend about one-fifth of class time each month in lecture-based classes and another one-fifth on teacher-guided student practice. Such distribution of class time is similar to averages reported by students from other countries participating in TIMSS. The distinction between Thailand and other countries lies in the limited opportunities for Thai students to apply knowledge to new situations or exercise creative thinking during the school day. In response to a question that asked students to identify activities frequently undertaken in the classroom, 91 percent reported that teachers actually showed them how to do their mathematics work.

More strikingly, only 19 percent of Thai students reported working independently on class mathematics projects, in contrast to Hong Kong (China) (67 percent) or Korea (46 percent). The international average was 36 percent. More than 90 percent of Thai students practice computational skills in most mathematics lessons; however, only 54 percent of students report that their teachers explain the reasoning behind an idea and a mere 12 percent report the use of tables, charts, or graphs to represent and analyze relationships. Some 93 percent of students report that mathematics teachers use the blackboard for presentations, but only 33 percent of students get called to the front of the class, compared with an international average of 60 percent. A similar trend can be observed in science instruction.

Science instruction does appear to adequately emphasize scientific investigation and practical application. A majority of Thai students report conducting experiments in science classes. More than half of students report that they spend more than 25 percent of class time in practical demonstrations always or pretty often (in contrast to an international average of 38 percent), which is largely on par with Singapore, Japan, Malaysia, and New Zealand.

Overall, these findings from TIMSS and PISA point to a need for targeted teacher support and policies to upgrade skills that complement existing shortfalls and imbalances in teacher performance. Enhancing teacher professional development could potentially translate into significant improvements in student learning.

There is an emerging recognition within the MOE that lasting changes in teacher education practices do not come about from one-time workshops, but rather are the product of sustained capacity development efforts. An ongoing pilot program has sought to train leader teachers (facilitators) and subject teachers through innovative distance training models. Leader teachers and education supervisors also provide continuous support through roving teams. They observe classrooms, make recommendations, and provide advice with teaching planning. This is a promising model. Research evidence suggests that among alternative quality improvement interventions at the school level, teacher training investments can have high payoff in terms of student retention, promotion, and, in particular, student learning (see, for example, Rowe 2003).

School Characteristics. The average student-to-teacher ratio in secondary education is 28:1, ranging from as low as 12:1 in Petchaboon to as high as 37:1 in Chiang Rai. Although student to teacher ratios generally stand below 30:1, class sizes in Thailand are notably larger. The average secondary school class size for Thailand is 43 students.

The relationship between class size and student achievement is difficult to extricate. Although TIMSS and PISA data concur that large class sizes do not appear to have a negative impact on student test scores in Thailand, many other factors influence the higher scores achieved by students from larger classes. Class size in East Asia tends to be larger than the international average, ranging from 36 in Japan to as high as 50 in the Philippines. In Thailand, about 75 percent of eighth-grade students tested in TIMSS enrolled in mathematics classes with 36 or more pupils, while less than 5 percent enrolled in a class with 1 to 20 students. Interestingly, students from larger classes achieved better scores in both mathematics and science (see figure 6.21). PISA results corroborate these findings. No negative effects of adding students could be discerned at any relevant class size in the PISA literacy or mathematics exams (OECD 2003). In Thailand, large classes are generally better equipped and in highly competitive schools. In those schools, students tend to come from higher socioeconomic backgrounds, therefore, receiving better support for education at home. Most schools with small class size tend to be located in rural areas where students are from less privileged backgrounds and cannot afford to attend large city schools.

PISA 2000 collected extensive data on principals' perceptions about the adequacy of school resources (OECD 2003). Based on their responses, a distinction can be drawn between the impact of physical infrastructure (condition of buildings, the instructional space, and heating, cooling, and lighting systems) and education resources (computers, library material, multimedia resources, science

Figure 6.21 Cross-National Comparison of Average Mathematics Achievement and Class Size, 1999

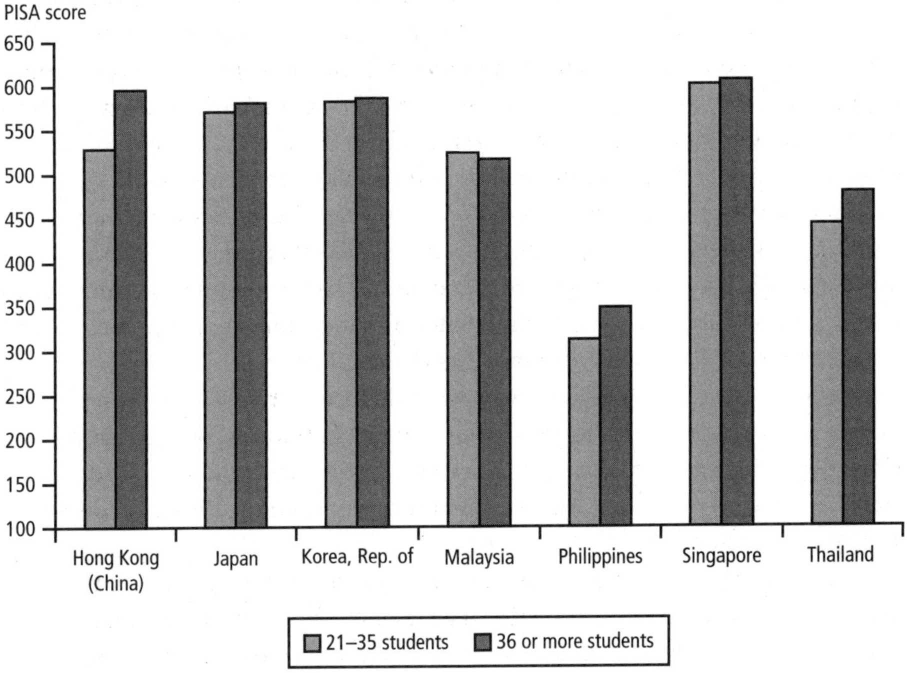

PISA score

Source: Mullis et al. 2000.

laboratory equipment, and facilities for the fine arts) to student learning. School principals perceived the quality of education resources to be a more important obstacle to student achievement than school physical infrastructure. According to Thai school administrators, the quality of school physical infrastructure is rated around the OECD country mean, while school education resources are rated more than two-thirds of a standard deviation *below* the OECD mean (−0.82).

Of particular concern is Thailand's position in the lowest decile among all PISA-participating countries with regards to the difference in the quality of school resources between the top and bottom quarter of schools as characterized by a proxy of school socioeconomic background (OECD 2005b). Moreover, school resources are inequitably distributed among schools. There is a statistically significant performance difference between schools in the top and bottom quarters of this education resources index.

The impact of school resources for instruction on student achievement in mathematics and science is complex, but overall, TIMSS data suggest that they play an important role in advancing student learning. TIMSS created an index of availability of school resources for mathematics and science instruction. This index includes general instructional items—such as basic materials, budget for supplies, instructional space—as well as more specific mathematics and science instructional items—such as computers, library materials, and audio-visual resources. Over half of the students in Thailand report that shortages affect instructional capacity some or a lot, compared with 18 to 20 percent internationally. Less than 40 percent of eighth-grade students had access to a calculator in mathematics class, compared with an international average of 73 percent. Not surprisingly, 85 percent of students have never used a computer in class. Countries that reported shortages in the availability of instructional materials were significantly below the international average in mathematics or science achievement.

Thus, the evidence gathered by PISA, TIMSS, and other research persuasively suggests that there is a shortage of resources for learning in Thai schools, and this is generally perceived as a constraint to higher student achievement. Greater investments in basic school resources to provide a minimum set of materials for effective use by teachers to support instructional content could well buttress student performance in Thailand and translate into higher learning outcomes.

Household and Individual Characteristics. It is widely acknowledged that higher family income and household resources have a positive effect on student achievement. Some of the obstacles that disadvantaged students face include poorly educated parents, greater demand to supplement family income through labor, peers with low academic performance, and lower expectations about the future.

Parents with more education tend to place greater emphasis and provide more support for their children's education. Students whose parents have more education score higher across subjects—reading literacy, mathematics, and science. According to TIMSS, eighth-grade students with parents who are well-educated tend to score better on mathematics and science tests.

Yet, as noted earlier, the differences among socioeconomic groups are not as stark in Thailand as in other countries. For instance, the variance in student performance on the PISA mathematics test was more than 15 percent below the OECD average variance (OECD 2003). Although children from wealthier households perform better than children from poorer households, the distribution of knowledge is fairly equitable across income groups.

Along these lines, parental education is not an influential factor shaping student aspirations for tertiary education in Thailand. Students tended to have high expectations independent from their parents' education background. Although 30 percent of Thai students had a parent who did not finish primary school and another 40 percent had a parent who did not complete upper-secondary school, 55 percent of students expressed an intention to graduate from university (Mullis et al. 2000).

Thus, it appears that efforts to improve student performance need not be primarily targeted along socioeconomic lines. Low-performing students are not concentrated among lower-income quintiles necessarily. Rather, given Thailand's low levels of academic achievement in absolute terms, policies to raise the overall performance level of the general student population are imperative, such as enhancing teacher preparedness and practice, providing adequate instructional materials, promoting performance incentives for school staff, encouraging greater accountability for results, and strengthening a formative evaluative culture.

QUALITY ASSURANCE MECHANISMS IN THAI EDUCATION

Since the NEA was promulgated, the quality of the Thai education system is officially evaluated both internally and externally. Internally, schools are expected to conduct self-assessments of their institutional quality. This process is meant to be woven into the administrative apparatus of each institution. Schools are expected to prepare annual reports that are then submitted to government agencies and made available to the public.

External assessments are meant to complement and follow up on school self-assessments. The NEA established ONESQA as the agency responsible for overseeing quality assessment studies of every education institution at least once every five years. These results are shared with relevant agencies and made available to the public, with the first assessments conducted in 2001. As of March 2005, nearly 98 percent of primary and secondary education schools had been evaluated. The assessments monitor student academic performance, teacher performance, administrator vision and leadership, as well as school laboratories and equipment.

The NEA authorizes ONESQA to submit corrective measures and actions for schools that are performing poorly to improve their function. If an institution continues to perform poorly, a report is submitted to the Basic Education Commission for further action. But anecdotal data suggest that the review process, frequency, and type of advice provided for school improvement by external independent evaluators is insufficient to generate actual changes in schooling practices. There is room for ONESQA's overall supervisory function to be further strengthened to translate the monitoring and evaluation process into tangible improvements in education quality.

The MOE has spearheaded selected research initiatives to further review and strengthen Thailand's education quality assurance mechanisms. A project initiated by the ONEC, now the OEC, strives to better understand how government agencies and schools can work together to improve student outcomes. In-depth data was collected from 250 schools in 2001 and 2002. One of the most notable findings is that education activities across different ministries need to be better harmonized. Recent reform efforts have attempted to streamline the administrative and operational work of government agencies, but schools still consider the system confusing and less than adequate. This situation has been further compounded by the ongoing education decentralization process, where the roles and responsibilities for service provision and administration are shifting and being redefined. Sustained coordination and cooperation between government agencies and education institutions is vital to improve quality assurance and enhancement mechanisms in Thailand.

The importance of the school governance structure in school improvement has received increasing recognition, in particular the role that school community leaders can exert (Gamage and Sooksomchitra 2004). A pilot program examining different types of school boards to explore ways to effectively improve the efficiency of local government and its role in supporting education development is ongoing. Training modules for school boards and administrators have been developed and are being evaluated for possible implementation nationwide.

Thailand's newly established framework for education quality assurance is promising, but at present, it is still at an early stage of development. Teachers and principals need better information about student performance so that they can adequately respond to the education needs of students. Policy makers need to understand the conditions that positively influence learning and identify shortcomings in education service delivery in a timely manner so that interventions can be put in place to support the instructional function of schools. For their part, parents must play a more active role in school decision making so that as partners in the schooling process they can better articulate their needs or aspirations as well as hold schools accountable for the quality of education services received.

EFFICIENCY OF THE THAI EDUCATION SYSTEM

This chapter outlines the basic characteristics of education spending in Thailand, including both public and private sectors, with a focus on secondary education. Secondary education financing in Thailand is confronted by the dual challenges of expanding access while improving quality. It is crucial not only to secure sufficient resources to finance the system, but also to ensure that those resources are apportioned in the most productive manner. Outlined below is an overview of salient issues on secondary education financing, followed by selected recommendations for possible improvements in allocation efficiency.

PUBLIC SPENDING ON EDUCATION

The RGT spends more than one-fifth of its total budget on education, but education allocation has shown a declining trend in recent years. Over the past decade, the Thai government allocated more than 20 percent of its total budget to education, accounting for 4 to 5 percent of the country's GDP. This level of allocation was maintained even through the economic crisis in the late 1990s. The budget

Table 6.10   Education Budget per Fiscal Year, 2000–05

	2000	2001	2002	2003	2004	2005
Education budget (million baht)	220,621	221,603	222,990	235,092	251,233	262,938
As a percentage of total government budget	25.7%	24.4%	21.8%	23.5%	24.4%	21.9%
As a percentage of GDP	4.5%	4.3%	4.1%	4.0%	3.9%	3.7%
Basic education budget as a percentage of total education budget	67.2%	68.1%	68.1%	69.3%	71.5%	70.2%
Basic education budget as a percentage of GDP	3.0%	2.8%	2.8%	2.8%	2.8%	2.6%

Source: Office of Education Council 2005; Office of National Education Commission 2001; and Bureau of the Budget Web site, http://bb.go.th/budget.

allocation for education as a share of GDP peaked in 2000 and has experienced a slight declining trend in recent years (see table 6.10). Conversely, the share of basic education in the overall education budget has been steadily maintained, with a slight upward trend.

More than 80 percent of the education budget is allocated to current expenditure. In 2003, education had the largest average per capita current spending rate of all sectors. Per capita current spending was at 2,425 baht, four times more than the sector with the second largest current spending rate, public order and safety affairs. Sixty percent of current expenditure is used to pay for salaries for permanent and temporary staff, while the rest pays for nonpersonnel items such as remuneration and other services. Education budget trends show that increasing resources have been allocated toward current expenditure in recent years. Although capital expenditures are not made on a regular basis, its share has been declining over time, from 25 to 6 percent between 1997 and 2002.

More than two-thirds of the education budget is allocated to basic education, with preprimary and primary levels receiving the largest proportion. Education expenditure is divided into six categories: preprimary and primary, secondary, tertiary, services not defined by level, education support, and miscellaneous. Almost 50 percent of education resources are allocated to preprimary and primary education levels, with another one-quarter spent on secondary education and 15 percent on higher education (see figure 6.22). Resources allocated to education support have increased recently, rising from 6 billion baht in 1996 to more than 28 billion baht in 2003.

Although basic education (primary and secondary levels) received almost 70 percent of the education budget, it accounts for 90 percent of all students enrolled in the Thai education system (see table 6.11). Tertiary education is given

Figure 6.22   Share of Education Budget by Spending Category, 1997–2004

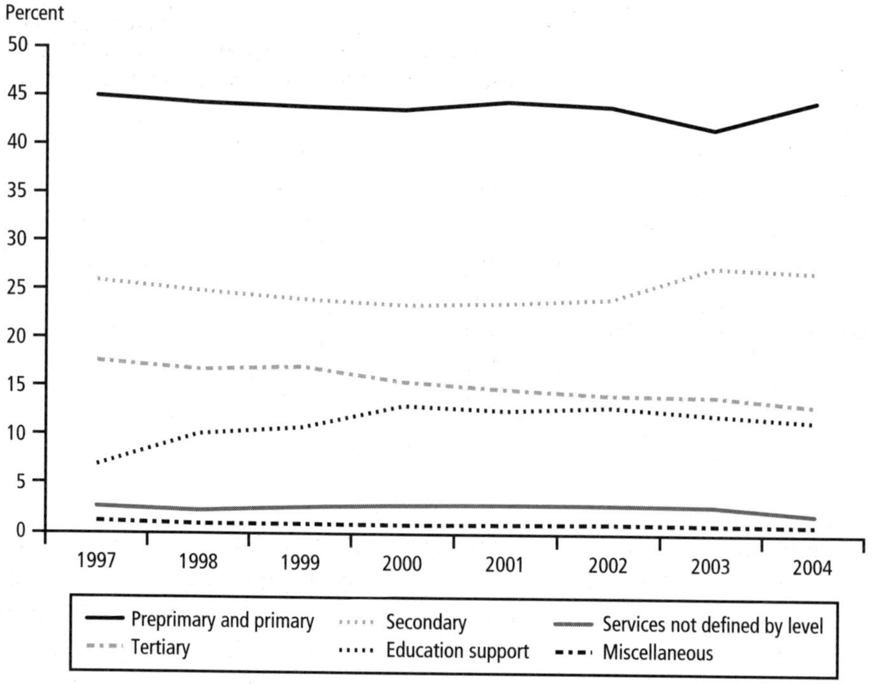

Source: Office of Education Council 2005; and Office of National Education Commission 2001.

Table 6.11   Education Budget Allocation and Student Enrollment by Spending Category, 2002

Level	Total (million baht)	Percent of budget	Percent of enrollment (GER)
Preprimary and primary	98,228	41.7%	62%
Secondary	64,770	27.5%	29%
Tertiary	33,348	14.2%	9%
Services not defined by level	3,377	1.4%	
Education support	28,868	12.3%	
Miscellaneous	6,854	2.9%	
Total	235,445	100%	100%

Source: Office of Education Council 2004b.

close to 15 percent of the budget, although only 9 percent of the total student population is enrolled at this level. In view of the higher cost structures associated with tertiary education, this apparent inequity is commonplace in education systems around the world.

Thailand allocated approximately 28 percent of its total education budget and 1.1 percent of GDP to secondary education in 2003, falling behind what countries

Table 6.12   Total Secondary Education Expenditure as Percent of GDP by Source of Funding, 2003

Country	Income level	Public resources (percent of GDP)	Private resources (percent of GDP)	Share of private resources in all domestic resources
Argentina	Upper middle	1.58	0.38	24%
Chile	Upper middle	1.49	0.70	47%
Colombia	Lower middle	1.53	1.00	65%
Hong Kong, China	High	1.50	0.75	50%
Indonesia	Lower middle	0.48	0.28	58%
Mexico	Upper middle	1.52	0.40	26%
Philippines	Lower middle	0.69	0.58	84%
Korea, Rep. of	High	1.83	0.60	32%
Thailand	Lower middle	1.13	0.06	5%

Source: UNESCO 2005.

with strong secondary education sectors typically spend. On average, in the same year, OECD countries spent 2.1 percent of GDP on secondary education. Lower-middle-income countries allocated on average 40 percent of their total education resources and 1.86 percent of GDP to the secondary level. The limited public financing for secondary education is further compounded by low shares of private resources contributed to secondary education compared with other countries. For example, although the Philippines only invested 0.69 percent of GDP in secondary education, the share of private resources was 84 percent or 0.58 percent of GDP. In Thailand, private sector contributions are equivalent to 5 percent of public sector financing, or 0.06 percent of GDP (see table 6.12). This suggests considerable opportunity for promoting private provision in secondary education.

Per student spending usually rises as students matriculate from primary to secondary to tertiary levels. In East Asia and the Pacific, on average, putting a student through secondary education during the school year 2002–03 was 74 percent more expensive than primary education. These countries spent US$1,711 on each primary level student and US$2,409 on each secondary student (in purchasing power parity converted terms). Among OECD countries, each primary school student cost US$4,818 and each secondary school student cost 28 percent more at US$6,688. Yet in Thailand, *the unit cost for secondary education is lower than the unit cost for primary education.* In 2000, the unit cost for preprimary and primary education was 13,770 baht; for secondary education, 8,564 baht; and for tertiary education, 32,336 baht. Similar trends persist in 2002 data: per student spending was estimated at 13,226 baht for primary education and 10,011 baht for secondary education.

Local governments are reliant on subsidies from the central government to finance education. The RTG has encouraged the decentralization of education management to improve local participation and ownership. Decentralization includes increasing the share of local government resources spent on education. Most local agencies, however, rely on subsidies from the central government to finance education. In general, resources from local government account for only 20 to 30 percent of education spending. Additionally, recent data from the MOE show that subsidies from the central government have been increasing in recent years, the opposite of what should have been observed (Punyasavatsut et al. 2005).

Budget allocation to local levels could be more equitable. Although guidelines to allocate the national education budget at the provincial level exist, they are not strictly followed. In practice, provincial budget allocations are calculated based on how much each province received the previous year. As a result, provinces that started off receiving larger shares of the national education budget continue to receive proportionately more each year, regardless of the number of schools, students, or teachers. Additionally, findings from a study funded by the Asian Development Bank point out that budget allocation at the secondary level favors wealthier provinces and that this trend has remained constant over time (Cresswell 1999). Conversely, the government tends to abide by the funding formula for the allocation of resources to ESAs, which considers such factors as enrollment, number and type of schools, student-to-teacher ratio, and number of classrooms. Yet when ESA budget allocations are disaggregated by gross provincial product, average spending per student appears to benefit the poor at the primary level. But this is not the case at the secondary level (Punyasavatsut et al. 2005).

Bangkok and its vicinity account for the largest share of total education expenditure. Unlike any other region, however, education expenditure is concentrated at the tertiary level in Bangkok, totaling more than preprimary, primary, secondary, vocational, and others combined. The northeast region spends the most on preprimary and primary levels and only about a tenth of that amount on tertiary education. A breakdown of data by per student spending paints a different picture, however (see table 6.13). Because of the large population of school-age children in the northeast region, the per student cost is 2,705 baht compared with 3,952 baht for Bangkok and its vicinity. At the secondary level, while per capita education expenditure in Bangkok and its vicinity is as high as 764 baht per head, the northeast region received only 575 baht per head, the lowest share across regions.

Although education receives the largest share of the national budget across sectors, whether those resources are equally and efficiently distributed among different income groups is debatable. We have estimated expenditure shares by per capita income quintiles. The results, disaggregated by levels of education, show that the poorest 40 percent of the population receives 56 percent of total spending in preprimary and primary levels, reflecting a pro-poor allocation of resources. The quintile distribution for the secondary level is also distributed relatively

Table 6.13   Per Capita Education Expenditure by Region, 2002[a]
(baht)

Region	BMR	Central	Northeast	North	South	National average	National average (without BMR)
Preprimary and primary	706	1,595	1,737	1,718	1,724	1,536	1,699
Secondary	764	699	575	623	760	663	643
Vocational	251	248	142	214	260	208	200
Tertiary	1,960	151	180	442	349	537	257
Others	271	96	71	110	87	118	87
Total	**3,952**	**2,789**	**2,705**	**3,107**	**3,180**	**3,062**	**2,886**

Source: Comptroller General's Department 2002.
Note: BMR = Bangkok Metropolitan Region.
a. Divided by entire cohort population, not the corresponding school-age groups.

Figure 6.23   Incidence of Public Expenditure across Income Quintiles by Education Level, 2002

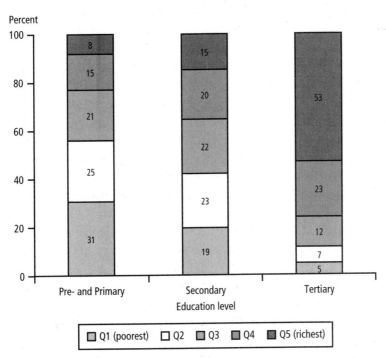

Source: National Statistics Office 2002.

equally and slightly skewed toward giving more to the poor (see figure 6.23). Spending for tertiary education is clearly regressive, regardless of which data are examined. The wealthiest 20 percent of the population receives 53 percent of total spending. Thus, although Thailand's education expenditure pattern is proportionately well distributed across income quintiles as a whole, there are some notable discrepancies.

HOUSEHOLD EDUCATION EXPENDITURE

The government is not the only source of education financing in Thailand. Households, the private sector, nonprofits, and international organizations all contribute to improving the Thai secondary education system (for examples, see box 6.4). As discussed, public resources account for about 95 percent of the domestic education

---

BOX 6.4 PRIVATE PARTICIPATION IN EDUCATION: EXAMPLES FROM KOREA, AFRICA, AND CHILE

In the Republic of Korea, the government introduced subsidies and tax exemptions in the 1970s. Such subsidies were based on the difference between the school's own budget and a standard budget for a public school of the same enrollment size and type. Private school institutions responded to the subsidies and tax exemptions by scaling up their capacity to reach more students. Consequently, as of 2000, private sector enrollment had reached 20 percent for middle schools and 55 percent for high schools.

In Africa, fees have been maintained at the secondary level, even in countries where free primary education is provided, such as Malawi, Uganda, Tanzania, and Kenya. Fees at the secondary level are controlled and increases beyond stated levels must be cleared with the Ministry of Education. The costs to poor families, as well as those with female children or living in hard-to-reach areas, are sometimes subsidized through scholarships.

Chilean schools were previously not allowed to charge fees if they were a public institution or a private school that received government subsidies. This policy was changed in the mid-1990s and private schools are now able to charge fees within certain parameters and can continue to receive subsidies. The Chilean system ensures that schools charging fees exempt a proportion of parents from fee payment and that they use some of the revenue to set up internal cross-subsidies from fee-paying parents to non-fee-paying parents.

Source: World Bank 2005.

Table 6.14 Household Expenditure on Education by Region, 1994–2002

	1994	1996	1998	1999	2000	2002
a. Average household expenditure on education (per year, real baht[a])						
Expenditure quintile						
Bangkok	6,278	6,564	9,666	10,553	10,428	9,585
Central	2,111	2,436	3,291	3,654	2,979	3,280
North	1,702	2,218	2,742	3,958	2,655	2,922
Northeast	1,429	1,579	1,887	1,933	1,665	1,753
South	2,300	2,411	2,815	3,043	2,948	2,882
Total	**2,452**	**2,738**	**3,426**	**3,912**	**3,394**	**3,449**
b. Share of total household expenditure (percent)						
Expenditure quintile						
Bangkok	2.3	2.3	3.6	3.9	3.7	3.2
Central	1.4	1.5	1.8	1.9	1.7	1.6
North	1.4	1.7	1.9	2.5	2.1	2.0
Northeast	1.3	1.5	1.7	1.9	1.7	1.6
South	1.6	1.7	2.0	2.2	2.1	1.8
Total	**1.6**	**1.7**	**2.2**	**2.5**	**2.3**	**2.0**

Source: National Statistics Office 1994–2002.
Note: CPI = consumer price index.
a. Prices are deflated by regional and yearly CPIs (base region = Bangkok, base year = 2002). Yearly CPIs: 1994 = 75.0, 1996 = 84.1, 1998 = 96.0, 1999 = 96.3, 2000 = 97.8, 2002 = 100.

budget for secondary education, with only a tiny share coming from local governments and 5 percent originating from private resources (UNESCO 2005). This section focuses on the current state of household spending on education, with a particular focus on differences between wealthy and poor families.

Average household spending on education in 2002 was 3,449 baht per year, but this expenditure varies dramatically across regions. It ranges from 1,753 baht in the northeast to 9,585 baht in Bangkok (see table 6.14). An analysis over time shows that households in the northeast consistently spend less on education than those in other regions. Education as a share of household expenditure also varies across regions. On average, households in Bangkok spend between 2.3 to 3.9 percent on education, but the share of household education expenditure in the northeast ranges between 1.3 and 1.9 percent.

Poorer households spend less on education. Average household spending by per capita income quintile in 2002 shows that the poorest quintile spends only 840 baht on education while the wealthiest quintile spends more than 7,870 baht (see table 6.15). The difference in spending across income quintiles is reflected not just in the absolute levels of spending on education but also as a share

Table 6.15   Household Expenditure on Education by per Capita Income Quintile, 1994–2002

	1994	1996	1998	1999	2000	2002
a. Average household expenditure on education (per year, real baht[a])						
Expenditure quintile						
Poorest	777	934	1,023	1,044	1,048	840
Second	1,145	1,314	1,432	1,538	1,415	1,322
Third	1,611	1,939	1,928	2,108	1,930	1,822
Fourth	2,445	2,916	3,455	3,325	3,024	3,214
Richest	4,981	5,268	7,237	8,940	7,471	7,878
Thailand	**2,452**	**2,738**	**3,426**	**3,912**	**3,394**	**3,449**
b. Share of total household expenditure (percent)						
Expenditure quintile						
Poorest	1.3	1.5	1.6	1.7	1.8	1.3
Second	1.4	1.5	1.6	1.8	1.8	1.5
Third	1.5	1.6	1.7	1.9	1.8	1.5
Fourth	1.6	1.8	2.2	2.2	2.0	2.0
Richest	1.8	1.9	2.7	3.3	2.7	2.7
Thailand	**1.5**	**1.7**	**2.0**	**2.2**	**2.0**	**1.8**

Source: National Statistics Office 1994–2002.
Note: CPI = consumer price index.
a. Prices are deflated by regional and yearly CPIs (base region = Bangkok, base year = 2002). Yearly CPIs: 1994 = 75.0, 1996 = 84.1, 1998 = 96.0, 1999 = 96.3, 2000 = 97.8, 2002 = 100.

of total household expenditures. Given that poor households spend most of their income on food and other basic needs, fewer resources are allocated for education. Hence, on average, poor households allocate around 1.5 percent of total household expenditures to education, compared with 2 or 3 percent in wealthier households. The financial burden on poor households is compounded during times of economic crises.

Wealthy households allocate more resources toward each secondary school student, and the spending gap between the rich and the poor has widened over time. Results from an estimation of per student spending from the SES show that real spending per student has increased between 1994 and 2002 at all levels of education, most notably at the primary and tertiary levels. This jump is not observed at the secondary level. Furthermore, household secondary expenditure widely varies across per capita income quintiles. In 2002, households in the poorest quintiles spent about 860 baht per secondary school student, compared with more than 6,800 baht in the wealthiest quintile, approximately 8 times as much. This gap appears to have widened over time. In 1994, household expenditure per secondary school student in the top quintile was about 4.5 times as much as that in the poorest quintile, while in 1999 it was 6 times as much.

RAISING EFFICIENCY OF SECONDARY EDUCATION FINANCING

Examining the efficiency of the Thai education system may be a key factor in improving student outcomes. On the one hand, Thailand allocates a significant share of its national income to the education sector. On the other hand, the secondary level captures less than a third of the overall public budget, and the private sector is a relatively minor player in secondary education financing. It has been argued that lower per student expenditures for secondary education, in contrast to primary education, are a reflection of the fact that school expenses are significantly subsidized by private contributions in the form of tuition fees or parental support. But evidence from the SES suggests that this is unlikely. In 2002, families spent on average 1,700 baht to educate a primary school child, while they spent 2,350 baht for a secondary school student. The premium paid by households for secondary education does not make up for the relative decline in public financing, even if primary and secondary education had similar per student costs. In summary, as measured by international standards, Thailand lags behind in providing resources for secondary education.

Despite relatively low levels of financial resourcing, as discussed above, Thai students perform, on average, above predicted levels when considering Thailand's economic developmental stage. Moreover, the distribution of knowledge across Thailand is fairly equitable. These successes on student outcomes indicate that the funding available for secondary education has been put to work in a relatively efficient manner.

Yet, it is also apparent by Thailand's performance in international assessments that student achievement levels are low. A vast proportion of students are functioning at or below the most basic level of language, mathematics, and science ability. Poor academic performance and low education quality have increasingly raised concerns regarding Thailand's competitiveness relative to more developed East Asian countries. Secondary education is an important tool for growth, economic development, and social stability. This raises the question of allocative efficiency in budgeting for the Thai education system. As already discussed above, greater investments in teacher training and education materials could be warranted.

Is there empirical evidence that financial resources act as a constraint for the improvement of student outcomes? Although results from international assessments demonstrate that the impact of socioeconomic background on student performance in Thailand is significantly lower than the OECD average, results from PISA also indicate that "among the more advanced group of students, home background makes a greater difference to student performance in mathematics. In other words, the greater the socio-economic advantage, the greater the advantage it has in terms of student performance" (OECD 2004b, 182). Households from the richest quintile more than double private expenditures on education than households in the fourth quintile. According to the SES, while the fourth quintile spent on average 2,960 baht in private education expenditures, the richest quintile spent 6,890 baht.

International experience points to the fact that quality improvements are costlier at the secondary level than at the primary level (and costlier at the tertiary level than at the secondary level). Thus, achieving universal secondary education will depend on concerted efforts to redirect resources to enroll poor children who are currently excluded. Given Thailand's already sizable investments in education, is there scope for a more efficient allocation of resources? Evidence from the benefit incidence analysis of public spending on education provides evidence that tertiary education investments have disproportionately benefited wealthier sectors of the population. Thus, there may be scope to further investigate the appropriate distribution of the education budget across levels to improve the efficiency of the Thai system. But as noted above, the greatest potential for drawing additional resources into secondary education seems to reside in private sector mobilization.

Another important indicator that should be examined within the context of raising school efficiency is the student-to-teacher ratio. There is a delicate balance between lowering the overall cost of education by minimizing the number of teachers to maximize teacher utility and raising achievement through the provision of more teachers who can then give individual attention to pupils. A study on the efficiency of expenditure in education provision compared PISA 2003 results with teachers per student and time spent at school. Its findings suggest that Thailand is performing significantly below the production function frontier for education. In other words, *inefficiencies in Thailand are relatively high compared with other countries*. These findings hold even when correcting for GDP per capita and parental education attainment under the assumption that wealthier and more cultivated environments are catalysts for better student performance (Afonso and St. Aubyn 2005).

The Thai government has sought in recent years to merge small rural schools together, wherever possible, to maximize efficiency. Scrutiny of other utilization ratios, such as the average number of students per class and the number of classes taught by teachers may shed light on ways to increase internal efficiency (see table 6.16). Conversely, teacher redeployment efforts must ensure that service delivery points remain within a reasonable distance from children's homes to remain accessible. Furthermore, any teacher redeployment effort must consider the needs of remote rural and other disadvantaged areas that experience teacher shortages and rely primarily on volunteer teachers for staffing.

Conventionally, an education system is considered internally efficient if it generates maximum output at minimal cost (Hossain 1996). Outputs are often measured by indicators such as transition rates or cohort survival rates. In Thailand, the transition rate is high from the primary to lower-secondary level, with an

Table 6.16 Utilization Ratios by Education Level, 2002

	Lower secondary	Upper secondary (general)	Upper secondary (vocational)
Number of students per class	39	35	37
Number of classes taught by teachers	1.63	1.59	1.48
Student-to-teacher ratio	24	22	25

Source: Office of Basic Education Commission 2002.

average of 90 percent of students from grade six continuing to grade seven. The rate declines to around 80 percent for students graduating from grade 9 and entering grade 10. The majority of lower-secondary graduates continue to the general, rather than vocational, track. An examination following the same cohort throughout the entire basic education system shows that only 40 percent of students entering grade 1 make it to grade 12. The RTG must continue to closely monitor transition rates, particularly at the junction between the lower- and upper-secondary levels.

Retaining a larger share of students in the education system will lower average per student expenditures per secondary school graduate. Annual public spending per student in 2002 was 13,226 baht for primary education. This means that for every student graduating from primary school, the government spent approximately 80,000 baht over six years. As for the secondary level, public spending per student was 10,011 baht in 2002, thus the total cost of producing one high school graduate is more than 60,000 baht. In total, this means that the government ideally spends almost 140,000 baht for 12 years of schooling. But with only 40 percent of students graduating from secondary school, per pupil expenditures for every secondary school *graduate* are considerably higher.

The NEA ensures that free basic education will be available to all students through government subsidies, whether a student attends public or private schools. The funding mechanism for the provision of free basic education is driven by the number of students at each school. Under the NEA, schools receive per pupil subsidies based on the expected number of students each year, in principle with differential formulas for different "types" of students to adjust for the fact that poor or other disadvantaged children may require additional resources to achieve a similar level of education output. Thus, student counts largely drive the resource allocation process. In addition, both private and public schools receive additional funds for expenditures such as equipment, buildings, and special programs through this funding mechanism. Because allocation of the education budget is dependent on the number of expected students, schools hopefully will become more competitive in an attempt to attract more students. School autonomy will be further encouraged through a proposed block grant system so that operational budgets, including both salary and nonsalary costs, are directly transferred to schools. Schools then have full authority to determine how to allocate funds. Block grants will continue to be calculated based on the number of students, giving an incentive for schools to improve quality and attract more students.

Along with this funding mechanism, a functional accountability system has not been established to act as another avenue for the promotion of education quality and efficiency enhancement. Maximizing the impact of schooling inputs can entail empowering principals and administrators to manage for results and making them accountable for these results. Adequate information allows local stakeholders to reflect on existing practices, support interventions to bring about efficiency changes, monitor performance, and demand results. The school external assessments conducted under the auspices of the ONESQA are in its infancy. The feedback loops to disseminate information and raise community awareness on school management issues are at present largely notional. Pilot programs on school governance and community boards are a promising development to improve oversight on school management practices, which can lead to efficiency gains, but these pilot programs operate on a small-scale basis. Although headed in the right direction, the current education system lacks a coherent framework of checks and balances that fosters greater accountability relations among schools and local actors as well as central administrators. The reforms proposed under the NEA are likely to remain incomplete until stronger accountability measures are put in place.

The NEA articulates a vision for free basic education during nine years of compulsory education. In addition, it proposes ambitious targets on education service provisions, including a student-to-teacher ratio adjusted to 25:1, a new teacher compensation structure, increased and better integrated use of information technology, and additional funds to encourage more children to enroll in the system. These are worthy goals. But these commitments require substantial funding upfront, either from the public or the private sectors. Current spending is insufficient to fulfill these commitments. A study estimating the costs associated with free basic education, based on several different scenarios, shows that an additional 188 to 229 billion baht would be required (Thailand Development Research Institute 2000). Changes to the teacher compensation scheme, increased use of information technology, and the cost to attract more children into the education system requires an additional 95 to 199 billion baht. Raising the cost-effectiveness and performance of the education sector will be imperative to enhance outcomes and contain costs. Without serious considerations to efficiency measures, many of the commitments promulgated under the NEA could remain elusive.

ADDRESSING THE NEXT GENERATION OF CHALLENGES

The 1999 NEA addresses critical issues and challenges faced by Thailand with regard to secondary education. Subsequently, the National Education Plan 2002–16 translates these issues into a plan that can guide education-related agencies toward their reform of Thai education administration and service delivery. The following provides an overview of current government initiatives and policy recommendations that embrace the MOE's vision for greater equitable access, better quality, and increased efficiency in its secondary education system.

INCREASING ACCESS AND EQUITY

The government's initial policies to expand secondary education focused on increasing the available infrastructure to accommodate classrooms beyond grade six. The use of excess physical facilities and teachers in primary schools, resulting from the declining primary-school-age population, helped promote a nearly universal transition rate for lower-secondary education.

In recent years, secondary enrollment expansion efforts aptly shifted focus from supply- to demand-side constraints. The MOE introduced a variety of schemes to tackle the cost barriers associated with schooling participation to realize the commitment to a "free" basic education provision inscribed in the NEA. The introduction of a variety of financial incentive schemes sought to reduce the cost burden on families. The effectiveness of these schemes could be enhanced through better targeting; however, a dearth of demand-side interventions remains at the lower-secondary level. To reach current excluded populations, the government will need to embark on a concerted effort to address cost barriers faced by the poorest children at risk of dropping out.

The Education Provision Policy for Disadvantaged Children lays down a vision to bring into the formal education system traditionally disenfranchised groups, such as children with disabilities and ethnic minorities, through specifically targeted programs. A clear blueprint to translate these ideals into a step-by-step implementation plan is missing. Key agencies responsible for assuming a leadership role in such programs should be identified and resources needed for implementation appropriately allocated.

Existing education guidelines regarding children living in Thailand without Thai citizenship need to translate into on-the-ground actions. Although non-Thai children are included as one of the 16 disadvantaged groups who can potentially benefit from existing education provision policies, in practice, the process is complex and unable to reach the majority of children outside the formal system. Currently, approximately 45,000 non-Thai children are in school and benefiting from per capita budget allocations from the RTG. However, the out-of-school population is estimated to be considerably higher.

The role of alternative education service modalities can certainly be strengthened. Existing programs, although encouraged by the NEA, are small and do not seem to satisfy potential demand. Flexible education arrangements can play a key role in providing opportunities to disadvantaged children in accessing secondary education. Greater flexibility in terms of learning sites, class schedules, and curriculum can provide a more suitable environment to fit the needs of children, such as rural migrant workers, who cannot participate in traditional school settings. To make better use of alternative education enrollments in reaching formal universal secondary education goals, a better understanding is needed of how these systems function. At present, no information is available regarding students between 12 and 17 years old who attend nontraditional secondary programs.

IMPROVING QUALITY

The heart of Thailand's education reform is to improve the human capital of Thai children by providing equal access to quality education. In reality, schools have varied degrees of readiness and resources to provide such education. Students' learning capacity also differs. Thus, the government has emphasized the need to ensure minimum quality standards for service provision for all, and to establish a "fast track" for those students who can cope with a more challenging program.

The Five New School Designs program, overseen by the Bureau for Innovative Development in Education, began in late 2003 in a small number of pilot schools nationwide on a voluntary basis. Autonomous schools decentralize authority in academic, financial, personnel, and general administrative activities. A participatory approach among involved parties is promoted through school committees. Buddhist Way Schools seek to apply teachings of "morality, meditative concentration and wisdom" in their students and in school management. Strategic Plans for Gifted Children emphasize science, music, sports, and Thai performing arts for high-performing children. Bilingual schools administer English Programs and Mini-English Programs through a language immersion curriculum. Schools can charge additional fees from their standard rates. The Information and Communication Technology (ICT) Schools integrate computers to teaching and learning, distance education, and university-school links.

In addition, the MOE has launched a separate initiative, "One District One Lab School" to break the perception that most "quality" schools are located in Bangkok and other large cities. The Lab Schools aim to establish centers of education quality in nonurban districts to reduce social disparities. Their methods will include learner-centered approaches as well as self-learning skills through the use of ICT.

These pilot programs are commendable and can provide important insights about various methodologies and approaches to improve education service provision, if properly evaluated. But these programs are relatively small and, although they could clearly benefit certain groups of students, there are concerns as to how they can be implemented on a large scale. There is also a question about how these initiatives link to other education reform efforts in Thailand and a need to avoid duplicating previous efforts. The bottom line is that, although these meritorious initiatives test innovative approaches to education quality enhancement, they do not add up to a cohesive plan for education quality enhancement and lack an overarching framework for systemic and progressive quality improvement.

Evidence gathered from international assessments indicates that the shortage of resources for learning in Thai schools is generally perceived as a constraint to higher student achievement. Greater investments in instructional resources and teaching aids may be warranted to endow schools with a minimum set of materials. The development of Local Learning Resource Centers can make an important contribution to expand the availability of instructional resources. However, the supply of materials is not a sufficient condition to make a difference in student learning. Teaching aids need to be put to use effectively by teachers to support instructional content delivery.

It is widely accepted that teacher quality is among the most crucial factors contributing to student learning achievement. The Office of the Teacher Civil Service Commission has developed a strategic plan and implemented several efforts to enhance teacher quality including pre-service and in-service development. A major task has been to develop criteria and methods to upgrade teacher standards and quality through a whole-school approach, in which capacity building for teachers and principals is tackled together. The Education Reform Program aims to provide an in-depth understanding of education management, curricular change, child-centered teaching, and classroom research. The MOE has espoused distance learning and computer-assisted instruction as possible media for capacity development and the creation of a master teacher network to exchange experiences with direct assistance from "mobile support teams," Rajaphat Institutes, and ESA staff.

These innovative approaches to capacity development and on-going pilot studies suggest promising results. Conventional teacher development approaches such as seminars or mass distance training have proven to be less effective, because they do not respond to specific needs of teachers. Again, the challenge lies on the translation from vision to implementation of this strategic plan, so that it reaches a scale with tangible national results and goes beyond small ad hoc initiatives.

Internal and external quality assurance mechanisms have been established. The relevance and quality of such assessments themselves needs to be guaranteed, however. Internal assessments and self-assessment are new to Thai culture, so it will take time for schools to assimilate this process as an organic part of school development planning and turn it into a meaningful reflective exercise. Ongoing capacity building efforts at the school and ESA levels will contribute to institutionalize this process.

The proposed approach for direct but constructive external assessment has the potential to improve education quality. The MOE has adopted a cautious approach to manage the "stakes" of this assessment, to encourage school staff to approach it openly as an opportunity for self-improvement. Again, this type of formative review is unfamiliar to Thai administrators and educators. Thus, it will take time to demystify the process and assimilate it. On the one hand, recommendations made by external evaluators must be tangible and achievable. And the quality of external independent evaluators itself needs to be monitored and evaluated for the process to be meaningful. On the other hand, school staff need to demonstrate action to turn around ineffective practices and improve student performance. Mechanisms to provide systematic rewards for improvements in academic or institutional outcomes could be weaved into the current system. Performance-based incentives could provide the necessary impetus to fuel administrative and instructional behavioral changes.

Enhancing accountability systems for school performance can operate as a strong incentive to improve education quality. The authority over curricula, personnel, and finance will be decentralized to ESAs once they have met "readiness" criteria. Significant citizen participation is expected to take place in the management of ESAs. Additionally, pilot programs examining different types of school boards to explore ways to enhance the relevance and responsiveness of education service delivery to local needs are under way. Training modules for school boards and administrators have been developed and are being evaluated for possible implementation nationwide.

A step-by-step implementation plan for decentralization of education provision and management, however, needs to be reinforced. The teacher transfer process has been slow to date. Teachers have been unwilling to renounce the terms of employment as civil servants under MOE for positions with local governments. Local bodies need to build their capacity. Existing technical assistance and institutional strengthening schemes have lacked planning and coordination. As administrative and service delivery functions are being devolved, a strong accountability system must be actively nurtured to foster a service-oriented culture that is responsive to local aspirations and needs.

ENSURING EFFICIENCY

The government has adopted an ambitious organizational reform program to enhance the efficiency of the national education system. The NEA specifies that the financing system will be restructured by providing block grants to ESAs and schools. These grants will be based on a standard capitation formula in addition to other per capita top-ups according to poverty levels and other provisions for disadvantaged students.

In principle, the decentralization process is expected to produce administrative savings. Estimates prepared under the RTG-World Bank Country Development Partnership for Governance suggest that if all the functional decentralization targets of the Decentralization Action Plan are realized, a substantial share of central government apportionments to local boards could be potentially reallocated from administrative to service delivery purposes. In practice, a significant share of local expenditures is centrally mandated, such as personnel expenditures. These central directives could lead to overstaffing and overspending. Moreover, ESAs are not necessarily co-terminous with local government boundaries or responsibilities, generating additional administrative demands. The current lack of clarity on specific duties to be conducted at different government levels also carries the risk of overlapping functions leading to resource waste. Overall, there has been reluctance in transferring functions, so central positions have not been eliminated. Local capacity to take on new functions and responsibilities has been slowly developing. Thus, at this stage, it is unclear to what extent decentralization will indeed materialize into a more efficient government administration.

Another possible avenue for raising efficiency could entail a careful review of student-to-teacher ratios. The average student-to-teacher ratio in secondary education is 28:1. Yet while the student-to-teacher ratio remains relatively low, class sizes are relatively large. The average secondary school class size is 43 students. The Thai government recently sought to merge small rural schools together, wherever possible, to maximize efficiency. Such school consolidation efforts must be balanced by assurances that service delivery points will remain within a reasonable distance from children's homes and that incentives are provided to staff remote rural and other disadvantaged areas that face severe personnel shortages. A functional review of teacher deployment and school staffing arrangements may help distribute staffing resources more equitably across schools and alleviate staffing constraints in establishments with large overcrowded classrooms.

A third possibility to improve systemic efficiency may entail reallocating resources from other education levels, such as tertiary, to secondary education. The bottom line is that secondary education access and quality are not likely to experience notable improvements without an infusion of additional resources. ESAs will be responsible for raising additional funding, but the level of local revenue generation is uncertain and, according to current estimates, likely to be low.

The private sector plays a small role in general secondary education, accounting for 11 percent of student enrollments in lower-secondary and 20 percent in upper-secondary education. Its overall share has either remained largely stagnant or diminished over the past decade. In terms of financial contributions, the private sector accounted for approximately 5 percent of overall domestic secondary education resources. Thus, there is plenty of potential for the private sector to expand its role in the provision of education. Although the government has sought to institutionalize formal channels to encourage funding from private firms, more aggressive promotion efforts are needed to increase the flow of private funds into secondary education.

Thailand has achieved remarkable improvements in the provision of and participation in secondary education. Much has been accomplished in the last decade. The RTG has now embarked on finding solutions to the next generation of challenges: consolidating equitable access, improving quality, and enhancing efficiency. An ambitious reform program is gathering momentum. Dedicated efforts and a continued focus in redressing existing systemic inefficiencies can realize the potential to fulfill the goal of a high-quality universal secondary education for all Thai children.

NOTES

1. Formal education consists of two levels: basic education and higher education. Basic education covers the 12 years of education completed before higher education. Higher education is further divided into two levels, lower than degree and degree levels. Formal education includes schools under the jurisdiction of the government, including institutions that provide schooling for students with disabilities, as well as welfare-based schools that address the needs of students who are socially disadvantaged. Other types of formal education include schools for the ecclesiastic, special education, and vocational and special vocational education, including sports and fine arts schools. Nonformal education reaches out to those outside the formal school system, including early childhood and adult education. Preschools, literacy programs, and certain adult vocational training fit under the nonformal education category. Finally, informal education promotes self-learning and often operates out of community-based locations such as learning centers, libraries, and museums.

2. In September 2000, the RTG, along with other governments, signed the Millennium Declaration, pledging a commitment toward achieving the Millennium Development Goals (MDGs), where achieving universal primary education is one of the eight goals. The first report on Thailand MDGs, launched in June 2004, assessed the current Thai education system and showed that Thailand has already achieved universal primary education in terms of its GER.

3. The SES is conducted every two years by the National Statistics Office. It contains information on household income, household consumption patterns, changes in assets and liabilities, ownership of durable goods, and housing characteristics. It was first conducted in 1957 with intervals of five years until 1988, after which point the survey has been undertaken every two years.

4. It should be noted, however, that many children with physical disabilities do not require additional support if the environment has been made accessible and they are provided with the necessary assistive devices.

5. These include the availability of a dishwasher, a room of their own, education software, a link to the Internet, and the number of cellular phones, television sets, computers, motorcars, and bathrooms at home. This type of variable has been used in many other studies as a good proxy for household welfare in the absence of consumption information (see Filmer and Pritchett, 1997).

CHAPTER 7

Education in Ireland: Evolution of Economic and Education Policies since the Early 1990s*

Daniel O'HARE

INTRODUCTION

Readers may wonder why the Irish education experience is included in a volume on education development in Asia. The reason is simple. The education lessons from Ireland are potentially relevant to the African audience to whom this publication is directed. Indeed, the parallels between initial circumstances in Ireland and those that currently prevail in many African countries are numerous. At independence, Ireland had to deal with a highly dependent agrarian economy, inexperienced leadership, and a period of civil unrest, circumstances also confronted by various African nations. It experimented with economic nationalism and protectionism. It wrestled with high graduate unemployment and brain drain, challenges that still prevail in many parts of Africa. Yet another parallel is found in Ireland's experience with structural adjustment made in response to deficit spending by earlier governments. Ireland faced the test of putting overseas development assistance to good use while accommodating the requirements of donor agencies.

---

*Careful readers of this volume will recognize similarities among the policies employed by Ireland and those of the Asian Tigers described in other chapters. Among them are a strong interventionist role by government on the supply side of education; an early demographic transition to lower fertility rates; favorable regulatory, tax, and investment conditions; initial achievement of universal primary education; subsequent emphasis on technical education at the senior secondary and tertiary levels; later attention to R&D capacities in science and technology; continuous concern with social equity and provisions for disadvantaged groups; and the development of lifelong learning programs to build and maintain worker competitiveness in knowledge and skills. Perhaps the most important common feature has been the sustained commitment by successive governments to fundamental policy goals, pursued in a climate of partnership between the government and key stakeholders and implemented with flexibility in response to experience acquired and changing circumstances.

Other similarities include its needs for public sector capacity building, its society's strong belief in the value of education, and its campaign to achieve universal basic education.

The story of Ireland's development—in both the economic and the education spheres—is a narrative of constant struggle, of thought and experimentation, of openness to new thinking, and of a willingness to discard old and failed policies as soon as it became clear that they were not working. Thus, no miracle occurred here. If a lesson is to be found in this history, it is simply that when governments work continually in the people's interest, and when the people work constantly in the nation's interest, much can be accomplished over time.

The following discussion first addresses Ireland's economic development experience. It then deals separately with the progression of its education system in primary and secondary education and higher education. The discussion is approached in this way because, whereas economic and education developments have clearly been intertwined in practice, the evolution of economic policy making has had its own dynamic. The same applies to education. It seemed that intermingling the two experiences might make it difficult for clear insights and lessons to emerge. Thus, a set of reflections unites these two historical streams, using each as a pillar in Ireland's overall development.

THE ECONOMIC DEVELOPMENT OF IRELAND, 1922–PRESENT

Ireland achieved its independence from Great Britain in 1921. The year 2006 therefore marked eighty five years of self-governance. It is useful to reflect on the strains and challenges the transition to independence placed on Irish politicians and leaders—many of whom were young and certainly inexperienced. They had no real understanding of national governance, policy formulation, industrial strategy, nor international financial issues—and, especially, of nation building. The first years of independence were hugely affected by a ruinous civil war. Families, communities, and the nation were divided. This division has had a strong effect on national politics since that time and, in fact, influenced national politics well into the 1990s, although to a hugely diminished degree. This wrenching experience has had many consequences. The most important of these has been the general absence of left-right politics and political philosophies. Instead, "civil war" politics have prevailed and, coupled with the pragmatism and inclusiveness of the two major civil war political parties, have ensured a generally weak labor political movement. The civil war political parties have embraced policies that would find comfortable homes in parties of the right or the left in other nations. On balance, however, Ireland's major political parties have never proposed radical left or right policies. In short, it has been a rather conservative country.

EVOLUTION OF THE IRISH ECONOMY

Since independence in 1922 the evolution of the Irish economy falls broadly into two main periods:

- The Era of Protectionism and Economic Nationalism, 1922–55.
- The Outward Orientation of Ireland's Economy, 1955–present.

These eras will be explored in turn.

THE ERA OF PROTECTIONISM AND ECONOMIC NATIONALISM, 1922–55

During this period, a decisive shift in political perspective occurred that favored economic nationalism and protectionism based on "infant-industry" arguments. This shift was in line with much conventional economic theory. John Maynard Keynes, for example, in a lecture delivered in Dublin in 1933, while warning against the dangers to be avoided in economic nationalism, advocated a policy of national self-sufficiency and advised: "Let goods be homespun wherever it is reasonably and conveniently possible, and, above all, let finance be primarily national" (Keynes 1993).

At the time, Ireland essentially had an agrarian economy. Those working in agriculture accounted for more than 50 percent of the labor force, and agricultural exports constituted almost 90 percent of exports. Beginning in the 1930s, efforts were made to build up an indigenous industrial capability by introducing *ad valorem* duties, which ranged from 15 percent to 75 percent and were applied to a variety of imported goods. Revenues were used for the parallel promotion of industrial enterprises in Ireland. State-owned banks were established to provide financing for industrial and agricultural development. The state became increasingly involved in the provision of transportation services, utilities, and the promotion of economic development. Legislation introduced in the 1930s stipulated that, in the case of all new manufacturing companies (unless they were specifically exempted from these requirements by the government), Irish nationals must hold 51 percent of the nominal share capital and two-thirds of shares with voting rights.

Protectionist and economic self-sufficiency policies, pursued during the 1930–60 period, generated only limited success. Undoubtedly, state involvement in the provision of utilities, including a national electrification program, and in internal and external transportation services (including rail, bus, sea, and air) created the basic infrastructural foundations for some advance in the state's conventional economic and social objectives. Similarly, state participation in promoting economic development through the provision of sectoral banking facilities and other activities produced occasional achievements. In the case of industry, total

Table 7.1   Changes in Population and Labor Force, 1926–61

	1926	1961
Population	3,010,000	2,818,000
Labor force	1,300,000	1,109,000
of which:		
Agriculture	653,000 (50%)	379,000 (34%)
Industry	162,000 (13%)	259,000 (23%)
Services	406,000 (31%)	415,000 (38%)
Unemployed	79,000 (6%)	57,000 (5%)

Source: Central Statistics Office Ireland.

employment increased by some 50 percent during the 1930s under the protectionist policies in place. Labor productivity in the manufacturing industry fell despite this relatively significant increase in employment within the sector. In a less protected environment, such employment growth might have been associated with new, more capital-intensive and productive enterprises.

But these policies, even if not effective at the time, produced as by-products two important national assets that would be drawn upon at a later stage. First, these initiatives provided valuable learning experiences with regard to effective state intervention in the economic development process. Second, they fostered an indigenous management capacity that would be put to good use in the longer term. In this way, Ireland avoided becoming an "absent landlord" or a dependent economy as a result of its human resource shortcomings at independence.

As a result of the complex of factors linked to protectionist policies pursued into the 1950s, Ireland's population and labor-force fell to their lowest levels since the emigration peak in the early nineteenth century. But at the same time, agricultural exports still accounted for almost two-thirds of total exports. The bulk of these were purchased by the United Kingdom (U.K.) which, pursuing urban-oriented "cheap food" policies, meant that the prices paid for these exports were low. Table 7.1 summarizes the performance of the Irish economy over the period from independence until 1961.

From independence until the early 1960s, Ireland's economy concentrated on the production of agricultural commodities, and the British market dominated as the main destination of Irish exports (92 percent in 1929 and 75 percent in 1960). Early indications of an export shift toward industrial exports were becoming apparent, however, as the share of agricultural exports fell from 50 percent to 34 percent, while industrial exports increased from 13 percent to 23 percent of the total.

THE OUTWARD ORIENTATION OF IRELAND'S ECONOMY, 1955–PRESENT

Beginning in the 1950s, economic policies in Ireland increasingly focused on export generation. In this context, the Irish economy opened to embrace international developments. Policy orientation during the past 50 years evolved throughout four broad phases:

- The Shift from Protectionism to Internationalism, 1955–73.
- The Impact of the International Oil Crisis, 1973–83.
- Crisis-Driven Adjustment, 1983–93.
- Period of Exceptional Economic Growth, 1993–present.

The Shift from Protectionism to Internationalism, 1955–73. The full impact of the relative failure of economic policies became clear with the 1961 Census of Population. It showed that the Irish population had fallen to 2.8 million—its lowest level in 200 years. Population had been driven down by emigration during the 1950s, which reached an intensity not experienced since the nineteenth century. This development triggered a series of policy changes that laid the foundation for high rates of economic growth of the 1960s and early 1970s. The principal policy changes were as follows:

- In 1951, an Export Promotion Board was established to help exporters.
- In 1952, the remit of the Industrial Development Authority (IDA), which had been established in 1949, was extended to promote foreign direct investment (FDI) and to encourage the establishment of new Irish-owned industries.
- In 1952, a new State body (*An Foras Tionscal*) was established to award grants for capital investment and training in industry and tourism—initially in the less-developed regions of the country but subsequently (1956) in all regions.
- In 1956, a 10-year moratorium (later extended) was introduced for taxes on corporation profits generated from export activities.
- In 1959, the Shannon Free Airport Development Company was created as the first customs free industrial zone in the twentieth century.
- The legislation introduced in the 1930s to ensure majority Irish ownership in new manufacturing plants established in Ireland was dismantled.

In 1958, the Department of Finance published a study advocating an integrated approach to economic development; this guided a series of economic development programs prepared by the government during the 1960s. This seminal policy document "Economic Development" was the brainchild of the Secretary General of the Department of Finance, Dr. T.K. Whitaker, and received support from the *Taoiseach* (the prime minister). This document recommended the following: (a) abandonment of the outmoded protectionist policy, (b) adaptation to a free-trade world, (c) encouragement of export-oriented industry, (d) expansion of industry and services—even if foreign owned, (e) an emphasis on productive investment in public capital budgets, and (f) a more coherent and planned approach to national development (Whitaker 1958). Whitaker's intuition as to "the psychological value of setting up targets of national endeavour, provided they are reasonable and mutually consistent," was amply confirmed by the unprecedented economic progress of the 1960s (Whitaker 1958). At this stage, Ireland began its transition to a market-oriented economy.

These programs had limited success in terms of achieving the specific growth targets that they put forward for different sectors of the economy, and they were consequently abandoned in the early 1970s. But they provided an impetus to the *process* of considering the development potential of the economy in a more integrated and forward-looking way, and they took into account international as well as purely domestic factors. During the 1960s, this process was further developed through the following policy initiatives:

- Ireland applied to join the European Economic Community (EEC) along with the United Kingdom in 1961. (This application was left moribund with the breakdown of negotiations on the U.K. application in 1963.)
- A phasing out of import quotas and tariffs was initiated.
- A series of studies of the industrial sector were undertaken by the state, employer bodies, and trade unions. These sector studies identified specific actions for industry to undertake to be able to compete effectively in a free-trade environment.
- Ireland became a full member of the EEC on January 1, 1973.

The results of these developments were significant in terms of Ireland's economic development. The economy (measured in gross domestic product [GDP]) grew at an average rate of almost 4.5 percent per year from 1960 to 1973. The population decline, which reached its low point in 1961, was arrested. Living standards increased markedly. Most important, a significant transformation took place within the structure of the economy:

- Manufacturing output increased by a factor of more than 2.5, in real terms, between 1958 and 1973.
- Exports, as a proportion of manufacturing output, increased from 5 percent in 1958 to 30 percent in 1973.
- The average annual rate of growth in the export of goods and services between 1958 and 1973 was more than double the highest rate achieved in any 10-year period since independence.
- Export markets diversified, with European exports doubling between 1960 and 1973, while increasing shares were destined to the United States and other countries.
- The proportion of national employment in the agriculture sector fell from 34 percent in 1961 to less than 25 percent in 1971.

The Impact of the International Oil Crisis, 1973–83. After a decade of unprecedented economic growth, Ireland's entry to EEC membership in 1973 generated high expectations of further economic advancement. These expectations were not realized, however. Unanticipated international oil price jumps in 1973 and 1979, the associated world economic recession, and inappropriate economic policy responses pursued by successive governments combined to frustrate these hopes.

At the outset of the 1970s, Ireland imported more than 70 percent of its primary energy requirements. Thus, the sharp rise in oil prices between 1972 and 1980 hit the economy hard. These difficulties occurred as major changes took place in the population and labor force. A now-increasing population was driven by a major turnaround in the pattern of migration. A net population *increase* of 103,000 resulted from immigration over the 1971–81 period, thus reversing a century-old trend in net outward migration. The influx of people to Ireland during the 1970s was a consequence of the noted high expectations of economic growth associated with EEC membership and the poor performance of the U.K. economy with which Ireland shared a joint labor market. By the mid-1980s, the Irish economy was in crisis. Although some increase occurred in GDP, the level of GNP actually fell, in real terms, between 1982 and 1986. Unemployment increased by 77,000 between 1980 and 1985, and the unemployment rate reached 16 percent by 1988. The traditional response pattern of high emigration resumed and accelerated during the 1980s. Net positive migration (inflow) to Ireland of 103,000 between 1971 and 1981 was followed by a net negative migration (out flow) of 208,000 over the following decade of 1981–91. The crisis was so severe that it forced sectional economic and political interests to be set aside in a common national effort that sought economic recuperation. Subsequently, consensus was forged around a national economic development strategy that set the stage for a period of exceptional growth stretching from the 1990s and to the present.

Crisis-Driven Adjustment, 1983–93. The economic crisis of the mid-1980s, fueled in large part by increased government borrowing, led to the negotiation of a three-year national agreement between the government, employers, and trade unions in 1987. At the core of this agreement was a decision to limit wage increases to 2.5 percent a year over the three-year period. The agreement included measures to balance public finances and to offset the low wage increases with reductions in personal taxation rates. Additionally, concurrence was achieved regarding the thrust of government policies in support of the industrial, services, and agricultural sectors. An important feature was the sense of common national purpose that the agreement established. A key outcome of the agreement was that it provided a framework within which the government could manage imbalances in public finances through cutbacks in public expenditure without creating social tensions and industrial unrest. These cutbacks included a refusal to continue subsidizing many traditional industries that were unable to meet the rigors of international competition. The agreement program, and the vigor with which it was implemented by the social partners, did much to restore investor confidence in the economy.

The success of this approach is supported by the following outcomes:

- Inflationary expectations in wage negotiations were broken.
- The average annual rate of GDP growth recovered to more than 5 percent.
- The Exchequer borrowing requirement as a proportion of GNP fell from 12 percent in 1986 to 2 percent by 1990.
- The national debt as a proportion of GNP fell from 125 percent in 1987 to 98 percent in 1990.
- Following the loss of some 75,000 jobs between 1980 and 1986, employment regained more than 50,000 of these positions over the following five years.

The success of the 1987–90 social compact led to a series of three-year social partnership programs. These have been extended, on a voluntary basis, to include local government and nongovernmental sectors in addition to employees, trade unions, and the government. As a result, a social partnership ethos has been embedded in the public policy area whereby all new policy initiatives are discussed under the social partnership arrangements before they are formally introduced. Needless to say, this represents an extraordinary national achievement as well as a sizeable national asset.

Period of Exceptional Economic Growth, 1993–Present. The difficult process of economic adjustment initiated in the mid-1980s, together with the key gains of earlier decades, produced a period of exceptional economic growth that continues today. GDP growth averaged 9 percent annually from 1994 to 2004. The average annual rate of inflation was 1.9 percent between 1993 and 1999, rising to about 4 percent in 2006. Other principal features of this transformation are given in table 7.2.

The accelerated rate of increase of per capita GDP in Ireland relative to the European Union over the past 30 years has been driven by two principal factors: strong productivity growth (output per head) as technology has been increasingly applied to the industrial sector; and a falling economic dependency ratio (that is, the ratio of total population to the number of people employed). Per capita GDP rose from 80 percent of the EU average in 1960 to 110 percent in 1999. The dependency rate in Ireland relative to the European Union has evolved from 140 in 1960 to 100 at present, which is the EU average (Economic and Social Research Institute 1999).

The evolution of Ireland's economy during the 1990s continued its long-term trend from a natural-resource, agriculture-based, inward-looking, narrow-export economy into a high-tech, knowledge-based, export-driven economy. Today, it is one of the most open trading economies in the world. Strikingly, the value of

Table 7.2 Ireland—Basic Data

	1993	2003
Population	3.6 m	3.9 m[a]
Unemployment (percent)	15.7	4.7[b]
Labor force	1.4 m	1.9 m
Government debt as percent of GNP	93	34
Corporation tax range (percent)	10–40	12.5–25
Personal tax range (percent)	27–48	20–42
Exports (€ billion)	12.4	123.5
Irish GDP per capita as percent of EU-15 GDP per capita	69	125

Source: Central Statistics Office Ireland.
Note: m = million.
a. 4.04 million in 2005.
b. 4.3 percent in 2006.

Table 7.3 Destination of Exports by Region, 1960–2005
(percent)

Year	United Kingdom	Rest of Europe	United States	Other	Total
1960	75	6	8	11	100
1970	62	11	13	14	100
1980	43	32	5	20	100
1990	34	41	8	17	100
1999	22	43	15	20	100
2005	18	46	18	18	100

Source: Central Statistics Office Ireland.

exports and imports combined amounted to more than 160 percent of GDP in 1999. Table 7.3 illustrates Ireland's progress in export market diversification.

The sectoral composition of GDP has undergone a dramatic change in emphasis over the past four decades. Whereas the services sector has remained stable at slightly less than 50 percent, agriculture decreased from 25 percent to 5 percent, while industry increased from 29 percent to 46 percent.

THE UNDERLYING REASONS FOR SUCCESS

In seeking to identify the underlying reasons for Ireland's impressive economic performance in recent years, it is useful to keep in mind the following facts. Indeed, they could well constitute applicable lessons for other countries in similar circumstances.

• There is no "silver bullet." No single unique reason caused the success achieved. The explanation resides in a combination of multiple factors.

- The success achieved is no overnight transformation. Many of the underlying factors that determined the success of recent years are rooted in actions taken during the 1960s and 1980s.
- The application of ideas and knowledge has transformed business and industry and has been crucial in the development of the Irish economy. (This is discussed more fully in the concluding section.)
- The Irish government's economic policies are directed toward the creation of a stable economic environment that is supportive of the needs of business.
- The forces of growth are firmly rooted in Ireland's economy in the form of favorable demographics, increasing investments in education, and a high rate of technology-oriented investments.
- Ireland is a small, open, trade-dependent economy. Its openness is reflected in the international mobility of its labor as attested by its strong migratory fluxes and of capital as evidenced by its high levels of FDI.

The following eight factors, alluded to in the historical review above, are among the most influential in explaining the success achieved in more recent years:

- Macroeconomic management.
- EU membership.
- Social partnership agreements.
- Research and development (R&D) investment.
- Taxation reform.
- Demographics, skills, and education.
- Public administration.
- Industrial policy.

Macroeconomic Management. Sound fiscal and monetary policies are an essential prerequisite for investor confidence and economic growth. At the low point of Ireland's economic performance (1986), the macroeconomic situation was difficult. The effectiveness of the government's combined policy interventions is evident in a comparison of the 1986 position with that of 2005 (table 7.4).

Table 7.4 Macroeconomic Management Indicators, 1986 and 2005

	1986	2005
Exchequer borrowing	Deficit	Surplus
National debt as a percent of GDP	122	28
Taxation as a percent of GNP	46	34
Prime lending rate (percent)	15	5
Annual inflation rate (percent)	20	4

Source: Central Statistics Office Ireland.

The turnaround associated with good macroeconomic management over the past decade has been remarkable, including control over public expenditure in line with the revenue potential of the economy and a reduction in the burden of taxation. It has laid a foundation of good fundamentals on which the exceptional economic performance of recent years, especially that of the industrial sector, has been erected. To achieve the necessary control over public expenditure, particularly in the earlier years of economic recovery, a national consensus on public expenditure priorities was painstakingly constructed. As noted, this consensus has been negotiated under a series of three-year Social Partnership Agreements since 1987.

EU Membership. EU membership has exerted a major and pervasive influence on Ireland's economic development in diverse ways not always fully recognized. The impact can be summarized under a number of headings:

Macroeconomic stability: The Maastricht criteria for European Monetary Union membership imposed an important external impetus toward achieving a more disciplined approach to the management of public finances. They helped to sustain consensus on the need to achieve a balance in the public finances included in the series of Social Partnership Agreements. The resulting improvements now underpin much of Ireland's good economic performance.

EU Transfers: Net EU financial transfers to Ireland peaked at 6.6 percent of GDP in 1991, with more than two-thirds of the revenues coming from FEOGA (the main EU Fund for support of the agriculture sector). By 1999, net receipts from the European Union had declined to 1.9 percent of GDP and FEOGA receipts accounted for about 60 percent of the total. A significant feature of recent years is the additional resources made available under the European Social Fund, Regional Development Fund, and the European Cohesion Fund to increase investments in human resources, R&D, and physical infrastructure, as well as to underwrite new business ventures, particularly in the Irish-owned enterprise sector. Ireland may soon be a net contributor to the EU budget rather than a net recipient.

Reform of the Public Finance System: EU transfers under the Community Support Framework have given impetus to the modernization of Ireland's public finance system. This has taken the form of longer-term planning, multiyear budgeting, the introduction of effectiveness evaluations, and value-for-money audits in a much more systematic way than had been the case.

Unified EU Market: The removal of barriers to the movement of goods, services, capital, and people within the EU has had a dynamic impact on opening this regional economy to external competition and stimulating firms toward productivity gains. This is essential for an economy dependent upon export-led growth, as is the case in Ireland. The progressive integration of Ireland's economy into a single EU market of 360 million people has been a determinant of Ireland's success in attracting FDI and in upgrading the performance of Irish-owned enterprises.

Social Partnership Agreements. The five national agreements negotiated among the social partners beginning in 1987 have been essential for Ireland's improved economic performance. They arose from a deep sense of crisis associated with Ireland's declining economic performance in the mid-1980s. The social partnership approach has stabilized risk and introduced predictability in the area of remuneration trends and industrial relations procedures. Specifically, these agreements have enabled the following:

- Modest levels of pay increases.
- Significant reductions in average tax rates on employee incomes.
- An improved industrial relations climate with fewer disputes and a 90 percent reduction in the number of working days lost because of strikes over a 15-year period.
- The flexibility required to achieve control of the public finances, to initiate a program of public sector reform, and to establish a macroeconomic framework consistent with Ireland's competitive needs and criteria for participation in the European Monetary Union.
- Record levels of employment increases.
- Significant improvements in living standards for employees.
- A central and positive role for the trade union movement, employer bodies, and other social partners in influencing government policies as a quid pro quo for a more modest stance on pay and industrial relations issues.

R&D Investment. As part of its Lisbon Strategy, the European Council decided that 3 percent of the EU's GDP should be spent on R&D by 2010. The *Irish Strategy for Science, Technology and Innovation, 2006–2013* (Department of Enterprise, Trade and Employment 2006) envisions that Ireland will reach 2.5 percent of GDP expenditure on R&D by 2013.[1] Although substantial increases in R&D expenditure have been achieved in Ireland, limited progress has been made in narrowing the gap between Ireland and the investment targets set by the European Union and the Organisation for Economic Co-operation and Development (OECD) as a share of GDP. At 1.4 percent of GDP, Ireland's present R&D investment remains about 0.5 percentage points below that of the European Union and 0.9 percentage points below that of the OECD.

In 2003, business expenditure on R&D in Ireland stood at €1,075.6 million. This represents a nominal average annual growth rate of 19.4 percent over the previous two years. In 2003, the government introduced R&D tax credits to encourage enterprises to invest in research and technological developments. Despite having one of the strongest growth rates in business expenditure on R&D, as a percentage of overall economic activity, this indicator has remained static. Strong R&D gains have been matched by equally strong economic growth.

Most business expenditure on R&D in Ireland is undertaken by foreign-owned companies. The *Irish Strategy for Science, Technology and Innovation, 2006–2013* proposes that R&D expenditures by indigenous companies will grow to €825 million by 2013, that is, 33 percent of the total target amount.

Ireland's higher education sector significantly raised its R&D spending from €322 million in 2002 to €492 million in 2004—a 53 percent increase. This increase outpaced economic growth, pushing up relative intensity. Expanding higher education R&D activities have been driven by direct government funding through Science Foundation Ireland (SFI) and the Higher Education Authority's (HEA) Programme for Research in Third-Level Institutions (PRTLI).

Links between the private sector and tertiary education in Ireland remain poor. Since the launch of government-sponsored PRTLI and SFI funding in 2000, the level of R&D expenditure by higher education has increased dramatically. But industry-financed R&D within the tertiary sector has remained static. Consequently, the share of overall higher education R&D financed by industry has fallen considerably, from 6.6 percent in 1996 to 2.6 percent in 2004.

The "R&D Action Plan for Promoting Investment in R&D" has set a target of 9.3 Irish researchers per 1,000 of total employment by 2010. Some progress has been made, with the number of researchers growing from 5 per 1,000 total employment in 2001 to 5.8 in 2004.

As a vibrant knowledge economy, Ireland has become the advertising message to the world from the government of Ireland. The ability to use knowledge quickly, flexibly, and creatively is a distinguishing feature for Ireland among many world-leading companies. Ireland is reinforcing this image through a new marketing campaign under the banner "Ireland, knowledge is in our nature." In testimony to this claim, more than 50 percent of jobs in 2005 required third-level or higher qualifications in a wide range of disciplines.

The breadth and depth of sophisticated R&D projects now being competitively awarded to Irish firms drives world-class innovation. Among the many significant R&D investment decisions favoring Ireland in 2005 were those of Bristol-Myers Squibb, Citigroup, Genzyme, Pfizer, and Xilinx. Global transformation has brought fresh opportunities in the types of functions being added by Ireland's existing companies and new entrants. Ireland now serves as a European Operations Hub for many companies across a range of sectors and activities, for example, Pfizer's financial shared services center, Kelloggs's marketing and sales, and Google's multilingual financial and administrative functions. These are a few examples of the range of companies, sectors, and functions that have flourished by recognizing Ireland's unique blend of language, communication, and technical skills enhanced by a demonstrably attractive living environment.

The addition of strategic functions such as R&D, intellectual property management, sales and marketing, and supply chain management by existing multinational investors in Ireland further attests to the attractiveness of Ireland for a new breed of investments based on knowledge. Ireland's future success will depend on its ability to foster an environment in which research and knowledge, high-level skills and expertise, high-quality infrastructure, and business services are combined in the flexible and creative ways needed to sustain productivity growth and competitiveness.

Taxation Reform. The Irish taxation regime has been significantly reshaped over the past 10 years and, particularly, over the past 5 years. Changes have encompassed income tax rates, bands and allowances, capital taxes, and corporation taxes. Personal income tax rates have fallen from 35 percent (lower rate) and 60 percent (higher rate) in the mid-1980s to 20 percent (lower rate) and 42 percent (higher rate) in the tax year 2001–02. The higher rate has been further reduced to 41 percent in the 2007 budget. A single 12.5 percent rate of corporation tax for commercial income in all sectors of the economy provides a major incentive for the development of the enterprise sector in Ireland.

Demographics, Skills, Education, and Attitudes. Ireland's total investment in knowledge (including investment in public and private spending on higher education) increased by an average annual rate of more than 10 percent during the past decade. This compares favorably with averages of around 3 percent by the European Union and the OECD. Surveys show that foreign investors consider the quality of work and the flexible can-do attitude of the Irish people to be two of the country's greatest advantages.

The availability, quality, and potential productivity of the Irish labor force have been major factors in attracting internationally mobile investment in the traded goods and services sector to Ireland. Areas of significant output and employment growth include electronics, financial services, pharmaceuticals, and computer software. These same factors underlie the fundamental transformation of Irish-owned industry in recent years. The Irish-owned software sector, for example, now employs some 10,000 people—up from low figures in the early 1990s. The value of software exports has been growing at more than 30 percent annually in recent years, and Ireland is now the biggest exporter of software products in the world.

The quality of the labor force reflects the high value that is widely attached to education and to the acquisition of skills and qualifications within Irish society. Ireland's education system also benefits from, and reinforces, important cultural characteristics, including the following: creativity, flexibility, pragmatism, agility, and informality. A long-standing public policy of providing universal (free) access to education opportunities beyond the primary school level—first and second level since the mid-1960s and subsequently at the third level since the early 1990s—ensures that financial barriers do not impede student access. Expenditure on education as a proportion of total public expenditure is higher in Ireland than in any other EU member state. These policies have resulted in 82 percent of the students who entered the second-level sector five years prior sitting for the School Leaving Certificate examinations in 2005 compared with only 20 percent in 1965.[2] Participation rates in the tertiary sector by 17 and 18 year olds rose from 11 percent in 1965 to 60 percent in 2005.

The education attainment of those employed in Ireland has increased substantially. The proportion of employees with third-level qualifications more than tripled from 12 percent in 1981 to more than 36 percent in 2006, and today is approaching 40 percent. In terms of higher education achievement, the percent of the population that has attained at least tertiary education in Ireland is greater than in France, Denmark, Germany, and the United Kingdom. Compared with other EU countries, Ireland ranks highly in education attainment, particularly in the areas of science and engineering. The independent *IMD World Competitiveness Yearbook* (1999, 2006) ranks Ireland among the top countries in Europe for the quality of the education received and the degree to which the education system meets the needs of a competitive economy. In fact, according to 2005 data, it scores higher than Belgium, the Netherlands, the United States, France, Germany, and the United Kingdom—in that order.

The acknowledged quality of the Irish labor force reflects positively on the education system in all of its facets. Human resource development is an area, however, in which significant advances are taking place in many countries. In Ireland, considerable scope for improvement can be found in the education attainment of older age-groups of the labor force and in the areas of adult literacy, early school-leaving, and education underachievement. In these areas, Ireland compares poorly with other industrial economies. Ireland will need to continue to invest at adequate levels in education infrastructure, curriculum development, teacher training, and research to ensure that the education system continues to produce a competitive workforce. Significant improvement in public finances provides one such opportunity to do this.

Public Administration. Although the role of the enterprise sector as the main engine of economic growth is widely acknowledged, the system of public administration also plays a major and complementary role. This is an important factor because public administration performance can help or hinder the development of the enterprise sector in significant ways. In fact it can do both—and often does so at the same time. Therefore, national approaches to enterprise policy will be much more effective if they are cross-sectoral as well as cross-functional.

In Ireland where, until recent decades, the internationally traded goods and services sector has been particularly weak, the public sector has played an important promotional role. Nowhere is this more apparent than in the work of the IDA in promoting foreign investment in Ireland. As explained, the efficiency and effectiveness with which a whole range of public policies are administered (for example, taxation, infrastructure, education, competition) are major determinants of the scope and pace of growth.

Global competition has been a major impetus for achieving improved efficiencies, good management, and operational change in the internationally traded sectors in Ireland over the past 20 years. The present challenge for the public sector is to achieve a similar degree of change in management and operational reform without the spur and "bite" that market forces provide. A process of public administration reform has started under the Strategic Management Initiative being led by the Department of *An Taoiseach* (prime minister). This initiative is still in its infancy, but initial results have been encouraging.

Industrial and Enterprise Policy. For many years, enterprise policy was viewed primarily as the activities of the industrial promotion agencies. For example, the mission of the IDA was typically seen as providing grants and advice to firms to create output and employment in Ireland. It was never, of course, that simple. A wide range of public sector policies and activities have always been at work behind bodies like IDA Ireland (the agency responsible for promotion of FDI in Ireland) and Enterprise Ireland (the agency responsible for the promotion of indigenous industrial development and trade). These policies set the framework within which these agencies conduct their work. They establish the fundamental parameters that support or hinder the promotional work of the agencies and determine their relative success or failure. For example, in the 1960s and 1970s public policies and programs that supported the promotion of investment in Ireland included the following:

- The Export Profits Relief Scheme under which profits generated from export activity in the manufacturing sector enjoyed a zero rate of corporation tax.
- The decision to reestablish bodies like the IDA, which operated within the civil service up to 1969, as separate agencies outside the civil service system to provide them with greater operational flexibility.
- The decision to remove the once deeply ingrained requirement that all manufacturing operations in Ireland had to have a majority ownership by Irish nationals.

Industrial or enterprise development policy is now accepted as encompassing numerous policy areas—for example, taxation, transportation, telecommunications, energy, competition, public sector administration, education, science and technology, and so on—as well as the promotional activities of the development agencies. This wider definition of enterprise policy has been accepted by successive governments. It does, however, pose a particular challenge for public sector management. It requires *horizontal coordination* across different sectoral and functional areas of the government—each generally under the control of a single department and minister that is charged with the administrative and political responsibility for a particular sector or function. This is not an easy goal to accomplish.

The governmental organization, *Forfás,* has been established to address this challenge. To make this broader definition of enterprise policy work effectively requires two things: (1) a widespread acceptance that the enterprise sector is the main engine of growth and the means through which the resources required to generate higher living standards, improved quality of life, redistributional equity, and social cohesion can best be achieved; and (2) close working arrangements among the government departments and agencies responsible for the wider range of enterprise policy instruments discussed earlier.

The progress of the enterprise policy agenda along this wider, coordinated path has been reasonably encouraging. Five examples attest to this:

- The adoption of a single low rate corporation tax of 12.5 percent for traded income in all sectors of the economy.
- The accelerated liberalization of the telecommunications sector in Ireland in advance of EU requirements.
- The additional, significant resource allocations by the government for the provision of high-tech graduates and technicians from the tertiary-level sector in the areas of information technology and life sciences.
- The upgrading of R&D and teaching facilities in the technology sector in response to the needs of the fast-growing information society and biotechnology related sectors in Ireland.
- The separate promotion of FDI by IDA Ireland and of Irish-owned firms by Enterprise Ireland, each program reflecting the different characteristics and promotional requirements of these respective sectors, each of which is crucial to national economic development in Ireland.

The high-tech industry sector was particularly important in driving the growth of the Irish economy during the 1990s. High-tech exports represented almost two-thirds of the total exports of goods and services in 1999, compared with some 47 percent of that total in 1993. These sectors presently account for more than 25 percent of GDP. The level of employment in these sectors has doubled to almost 140,000 in that same time. Pharmaceuticals, electronics, telecommunications, electrical equipment, instrument engineering, and software development have all increased their output, exports, and employment at a rapid pace. Irish-owned firms have developed strongly in these sectors in recent years, particularly in the software development sector. Since 1980 some 40 percent of all new U.S. investment in European electronics have been located in Ireland, and this trend continues. In 1999, Ireland became the largest exporter of software products in the world in terms of the absolute value and volume of exports.

A fundamental reason for the development of a strong, expanding, high-tech, industrial sector in Ireland lies in the fact that Ireland is the most profitable location for investors in Europe. This profitability is due to the low operating costs, low corporate taxes, and generous incentives available for investment. U.S. Department of Commerce figures show that for more than a decade U.S. manufacturing companies have achieved average aftertax returns of 24 percent per year on their investments in Ireland (U.S. Department of Commerce 1998). A more recent calculation by Deloitte and Touche in 2006 expresses this reality somewhat differently. They calculate the percentage increase in profit that would be needed in a number of other countries to achieve the same distributable income that is available in Ireland: Netherlands, 24 percent; United Kingdom, 25 percent; China, 31 percent; Germany, 42.5 percent; and the United States, 45 percent.

The development of the International Financial Services Centre (IFSC) in Dublin is a good example of how Irish industrial development policy has evolved in response to changing domestic and international factors over the years. The government decision to establish such a center was taken in 1987. Today, the IFSC has become a vital part of Ireland's economy, directly employing more than 7,500 persons in corporate treasury management, fund management, futures and options trading, securities trading, and insurance and reinsurance. In addition, significant numbers are employed in professional support services to the center in areas such as taxation, legal services, and banking.

LOOKING TO THE FUTURE: KEY POLICY ISSUES

One reason so many companies choose Ireland is because of its unique workforce. Ireland has one of the youngest populations in Europe with more than 36 percent under the age of 25 years. Ireland's population and age structure advantages are expected to continue for the next 15 years. In a study of demographic trends, economists at NCB Stockbrokers forecast population declines across much of Europe and suggest that Ireland's already strong economy will look even more attractive in a European context over the next decade. In many ways, Ireland is now at a pivotal point in the evolution of its economy. Much of what has been achieved in recent years is a result of wise decisions made in a number of areas in prior decades—10, 20, and perhaps even 30 and 40 years ago—particularly in the areas of investment in education and in the orientation of industrial policies. The response to the crisis, which affected the Irish economy in the mid-1980s, built as it was on social consensus and partnership, has been crucial. These policies, in conjunction with an external international economic environment favorable to the policies established by Ireland, which give a high priority to export-led growth, have brought Ireland to its highest-ever plateau in economic performance and development.

But these policies have made their contributions, and the unrelenting pressure of global competition means that Ireland must continue to be innovative if it wants to maintain its hard-won gains. Ireland can no longer count on a sense of national economic crisis to provide the focus and cohesion that enabled it to move forward in the mid-1980s. Neither can it simply refer to the need to meet the Maastrict Criteria of 1992—the macroeconomic conditions necessary to enable Ireland to become a founding member of the European Monetary Union—as a substitute for conscious policy analysis and difficult choices. Ireland must now determine its future prospects by further developing capacities for systematic and well-researched approaches to policy formulation and implementation without the stimulus of an economic crisis to concentrate minds on a common national effort.

In this context, the critical policy issues to be addressed seem to be as follows:

- Maintaining the recognition achieved in recent years in overall policy formulation that the enterprise sector is the main engine of economic growth.
- Actively fostering a sense of national cohesion and partnership through the formally negotiated national partnership arrangements of recent years.
- Placing a concomitant emphasis on creating a regulatory and competitive environment within which the enterprise sector can continue to flourish as the principal engine of sustainable economic growth and development.
- Establishing a sense of strategic direction for decision making in both the public and private sectors by setting out and widely disseminating government views on the medium- and longer-term needs and objectives of the economy, the policies needed to achieve these objectives, and the policy milestones against which progress in the right direction is gauged.
- Continuing the downward pressure on public expenditure, public debt, and taxation as a proportion of GNP in support of the fundamental objective of ensuring that the enterprise sector remains the main engine of economic growth.

These broad goals suggest that policy leverage might be gained by placing particular emphasis on the following:

- Significantly increasing investment in *infrastructure provision.*
- Continuing investment in *education and training* to ensure that the knowledge and skills base of the economy is high relative to that of other industrial countries.
- Promoting the investment and training needed to achieve widespread involvement of both enterprises and individual citizens in *e-commerce and the information society.*
- Pursuing additional investment and further regulatory reform in the *telecommunications* sector.
- Promoting increased investment in *R&D* and related support activities to improve the *innovation capacity* of Ireland's economy.
- Moving further up the value added chain in *the type of FDI investment promotion in Ireland* to increasingly sophisticated, knowledge-based activities and in the

sectoral repositioning of Irish-owned enterprise to compete more effectively in an open global economy.

- Recognizing that Ireland's relationship with the European Union is undergoing fundamental changes at present and will be different in the future. These changes require the development of additional competence in public administration to reflect this changing relationship and to *engage more fully in shaping the strategic evolution of the European Union.*

The government's National Development Plan (NDP) 2000–06 addresses many of these issues in a comprehensive way. The range of issues targeted makes the point that enterprise policy in today's world is a complex matter involving numerous variables. The trick is to ensure that the policy levers are those relevant to the needs of the enterprise sector at the time and in the period immediately ahead. It remains true that the policy foundations laid today determine the performance of the economy tomorrow. Ireland's current challenge is to determine how it can manage economic success in a way that maintains its significant recent achievements.

In engaging this challenge, Ireland has significant strengths on which it can build. These include its success in attracting high levels of overseas investment, its competitive personal and corporate tax rates, its young and capable labor force, its improving school completion and higher education participation, its low levels of regulation, its high levels of public investment, and its high productivity levels in modern export-oriented manufacturing and services sectors. It currently leads the world in several competitive business environment categories: (a) science and technology graduates per 1,000 is the highest internationally at 23.2 (Eurostat 2003); (b) worker motivation at 7.68 leads all others, with Japan second at 7.21 (IMD 2006); (c) labor productivity at US$47.18 (GDP per person employed per hour) is ranked first with France and second with the United States (IMD 2006); (d) flexibility and adaptability of the workforce when faced with new challenges (IMD 2006); (e) the percent of the population with at least tertiary education (IMD 2006); (f) the degree to which the education system meets the needs of a competitive economy (IMD 2006); and (g) with a score of 8.33, Ireland leads in the worldwide quality of life index (Economist Intelligence Unit 2005).

Offsetting these assets is a series of weaknesses that must be addressed if Ireland is to continue to prosper. Its trade performance is weakening and it has begun to lose employment in manufacturing. Ireland's cost-competitiveness recently has begun to erode. The country's infrastructure remains relatively poor, and it is not yet maximizing the potential of information and communication technology. In particular, its R&D system is still developing, and its education system suffers from low levels of engagement in lifelong learning and less-than-desirable average education performance.

Figure 7.1 Education System in Ireland

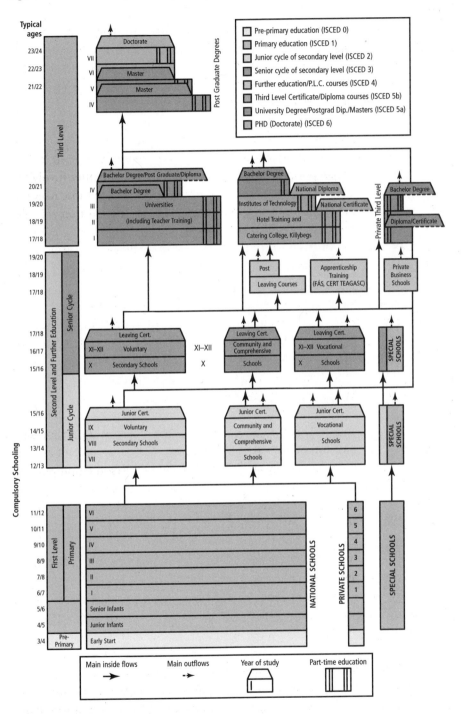

Source: Department of Education and Science 2004.
Note: Infant classes correspond to Pre-Primary in the International Standard Classification of Education.

The primary factors in Ireland's success to date have been the value of its unique social compact, the importance of major financial subsidies from the European Union, the highly complementary role of sustained education sector investments, a public policy emphasis on creating a probusiness environment, and the positive characteristics of Irish culture. But the future will be different, and existing solutions are unlikely to hold. The most likely conclusion is that the enterprise model that has worked so far in delivering unprecedented growth will have to be modified considerably. Perhaps the most encouraging sign is that far from ignoring the latter challenge, the Irish public actively debates it. The government is intent on using its now considerable financial resources to address this challenge. Little or no complacency is evident and that, surely, is the first requirement if Ireland is to secure a bright future.

EDUCATION DEVELOPMENTS: PRIMARY AND POSTPRIMARY

A society which rates highly spiritual and moral values and seeks to develop the mental and physical well-being of its people will devote a substantial part of its resources to education. There are, in addition, social and economic considerations which reinforce the claim of education to an increasing share of expanding national resources. Improved and extended educational facilities help to equalise opportunities by enabling an increasing proportion of the community to develop their potentialities and raise their personal standards of living. Expenditure on education is an investment in the fuller use of the country's primary resource—its people—which can be expected to yield increasing returns in terms of economic progress.

—Second Programme for Economic Expansion 1963

Recent estimates suggest that improvements in labor quality, due to rising education levels, particularly in the 1980s and 1990s, accounted for almost 20 percent of total growth in output.

—Economic Social Research Institute 2001–07

HISTORICAL BACKGROUND OF PRIMARY, SECONDARY, AND TECHNICAL EDUCATION

At the establishment of political independence in 1922, the Irish state inherited a school system of a rather unusual character. To understand the structure of the modern Irish school system it is necessary to appreciate the earlier historical circumstances that shaped it. Before the introduction of state support for primary and secondary education in the nineteenth century, Ireland had a long history of schooling and, particularly in the case of primary education, school provision was widespread. Through the nineteenth century, the English administration for Ireland decided to provide state support for the promotion of primary, secondary, and technical education. The nature of this support has had a long-lasting effect on the configuration of Irish schooling.

In 1831, when the English government decided to establish the national school system (for primary education), it had politicization and socialization as well as education aims. A state-aided system was conceived, which proved to be popular and successful, gradually replacing the older pattern of schooling. The essence of the new system was that the state was prepared to give financial support to approved local initiatives taken to establish national schools. The local patron sought support from the newly established Commissioners of National Education in return for which the patron agreed to abide by the rules and regulations of the Commissioners. In most cases, the ownership of the school and the local management resided with the local patron. The original intention was that the system would be multidenominational, but almost all the patrons were clergymen and the various churches succeeded in making the system a de facto denominational one. As time went on, the state gradually took over the vast expenditures associated with the national school system, including teacher salaries. Yet the schools never became state schools per se, and they continued to be state-aided schools de jure.

At the postprimary level, two state-aided systems—secondary and technical education—had been put in place by the end of the nineteenth century. Secondary schools were strictly private institutions. Under the Intermediate Act of 1878, the state devised a scheme to give financial support to secondary school managements. The mechanism allowed for payments to school managements on the basis of the success rates of pupils in the new public examinations, which were introduced under the Act. Apart from setting out syllabi and rules for the conduct of public examinations, the state took no active role with regard to founding schools, managing secondary schools, paying teachers, or regulating school standards. The secondary schools were denominational, with the exercise of a conscience clause, allowing pupils to withdraw from religious classes if they had conscientious objections.

Public vocational-technical education traces its origin to the establishment of the Department of Agriculture and Technical Instruction in 1899. This technical education system operated differently than secondary education. The schools were public schools in that they were jointly funded by the state and local authorities and they operated under democratically elected local authority committees. But for a long time, the numbers of these schools and pupils remained but a small portion of overall schooling provision.

Following the achievement of political independence in 1922, the state-church interface on the ownership and management of schooling persisted with a remarkable degree of continuity. The state did not alter in any significant way the balance of control and ownership of the school system that it inherited. Thus, the primary schools remained under the ownership and management of religious denominations in almost all cases. Secondary schools were left as private institutions, and the state took on no responsibility for building or management. The government of the newly independent state began by concentrating on curricular rather than administrative change. Inspired by the ideology of cultural nationalism, the state introduced radical changes into the prevailing curricula, giving priority to the Irish language and Gaelic cultural heritage. Under the newly established Department of Education (1924), the state took control of curricular policy for all schools and also centralized public examinations for secondary schools. In addition, it set up an incremental salary scale and superannuation scheme for secondary teachers. Under the Vocational Education Act of 1930, the technical school system was restructured, and the new vocational schools operated as publicly owned and controlled schools.

In the early 1960s, the Department of Education, in association with the OECD, commissioned a detailed statistical survey of education provision in the country. Its report, *Investment in Education* (1966), proved to be a catalyst for the restructuring and modernization of the school system. The report recommended that the Department should establish a development branch for planning. This branch was set up and contributed to changes made, but was subsequently discontinued in 1973. Indicative of a changing climate, an Educational Research Centre was established in 1966 with a particular brief to conduct experiential research studies on qualitative aspects of the education service. In the context of significant education reforms that occurred in the 1960s, the state upgraded the status of vocational schools, gave the first capital grants to the private secondary school sector, and established two new types of postprimary schools—the comprehensive and the community school. These latter schools were designed more in the tradition of public schools and mainly managed by boards representing the state, the local authority, and denominational interests, to which parent and teacher representatives were added later. The state now espoused a comprehensive curriculum for all postprimary schools. Enrollments in postprimary education began to expand greatly.

Today, practically all schools depend almost entirely on the state for their capital and current costs, including teacher salaries, and are governed by state rules and regulations. They observe the state curricula and participate in the public examinations administered by the state. In the education statistics issued, all publicly funded schools are categorized together. Thus, although the ownership and trusteeship of most schools are still vested in private agencies, with a smooth division of powers between state and private interests, the profile of the Irish schooling system is regarded as public. Virtually all schools are governed by boards of management including trustees, parents, teachers, and the community. For the most part, a strong denominational tradition characterizes school provision in Ireland.

But some variations on the predominant model have emerged. Article 44 of the Constitution guarantees equity regarding state aid for schools under the management of different religious denominations and respects their property rights. In recent decades, groups of parents in the Educate Together movement have succeeded in establishing 25 multidenominational primary schools. Although the Constitution upholds the right of children to attend a school receiving public money without being required to undergo religious instruction in that school, it is often difficult in practice for nonbelieving parents to find fully secular schools for their children. Other parents remain dissatisfied with the shortage of schools in which the instruction is conducted in the Irish language. These parents have established a range of such schools at preschool, primary, and secondary levels under the organization, *Gaelscoileanna* (Irish Schools), with state support.

PRIMARY-LEVEL EDUCATION

Schooling is compulsory from the age of 6 to 16 years. But about 60 percent of four year olds and 95 percent of five year olds attend the national (primary) schools. Thus, 85 percent of children ages four to five are in regular attendance in both urban and rural areas. Overall, 96 percent of Irish children of primary school age attend school. Universal compulsory schooling was brought into force for children ages 6 to 14 from January 1927, by virtue of the School Attendance Act. The age bracket for compulsory schooling was expanded to 15 years in 1972 and to 16 years in 1996.

Overall, about 444,000 pupils are enrolled in the primary schools, most of which are coeducational. In 2000–01, the average pupil-to-teacher ratio was 19:1. The state provides for free education in all primary schools. The vast majority of primary schools (3,157) are, however, state-aided parish schools that were established under diocesan patronage. Another 109 primary schools are special schools for children with disabilities. Additionally, 68 privately owned primary schools follow the state curriculum, although they do not receive state aid and enroll less than 2 percent of the age-group.

The typical primary school enrolls pupils by age into eight consecutive year-groups or classes, ranging from junior infants to sixth class. The vast majority of schools are "all-through" schools, catering to pupils from infants to sixth class. Most pupils transfer to postprimary school at age 12. Slightly over half of the primary schools have fewer than 100 pupils, and thus have four or fewer teachers (data for 2003–04). Some 22 percent of primary school pupils attend these smaller schools. In 2000, 57 percent of all classes were single-grade classes. But more than 25 percent of all classes are consecutive-grade classes (that is, classes in which two consecutive age-groups are combined, for example, first and second classes together). In addition, 16 percent of classes are multigrade classes, in which one teacher handles a sequence of three class standards (one, two, and three; or four, five, and six).

The primary schools are governed by management boards, the main pattern of participation being two representatives of the trustees, two elected parents, two teachers, and two members of the community co-opted by the other six members. Most schools hold formal parent-teacher meetings to discuss children's progress and share important information. A range of targeted schemes operate to alleviate difficulties being experienced by schools serving areas of serious socioeconomic disadvantage.

The late 1960s saw the preparation of a new curriculum for national schools that became official policy in 1971. In its ideology, content, and format, this curriculum was a radical contrast to that which had existed. Based on the ideology of child-centered education, it offered a wide subject range and encouraged discovery-type teaching methods with pupil interest and involvement as the prime objectives. Unfortunately, a lack of coordination and the failure to plan an education program in sequential stages appropriate to age and intellectual capacities from the early primary level upward caused considerable problems for pupils and teachers. This led to the establishment in 1978 of a special committee on the transition from primary to postprimary schooling.

Throughout the 1990s, the National Council for Curriculum and Assessment (NCCA) worked to revise the primary school curriculum. Intended to update the new curriculum introduced in 1971, the revisions covered art and crafts, an expanded music program, elementary science, and physical education for the first time. On NCCA advice, the Department of Education and Science adopted this revised curriculum in 1999 and implemented it on a phased basis. The three general aims of primary education as outlined in the curriculum are as follows:

- Enable the child to live a full life as a child and to realize his or her potential as a unique individual.
- Enable the child to develop as a social being through living and cooperating with others and so contribute to the good of society.
- Prepare the child for further education and lifelong learning.

The curriculum continues to be child centered rather than subject centered, and it allows for flexibility in time-tabling and teaching methods. The curriculum comprises six main areas: language; mathematics; social, environmental, and scientific education; arts education; physical education; and social, personal, and health education. A separate religious education program is devised by religious authorities. The subject matter of these curricular areas and associated pedagogic approaches are set out in a suite of 23 curriculum documents published by the Department of Education and Science. The revised curriculum has been warmly received, with much in-service education for teachers supplemented by assistance to schools of a full-time support team. In 2003, an interesting curriculum proposal was put forward by the Enterprise Strategy Group, which called for the introduction of entrepreneurship into the curriculum.

Since 1973, the basic qualification for primary teachers has been the education bachelor's degree. In general, teachers are trained at a pre-service level in group, individual, and class teaching methods. The principle of subject integration is promoted in both pre-service and in-service education. A variety of teaching methods are encouraged.

Each class teacher is responsible for the evaluation of her or his own pupils in primary schools. Teachers carry out their own assessment of pupil performance, either through standardized tests or their own tests based on aspects of the curriculum. Increasingly, standardized tests are used as the Department seeks objective data on pupils for national statistics. These test assess school applications for learning support or resource teaching personnel. Although a formal national examination at the end of primary school was in place from 1943 to 1967, it no longer exists. Instead, primary schools are required to prepare formal report cards on pupils on transfer to postprimary school.

Although the facilities available in schools vary considerably, an increasing number now use television and video. Since 1999, all schools are connected to the Internet and many are using computer-assisted learning.

SECONDARY-LEVEL EDUCATION[3]

The period from independence to 1960 was marked by a traditional and conservative approach to education at all levels. Little structural or curricular change was undertaken, and access to postprimary education (and especially to higher education) was far from being equitable. But education changes were introduced in the late 1950s that reflected the broader changes of attitude that were occurring in Irish society generally. A notable landmark was the publication in 1958 of the government *White Paper on Economic Expansion*, which led to the first economic program and affected public attitudes toward economic and industrial development. Economists were now emphasizing education as an economic investment rather than taking the traditional view of education as a consumer service. The returns on investment in education, both individually and socially, were held to be as important as investment in capital plant. The prosperity of a modern technological society, it was argued, depended on the availability of an educated workforce. Increased economic growth and production in turn allowed for greater financial resources to be applied to education. New emphasis was put on slogans such as "a nation's wealth is its people."

Furthermore, it was felt that society needed to draw on the full potential of its pool of talent. Many commentators remarked that existing education provision was not facilitating that potential. New policy thinking was influenced by Ireland's links with international organizations such as the United Nations, the Council of Europe, and OECD, and its hopes of joining the EEC were high in the early 1960s. Irish representatives participated in international conferences and symposia on education affairs, which tended to bring in wider perspectives that reduced insularity.

By the late 1950s, signs from government indicated that new education initiatives were likely and the 1960s saw the introduction of significant reforms. The minister of education announced in 1963 the construction of postprimary schools, called comprehensive schools, which would be coeducational and open to all classes and ability levels within a broad curriculum. Subsequently, the Department of Education began to decentralize education provision on a catchment area or district basis. Transport would be provided within this service area to facilitate student attendance at their local school. In his policy statement, the minister stated, "there are still areas of the country which have neither a secondary nor a vocational school within easy daily reach of potential pupils and where, under the existing system, such is not likely to be available in the foreseeable future" (Hillery 1963). In addition to transportation, another obstacle to access to education for children of poor parents was the cost involved. In 1961, the government intervened to bolster an existing but poorly funded scholarship scheme for disadvantaged students at the secondary and university levels, raising the number of awards from 2,609 in 1960 to 9,614 in 1966.

Perhaps the most far-reaching and innovative initiative ever to be undertaken by a minister of education was announced in September 1966. He announced that free postprimary education would be made available throughout the country from the beginning of the new academic year 1967–68. This applied to all students in all grades simultaneously. This reform was directed, he said, at "the basic fault of our present educational structure . . . the fact that many families cannot afford to pay even part of the cost of education for their children" (Randles 1975).[4] School managements were compensated for the loss of fee income through the provision of a grant per student in lieu of fees. School authorities found that these amounts did not reimburse them fully and introduced voluntary financial contributions from parents to bridge the funding gap.

Whereas secondary enrollments grew gradually during the early years of the decade, they leaped ahead dramatically between 1966–67 and 1968–69

Table 7.5   Secondary Enrollment Growth in Ireland

Year	Secondary enrollment
1966	148,000
1968	185,000
1974	239,000
1985	334,692
1995	374,230

Source: Central Statistics Office Ireland.

(see table 7.5). This increase was triggered by a large influx of new students who responded to the free fees and free transport initiatives. The school-leaving age was raised to 15 years in 1972. This meant that most pupils would obtain two or three years of postprimary education—the age of transition from primary school being 12 years. This decision increased second level enrollments considerably. To a lesser extent, efforts to reduce dropouts throughout the years of secondary education also contributed to enrollment growth. Enrollments peaked in 1995, but birth rates began to fall in 1981 and this began to affect secondary enrollments from 1997.

This huge increase put pressure on the provision of school buildings, requiring the use of temporary buildings. Since the schools now brought together pupils with a wide range of intellectual abilities and social backgrounds in crowded classrooms, the pressure on teachers was intense. Teacher numbers increased for a time but not immediately.[5] The consequences were that class sizes increased significantly for a time.

Many of the education policy measures introduced were closely linked to perceived socioeconomic needs. The state attempted to amalgamate schools at the primary and postprimary level, so that larger units would allow for more economical capital and running costs, more satisfactory use of teaching resources, and the provision of better equipment and facilities. The proliferation of small national schools in Ireland, as well as the decline in population up to 1966, left many rural schools with small numbers on the roll. It was difficult to equip and staff them in line with modern thinking and requirements. Many of the schools were old and in disrepair. Meanwhile, public expectations of the standards of hygiene, heating, and facilities had risen in line with general improvements in domestic housing. The development of education technology in the form of language laboratories, tape recorders, educational radio and television, and film projectors highlighted the need to rationalize school provisions. A policy of closure or amalgamation of small national schools was adopted and larger postprimary units were encouraged. The increasing availability of automobiles reduced the physical hardship of travel to school and an expanded bus transport scheme was introduced to facilitate further centralization of schools.

Another dramatic development was the establishment of community schools in October 1970. The community school was an outgrowth of the comprehensive school. It provided free comprehensive schooling to all pupils in a catchment area without any pupil selection procedures. The schools were viewed as a further step toward equality of education opportunity, the reduction of overlapping resources, and the elimination of the binary pattern of vocational and secondary schools. A significant new element, however, was the special emphasis placed on the reciprocal relationships between the school and its surrounding community. No longer was the school seen as an institution concerned solely with the responsibility of educating the young; it was charged with fostering many forms of youth and adult education and making its facilities available to the wider community. By 1974, the comprehensive school model had been largely replaced with the wider community schools approach.

THE SYLLABUS

Three national examinations were introduced during the twentieth century: the Intermediate Certificate, the Leaving Certificate, and the Group Certificate. The Intermediate and Leaving Certificate examinations were established in 1924. The former was taken after three years of study, while the latter was taken following a further two years. The Group Certificate was introduced in 1947 and was based on an examination to be taken at the end of two years of study in vocational-technical postprimary schools. It has become the basic entry qualification for apprenticeship. In 1992, the Intermediate and Leaving Certificates were replaced by the Junior Certificate. The objective of the junior cycle, which has a three-year duration, is ". . . to provide a well-balanced, general education suitable for pupils who leave full-time education at the end of compulsory schooling or, alternatively, who wish to enter on more advanced courses of study" (Department of Education and Science [Ireland] 1992).

Several important initiatives introduced changes in the syllabus of postprimary subjects regarding both content and methods, starting in the early 1960s. Efforts were made to give science teaching a more experimental base. Grants were provided to schools for science laboratories, and special gratuities were awarded to science graduates who entered teaching. An annual competition known as "Young Scientist Exhibition" has done a great deal to foster science experiments in schools, as well as to promote general public interest in science. At the same time, much work was put into changing the mathematics courses and this resulted in the introduction of what were popularly known as new maths.

The introduction of the common Intermediate Certificate course in 1966 contributed to a wider subject range and placed a greater emphasis on practical subjects. The vocational and new comprehensive schools offered practical subjects, and many secondary schools adopted a more comprehensive curriculum in the late 1960s. The Department of Education encouraged a group scheme of subject choice for the Leaving Certificate in 1969. From a range of five groups—languages, commerce, science, technical studies, and social studies—students were to choose at least three subjects from one of the groups. This would have introduced an element of specialization at senior cycle. But the established tradition of a general education was preferred by the public, and the group scheme was eventually rejected.

This period also saw the introduction of guidance teachers in Irish postprimary schools to provide pupils with academic counseling and vocational guidance. By 1979 about half of the postprimary schools contained guidance counselors. In addition to helping the students, they also worked with the Department's psychological service and guidance clinics.

Despite considerable curricular change, the examination structure remained traditional with its three national certificate examinations (that is, the Group, Intermediate, and Leaving Certificates). A study of the Leaving Certificate in 1968 found that it was unreliable, that it sought too much factual information, and that it placed a heavy burden on pupils because it was used as the test to qualify candidates for entry to many occupations. In 1969, the "honors-pass" nomenclature was dropped and a grading system with six categories from A to F was introduced. The centralized public examinations have continued to exercise a strong influence on teaching in the schools. A further pressure was placed on the Leaving Certificate examination and the university matriculation examinations in 1968, when universities began to operate a points system to select candidates for entry into some faculties where student applications were highly competitive because of the growing numbers of secondary graduates. Ironically, the tertiary student grant scheme introduced in 1968 tended to lessen the economic competitiveness that had existed for university scholarships, but the introduction of the points system in the same year replaced this with academic competitiveness. Today, many teachers and parents continue to feel, some 40 years later, that the examinations and entry requirements to the tertiary level have distorted the whole process of second-level education.

CURRICULUM AND THE NATIONAL ECONOMY

Other curricular changes were periodically introduced into postprimary schools. A highly influential factor here was the pressure for a closer alignment of school curricula with the needs of a more industrialized economy. Changes occurred in the content of existing subjects and the pedagogic approach to them, with technical and applied subjects receiving more official support.[6] These curricular changes preceded with little account for curricular developments at the primary level. Computer studies, as a course module in mathematics, were introduced in 1980. Since 1977, pre-employment courses have existed in many postprimary schools, particularly in the vocational schools. These are post-junior-cycle courses aimed at pupils who do not go on to study for the Leaving Certificate, but who do not, or cannot, go straight into employment. The programs combine social, general, and technical education with work experience in industry or commerce. Many post-primary schools also offer one-year secretarial courses that may involve a work experience component.

These curricular initiatives reflect widespread concerns and continuing debate regarding secondary curriculum. Although the content of individual subjects may be adequately covered in secondary school, the presumed value of such study in terms of personal development may not be realized. Parent groups felt that more specific provision should be made for social, health, and sex education in the schools as a preparation for adult life. Others argued that the arts were being seriously neglected in the education system. Industrialists and politicians commented that the school programs were not sufficiently aligned to the technological changes in areas such as electronics and bioengineering. Scientists observed the implications of developments in the microchip and called for curricular change. Some teachers and researchers in curriculum development argued in favor of more integrated courses, particularly at the junior cycle, and proposed alternative examination programs. It may be that society is expecting too much from its schools or poses too many conflicting goals for them. Nevertheless, momentum is gathering for further revisions of postprimary curriculum.

The postprimary curriculum offers a wide range of subjects. This, in itself, may pose significant problems for pupils in deciding which subjects or combination of subjects they should pursue, bearing in mind their ability and aptitudes as well as the subjects required by certain careers or third-level institutions. These early decisions have long-term consequences on the options and institutions that are available to students at a later stage. A great deal of information and data on regulations for examinations needs to be communicated intelligibly to students. Increasingly, the importance of pupil and career guidance has been recognized by schools, and the guidance of career guidance counselors, particularly for Leaving Certificate students, has been helpful to many students as they make their subject choices. A high degree of competitiveness at the Leaving Certificate level imposes considerable strain on students in their adolescent or early adult years. Additionally, the number of "grind" schools, which provide extra instruction in the hope of improving examination performance, is growing. Some people are concerned that the examinations have become the raison d'etre for postprimary schooling to the detriment of the more humane concerns of education. As is the case in many other countries, however, the public is reluctant to see the public examinations dismantled and the level of competitiveness reduced, particularly with the increased participation rate in education and without corresponding expansion of job opportunities and third-level education.

The 1980s opened with a government *White Paper on Educational Development*, which included a wide-ranging review of education topics. It was especially interesting because of its emphasis on labor market needs. For example, it recommended that "the outcomes of the Second Conference on Engineering Manpower for Economic Development be taken into account." This was followed in 1984 by the *Programme for Action in Education 1984–1987* after a change of government. It recommended that "major needs will be the reform of curricula and the development of more flexible organisations with particular regard to the needs of lower achievers, and the establishment of a more effective relationship between the (second level) education and training system and the world of work." Its thrust was much the same as the earlier *White Paper*, although it placed a new emphasis on the regionalization of education administration—a policy that was rejected by all subsequent governments.

Raising the compulsory school-leaving age from 15 to 16 years in 1996 proved to be a particularly progressive decision. It stemmed from the 1992 Green Paper, "Education for a Changing World." Following extensive public consultation, which included the convening of a National Education Convention (NEC) in 1993, it led to government adoption of the 1995 *White Paper on Charting Our Education Future*. The NEC was an unprecedented event in the history of Irish education. It brought together representatives from 42 organizations, representing education bodies, trade unions, business and enterprise, and the Department of Education, to engage in sustained discussion of major issues of education policy in Ireland. It asked participants to clarify viewpoints; to question, probe, and analyze varying perspectives; to foster multilateral dialogue; to improve mutual understanding between sectoral interests; to explore new ways of doing things; and to identify areas of actual or potential agreement between different interest groups.

Government emphasis on the importance of education for the economic development of the nation was emphasized and reemphasized throughout the convention. At a time of high unemployment (17 percent), the following statement in "Charting Our Education Future" captures this view:

> Links between education and the economy, at national and international levels, are important. This has been recognized by successive governments, the social partners and various expert bodies. The contribution of education and training to economic prosperity has been underlined in successive national understandings with the social partners and in independent studies carried out by, for instance, the National Economic and Social Council and the Organisation for Economic Co-operation and Development. These developments have placed education at centre stage as part of more broad based economic and social policies. The government is committed to continuing this process (Government of Ireland 1995).

TRENDS

Enrollments: Trends over the past five decades are presented in table 7.6. As noted earlier, population dynamics—in terms of migration movements and fertility

Table 7.6 **Full-Time Students in Institutions Aided by the Department of Education** (thousands)

Level	1965/66	1975/76	1985/86	1995/96	2004/05
First level	481	528	567	479	449
Second level	132	268	335	370	335
Third level	19	32	53	95	134
Total	632	828	955	944	918

Source: Department of Education and Science Statistics.

patterns—played an important part in these fluctuations. The peak in primary enrollments that occurred in the 1980s was replicated in secondary enrollments in the 1990s. In turn, this has given way to sharp growth in tertiary enrollments since 1995.

Rate of Retention: The rate of retention in second-level schools—that is, the percentage of students enrolled in year one who pass the Leaving Certificate examination some five or six years later—has increased progressively from some 20 percent in 1965 to 60 percent in 1985 and to nearly 82 percent in 2004.

Pupil-to-Teacher Ratios: The pupil-to-teacher ratios have fallen in the period from 1994 to 2004 from 24:1 to 17:1 in primary schools, and from 17:1 to 14:1 in postprimary schools.

Government Expenditure: Exchequer spending per student in constant 1999 prices increased steadily from about €1,250 in 1965 to nearly €3,500 in 2000. The expenditure per pupil for primary education in 2002 was €3,600 compared with €4,200 in the European Union. The corresponding figures for secondary education were €5,000 and €5,600 (see table 7.7 and table 7.8).

Table 7.7 **Percent of GNP Spent on Secondary and Higher Education**

Year	GNP (£ millions)	Education expenditure	Percent of GNP	Percent on higher education	Percent on secondary
1985	16,611	1,108	6.67	18	41
1990	24,056	1,757	6.06	20	37
1995	36,817	2,173	5.90	22	39
2000	68,614	3,264	4.76	28	39

Source: Department of Education and Science.

Table 7.8 **Current Expenditure per Pupil/Student** (2004 prices, €)

Level	1994	1999	2004
Primary	2,253	3,019	5,000
Postprimary	3,557	4,430	6,788
Higher	6,766	8,049	8,914

Source: Department of Education and Science.

NEW PROGRAMS

The 1990s witnessed the launch and development of new programs that focused on preparation for work and independent learning.

Transition-Year Program. This year of study has been interposed between the junior cycle and the Secondary Leaving Certificate (the final two years at second level). It was introduced to give students enhanced opportunities for personal development; it is interdisciplinary and student centered. It provides a bridge to enable pupils to make the transition from the more dependent type of learning associated with the junior cycle to the more independent learning environment fostered under the senior cycle. It encourages personal and social development and recognizes the need for students to grow in independence. It fosters academic achievement as students prepare for a Leaving Certificate program, further study, and adult and working life. It encourages the development of a wide range of transferable critical-thinking and creative problem-solving skills. By freeing students to take responsibility for their own learning, the program helps them to acquire skills and to evaluate life in ways and in situations that arise outside the boundaries of the certificate programs. Students mature greatly during this year, and this time leads some to revise their subject and career choices.

Leaving Certificate (LC) Examination. The LC examination is the terminal examination of postprimary education and is held at the end of the senior cycle in postprimary schools. The senior cycle caters to students in the 15- to 18-year-old age-group. Students normally sit for the examination at the age of 17 or 18, after five or six years of postprimary education. Numbers of students sitting for the LC examination have declined from 42,500 in 2002 to 39,800 in 2005. This drop is explained by the reduction in the relevant age cohort, a consequence of the decline in births that began in 1981. The expansion of the Leaving Certificate Vocational Programme and the Leaving Certificate Applied Programme as competing education options have further contributed to this decline.

Leaving Certificate Vocational Programme (LCVP). The LCVP is the normal LC with a concentration on technical subjects and a few additions. It was introduced in 1989, and in 1994 was expanded to broaden the choice of subjects and to strengthen the vocational content. The strong vocational focus of the LCVP is achieved by arranging LC subjects into Vocational Subject Groupings, which is done through the provision of linked modules. Pupils take five LC subjects, including two from a set of vocational subjects, a recognized course in a modern European language, and three mandatory linked modules. Enrollments have increased from 16,500 in 1996–97 to nearly 29,000 in 1999–2000. Students opting to sit for the examination have risen from less than 13,000 in 2001 to about 14,250 in 2005.

Leaving Certificate Applied Programme (LCAP). The LCAP was initiated in 1995. It is a distinct, self-contained two-year program aimed at preparing students for adult and working life. It responded to concerns that the established Leaving Certificate Programme did not meet the needs of all students. The program includes a range of courses designed on a modular basis. The number of modules depends on the course. Each year of the two-year program is divided into two sessions, September to January and February to June. A module within a given course is usually completed within one session. Over the two-year duration of the program, participants complete 44 modules, that is, 11 modules per session. Candidates are required to take final examinations in the following subjects:

- English and Communications.
- Mathematical Applications.
- Social Education.
- Gaeilge Chumarsaideach (Irish Language).
- Modern European Language (that is, French, German, Spanish, or Italian).
- Two Subjects from the vocational specialization (for example, Agriculture/ Horticulture, Engineering, Childcare/Community Care, Technology, Hair and Beauty).

The number of LCAP candidates increased from 3,026 in 2002 to 3,520 in 2004, but then decreased to 3,353 in 2005. As a proportion of the total number of LC candidates, however, the LCAP has increased in popularity from 5.2 percent in 2002 to 5.8 percent in 2005. An approximately equal number of males and females sat for the exam in 2004, at 49 percent and 51 percent, respectively.

Post-Leaving Certificate (PLC) Courses. PLCs are aimed primarily at those who have completed their senior cycle. PLC enrollments have grown from 17,644 in 1994–95 to 29,303 in 2004. The PLC program includes full-time one- and two-year (and some three- and four-year) courses of integrated education, training, and work experience provided in schools and colleges outside the third-level sector. Their objective is (a) to provide skills to meet the needs of the economy, (b) to equip young people with the vocational and technological skills necessary for employment and progression to further education and training and (c) to foster innovation and adaptability in participants. The majority of courses are placed at level five on the National Framework of Qualifications, and a few courses are placed at level six. All PLC programs follow an agreed format with the following components:

- General Education: the core skills needed for all types of employment such as literacy, numeracy, communications, new technology, decision making, and so on.
- Technical Knowledge: the skills needed for particular occupational groups.
- Work Experience: preparation for work and experience.

In 2004, roughly 29,300 students were taking PLC courses. This is an increase of 27 percent over 2001. The majority (72 percent) of participates are female.

THE STANDARD-BASED APPRENTICESHIP

The standard-based (designated) apprenticeship system was introduced in 1991 and fully implemented in 1993. Apprentices are required to follow a specific course of training and undergo a series of assessments to confirm that they have reached the required standard. The apprenticeship has seven phases, three off the job and four on the job. Apprentices are deemed to be qualified when they have successfully completed all the on- and off-the-job phases of their apprenticeship. This completion usually requires a minimum of four years from the date of registration with the national training authority (FÁS). FÁS and the Department of Education, through the Institutes of Technology, are responsible for arranging the off-the-job training.

Currently, instruction in 25 apprenticeship trades is offered within the broad categories of construction, mechanics, electrics, printing, and engineering. The apprenticeship lasts four years, leading to a National Craft Certificate awarded by the Further Education Training and Awards Council (FETAC), which has been placed at level six on the National Framework of Qualifications. A few level-seven learning outcomes are associated with apprenticeship.

New Registrations. The number of new apprentices has increased by one-third from 6,325 in 1998 to 8,236 in 2004. Males represent 99.5 percent of new registrations in all years. The work-and-study format of the apprenticeship programs now attracts in excess of 20 percent of the male 16 to 18 age cohort. Campaigns to attract females into the trades have been unsuccessful. The construction trades attracted the greatest number of new registrations in 1998 and 2004. Within this group, carpentry and joinery have the largest number of new registrations with registrations almost doubling over the six-year period—from 1,180 in 1998 to 2,089 in 2004. Electricians are the second-largest group of apprentices, with new registrations increasing from 1,660 in 1998 to 2,029 in 2004. New registrations to the printing trades have declined significantly, mainly because of the increased automation of the printing process. In 2004, 65 percent of all new registrations were in three trades—carpentry/joinery, plumbing, and electrical—all heavily influenced by the ongoing boom in the construction industry.

National Craft Certificates. The National Craft Certificates are awarded by FETAC. The number awarded in all apprenticeship trades increased from 478 in 1998 to 5,437 in 2004. The construction trade has the greatest output of apprentices with more than 2,000 graduates in 2004. As with new registrations, awards granted are dominated by three trades—carpentry/joinery, plumbing, and electrical—accounting for 57 percent of all National Craft Certificates awarded in 2004.

The National Training Fund. New legislation was introduced late in 2000 to expand the financing of training in Ireland. The National Training Fund Act represents a significant change in the way training for employment is funded. The Fund, derived from a levy of employer social insurance contributions, replaces the previous sector-based levies—the Apprenticeship Levy and the Levy Grant schemes. The Fund supports a range of schemes to better the skills of those in employment and provide training for those seeking employment. These employment training initiatives include company-specific and sectoral training programs, apprenticeships, traineeships, and employment-related training programs for the unemployed. A significant feature of the Act is its provision for consultation with employer and employee representatives. A National Training Advisory Committee facilitates this consultation process and ensures that national training policy is responsive to the needs of enterprises. The Committee advises on emerging trends and specific skill needs in relation to training and ensures a coordinated approach.

VOCATIONAL EDUCATION

Vocational and technical schools were established under the aegis of the Vocational Education Act in 1930. Their role was limited to the first two years of secondary education and to the vocationally oriented Day Group Certificate. This was regarded as a preparation for entry into certain skill-based occupations and to apprenticeship training. It was a system that did not enjoy popular regard, although it was administered on a local basis through Vocational Education Committees. The minister of education, in a 1963 policy statement, saw "the bringing of the vocational stream throughout the country to a parity of standard and evaluation with the secondary school stream" as constituting "a very important educational and social reform" (Hillery 1963). This goal was reaffirmed in the *Second Programme for Economic Expansion.* The Group Certificate was eliminated in 1963 with the introduction of the three-year Intermediate Certificate, which was common to both secondary and vocational schools alike. The Technical Leaving Certificate was announced at that time, thus allowing the vocational schools to extend their reach to that level also.

At the tertiary level, a number of Technical and Vocational Colleges had been operating since the late-nineteenth century in Dublin, and in Cork principally, under various arrangements. They were principally involved in apprenticeship education and offered a number of professionally oriented programs, including architecture, quantity surveying, medical laboratory technology, and marine radio. In the absence of an Irish accrediting body, a number of programs were accredited by the City and Guilds of London Institute.

This situation was transformed with the establishment of the regional technical colleges (RTCs) in 1969 (described in the following section). These colleges offered apprenticeship programs, both day and block release, and short-cycle programs in science, technology, business, and art and design. From the late 1970s onward, they also offered a limited number of bachelor's degrees in these areas. This initiative was the result of university reluctance to respond to manpower shortages at the degree level in Ireland at that time. More recently, the technical colleges have been redesignated as Institutes of Technology. Today, 13 institutes now offer master's programs and, in a number of cases, doctoral programs. The final step in the development of the technical education system is the government's decision, taken in early 2007, to designate these Institutes as higher education institutions. This designation places them under the aegis of the HEA, the intermediate body that traditionally had been responsible for the universities alone. Notwithstanding government insistence that the binary system should remain in place, a number of Institutes have made it clear that they aspire to full university status. But such a decision can only be made by the government.

HIGHER EDUCATION: CHANGE AND DEVELOPMENT

Irish workers are not just good at accumulating knowledge. They are also very good at applying it. There is an eagerness to get things done right the first time, and to do it better, faster. The interest in continuous knowledge building and learning by the Irish workforce is a keen competitive advantage that enables them to be multifunctional across business processes.

—Bernard Collins, former vice president of International Operations
and director of the International Board, Boston Scientific

CONTEXT

The education roots of Ireland's economic miracle stretch back more than a quarter of a century. At that stage, tertiary education was a luxury restricted mostly to the middle classes. But the last three decades have witnessed an extraordinary expansion in third-level education. The increase in participation rates has been remarkable. For example, in 1984–85, around 39 percent of 18 year olds were engaged in full-time education. Ten years later that figure had risen to 61 percent. Among those age 20 years and older, the rate of participation had risen from 8.9 percent to 18.2 percent—a twofold increase in the space of a decade. The effects of third-level expansion are demonstrated by the fact that Ireland now ranks above the OECD average for the proportion of first degree graduates in the population. It has a higher proportion of scientific and technological graduates in the general population than all other OECD countries, including Japan. Although much progress has been achieved in meeting the demand for places, the country is still conscious of the need to further expand access to tertiary education.

Given the twenty-first-century global economy, the Irish population is widely aware that the development of their education and skills is as important a source of wealth as the accumulation of more traditional forms of capital.[7] Time and again human resource development has been identified as the critical basis of economic and social well-being in modern society. According to the OECD, investment in education is as effective a form of capital accumulation as investments in physical capital. In other words, investment in people and their futures plays a critical role in economic and social progress. At an individual level, the advantages of improved education access and quality are immediately obvious. Those already in employment benefit from higher earnings derived from better qualifications. OECD figures clearly show that, in Ireland in particular, the pay differential between those who have gone on to higher education and those who have not is substantial. In 1997, Irish women graduates in midcareer could expect to earn double that of women who had left education following the LC exam. In all OECD countries, without exception, education attainment remains a significant factor in explaining differences in employment earnings.

In view of Ireland's economic circumstances, its record growth rates, its low inflation, and its competitive economy, it would be easy to be complacent. But to do this would be to ignore the reality of the modern world: If a society does not make the effort to maintain its economic advantages, they will be lost to harder-working competitors.

Over the last 30 years, Ireland has undertaken significant investments in technological and vocational education. Its current level of economic prosperity is due in no small way to this investment, which produced a significant increase in the number of well-equipped workshops and other physical facilities for the training of highly skilled craftsmen and technicians in the Institutes of Technology. The need for ever-improved standards of education to ensure that those entering the workforce have the requisite skills to compete in an increasingly technological world is widely acknowledged. Employers feel more than ever the need for new employees to be well educated in the broadest sense. These employees are adaptable, multiskilled, good communicators, capable of making decisions, and have the potential to be lifelong learners. The days of cramming individuals with facts and sending them out to perform a narrowly specified task are long gone. The key to productivity today lies in adaptability.

It is within this perspective that significant improvements were made to the education system through the restructuring of the senior cycle for students at the second level. As discussed, the system was tailored to meet the needs and abilities of the individual student, providing them with valuable insights into the working world, and preparing them for the demands that the job market would place on them. To present the story of Ireland's education development in higher education, we turn to the 1960s.

HINDSIGHT

Just over 30 years ago, the Commission on Higher Education published a long-awaited report on the status of higher education, the *Investment in Education Report* of 1967. The Commission's assessment of the existing situation in higher education painted a rather dismal picture. It criticized the piecemeal character of the system and its lack of planning machinery. It believed that increasing numbers of students, low entry standards, inadequate staffing, and insufficient accommodation placed academic standards in jeopardy. The Commission was also unimpressed with the level of postgraduate studies and research, where it found that "the insufficiency of staff, equipment and accommodation has been especially frustrating" (Commission on Higher Education 1967). It criticized the academic appointment procedures, the constitutions, and the administrative structures of the higher education institutions. Overall, the Commission considered the shortcomings "so grave as to call for a concerted effort to remove them." Although the Commission referred to "increasing numbers of students," in fact only about 4 percent of the age cohort progressed from second-level to university education. Moreover, it demonstrated a massive social imbalance, whereby 85 percent of places available in university were held by students from families in the top three categories of an occupational matrix devised by the researchers.

Within a generation, the profile of higher education in Ireland has changed dramatically. The role of higher education has become recognized as a central one in the economic, social, and cultural life of society in all countries of the industrial world. This role has been increasingly emphasized in Ireland in a range of public documents. Notably, public confidence in the investment value of higher education received a strong external endorsement by the OECD *Economic Survey on Ireland* (1995), when it stated:

> On the basis of the current system of financing higher education and current income and indirect tax rates, the rate of return to government would appear to be around 12 percent, which is higher than the rate of return on government bonds and the long-run private rate of return on equities." It also noted that ". . . the social rate of return would appear to be somewhat higher than this (OECD 1995).

Building from a modest base in the mid-1960s, policy measures were implemented over the succeeding three decades that transformed the structure and character of higher education in Ireland. The key features of the changed configuration of higher education include the establishment of a strong binary tradition whereby the RTCs, the Dublin Institute of Technology, and the National Institutes for Higher Education (NIHEs) in Limerick and Dublin formed strong pillars of the extra-university sector. The designation of the NIHEs as the University of Limerick

Table 7.9 Full-Time Student Numbers by Sector, Selected Years, 1965–66 to 2003–04

Institutions	1965–66		1985–86		1995–96		1999–2000		2003–04	
	Number	%	Number	%	Number	%	Number	%	Number	%
Universities/RCSI/NCAD	16,007	77	32,388	59	56,698	56	66,914	54	79,120	56
RTCs/DIT	1,007	5	18,953	34	38,130	37	47,858	39	53,386	38
Colleges of education/ other aided	1,679	8	2,212	4	1,982	2	2,602	2	2,810	2
Nonaided	2,005	10	1,534	3	5,518	5	6,000	5	6,373	4
Total	20,698	100	55,078	100	102,328	100	123,374	100	141,689	100

Sources: Higher Education Authority 1995, table 1.1, 24; figures supplied by the Higher Education Authority and the Department of Education.

Note: DIT = Dublin Institute of Technology; NCAD = National College of Art and Design; RCSI = Royal College of Surgeons; RTC = regional technical college.

and Dublin City University in 1989, the first universities established in independent Ireland, did not impair the binary approach. Indeed, they emphasized the importance of creating an institutionally diversified tertiary education system.

At the same time, system support agencies were created to guide the tertiary sector. The HEA was set up in 1968 and given significant responsibilities for higher education, particularly for the universities. The National Council for Educational Awards was created in 1971 and charged with academic responsibilities for the extra-university sector. These were pivotal institutions during this developmental and expansionary era. The diversification provided by many new types of higher education institutions was matched by the expansion of established institutions and by the introduction of new and restructured course offerings. Table 7.9 sets out an overview of the general pattern of full-time students participating from 1965 to 2004, showing the substantial increase in technology enrollments during this period.

The impressive expansion in the provision of diversified forms of higher education placed heavy demands on the national exchequer. The current expenditure increased from about €13 million in 1965 to €1,237 million in 2002. The capital expenditure from public sources increased from €14 million in 1965 to nearly €200 million in 2002. The OECD figures in *Education at a Glance* (2004a) indicate that expenditure in Ireland on higher education, as a percentage of total expenditure on education, is close to the OECD average, at around 25 percent. State funding of higher education has increased significantly with the current and capital state expenditure increasing from €371 million in 1990 to €565.5 million by 1994. Table 7.10 charts the steep rise in funding from 1995 to 2004.

Over the 10-year period, total education expenditure rose by €872 million, representing an increase of 127 percent.

As its investments in higher education have grown, the government has assumed a much more involved and directive role in this subsector. As well as

Table 7.10   Public Expenditure on Third-Level Education, 1995–2004
(€ millions)

	1995	1996	1997	1998	1999	2000	2001	2002	2003	2004
Current	559.4	632.0	784.6	754.2	855.2	948.1	1,103.0	1,236.9	1,313.8	1,370.0
Capital	46.9	59.7	68.3	198.0	154.3	188.0	198.3	183.9	124.0	108.0
Total	606.3	691.7	852.9	952.2	1,009.5	1,136.1	1,301.3	1,420.8	1,437.8	1,478.0

Sources: Key Education Statistics 1994–2000; Finance Unit Estimates 2001–04.

expanding participation in line with social demand, it sought to ensure that higher education was responsive to the perceived economic and social goals of society. These trends were not without their tension, and academics have voiced concerns about the danger of an imbalance in higher education that underestimates the importance of basic research in the humanities and social sciences. By 1997–98, the gender imbalance that was so evident in 1965–66 had been rectified. Whereas the ratio of male to female students was roughly 2 to 1 in 1965–66, it had adjusted itself to 1 to 1 parity by 2003–04.

The drive by many countries to boost the participation of disadvantaged students in higher education has only been partially successful, and Ireland is no exception. Growth in the participation rate for young adults from lower socioeconomic groups failed to match the growth in overall student numbers in all countries except for the United States. Table 7.11 summarizes the impact that these changes have had on education attainment in the Irish labor force.

Regarding the number of science and engineering graduates per 1,000 of the population ages 20 to 29, Ireland's position in comparison with other countries is instructive. In 2002, Ireland occupied the top position (20.5 percent), followed by France (20.2 percent), United Kingdom (10.5 percent), Finland (17.2 percent), Denmark (12.2 percent), and the United States (10.2 percent). This outcome would not have been predicted or even aspired to in the 1960s.

Table 7.11   Education Attainment of the Irish Labor Force
(percent distribution)

Highest level attained	1991–95	1996–2000	2001–05	2006–10
Primary	22	16	12	9
Junior certificate[a]	26	25	23	21
Leaving certificate[b]	30	31	33	33
Third level	22	28	32	37
Total	100	100	100	100

Source: Central Statistics Office Ireland.
a. This is the examination for which students sit after three years of secondary education.
b. This examination is taken after five or six years of secondary education (that is, after six years for those who choose to add the Transition Year after receiving their Junior Certificate).

INFLUENCES

The period from the mid-1960s has been, arguably, the most exciting period in the history of Irish higher education. Many influences have combined to generate this excitement and dynamism, quite apart from the well-established positive attitude of Irish people toward education as the means to a more fulfilling life.[8] These influences emanated from various sources over four decades, and reflect the interplay of ideas between national and international players.

- 1958: The new policy emphasis by government on industrialization and internationalization.
- 1964: The OECD assessment, *Training of Technicians in Ireland*.
- 1965: The OECD's persuasive report, *Investment in Education*.
- 1967: The Commission on Higher Education's *Investment in Education Report*.
- 1967: Government report on *Technological Education*.
- 1973: Ireland's admission to the European Union (then the EEC).
- 1980: Financial assistance provided by the European Social Fund, European Development Fund, and Community Support Framework of the European Union from the 1980s onward.
- 1989: The OECD's pioneering report on *Education and Economy in a Changing Society*.
- 1993: The National Economic and Social Council's *Strategy for Competitiveness, Growth and Employment*.
- 1994: The European Union's White Paper on *Growth, Competitiveness, and Employment*.
- 1994: The government's *Industrial Policy Review Group Report*.
- 1995: Government report on *Education and Training Policies for Economic and Social Development*.

In its 1989 report *Education and Economy in a Changing Society*, the OECD emphasized that a high standard of general education was an essential prerequisite for a vocationally skilled and adaptable workforce. The report further stressed the importance of the role played by initial education and training, before the student entered employment, to promote successful economic performance and the functioning of these countries as democratic societies. The subsequent 1994 OECD *Jobs Study* concluded that ". . . extending and upgrading workers' skills and competences must be a life-long process if OECD economies are to foster the creation of high skills, high wages." These influential publications argued that education and training policies should be directed at achieving this goal as well as at pursuing other fundamental social and cultural objectives. An important aspect of the Irish government's industrial strategy, arising from the implementation of the

1994 report of the *Industrial Policy Review Group* was the high priority attached to the acquisition of high-quality technical and vocational education.

The government's 1995 White Paper on Education, "Charting Our Education Future," was informed by these and other themes that linked education achievement to economic performance. For instance, it states under the heading "Rationale for Future Development" that

> The achievement of economic growth and development is dependent significantly on the availability of suitably qualified and adaptable personnel with the necessary personnel and vocational skills. The availability of skilled personnel, in turn, is dependent on the efficiency and effectiveness of initial vocational education and training and the updating of skills on a continuous basis throughout life (1995).

These positive attitudes toward the importance of vocational and higher education are a far cry from the uncertain and questioning stance of the 1980s when unemployment was high (17 percent) and when emigration was extensive. This worry is best captured in the following extract from the government's *Programme for Action in Education 1984–1987*:

> A major challenge faces the country in planning for the future of third level education. It is at this level that the greatest demand for increased places will arise in the coming decade and it is here that the costs are greatest. Some important questions of principle arise as to the extent to which enrolment at third level should be allowed to grow. The benefits accruing to society as a whole from having a well educated, highly skilled population must be recognised. On the other hand, there is an argument that a large expansion in third level education would increase the supply of highly-qualified graduates in various disciplines beyond national manpower needs and would, in effect, be educating people for emigration or unemployment and in a particularly expensive way. It is recognised however, that there are serious reservations about planning on the basis of manpower projections alone. Account must be taken of the extent to which a well educated cadre of people can, of itself, contribute to economic recovery (1984).

Later in this same document, however, the government asserts that

> Priority in financial support will be given to those academic developments, either by way of new courses or extensions to existing courses, which are geared to development in modern society and thus ensure that our graduates are kept abreast of rapidly changing technology and can compete with graduates of other countries. In submissions received from the Higher Education Authority (HEA) and from individuals, examples were given of several such academic developments planned by the institutions. Analysis of labour force

requirements for the coming decade reveals an increased demand for highly skilled, creative and adaptable people. While the natural growth in the labour force is slowing, there will be a significant increase in the educational level of entrants to the labour force in the years ahead (1984).

As can be seen from the growth figures for student numbers, these circumstances did not limit growth in provision. But they did reflect the government's reaction to the huge burden of public debt that the government of 1977 had incurred in a (failed) attempt to "turn around" the economy.

The influence of EU thinking was a significant external factor. As expressed in its 1994 White Paper on *Growth, Competitiveness, and Employment,* it recognized the critical role of education and training in ensuring the continued competitiveness of the European economy. The Irish government, in formulating its approach to the Community Support Framework, 1994–99, accepted this role of education and training to achieve its objective of maximizing the potential of young people. The analytical rigor of the European Union from the late 1980s onward required the government to measure its return on investment in many areas, including education.

The EU approach and requirements in relation to analysis of outcomes, in relation to the importance of investment in R&D, in requiring that environmental impact statements be researched and provided when new infrastructural projects were being considered, and in requesting that value for money studies be undertaken in relation to new investments (for example, in relation to national and local infrastructural projects) has had a profound influence in the way that the Irish government now assesses policy formulation and implementation. This approach required the collection of sophisticated planning data and the creation of technical capacities that had not previously existed. These capacities added a rigor to the public policy process that had not always been evident.

DEVELOPMENTS AND INITIATIVES

This exciting history was clearly set in motion by the interplay of Irish, OECD, and EU thinking.[9] But what were the particular steps taken to carry out this transformation?

Institutional Development. The main institutional capacity-building actions in higher education were as follows:

- The establishment of the RTCs from 1969 onward.
- The creation of the NIHE (Limerick and Dublin) in 1970 and 1975, respectively—since transmogrified into the University of Limerick and Dublin City University.
- The European Regional Development Fund and its 1989–93 program, in particular.

Before the 1970s, the strongest institutions in the Irish higher education sector were the universities and the teacher education colleges. The universities were underfunded and, more worryingly, were conservative and inward-looking institutions. Dominated by their arts and humanities faculties, they rejected the recognition of "business and commerce" as worthy academic subjects. The economists were particularly unsympathetic to such recognition and felt, in effect, that to interact with business (much less respond to its needs) was academically degrading and a betrayal of the cultural traditions of learning and intellectual rigor that were synonymous with the university.[10]

The OECD's *Training of Technicians in Ireland* (1964) report changed all of that. Or rather, it played a major role in revising such attitudes. The government responded quickly to the OECD's identification of a huge gap in the supply of skills (namely, middle-level technicians). It established a study group that, when it reported in 1967, proposed the establishment of the RTCs throughout the country. The government moved quickly to build seven of these (later to increase to 13), which were distributed across rural Ireland in regionally important towns and cities. These colleges focused on providing middle-level technician education programs in science, engineering, business, and art and design, while also creating the basis for economic growth poles. This was a huge supplement to the rather modest efforts of the four technical colleges of the City of Dublin Vocational Educational Committee, which had not made much of an impact in their 80-year existence. All of the new RTCs provided training for large numbers of apprentices. These RTCs were applied in their emphasis, worked closely with business and government, attracted large numbers of school-leavers, and were hugely successful in supporting industrial development within their regions.

The RTCs were projected to function as sources of innovation in their respective regions. Thus, all of the first presidents of these new institutions were appointed at a young age—28 years to 34 years old. The inspectorate of the Department of Education influenced the decisions of the selection boards to appoint young, dynamic, and creative people who had acquired foreign experience and who were not immersed in the prevailing culture and ethos of the existing higher education institutions. They also ensured the space necessary for innovation. Considerable freedoms were accorded to the leaders of the new institutions to create and innovate with little or no intervention from the Ministry. In their turn, the leadership focused on recruiting like-minded innovative faculty and staff at all levels of their institutions. The same approach distinguished the NIHE, soon to become the new universities. Many faculty members were recruited from abroad—Irish and non-Irish—and also from existing institutions. In most cases, they were attracted to the new institutions by the prospect of being able to shape a new approach to higher education, untrammeled by the traditions of the older colleges and universities. The outcome was that school-leavers now had options for tertiary education, often close to home. The expansion of higher education is evident in the data included in tables 7.9 and 7.11. The universities were beginning to feel that they had competition.

When the NIHEs in Dublin and Limerick opened, this competition and rivalry intensified. The government wished to expand the number of places available for students in higher education, but not in the traditionally titled and structured academic programs. The minister of education, in addressing the *Dail* (Irish Parliament) in 1970, characterized the NIHE/Limerick, as "Ireland's MIT." This was meant to be—and was—a succinct statement of government policy in relation to higher education provision—that is, a strong emphasis on science, technology, and business that included interaction with businesses.

The NIHE programs became hugely popular with students. For instance, admission to NIHE/Dublin bachelor's program in International Marketing and Languages required a higher grade point average than did entry to medical school in the traditional universities. The NIHEs consulted with business and introduced many innovative programs—for example, software engineering (with computer science), communications, biotechnology (not biological science), analytical science, and accounting and finance. All programs included an industrial placement period of six to nine months. Basic and applied R&D were also promoted by the NIHE. The government, European Union, business, and industry reacted positively and made funding available to these institutions for this purpose. To the great credit of the older universities, they responded by introducing new programs (for example, international commerce, materials science, software engineering, biotechnology). They also began to undertake a certain amount of the applied research. Innovation and business incubator centers were established on NIHE and university campuses. Industrial advisory bodies were put in place for a number of universities.

Ireland's IDA was charged with developing business in the country and, most important, attracting FDI to Ireland. Its portfolio of incentives encouraged a greater output of skilled apprentices and, in particular, technicians throughout Ireland. The regional distribution of these skilled human resources helped IDA to interest foreign companies in locating to these regional centers. As part of its strategy, it endeavored to convince foreign businessmen that the Irish education system was responsive to the needs of business to a greater degree than in other countries. Presidents of institutions, professors, and faculty members participated in those promotional efforts to support the IDA contention and claims. They attended public functions, private breakfasts, lunches, and dinners, and they traveled to the United States and Japan. Members of the education community engaged willingly and without recompense in these and many other such activities. There was the strong sense that the higher education could help develop the nation. In this sense, such efforts by many academics were an expression of their patriotism.

These various changes affected the distribution of students by field of study. In 1950, only 20 percent of all full-time university students were enrolled in faculties of science and engineering. But by 1985, this proportion had grown to 30 percent. A similar surge in student enrollments occurred in commerce and business studies. For example, at the National University of Ireland in 1960, fewer than 5 percent of all full-time students were pursuing commerce or business studies. By 1985, this share had risen to 12 percent.

Philanthropy. Private fundraising for higher education began in earnest in the late 1980s, when universities organized themselves to seek donations of money, equipment, and services from business and wealthy individuals both in Ireland and in the United States. Those latter efforts were particularly successful. The universities persuaded the government to match many donations on a one-to-one basis (that is, one dollar from the government for every dollar raised by the universities). In this way, US$750 million was raised over a 10-year period. When government matching funds were added, this amount totaled US$1.5 billion for capital projects benefiting higher education.

R&D. Beginning in the late 1990s, the Irish government began to invest seriously in R&D. This funding responded to incentives from the European Union under its European Regional Development Fund programs. Another key influence was the Atlantic Philanthropies Foundation, which encouraged government interest in funding research in a substantial manner. The Foundation informed the government that it was prepared to donate some €200 million (initially some €100 million) to the creation of a fund—PRTLI—if the government would match it with a similar sum. This successful proposal in turn laid the groundwork for the establishment of Science Foundation Ireland (a Technology Foresight Study had recommended such an initiative), to which the government allocated significant funds—some €600 million over seven years.

Industrial Work Experience. The introduction of industry work placements to programs in universities had a number of significant outcomes as follows:

- Work experience for students.
- Career opportunities, because satisfied employers often would offer positions to students upon graduation.
- Final-year student projects brought back to university from the company (companies generally would fund these).
- Good relationships with many industrialists (academics would visit students), which, at times, resulted in joint R&D projects.
- Feedback on industry needs and feedback on the content and standards of the relevant university program.
- Donations of money or equipment by the business community.

Reaching Out to the Community. Other developments put in place have included a National Distance Education Centre and programs at Dublin City University. This Distance Education Centre went on to become considerably effective in its open-learning programs. Its main offerings included software engineering, humanities, nursing, project management, and accounting.

Formal Business Links. The universities, through the Conference of Heads of Irish Universities—now named the Irish Universities Association (IUA)—formalized their interactions with the Irish Business and Employers Confederation (IBEC) by establishing a joint council between the IBEC and the IUA. This forum discusses matters of common concern, devised joint ventures, and negotiates coordinated approaches to government. Many universities and faculties have gone on to establish Business Advisory Boards. The Institutes of Technology followed similar patterns.

External Stakeholder Membership on Governing Authorities. With the creation of the RTCs/Institutes of Technology in the early 1980s, a tradition of external stakeholder membership on institutional governing bodies began. When the NIHEs were established, their governing authorities were given extensive external membership, including an external chair. The Colleges of the National University of Ireland had some external representation—local authority members and representatives of the churches—on their governing bodies. Trinity College Dublin was unique in that its governing board consisted entirely of internal members. In addition, all higher education institutions typically included one or two student members on their governing authorities. The Universities Act of 1997 formalized this practice by making external members an explicit requirement.

Skills Planning. From the early 1980s, concerns had been expressed with regard to the need for an increased output of trained technicians and graduates from the Institutes of Technology (the former RTCs) and universities. In eventual response to these growing pressures, the government established in 1997 the Expert Group on Future Skills Needs (EGFSN) (see http://www.skillsireland.ie/index.html). This group was charged with the development of national strategies to tackle the issues of skill needs, manpower forecasting, and education and training programs for business. Membership of the EGFSN united business people, educationalists, training providers, trade unions, policy makers, public servants, and industrial support and promotion agencies. The EGFSN made significant inputs to government policy and actions since its formation. It has published various reports that have identified, in a systematic way, the skill needs of different sectors, and it has advised on the actions needed to address them. It has recommended how to improve the awareness of job seekers concerning sectors in which the demands for skills are strong. Through its Skills Awareness Campaign, the EGFSN has informed the public of the qualifications required and how they can be obtained.

Discover Science and Engineering Programme. Since the year 2000, Ireland has suffered a drop in the popularity of science and technology courses with young school-leavers. In response, a number of efforts—all of them initiated in parallel and not coordinated—were launched to promote careers in science and technology with teenagers at various stages in their secondary education. These efforts considered it particularly important to reach students in their final years of secondary schooling, that is, in the final three years leading to the School Leaving Examinations.[11] The problem was considered so important by industry bodies and major employers that they sponsored numerous promotional programs. Separate activities were undertaken by the higher education sector and by the government. The Government Task Force on the Physical Sciences, convened in 2003, recommended that these disparate programs should be integrated into one comprehensive promotional agency. The result was the national Discover Science and Engineering Programme, which has been extremely active in the promotion of science and technology. For example, it has sponsored a countrywide Science Week each year with events, displays, and competitions organized around a chosen theme.

NEW INITIATIVE: THE STRATEGIC INNOVATION FUND

For some time, the higher education sector had been complaining that the government was not providing adequate resources for the sector and that funding was not keeping pace with national inflation. It became clear that the government was reluctant to invest when it was not convinced that the tertiary institutions were committed to a reform agenda. The IUA recognized this credibility gap between the universities and the government. It proceeded to elaborate a document setting out its policy proposals for reform of the sector. Under the title of *Reform of Third Level and Creation of Fourth Level Ireland—Securing Competitive Advantage in the 21st Century*, these recommendations, bearing the stamp of the university community, were presented to the government in October 2005.

The government response was to create a Strategic Innovation Fund (SIF) in 2006. Funded by €300 million over five years, the SIF will encourage and facilitate innovation in higher education institutions. A main thrust is to foster new approaches to enhancing quality and effectiveness within higher education and research, in part by making use of existing resources (including capital resources) more effectively. In the national context, the Fund seeks to achieve the following:

- Underpin economic and social development through widening third-level participation and lifelong learning programs that will meet diverse student needs and improve the skills of those already in employment.

- Produce a highly skilled cadre of graduates who can foster and sustain research-based development and innovation that will evolve into a world-class fourth-level (postgraduate) higher education that can underpin Ireland's future economic prosperity.
- Protect and reinforce the roles of higher education as a key driver of economic development, as the provider of independent intellectual insights, and as a primary contributor to the country's social, human, and cultural understanding.

The primary objectives of the SIF are as follows:

- To enhance the delivery of the core activities of education and research through effective and creative institutional and interinstitutional collaboration including, where necessary, appropriate internal restructuring and rationalization efforts.
- To support innovation and quality improvement in teaching and learning, including enhanced teaching methods, program restructuring, modularization, and e-learning.
- To support access, retention, and progression at the individual institutional level through interinstitutional, sectoral, and intersectoral collaboration.
- To support enabling measures that lay a foundation for the expansion of postgraduate education (including the development of graduate schools), including both intra- and interinstitutional collaboration.

To this end, the Fund will make financing available to achieve the following:

- Provide incentives and rewards for internal restructuring and rationalization efforts.
- Provide for improved performance management systems.
- Meet staff training and support requirements associated with the reform of structures and the implementation of new processes.
- Implement improved management information systems.
- Introduce teaching and learning reforms, including enhanced teaching methods, program restructuring, modularization, and e-learning.
- Support quality improvement initiatives aimed at excellence.
- Promote access, transfer, and progression and provide incentives for stronger interinstitutional collaboration in the development and delivery of programs.

The SIF may be a precursor of future trends in higher education funding. Specifically, higher education will be expected to make a persuasive case for additional government funding and, in particular, it will need to specify the uses for which additional funds can be applied. Interinstitutional competition and collaboration will be particular drivers in this allocation process.

SUMMARY

The past 25 years or so have been a period of substantial development and innovation in Ireland as a whole and in its higher education sector in particular. Why, it is legitimate to ask, did this happen? Are there lessons for other countries? Are the conditions so unique that there is little to be learned from the Irish experience? These are questions that others will certainly investigate, but perhaps the following observations may assist them in doing so.

Industry and the government attribute the recent economic success of Ireland to the critical role of education in combination with other factors. To a large extent, the policy priority accorded to education development was not based on in-depth technical analysis but on traditionally held beliefs that the education of Ireland's youth was a right that should not be denied them. But other influences were also at work. International experts, and the education reports and industrial policy analyses that they produced, not only reaffirmed this national viewpoint but also stressed the relevance of matching the type of education to national development needs. Moreover, they positioned this task within the context of challenging traditional attitudes with regard to what, where, and how education was to be provided.

Policy makers recognized that the nation was in deep trouble and that it needed fresh leadership if it was to develop and thrive. The government created new types of tertiary institutions—RTCs and NIHE—and encouraged them to grapple with the needs of the developing economy, to experiment, and to innovate. This encouragement signaled the government's willingness to provide resources for those institutions and programs that would support government ambition.

This, in turn, stimulated healthy interinstitutional competition. The new institutions developed programs that were unique in Ireland and that the traditional institutions ignored or frowned upon. Examples included bachelor's degrees and short-cycle certificate, diploma, or associate degrees in such areas as analytical science, computer applications, communications, mechatronics, sports science, biotechnology, business and language, accounting and finance, translation and interpretation, and journalism. These programs were so popular with student applicants that the traditional institutions replicated many of them, thereby generating a much more diverse number of career options for the Irish school-leaver.

From the late 1980s, the analytical rigor of the European Union obliged the government to develop greater capacity and technical sophistication in its policy and planning process. The European Union required the government to measure its anticipated return on investment in many areas, including education. These studies were undertaken by the Economic, Social and Research Institute (ESRI) during the 1990s. Its staff concluded that the country's investments in education had indeed made a significant and discernible contribution to national development, and could perhaps be credited with 20 percent of the total economic gains achieved. These studies confirmed much anecdotal evidence, such as the views of foreign companies that their decision to locate in Ireland was related to the quality and quantity of the provision of education.

REFLECTIONS ON IRELAND AND THE KNOWLEDGE-BASED SOCIETY

Ireland's ESRI reported a positive link between investment in skill development and economic productivity at the end of the twentieth century. But long before such evidence became available, the country's citizens and policy makers intuited that higher levels of education and training would lead to increased wealth and higher living. Through a process of consultation, experimentation, modification, and rethinking, the government shaped a new strategic direction for enterprise development in Ireland that reflected this belief. In so doing, it identified skills development, education, and training as an area in which Ireland could build sustainable competitive advantage at the international level.

Within this context, we can examine Ireland's readiness for the economy of the future from a skills perspective. Skills, education, and training exert a significant influence on society that goes far beyond their impact on the economy. A participative and inclusive economy is one in which the wider social and societal impacts of skills development are acknowledged and considered. These potential collateral impacts include social cohesion benefits, health benefits, and a reduction in crime, poverty, and social welfare dependency.

In a modern society, education should satisfy social, cultural, and economic needs. From an enterprise perspective, the ability of the education system to respond flexibly to economic and social change is critical to the supply of appropriate skills for the effective functioning of the economy. Ireland's future economic development will depend to a large degree on knowledge management and innovation, both of which are essential in transitioning to higher-value activities that are necessary for continued economic growth and wealth creation. People are the enablers of such activities. Thus, the education and training system must continually adapt to produce the skills needed to drive successful enterprise.

GROWING IMPORTANCE OF KNOWLEDGE

Companies increasingly face global competition and seek new ways to compete effectively. Unable to compete on the basis of low costs, companies in industrial economies strive to identify and build new sources of competitive advantage based on knowledge and expertise, which often translate into efficiency and productivity gains. Despite a widely held belief that the Irish education system is world class, further improvements will be necessary if it is to sustain enterprise development and economic growth in the coming decade. For example, R&D investment levels, although rising in recent years, are still considerably below OECD averages.

Five sources of competitive advantage can enable enterprise in Ireland to achieve this goal. Three of these build on areas of national competitive advantage in which Ireland has competed and excelled in the past. These are (a) its education and training systems, (b) its stable and advantageous taxation regime, and (c) its reputation for an effective and agile government, which has been responsive to the needs of enterprise. In these areas, it is necessary to retain or regain Ireland's leadership position. Two additional sources of competitive advantage focus on (a) expertise in sales and marketing and (b) the application of R&D and technology to the creation of new products and services. These five aspects are expected to attract considerable policy attention in the years ahead and likely will frame a decisive new orientation of Irish enterprise policy.

The below discussion will focus on efforts needed to enhance Ireland's expertise in, respectively, technology and education and skills development.

EXPERTISE IN TECHNOLOGY

Policy makers in Ireland have already taken major steps to build expertise in science and technology through SFI and PRTLI. These investments in basic research are essential for further scientific advancement through new discovery as well as for enhancement of the country's ability to absorb and apply new technological developments. In particular, these investments should produce the skilled people necessary to build product development capacity in the enterprise base. Close-to-market and applied research capabilities must be promoted to facilitate greater synergy between those who generate knowledge and those who transform it into saleable products and services.

As a small country, Ireland has limited resources. It must be selective and restrictive in the areas in which it chooses to focus policy and investment resources. Developing an appropriate focus can be assisted by the identification of strategic technology platforms—areas of technology (for example, biometrics) that draw on several basic fields of knowledge (such as mathematics, physics, and computing) for application to a range of new products. Consultation and collaboration have proven essential in both the identification and exploitation of such platforms. In particular, interaction among industry, academia, and the state in this area must be fostered. European initiatives in this respect should be examined for their learning potential. The strategic objective is to achieve a critical mass of leading-edge expertise in particular areas or niches.

Not all product development and process advancement is technology driven. Process improvements, design enhancement, and changes in the composition and delivery of a product can also be innovative. Nontechnological innovation is particularly relevant to services, and achieving a competitive advantage in this area would enhance success in Ireland's knowledge-based services.

From an education perspective, Ireland should recognize the constant need to improve the skills of the general workforce and achieve distinction in the quality of graduates from higher education. Ambitious targets must be set to improve education and skills attainment across all levels. Governance of higher education must be reviewed to ensure that it is capable of flexible responses that match the increasing pace of change in the global environment. In view of the country's aspiration to increase its application of knowledge in the enterprise sector, it will be necessary to increase the number and quality of higher education graduates at all levels. To realize these objectives, new approaches to the funding of higher education are likely required. Attention must be given to maintaining and redefining the differentiated but complementary roles of the universities and the institutes of technology.

Lifelong skills development will become progressively more important in the decade ahead, particularly as the fast-changing nature of the workplace and the rapid expansion of knowledge require people to be progressively more flexible and adaptable.

THREE CRITICAL AREAS IN EDUCATION AND SKILLS DEVELOPMENT

Three aspects of education and skills development are critical to the future vitality of the enterprise sector:

- An adaptive and responsive higher education sector must be able to create and exploit knowledge and produce the number and quality of graduates necessary to support the knowledge economy. The numbers entering higher education may need to rise further. Investment in higher education and research is essential to generate the intellectual capital required to fuel an innovation-driven economy. Expanded postgraduate programs will have an important role to play in this effort.
- Improved skills of the existing workforce and increased education levels are essential in an environment of constant change and global competition. To foster the continual acquisition of knowledge, skills, and competencies, formally structured approaches to lifelong learning must be introduced and corresponding delivery structures must be put in place. Particular policy intervention will be required to ensure that the low skilled are not left behind in the move toward a knowledge society.

- New ways to expand the workforce to meet growth forecasts are needed. Specifically, an appropriate skills-based immigration strategy will be required to deal with demand for skilled workers that cannot be satisfied from within Ireland or the European Union.

An Adaptive and Responsive Higher Education Sector. The future development of the higher education sector will depend on institutional capabilities to achieve the following:

- Respond quickly to shifts in the global market, demands for skills, and advances in knowledge.
- Be flexible and adaptive to the needs of students and enterprise.
- Be creative and innovative in cost-efficient delivery methods.
- Support high levels of participation in lifelong learning.
- Be innovative in pursuing the commercialization of research.
- Facilitate the mobility of staff between academia and enterprise.

To achieve this, changes will be required in the way institutions are funded, governed, and managed, and additional institutional autonomy will be advantageous.

Integrated Higher Education Policies: Higher education should be underpinned by a coherent policy approach that includes the public and private sector (including the universities, institutes of technology, colleges of education, and private higher education colleges, and so on). A cohesive policy should be agreed on between education, enterprise, and the government to ensure that the skills necessary for enterprise success are developed in time, in sufficient quantity, and to the required standard of quality. The focus of policy in this area should be on outcomes, with quick and efficient adaptation and delivery of responses and regular monitoring and review.

Financing Higher Education: The higher education institutions must be adequately funded if they are to meet the goal of increased quality and quantity of graduates. At present, core funding for higher education in Ireland is provided predominantly from public sources (about 80 percent). An element of this public funding should be tied to performance and allocated on a competitive basis subject to the successful achievement of outputs. This would allow for flexibility and responsiveness to react to national strategic goals. The first steps have been taken with the establishment of the SIF. To augment public funding, the higher education institutions should be permitted to pursue additional funding from diverse sources, including commissioned R&D, commercialization of intellectual property, and other forms of collaboration with the private sector. A new funding framework that combines core funding with a competitively based element, allocated on the basis of performance, including the active encouragement of additional diverse sources of private funds, has been put in place recently and will be instructive to track performance and impact.

Facilitating the Development of Enterprise: After education and research, education institutions have a third role—that is, the promotion of enterprise.[12] The higher education institutions already support enterprise in many individual ways. But it would be important to provide more systematic support for this role. The exploitation of knowledge and commercialization of research must become rooted in the culture and infrastructure of the higher education system. This means continued attention to new campus company start-ups, a pro-innovation culture of intellectual property protection and exploitation, programs in entrepreneurship, consulting services, information services, new types of postgraduate programs, and additional links between higher education institutions and private enterprise.

Improve Skills of the Existing Workforce and Increase Education Levels. Given the critical importance of education for Ireland's future competitiveness, ambitious targets are being set for its education and training performance across the full spectrum of education levels, from primary to lifelong learning. These include increasing the proportion graduating from second-level education and facilitating access to higher education for a wider share of the population, raising overall education attainment levels, and supporting a high level of participation in lifelong learning.

Secondary Level: A dropout rate of almost 17 percent from secondary education is a disadvantage not only for the students involved but also for the economy. In fact, it limits the capacity to produce a workforce with the knowledge and skills required to drive and sustain a knowledge economy. Hence, a reduction in the dropout levels for early school-leavers would raise cost-effectiveness within the education system. Additionally, efforts should be made to ensure that all young people leaving education have acquired a recognized qualification that is relevant to the needs of the labor market. This is the key to maintaining high levels of employment. Because most education and training programs for medium- and high-level skills require a School Leaving Certificate as a prerequisite, this would be the appropriate qualification requirement.

A wide range of training and education approaches can be employed to attain equivalent results. The apprenticeship scheme has been one of the more successful elements of the Irish education and training system in recent decades. It has produced generations of world-class crafts and trades people who have made a major contribution to Irish economic development. Currently, some 27,000 people are undertaking apprenticeship programs for some 25 occupations, and the possibility of extending the apprenticeship model to additional occupations is currently being examined. Similarly, work-study approaches are being used in other parts of the education and training system, most notably in the hospitality sector and in parts of the formal education system. Additional work-study programs that integrate and accredit both experiential learning in a supervised work placement and formal study need to become more widespread. Specifically, work-study programs should target middle-skill occupations experiencing growth that are not currently listed among designated crafts.

Over the past decade, traineeships have been developed by FÁS (the national training authority) to provide shorter-duration training for entry into a number of occupations not covered by the formal apprenticeship system. These jobs are generally in expanding parts of the services sector, including security services, financial services, personal and leisure services, and child care. Almost 1,900 people undertook occupational skills development through this route in 2003. The ambition is to increase the current LC completion rate to 90 percent and to provide training for a broader range of occupations. These occupations should be offered to those students not completing the LC program and through new work-study programs that are relevant to the needs of the labor market. Qualifications from these programs should be equivalent to the LC standard.

Lifelong Learning: Although the concept of lifelong learning is well established, participation by adults in education and training is still significantly underdeveloped in Ireland compared with other countries, particularly regarding entry to higher education. Greater employee participation in lifelong learning can be encouraged in three ways:

- Improving skills—increasing on-the-job levels of skills and qualifications.
- Broadening skills—acquiring skills and knowledge in complementary new areas, particularly by combining skills from different disciplines.
- Continually developing skills—periodically renewing existing skill levels to stay abreast of technological or other developments.

Embracing lifelong learning as a strategic commitment requires combined effort in a number of areas, including the following: (a) a balancing of the rights and responsibilities of employers, individuals, and the state; (b) a cultural and attitudinal shift on the part of learners, employers, and the state, including the recognition of learning as an investment, not a cost; (c) greater flexibility in the provision of higher education; (d) addressing the anomaly between part-time and full-time fees; and (e) the elimination of other nonfinancial barriers, particularly in the areas of access, transfer, and progression. Most recent evidence on education and training of the employed suggests that there are particular problems in relation to the needs of low-skilled employees. In essence, those with lower-level education qualifications and those working in lower-level occupations are much less likely to receive education or training.

Augmenting the Skills Pool. With the number of school-leavers declining and the population aging, skills and labor market policies will have to be adjusted to ensure an adequate supply of skilled people, both in terms of quality and quantity. Although Ireland is near full employment, continued efforts should be made to attract more people into employment. These efforts need to focus on those groups in which there is scope for increased participation in working life, including females, older people, and the disabled. A greater commitment to policies that encourage participation, including tax incentives (particularly targeted at those with low incomes), child care support, and flexible working arrangements, including part-time work, would help to meet this objective.

Current projections indicate that approximately 420,000 new workers will be required over the period from 2001 to 2010. As available domestic sources are diminishing, Ireland will need to attract a considerable number of highly skilled immigrants. In fact, this is already occurring, with net migration registering an inflow of some 60,000 per year over the past number of years. The expansion of the European Union should allow for most of Ireland's immigration needs to be filled from within the Union.

But it is possible that the demand for particular skills, for example, research skills, will not be fully satisfied by migration from within the European Union. On one hand, the demographic profile of most EU countries shows an even more acute shortage of young people entering the higher education system. On the other hand, almost all industrial economies are actively seeking highly skilled immigrants. In trying to attract knowledge workers, Ireland will face intense competition from advanced economies, including other EU countries and the United States. To succeed in this, Ireland will have to be seen as an attractive place to live and work, with a welcoming attitude to immigrants and a vibrant, diverse cultural life. For these reasons, attention should be given to a planned, coherent immigration policy that is carefully managed and regulated and is consistent with the skill requirements of the economy.

TOMORROW'S SKILL NEEDS: TOWARD A NATIONAL SKILLS STRATEGY

The EGFSN's national strategy presents clear long-term objectives for the education and training requirements needed to develop Ireland as a knowledge-based, innovation-driven, participative, and inclusive economy with a highly skilled workforce by 2020. The strategy identifies Ireland's current skills profile, provides a strategic vision and specific objectives for Ireland's future skills requirements, and sets out a road map for how the vision and objectives can be achieved. It is expected that the implementation of this strategy will secure the future competitive advantage of enterprises in Ireland and enhance future growth in productivity and living standards. The EGFSN believes this vision is achievable. The strategy is complementary to the Strategy for Science, Technology, and Innovation launched in 2006.

Key performance targets for 2020 are as follows:

- 48 percent of the labor force should have qualifications at National Framework of Qualifications (NFQ) levels 6 to 10 (from National Certificate to the doctoral level).[13]
- 45 percent should have qualifications at NFQ levels four and five (equivalent to the LC examination).
- 7 percent should have qualifications at NFQ levels one to three (below junior certificate) while aiming to transition to higher levels.
- 500,000 individuals in the workforce will improve their skills by at least one NFQ level over and above their current level of education and training.
- The LC retention rate for young people should rise to 90 percent.
- By 2020, the proportion of the population ages 20 to 24 with NFQ level four or five (LC or equivalent) should be increased to 94 percent.
- The progression from second- to third-level education should increase from 55 percent to 72 percent.

The strategy also highlights the need for additional policy attention to the following issues:

- Integration of immigrants into the education and training system, at all levels.
- Career guidance and mentoring for those at work.
- Assistance for individuals and companies in identifying their skills needs.
- More awareness programs that highlight the benefits of education and training.
- Education and training provision to be flexible and responsive to the needs of employers and employees.

NATIONAL DEVELOPMENT PLAN, 2007–13

The importance of investing in education has received further reinforcement by the government in the recent statement by the minister of finance regarding Ireland's current NDP in the National Development Plan (2006):

> Investment in education will also be a core part of the NDP. We will build on the wise harnessing of Exchequer Social Fund monies which was a hallmark of previous plans. This is investment which has and will continue to deliver major returns. The Government has placed research and development (R&D) at the heart of its economic development strategy in order to build the skills necessary for a modern knowledge based economy and to strengthen our research base. We are committed to making a quantum leap

forward in the area of R&D and to move Ireland from impressive latecomer to acknowledged leader in this critical area. The next NDP will provide the investment to advance this objective. The Programme for Research in Third Level Institutions is playing an important role in facilitating the strategic development of institutional research capabilities, enhancing the numbers, quality, and relevance of graduate output and supporting high quality inter-disciplinary and inter-institutional research. The further development of our knowledge economy has made reform of our third level sector imperative in order to enhance the quality of teaching and of the student experience, to increase participation in third level education and meet up-skilling needs and, of course, to support research programs, both basic and applied.

CONCLUSION

The issues and challenges facing Ireland in transitioning to a knowledge-based economy are daunting, although they are buttressed by a successful experience in economic development. There is a danger of complacency resulting from this success. Such complacency would be unforgivable when one considers the struggles of the many generations of Irish people who built the current success that is the Irish economy. This chapter outlines clearly what must be done to sustain this success. Other nations will learn quickly from Ireland's success stories. Competition, which has always been acute, will intensify. The government and citizens alike must focus on collaborating to ensure Ireland's place in the more sophisticated and demanding world that stretches out before us in the globally competitive, knowledge-based economy and society of the twenty-first century.

NOTES

1. The *Irish Strategy for Science, Technology and Innovation* has set a target of €2.5 billion (constant prices) for business expenditure on R&D by 2013.

2. The School Leaving Certificate is the terminal examination in secondary school; students typically move on to higher education at that point.

3. The Irish secondary education system includes a junior cycle of three years and a senior cycle of two to three years.

4. The 1965 OECD-sponsored report *Investment in Education* had a notable influence on this decision, as did the comments of the National Industrial Economic Council. A detailed chronicling of this period and its reform initiatives can be found in *Post–Primary Education in Ireland, 1957–1970* (Randles 1975).

5. In primary schools, many unqualified teachers were recruited and, later, graduates were recruited and provided with in-service programs. Recently, a graduate entry stream has been introduced in the teacher training colleges whereby graduates undertake an

18-month program before qualification. Graduates may become qualified through a distance education program provided by Hibernia College, a private sector body; the program is recognized and approved by the Department of Education.

6. A number of curriculum projects that cover the transition from school to work benefited from the financial support of the European Union.

7. The OECD *Jobs Study—Facts, Analysis, Strategies* (1994) identifies three key areas in relation to education and training on which policy should be focused. The first of these is to ensure a sufficiently high standard of initial (basic) education, the second is to facilitate the transition from school to work, and the third is to upgrade skills among the adult population.

8. This strongly held attitude dates back to the 17th and 18th centuries when the British administration of the time prevented the native Irish from accessing even the most basic education.

9. The World Bank also contributed financing and technical assistance to this transformation. For example, the first building at Dublin City University was built with a World Bank Loan, and the RTCs (later the Institutes of Technology) were the beneficiaries of its last loan in 1974.

10. This attitude was, of course, not unique to Ireland.

11. Some 97 percent of students study science for the first three years of the six-year secondary school cycle and all students study mathematics in each year of secondary school.

12. This view is an Irish modification of the university's traditional third role of community service.

13. The report uses the National Framework of Qualifications as a basis for its projection. The NFQ comprises 10 levels of qualifications, with each level based on nationally agreed standards, skills, and competence. These standards define the learning outcomes to be achieved by learners seeking qualifications at each level. The 10 levels include qualifications gained in such settings as schools, places of work, the community, training centers, and colleges and universities, from the most basic to the most advanced levels of learning. Information on the NFQ is available at www.nfq.ie.

References

Adams, Arvil V. 2007. "The Role of Youth Skills Development in the Transition to Work: A Global Review." The Human Development Network Children and Youth Department, World Bank, Washington, DC.

Afonso, Antonio, and Miguel St. Aubyn. 2005. "Cross Country Efficiency of Secondary Education Provision: A Semi-Parametric Analysis with Nondiscretionary Inputs." Working Paper Series No. 494. Institute for Economics and Business Administration (ISEG), Technical University of Lisbon, Portugal.

Ang, Wai Hoong. 2006. "Singapore's Textbook Experience 1965–1977." In *Toward a Better Future: Education and Training for Economic Development in Singapore since 1965*, eds. Lee, Sing Kong, Goh Chor Boon, Birger Fredriksen, and Jee Peng Tan. Washington, DC: World Bank.

Beck, Lynn, 1994. *Reclaiming Educational Administration as a Caring Profession*. New York: Teachers College Press.

Bhangananda, Kulvitra. 2003. "Educational Development toward a Knowledge-Based Economy." In *Human Resource Development Toward a Knowledge-Based Economy: The Case of Thailand*, ed. Minoru Makishima and Somchai Suksiriserekul, 41–82. Tokyo: Institute of Developing Economies (Japan External Trade Organization).

Bray, Mark. 1999. *The Shadow Educational System: Private Tutoring and Its Implications for Planners*. UNESCO IIEP.

Bunnag, Sirikul. 2006. "Free Schooling Cuts Abuse." *Bangkok Post*, General News. Available at http://www.bangkok post.com (accessed August 3, 2006).

Business Times. July 8, 1980.

Central Committee of Vietnamese Communist Party. 2006. "Report on the Direction and Tasks for 5-year Socio-Economic Development for 2006–2010 Period." Hanoi: National Political Publishing House.

Chan, Chin Bock, ed. 2002. *Heart Work: Stories of How EDB Steered the Singapore Economy from 1961 into the 21st Century*. Singapore: Singapore Economic Development Board.

Chiang, Mickey. 1998. *From Economic Debacle to Economic Miracle: The History and Development of Technical Education in Singapore*. Singapore: Times Edition.

Chong, Guk Lee. 2001. *Hankukeui Kyokwaseo Chulpan Byuncheon Yeongu (Transition of Textbook Publishing in Korea)*. Seoul: Iljin-sa.

Chung, Kwang Hee et al. 2004. "KEDI Eight Year Study for High School Education and the Improvement of the University Admission Selection System." KEDI Research Paper RM 2004-69, Korean Educational Development Institute.

Chung, Tae Su. 1991. *The July 30 Kyo Yuk Kae Hyuk (The July 30 Educational Reform)*. Seoul, Korea: Yeji-kak.

_____. 2006. *Occupational Training, Korea's Human Resource: Challenge and New Paradigm*. Seoul: Beop mun-sa.

Chung, Tae Su. et al. 2004. *Kyo Yuk Hang Jeong Jae Jeong Sa (The History of Educational Administration and Financing in Korea)*. Seoul, Korea: Hankuk Kyo Yuk Sahak Hoe.

Circular No. 114/TTg. March 27, 1957. "Central Steering Committee on the Elimination of Illiteracy."

Clark, David. 1971. "Manpower Planning in Singapore." *Malayan Economic Review* XVI, no. 2 (October).

Colony of Singapore. 1954. "Report of the Industrial Resources Study Groups, September 1954." In *Andrew Gilmour, Official Letters, 1931–1956*, Mss. Ind. Ocn. s. 154., para 86, p. 13.

_____. 1955. *Annual Report*. Singapore.

Commission on Higher Education. 1967. *Investment in Education Report*. Stationery Office, Dublin.

Cresswell, Anthony M. 1999. *Educational Finance in Thailand: A Review and Recommendations for Improving Allocative Efficiency*. Bangkok: UNESCO-Bangkok for the Asian Development Bank Social Sector Program Loan.

Daehan Printing and Publishing Company. 1988. *Daehan Kyokwaseosa (The History of the Korean Textbook)*. Seoul: Daehan Printing and Publishing Company.

de Ferranti, David et al. 2003. *Closing the Gap in Education and Technology. World Bank Latin American and Caribbean Studies*. Washington, DC: World Bank.

Department of Education (Ireland). 1994. "Transition Year Guidelines." Dublin.

Department of Education and Science (Ireland). 1992. The Junior Certificate Examination, Rules and Programme for Secondary Schools, Dublin.

_____. 2004. *A Brief Description of the Irish Education System*.

Department of Enterprise, Trade and Employment (Ireland). 2006. *Strategy for Science Technology and Innovation, 2006–2013*. Dublin.

Department of Statistics (Singapore). Various years. *Yearbook of Statistics*. Singapore: Department of Statistics.

di Gropello, Emanuela. 2006. *Meeting the Challenges of Secondary Education in Latin America and East Asia: Improving Efficiency and Resource Mobilization*. Washington, DC: World Bank.

Dixon, Chris. 1991. *South East Asia in the World Economy*. Cambridge: Cambridge University Press.

Dong-a Il bo International Department. 2006. *The World's Noble Technical Vocational School*.

Economic and Social Research Institute. 2000–06. Medium Term Review (National Development Plan). Economic Social Research Institute, Dublin.

Education for a Changing World. 1992. Stationery Office, Dublin.

The Education Law of the Socialist Republic of Vietnam. 2005. Hanoi: Education Publishing House.

Emi, Koici. 1968. "Economic Development and Educational Investment in the Meiji Area." In *Readings in the Economics of Education*. Paris: UNESCO.

Enterprise Strategy Group Report. 2003. Stationery Office, Dublin.

European Union. 1994. "Growth, Competitiveness, and Employment."

Expert Group on Future Skills Needs. "Tomorrow's Skills: Towards a National Skills Strategy." Available at http://www.skillsstrategy.ie.

Filmer, Deon, and Lant Pritchett. 1997. *Child Mortality and Public Spending on Health: How Much Does Money Matter?* Washington, DC: World Bank.

Fredriksen, Birger. 1981. "Progress Towards Regional Targets for Universal Primary Education: A Statistical Review." *International Journal of Education Development* 1, no. 1 (April).

———. 1985. "Norway and the World: The Economic Dimension." In *Norwegian Foreign Policy in the 1980s*, ed. J. J. Holst. Oslo: Norwegian University Press.

Gamage, David, and Pacharapimon Sooksomchitra. 2004. "Decentralisation and School-Based Management in Thailand." *International Review of Education* 50: 289–305.

Goh, Keng Swee. 1972. *The Economics of Modernization.* Singapore: Asia Pacific Press.

Goh, Keng Swee and the Education Study Team. 1978. "Report on the Ministry of Education, Ministry of Education." Singapore.

Gopinathan, S. 1999. "Preparing for the Next Rung: Economic Restructuring and Educational Reform in Singapore." *Journal of Education and Work* 12 (3): 296–97.

Government of Ireland. 1995. "Charting Our Education Future." White Paper on Education, Dublin.

———. *Programme for Action in Education 1984–1987.*

Hahn, Man-jung. 2003. *Sakyo Yuk Munje eh daehan Inshik kwa Haekyon Bang An (Consciousness of Private Education Problems and Solution).*

Han, Yu Kyoung 2001a. "Assessment of Overseas Loan Projects for Education Implemented in Korea during 1969-1999." *Journal of Educational Research* 39 (2).

———. 2001b. *The Efficiency of Educational Loan.*

Hayashi, T. 1990. *The Japanese Experience in Technology: From Transfer to Self-Reliance.* Tokyo: United Nations University Press.

Higher Education Authority (HEA). 1995. *Interim Report of the Technical Working Group.* Dublin: HEA.

Hillery, P. J. 1963. Minister for Education, Press Conference, May 20.

Hossain, Shaikh I. 1996. *Making an Equitable and Efficient Education: The Chinese Experience.* Washington, DC: World Bank.

Hsien Loong, Lee. 1988. "Parliamentary Debates." *Official Reports* 50 (March 28).

IMD. *IMD World Competitiveness Yearbook.* 1999. Lausanne, Switzerland: IMD.

———. *IMD World Competitiveness Yearbook.* 2006. Lausanne, Switzerland: IMD.

Industrial Policy Review Group Report. 1994. Stationery Office, Dublin.

Inter-Agency Commission, WCEFA (UNDP, UNESCO, UNICEF, World Bank. 1990 *World Conference on Education for All: Meeting Basic Learning Needs. Final Report*, March 5–9, 1990, Jomtien, Thailand.

Irish Universities Association. 2005. *Reform of Third Level and Creation of Fourth Level Ireland—Securing Competitive Advantage in the 21st Century.* Dublin: IUA.

Jang, Suk Min. 1999. *Han Guk Kyo Yuk Pyoung Ron (The Crisis of Technical Vocational School and Correspondence Direction).* Seoul: Korean Educational Development Institute.

Jones, Gavin. 1975. *Population Growth and Educational Planning in Developing Nations.* New York: Irvington Publishers, Inc.

———. 2003. "Strategies and Achievements in Expanding Lower Secondary Enrollments: Thailand and Indonesia." Asian MetaCentre Research Paper Series, No. 13. National University of Singapore.

Jung, Tae Hwa. 2006. *The Problem and Tasks of Technical Vocational Education, Korea's Human Resource: Challenge and New Paradigm.* Seoul: Beop mun-sa.

Junior Certificate Examination. 2004. *Rules and Programme for Secondary Schools.* Department of Education, Ireland.

Kang, Sung Guk. 2006. *Analysis on the Growth of Korean Education for 60 Years.*

Kang, Sung Guk, et al. 2005. *Analysis of Educational Indicators about the Sixty Year Educational Development of South Korea.*

KDI. 1997. *The Korean Economy 1945-1995: Performance and Vision for the 21st Century.* Seoul: KDI.

Keynes, J. M. 1933. "National Self Sufficiency," *Studies* 22: 177–193.

Kim, Chol-su. 1998. *Honbob Hak Kaeron (The Theory of the Constitution)*. Seoul: Park Young Sa.

Kim, Jong Chol. 1989. *Hankuk Kyo Yuk Jeongchak Yeonku (Study on the Educational Policy in Korea)*. Seoul: Kyo Yuk, Kwahak Sa.

Kim, Ki Suk, Bang Ran Ryu, Sung Chul Sung, Han Gu Ryu, and Hyang Kyu Lee. 1996. *100 Years of Education in the South Korean School System and Transition of Population Statistics*. Seoul: Seoul National University Education Research Institute.

Kim, Young Hwa. 1997. "Development of Korean Education and the function of Education." *The Study of Educational Finance and Economy* 6, no. 1 (June): 31–63.

Ki-Zerbo, Joseph. 1990. *Eduquer ou périr*. Paris: Edition Lieu/Pl Publication.

Koh, Thiam Seng and Lee Sai Choo. 2008. "Digital Skills and Education: Singapore's ICT Master Planning for the School Sector". In *Toward a Better Future: Education and Training for Economic Development in Singapore since 1965*, eds. Sing Kong Lee, Goh Chor Boon, Birger Fredriksen, and Jee Peng Tan. Washington, DC: World Bank.

Korea Education Publishing Committee. 1960. *Hankuk Kyo Yuk Sip Nyon Sa (The Ten Year History of Korean Education)*. Seoul: Tong'mun-sa.

Larach, Linda. 2001. "Brazil Secondary Education Profile. A Summary of Secondary Education: Time to Move Forward." Secondary Education Series No. 24555. Human Development Network, World Bank, Washington, DC.

Le defi XXI, 2005. *Relier les Connaissances-21st Century Challenges, Knowledge Linkages*, ed. Edgar Morin (Vietnamese Version). Hanoi, Vietnam: Hanoi National University Publishing House.

Lee, Hi-suk. 2003. "Kwa Woe Hang Wi eh kwanhan Ga Im Ironjok Jeopkeun" ("A Game Theoretical Approach to Extra-Curricular Behaviors"). Master's dissertation, Seoul National University.

Lee, Hsien Loong. 1988. "Parliamentary Debates". *Official Reports* Vol. 50, Singapore (March 28).

Lee, Chong Jae. 2004a. "Education in Korea." PowerPoint presentation to ENERP Seminar at Graduate School of Education, University of Pennsylvania, Nov. 18, Philadelphia.

———. 2004b. "Sakyo Yuk Munje eh daehan Daechak: Kong Kyo Yuk Kanghwa reul Jongsim euro" ("Policy Measures for the Problems of Private Education; To Strengthen Public Education"). *KEDI Position Paper* 1 (1).

———. 2005. "University Restructuring in Korea." PowerPoint presentation to UNESCO, May.

———. 2006a. "The Development of Education in Korea: Past Achievement and Current Challenges." PowerPoint Presentation to "The East Asia Study Tour Seminar for Senior African Educational Policy Makers," World Bank, June 19–23, Singapore.

———. 2006b. "Chisik Kiban Sahoe eui Hakop Seong Chwi wa Hakyo Hyuk Shin" ("Achievement in the Knowledge-Based Society and the Innovation of School"). PowerPoint presentation to Seoul National University College of Education, June 9, Seoul.

Lee, Ju Ho., et al. 2000. *Economic Analysis of Teacher Remuneration and Policy Reform*.

Lim Joo-Jock. 1980. "Bold Internal Decisions, Emphatic External Outlook." In *Southeast Asian Affairs 1980*. Singapore: Institute of Southeast Asian Studies.

Lin, Cheng Ton. 2002. "Training a New Breed of Technologists." In *Heart Work: Stories of How EDB Steered the Singapore Economy from 1961 into the 21st Century*, ed. Chan, Chin Bock. Singapore: Singapore Economic Development Board.

Lockheed, M. E., and A. M. Verspoor. 1990. "Improving Primary Education in Developing Countries: A Review of Policy Options." Background Paper prepared for the World Conference on Education for All, Jomtien, Thailand, March 5–9, 1990, World Bank, Washington, DC.

Low, Linda, M. H. Toh, and T. W. Soon. 1991. *Economics of Education and Manpower Development: Issues and Policies in Singapore*. Singapore: McGraw Hill.

Martin, Michael O. et al. 2000. *TIMSS 1999 International Science Report*. Hamburg, Germany: International Association for the Evaluation of Educational Achievement.

Mass Communications Organization of Thailand (MCOT). Thai News Agency (TNA). 2006. "Free Education Not Really Free." Available at http://etna.mcot.net (accessed July 31, 2006).

Metzger, Christoph. 2005. *Differing Paths, Similar Pursuits: Alternatives to College Bounded Secondary Education—the Experience of Switzerland*.

Mingat, Alain. 2004. "La rémunération des enseignants de l'enseignement primaire dans les pays francophones d'Afrique sub-saharienne." Africa Region Human Development, Department, World Bank, Washington, DC.

Ministry of Education (Korea) and KEDI (Korean Educational Development Institute). *Statistical Year Book of Education*.

Ministry of Education (Korea) and Human Resource Development. 1960–2005. *The Statistical Year Book of Korea Education*.

_____. 1998. *The 50-Year History of Korean Education*. Seoul: Minstry of Education (Korea).

_____. 2002a. *Kong Kyo Yuk Jindan mit Naesilhwa Daechak (Diagnosis of Public Education and Measures for Improvement)*, March. Seoul: Ministry of Education (Korea).

_____. 2004. *Kong Kyo Yuk Jeong Sang Hwa reul wihan Sa Kyo Yuk bi Kyong Kam Daechak (Ways for Reducing the Cost of Private Education for the Normalization of Public Education)*. February 13. Seoul: Ministry of Education (Korea).

Ministry of Education (Korea). 1980. *The 30 Year History of Korean Education*. Seoul: Ministry of Education (Korea).

_____. 2001. *The 100 Major Educational Reforms of the People's Government*. April 25. Seoul: Ministry of Education (Korea).

_____. 2002b. *Kong kyo Yuk Naesilhwa Daechak kwa Sa Kyo Yuk Daechak (Measures for the Improvement of Public Education and Private Education)*. Seoul: Ministry of Education (Korea).

_____. 2003. *White Paper of the People's Government*. January. Seoul: Ministry of Education (Korea).

_____. "The Statistical Book of Korea Education (1960–2005)."

_____. 2008. *Daehak Jeon Hyong Kibon Kye Hoek (Basic Plan for the 2008 University Entrance Examination)*. Seoul: Ministry of Education (Korea) and Human Resource Development.

Ministry of Education (Singapore). Various years. *Annual Report*. Seoul: Ministry of Education (Korea).

_____. 1966. "Progress in Education in Singapore, 1959 to 1965."

_____. 2005. *Education Statistics Digest 2004*. Seoul: Ministry of Education (Korea).

Ministry of Education (Thailand). 2004. "National Report." In *Quality Education for all Young People: Challenges, Trends and Priorities: Forty-Seventh Session of the International Conference on Education*, September 8–11, 2004. Geneva: International Bureau of Education, UNESCO.

Moreno, Juan Manuel. 2005. "Changes in Secondary Education: From Weakest Link to Cornerstone." In International Semimar on Growth Strategies for Secondary Education in Asia, September 19–21, 2005. Kuala Lumpur: World Bank.

Mullis, Ina V.S. et al. 2000. *TIMSS 1999 International Mathematics Report*. Hamburg, Germany: IEA.

Nagao, Masafumi. 2007. "Can Japan be a Successful Mathematics and Science Education Teacher for Africa?" In *Mathematics and Science Education in Developing Countries: Issues, Experiences, and Cooperation Prospects*, ed. Masafumi Nagao, John M. Rogon, and Marcelita C. Magno. Quezon City: The University of the Philippines Press.

National Center for Education Statistics and Information (Korea). 1985–2005. Available at http://std.kedi.re.kr/index.jsp.

National Development Plan (Ireland). 2000. "National Development Plan 2000-2006." Dublin: Government Publications, Stationery Office.

———. 2006. "National Development Plan 2007–2013." Dublin: Government Publications, Stationery Office.

National Economic and Social Council. 1993. "Education and Training Policies for Economic and Social Development." Dublin.

———. 1993. "Strategy for Competitiveness, Growth and Employment." Dublin.

National Institute for Educational Strategy and Curriculum. 2001–05. Draft Report on Phase I (2001–05) implementation of the Strategic Plan for Educational Development during 2001–10 period. National Institute for Educational Strategy and Curriculum.

National Science and Technology Board (Singapore). 1992. "National Survey of R&D in Singapore." National Science and Technology Board, Singapore.

National Statistical Office (Korea). 1965–2005. Web site database. Available at http://www.nso.go.kr.

National Statistics Office (NSO) (Thailand). 1994–2002. Household Socio-Economic Survey. Bangkok: NSO.

———. 2002. Children and Youth Survey. Bangkok: NSO.

"New Criteria Announced for Granting Scholarships." 2006. Bangkok Post. May 7, 6.

Ng, David Foo Seong. 2008. "Strategic Management of Educational Development in Singapore (1965–2005)." Towards a Better Future: Education and Training for Economic Development in Singapore since 1965, World Bank/Singapore National Institute of Education, Washington, DC.

NIEC. 1965. Comment on "Investment in Education." Report No. 16. Stationery Office, Dublin.

Oh, Chon-seok. 1964. Hankuk Sin Kyo Yuk Sa (New History of Korean Education). Hyundai Kyo Yuk Chulpan Sa.

Oh, Won Chul. 2006. How Park Jung Hee Made Korea Economic Power. Dong-Seo Munhwasa.

Office of Basic Education Commission (OBEC). 2002. Education Information 2002. Bangkok.

Office of Education Council (OEC). 2004a. Education in Thailand 2004. Bangkok: OEC.

———. 2004b. Thailand Education Statistics 2003. Bangkok: OEC.

———. 2005. Thailand Education Statistics 2004. Bangkok: OEC.

Office of National Education Standards and Quality Assessment. 2006. Functions. Available http://www.onesqa.or.th (accessed June 27, 2006).

Organisation for Economic Co-operation and Development (OECD). 1964. Training of Technicians in Ireland. Paris: OECD.

———. 1966. Investment in Education. Paris: OECD.

———. 1989. "Education, and Economy in a Changing Society." OECD, Paris.

———. 1992. Technology and the Economy: The Key Relationships. Paris: OECD.

———. 1994. "Jobs Study—Facts, Analysis, Strategies." OECD, Paris.

———. 1995. "Economic Surveys on Ireland." OECD, Paris.

———. 1997. "Education at a Glance." OECD, Paris.

———. 2001. Knowledge and Skills for Life: First Results from PISA 2000. Paris: OECD.

———. 2001. The Well-being of Nation: The Role of Social Capital. Paris: OECD.

———. 2003. Literacy Skills for the World of Tomorrow: Further Results from PISA 2000. Paris: OECD and UNESCO.

———. 2004a. Education at a Glance. Paris, OECD.

———. 2004b. Learning for Tomorrow's World: First Results from PISA 2003. Paris: OECD.

———. 2005a. "Education at a Glance 2005, Tables." Education and Training: Statistics. Available at http://www. oecd.org (accessed June 28, 2006).

———. 2005b. School Factors Related to Quality and Equity: Results from PISA 2000. Paris: OECD.

Pang Eng Fong. 1982. *Education, Manpower and Development in Singapore*. Singapore: Singapore University Press.

Park, Jong Ryol et al. 2005. *Koryonghwa Sahoeesoi Haksang Inku Byunhwa Joon-mangkwa Kwa Je (The Prospect for the Change of School Population in the Aged People Society and Tasks)*. March 27.

Parliamentary Debates Singapore. 1970. *Annual Budget Statement* (March 9).

Patrinos, Harry Anthony. 2002. *A Review of Demand-Side Financing Initiatives in Education*. Washington, DC: World Bank.

Phongpaichit, Pasuk, and Isra Sarntisart. 2000. "Globalisation and Inequality: The Case of Thailand." In *Poverty and Income Inequality in Developing Countries: A Policy Dialogue on the Effects of Globalisation*. Paris: OECD.

Programme for Action in Education. 1984–87. Stationery Office, Dublin.

Punyasavatsut, Chaiyuth, et al. 2005. "Technical Consultancy for the Country Development Partnership Program in Education-Component 1: School Finance Reform." Bangkok: Unpublished manuscript.

Randles, Eileen. 1975. *Post-Primary Education in Ireland 1957-1970*. Dublin: Veritas Publications Dublin.

Reich, Robert B. 2001. *The Future of Success*. New York, Alfred A. Knopf.

"Report on the Directions and Tasks for Five-year Socio-Economic Development for 2006–10." Presented at the 10th Congress of the Vietnamese Communist Party.

Rice, Jennifer King. 2003. *Teacher Quality: Understanding the Effectiveness of Teacher Attributes*. Washington, DC: Economic Policy Institute.

Richter, Kaspar. 2006. "Thailand's Growth Path: From Recovery to Prosperity." Policy Research Working Paper No. 3912. World Bank, Washington, DC.

Rivkin, Steven G., Eric A. Hanushek, and John F. Kain. 2005. "Teachers, Schools, and Academic Achievement." *Econometrica* 73: 417–58.

Rowe, Ken. 2003. "The Importance of Teacher Quality as a Key Determinant of Students' Experiences and Outcomes of Schooling." In *Building Teacher Quality: What Does the Research Tell Us?*, 15–23. Camberwell, Australia: Australian Council for Educational Research.

Second Programme for Economic Expansion. 1963. Stationery Office, Dublin.

Seo, Jung Hwa. "Kyo Yuk Chujin e-daehan Banseong kwa Hyang Ju Kwaje" ("Review of the Educational Reform and Tasks for the Future"). November 11–12.

Sharpe, Leslie, and S. Gopinathan. 2002. "After Effectiveness: New Directions in the Singapore School System?" *Journal of Education Policy* 2 (17): 151–66.

Song, Byung-Nak. 2003. *The Rise of the Korean Economy*, 3rd edition. Oxford University Press.

Steering Committee on Technical Education. 1967. Report to the Minister for Education on Regional Technical Education. Stationery Office, Dublin.

Straits Times. September 26, 1965.

———. November 25, 1965.

———. April 10, 1968.

———. March 24, 1976.

———. August 9, 1976.

———. August 11, 1978.

———. July 8, 1980.

———. February 18, 1981.

———. December 30, 1993.

———. June 14, 1994.

Suwansathit, Savitri. 2002. "Quality and Equity in Education." The 8th International Conference on Education, *Innovations in Secondary Education: Meeting the Needs of*

Adolescents and Youth in Asia and the Pacific, November 26–29, 2002, UNESCO Asia and Pacific Regional Bureau for Education, Bangkok.

Tan, Jee-Peng. 1991. "Thailand's Education Sector at a Crossroads: Selected Issues." In *Decisions and Change in Thailand: Three Studies in Support of the Seventh Plan.* Asia Country Department 2, World Bank, Washington, DC.

Thailand Development Research Institute (TDRI). 2000. *Financing Basic Education under the New National Educational Act.* Bangkok: TDRI.

Tran, Hong Quan, Pham Minh Hac, Tran Chi Dao et al. 1995. *50 Years of Development of Vietnamese Education and Training Cause (1945–1995).* Hanoi: Ministry of Education and Training (MOET), Education Publishing House.

UNESCO. 1999. *Statistical Yearbook 1999.* Paris: UNESCO.

United Nations Educational, Scientific, and Cultural Organization (UNESCO). 2002a. "Development of Education in Africa: A Statistical Review." Document presented at the Eight Conference of Ministers of Education of African Member States (MINEDAF VIII), December 2–6, 2002, Dar es Salaam, Tanzania.

UNESCO. 2002b. *EFA Global Monitoring Report 2002.* Paris: UNESCO.

———. 2003a. The 8th International Conference on Education, *Innovations in Secondary Education: Meeting the Needs of Adolescents and Youth in Asia and the Pacific,* November 26–29, 2002. Bangkok: Asia and Pacific Regional Bureau for Education, UNESCO.

———. 2003b. *EFA Global Monitoring Report 2003/04.* Paris: UNESCO.

———. 2004. *EFA Gobal Monitoring Report 2005.* Paris: UNESCO.

———. 2005. *Global Education Digest 2005.* Montreal: UNESCO Institute for Statistics.

———. 2006. *EFA Global Monitoring Report 2007.* Paris: UNESCO.

———. 2007. *EFA Global Monitoring Report 2008.* Paris: UNESCO.

UNESCO-Breda. 2005. "EPT, repères pour l'action Dakar+5." UNESCO-Breda, Pôle de Dakar pole, Paris.

UNESCO, Institute for Statistics. 2006. *Global Education Digest 2006.* Montreal: UNESCO.

Verspoor, Adriaan M. and others. 2008. *At the Crossroads: Choices for Secondary Education in Sub-Saharan Africa.* Washington, DC: World Bank.

Whitaker, T.K., 1958. *Economic Development.* Dublin: Department of Finance/Stationery Office.

Witte, Ann Dryden, and Helen Tauchen. 1994. *Work and Crime: An Exploration Using Panel Data.* Cambridge, MA: National Bureau of Economic Research.

Witte, Johanna. 2000. "Education in Thailand after the Crisis: A Balancing Act between Globalization and National Self-Contemplation." *International Journal of Educational Development* 20: 223–45.

The Works of Ho Chi Minh, Volume IV. 1984. Hanoi: Su That.

World Bank. 1987. "The Korean Labor Market: Emerging Policy Issues." Report No. 6478-KO, Korea and South East Asia Division, East Asia and Pacific Regional Office, World Bank, Washington, DC.

———. 1988. "Education in Sub-Saharan Africa: Policies for Adjustment, Revitalization, and Expansion." World Bank, Washington, DC.

———. 1992. "Revitalizing Higher Education in Senegal: The Challenge of Reform." Population and Human Resources Division, Sahelien Department, Africa Region, World Bank, Washington, DC.

———. 1993. *The East Asian Miracle: Economic Growth and Public Policy.* Washington, DC: Oxford University Press and World Bank.

———. 1998. *Thailand: Education Achievements, Issues, and Policies.* Washington, DC: East Asia and the Pacific Region, Education Sector Unit, World Bank.

———. 1999. *Thailand Social Monitor: Coping with the Crisis in Education and Health.* Bangkok: World Bank.

———. 2000a. *Can Africa Claim the 21st Century?"* Washington, DC: World Bank.

———. 2000b. *Turkey—Economic Reforms, Living Standards and Social Welfare Study.* Washington, DC: Poverty Reducation and Economic Management Unit, Europe and Central Asia Region, World Bank.

———. 2000c. "Republic of Korea: Transition to a Knowledge-Based Economy." Report No. 20346-KO. June 29. World Bank, Washington, DC.

———. 2001a. "Poverty and Public Policy." In *Thailand Social Monitor Report.* Bangkok: World Bank.

———. 2001b. *Thailand: Secondary Education for Employment,* Volume 1. Bangkok: World Bank.

———. 2001c. *World Development Indicators 2001.* Washington, DC: World Bank.

———. 2002. *Education and HIV/AIDS: A Window of Hope.* Washington, DC: World Bank.

———. 2003. *World Development Indicators.* Washington, DC: World Bank.

———. 2004. "Republic of Korea, Four Decades of Equitable Growth." Working Paper No. 30781. World Bank, Washington, DC.

———. 2005. *Expanding Opportunities and Building Competencies for Young People: A New Agenda for Secondary Education.* Washington, DC: World Bank.

———. 2006a. *Africa Development Indicators 2006.* Washington, DC: World Bank.

———. 2006b. "Summary Education Profile." EDSTATS - Global Country Data. Available at http://devdata.world bank.org/edstats/cd1.asp (accessed August 30, 2006).

———. 2006c. *World Development Indicators Database.* Washington, DC: World Bank.

World Bank and Pôle De Dakar. 2003. "Rapport d'Etat du Système Educatif National Camerounais: Eléments de diagnostic pour la politique dans le contexte de l'EPT et du DSRP." Report prepared by a team comprising Cameroonian experts and staff from the World Bank and the French Cooperation, Washington, DC.

Yoon, Yang-Ro. 2001. "Effectiveness Born out of Necessity: A Comparison of Korean and East African Education Policies." ECSHED, World Bank, Washington, DC.

Ziderman, Adrian. 2003. *Student Loans in Thailand: Are they Effective, Equitable, Sustainable?* Bangkok: UNESCO.

———. 2004. *Policy Options for Student Loan Schemes: Lessons from Five Asian Case Studies.* Bangkok: UNESCO.

Index